Coercion to Speak

COERCION TO SPEAK
Conrad's Poetics of Dialogue

Aaron Fogel

Harvard University Press
Cambridge, Massachusetts, and London, England
1985

Publication of this book has been aided
by a grant from the Andrew W. Mellon Foundation

This book is printed on acid-free paper, and its binding
materials have been chosen for strength and durability.

Library of Congress Cataloging in Publication Data

Fogel, Aaron, 1947–
Coercion to speak.

Bibliography: p.
Includes index.
1. Conrad, Joseph, 1857–1924—Technique.
2. Dialogue.
3. Speech in literature.
I. Title.
PR6005.04Z69   1985   823'.912   85-775
ISBN 0-674-13639-X (alk. paper)

Acknowledgments

Some passages in Chapters II and IV have appeared, in different form, in *Conradiana*, 15, no. 2 (1983).

I am grateful to Quentin Anderson for his enthusiasm and indispensable criticism of this work in its early stages; to Robert Caserio for his close readings of extended sections, and for sharing ideas important to the book's definition; and to Helen Vendler for her consistent encouragement and insight during the later stages of composition. Colleagues and friends at Boston University—William Carroll, Emily Dalgarno, Eugene Green, Robert Levine, Gerald Fitzgerald, and David Wagenknecht—have read sections and offered helpful thoughts and criticisms. Other friends—Susan Monsky, Roy Skodnick, Mitch Sisskind, Patrick West—read and commented on parts of the manuscript. Lynn Ouellette of Boston University went out of her way to make word processing readily available to me during the last summer of writing.

Finally, Barbara Bliss, my wife, has worked and talked with me for years, giving me ideas, commenting on organization, and patiently rereading. I think the book would not have been written without her. This book is for her and for our son, Adam.

Contents

Coercion to Speak

I

Ideas of Dialogue
and Conrad's Forced Dialogue

IN 1912, in two scalding and irritated essays about the *Titanic*, Conrad
voiced some unusually direct public anger.[1] The shipwreck gave him
the chance to comment as a sailor on the bad architecture of large modern ships, and more generally to criticize technological grandiosity. But
though they are nautical polemics, the essays also read like prose
poems: they deploy, with casual force, some of the key words and
images of his fiction. A reader following changes in the fiction to this
year has to notice that some of Conrad's terms reapply almost too easily—almost as in a parody of his typical scenes—to his account of the
Titanic. He emphasizes, among other things, disproportion, stupidity,
and "detonation." In its totality the sinking is to him not a tragedy but a
"stupid catastrophe" of misunderstood navigational scale. He treats it
partly in the style of Augustan satire, as if *Peri Bathous: The Art of Sinking
in Poetry*, Pope's guide to writing bad poetry by abandoning any sense
of proportion, could now be translated back again into a modern anti-
handbook of navigation, in which the new first principle would be technological madness. He writes, for example, that since side-swiping
while trying to avoid the iceberg had probably caused the sinking, "the
new seamanship" will require great ships, on sighting icebergs, to ram
them head on.[2] The *Titanic*, like the big Russian novels Conrad tried to
despise, had been a technical "elephantiasis," the result of a naive
equation between size and progress. Modern failures of scale cause
stupid disasters in both navigation and writing.

But for all this nautical conservatism, or even reaction, the two essays
are at the same time, and as usual, politically hard to locate, because of
their protest for the working people destroyed by the stupidity. The *Ti-*

tanic figures as a class disproportion, a grand hotel with too great a gap between its leisure-class tourists and its sailors, with unnecessary luxuries aboard—French cafés and smoking-rooms nearly in the "style of the Pharaohs or . . . Louis Quinze"—and with the sailors degraded not by hard labor, but by its trivialization, including the final demand that they die for a commercial extravagance. Any elegy is for the sailors, not the passengers. From the failure of what Conrad presents as the older value of handling at sea, both in physics and in social relations, there follows the scene of oblique, unlikely collision, between the ship, now relatively small, and the iceberg, immense. "All the violence of that collision," the narrator had told us about a similar collision in *Nostromo*, "was, as usual, felt only on board the smaller craft" (291). This is commonsensical physics used to illustrate the most ordinary moral fact of power: the smaller unit always suffers, as the engineers trapped below on the *Titanic* die the worst death, and as Poland, a smaller large nation, has suffered in relation to Russia.

In this poetics of social and physical disproportion leading to disaster, one result of the collision is a mystifying "detonation"—a muffled explosion as the ship goes down—a sound, a "report," caused, Conrad insists, simply by the underwater collapse of decks, but now misunderstood by some landlubber inquirers as a mysterious hint that there may have been foul play.[3] The disproportionate collision with its resulting "detonation" recalls similar moments elsewhere—Gould's threatened detonation of his mine in *Nostromo*, the Professor's pocket detonator in *The Secret Agent*, the final explosion of the ship *Emma* (which is being used as a magazine) in *The Rescue*, and the most impressive and understated, the two "detonations" of Razumov's eardrums toward the end of *Under Western Eyes*. "Detonations" are, in Conrad's poetic glossary, oxymoronic: loud explosions which are at the same time silencings, muffled events: "de-tonings," or final losses of any clear tonality, and of the conventional expressive difference between loudness and silence. Detonation is probably his strongest and most typical closure: the loud silence which absorbs, without completely resolving or explaining, all the conflicted political noises and silences that have accumulated in the course of the action.

"There is reason in things,"[4] Conrad insists here, appealing to the idea that instrumental reason and moral reason are allied. This "reason in things" can only be understood in and through active labor. Responsibility involves a grasp of kinetic reason, a recognition of physical limits and working ratios; moral awareness grows partly out of the experience of physical obstacles during real work. Instruments represent fixed uses rather than new possibilities. By comparison to Conrad's characters, Thomas Hardy's people, though caught in even more fatal personal patterns, show much more incidental "ingenuity," or physical wit in converting old instruments to new uses. In *Jude the Obscure,* for instance, the farmer takes a thwacker meant to scare birds and beats young Jude with it; Jude converts his baker's wagon into a reading stand; Arabella uses what she says is the folk custom of incubating birds' eggs between her breasts to tempt Jude; little Jude, in a final act of ingenuity, uses nails meant for hanging clothes to kill himself.[5] Acts like this make Hardy's people seem, though certainly not free, at least tragically witty with old things, able to reuse agencies at will, and so to express personal humors. But it is hard to think of a Conrad character who revises an instrument in this way, whom we come to know and like for "ingenuity." Things—both natural givens and old instruments—have permanent, inherent uses, scale, and rules of handling; and the carefully chosen verb of motion is at the center of his style. But there are tragically ingenious reuses in Conrad as in Hardy, only they are more obviously political: the treatment of persons as reusable instruments. Living subjects are reused inventively, as Razumov is converted into a spy, Stevie into a bomb carrier, or the skulls of natives into warning signs around Kurtz's house. Persons, not things, are the typical reusables. Storytelling itself is apprehended as a forced, disproportioning reuse of the person represented. Even the most tactful narrator, when describing a life, forces it into disproportion. Marlow is angelically self-conscious about the ways in which he forces Kurtz or Jim into narrative realization. As the story goes on, this moral narrator is also seen, as if to confirm the guilt of telling, to have participated unwillingly in the destruction, rather than the rescue, of the subject. Readers are repeatedly shown by Conrad's methods that "communication" and "information," far from being good or neutral or innocent, can be given only in and through conditions of participatory disproportion and force that resemble those of the physical world. Narration occurs not as a complex of freely various "points of view," but within a political force field of disproportions, hearsays, pressures, and overhearings. This is not new: what is original is Conrad's imagery of "reports" and "detonations"—which take place as strange composites of silence and explosive exaggeration. The modern tale has to represent and include the danger that tone is being removed by a steady onslaught of exaggerations and silences, not unrelated to the commonplace and banal complaint we hear now about the news as so much numbing hyperbole, disinformation, and censorship. Hardy begins *Jude the Obscure* with the image of a pianoforte stored in a tool shed—the expressive romantic instrument put away so that he can write a more flatly adaptive prose.

Conrad repeatedly and variously dramatizes the ways in which a social and political world of plural "intonations" ends in forced resolutions of "detonation."

One job of prose imagery in this context is to remind readers forcibly and sometimes crudely of the necessary disproportion in all information and in the methods of reason itself. To illustrate the structural weakness of the *Titanic*, Conrad compares its construction unfavorably to that of "a Huntley and Palmer biscuit-tin"—a comparison possibly lifted from Stephen Crane[6]—and writes a little rudely that this sort of tin is "probably known to all my audience" (233). This audience, distant from sea life, not knowing about proverbial "biscuit-tins" like Marlow's boat in "Heart of Darkness," has figured in the writing at least since the Preface to *The Nigger of the "Narcissus"*: an audience that must be "impressed" by sharp disproportions and crudely "made to see" the facts of working life it doesn't know. To understand the *Titanic*, first understand a tin can. Heyst's glowing cigar resembles a distant volcano. Deliberately stupid, funny, or childish comparisons like these are aimed at the assumed naive disproportion in the reader's mind, and so are comically wise: "In my varied and adventurous career I have been thrilled by the sight of a Huntley and Palmer biscuit-tin kicked by a mule sky-high, as the saying is. It came back to earth smiling, with only a sort of dimple on one of its cheeks" (233). Subtlety isn't the purpose here. The illustration, a sort of elementary physics textbook analogy—and a little in the kindergarten voice—suggests that the average biscuit-tin is more soundly built than the *Titanic*, and can take a kick from the Ass of circumstance better. The tone is Menippean,[7] vulgarly commonsensical, against grandeur and titanism, mock-sublime. We're not supposed to wonder, mainly, where or whether Conrad saw some mule kick a tin but to see a popular iconography in all of it, mules in Conrad emblematizing labor, practical work, everyday physics, and the "asinine" as in some respects the stubbornly intelligent. When MacWhirr's father says of him, "Tom's an ass," [8] it's to be understood as part praise. Though a social fool, Tom has a sort of Menippean virtue in contrast to philosophers and other abstract thinkers—a physical grasp of work and things.

All these motifs—"handling" as analogous to moral reason; physical and informational disproportions; "detonation" as loud silence; the simple division of humanity into the two classes of the idle and the laboring; animality or *bêtise* as a fundamental perspective on existence; the ironies of "overhearing"; and the reader's need to be impressed by hyperbole—are interrelated, and contribute to the feeling that the essays on the *Titanic* are exemplary Conradian prose-poetic sketches.

They deserve a little more attention than they have received, because they repeat in compact and acerbic form his dramatic idea of the route to disaster. But in listing these typical features of the two essays I have so far left out the one major motif which is for this study of Conrad the most important. The specific occasion of the two essays is not, to be exact, the sinking itself, which is too large and potentially pseudosymbolic an event to tackle. Instead, Conrad begins to write out of a specific practical annoyance at the United States Senate for setting up an instant inquiry. The second of the two essays pretends to apologize for, but actually reinforces, the first essay's contempt for this senatorial meddling (a protest letter had come from a friend in America defending the good will of the senators), and carries the nearly Swiftian title "Certain Aspects of the Admirable Inquiry into the Loss of the *Titanic.*" Conrad denies a satiric intention like Swift's, and tries to compare his tone to W. S. Gilbert's.[9] But in fact, he is closer to Swift, and for all his angry disgust about the physical mishandling, what gets him writing, what he efficiently makes the occasion of these essays, is the image he has of a dialogical practice, the "bullying and badgering" interrogation of the second officer and of the "Yamsi" (businessmen and planners involved in the ship)—the "lot of questions" thrown at them by a group of politicians who, though perhaps under the guise of a "praiseworthy desire for information," do not even understand the work-reality about which they inquire. Conrad obviously has a picture of this other disproportion—dialogical but virtually physical in its misapplied force—a useless scene of disproportionate coercion to speak which has become representative for him of a general condition. Even though he sees its inevitability, it annoys him no end and starts him writing with unusually direct and fluent belligerence, in contrast to his more usual posture in England of taut politeness. He seems to feel that inquiry must by nature be disproportionate and forced, but at the same time to resent the fact.

These minor essays on the *Titanic* serve as a suggestive model for the organizing principle of Conrad's prose craft, or prose poetic: events that are physically and socially too big, intractably disproportionate, are given shape through a focus on a picturable imbalance or disproportion in the dialogue of inquiry. The "idea" of disproportionate forced dialogue ironically gives beginning, occasion, coherence, and shape to events which in themselves might be uncontrollable by representation. Disproportions and coercions in dialogue are among the main Conradian prose instruments for handling the modern event. Here, by their mishandling of the dialogue of inquiry, the senators unconsciously mimic, and therefore reenact, the prior mishandling of the ship's construction, and the mishandling of class relations aboard. The mistaken dialogue technique is linked, as a practice, to the mistaken physical technology which produced the *Titanic*. They are at the very least analogous, and at the most, twin expressions of the same relational ignorance. Dialogue and physical labor are not two different spheres of imagination.

Dialogue as an instrumental practice, conceived on a model of physical events, involves the application of force between persons, which like force in work can be creative or annihilating. As in physical events, disproportion and force create movement. There is, further, a sense of "measure" in dialogue, which makes the *relative amount spoken* by the persons (very visible on the page and highly formalized, especially from the period 1902–1912, roughly Conrad's "middle period") one of the most important features of many of his scenes of speech—more important, say, than the more usual features of dialect and idiolect,[10] interference, mannerism, or even sympathetic understanding and intimacy. Though these other dialogue motives appear to one degree or another, the primary "keys" to his dialogue[11] are much more often what he calls "force" (most dramatically coercion to speak itself) and the relative amount spoken—notions we will see played out with extraordinary scope of representational and formal vision and profound understanding of the history of dialogue forms. No other novelist makes the abstract proportional model (the relative amount spoken) a figure on the page to be *seen* so consistently, so forcibly, or with such cumulative effect as Conrad does in his "political" works. It is most obvious, probably, to the new reader either in the famous last dialogue between the Verlocs leading to her murder of him, where he wants her to speak and she remains largely silent for about twenty pages; or in Marlow's lengthy talk contrasted to the occasional grunts of his listeners, itself ambiguously parallel to Kurtz's reported verbosity. Undoubtedly, Conrad might be said to have instituted these principles of radical dissymmetry and coercion to speak in dialogue just because he could not institute the more conventional conversational ones with any success, for the obvious reason that he was not a native speaker of English, and perhaps for the less obvious reason (familiar to readers of memoirs about him) that he was probably uneasy in most polite conversational settings, and might himself have had some of the "taste for silence" that he gives to Axel Heyst in *Victory* and to many other characters. But these are not really good reasons. The "lack"—the negation of "conversation," with its substitution of a view of dialogue as labor and force—whatever its source, turns out to be a great gain. Though it makes Conrad's work weak just where the other novelists in Leavis' "great tradition" (Austen, Eliot, James, Lawrence) are strong—in rendering conversational contact—it introduces the question of dialogue as proportion and production, which had not been seen enough in serious English novels, to displace the more intrasocial questions of conversational intimacy, irony, sympathy, and repartee. This new measure of dialogue yields a whole set of insights into the history of dialogue itself, in many different literary genres and social settings; it allows Conrad also to cut across the usual categories separating "political," "metaphysical," "aesthetic," and "psychological" ideas of dialogue from each other, to give an interpretation of human relations in dialogue as primarily nonconversational and relatively unfree. In other words, Conrad for his own tragic and political purposes often undoes the conversational idea of speech in the high English novel. His work invites instead a cumulative contemplation of disproportional and coercive dialogue scenes—as in filibuster; yarning; extorted speech (from inquisition to selling); remaining abnormally silent (a well-known and early observed feature of many strong Conrad characters); overhearing (as coercion to hear and in the sense of overreacting to what is heard); and operatic high-pitched duets. Comparison of such scenes with each other often generates much of the formal power of his stories and novels.

Dialogue form as a visual image—and therefore as a kind of "idea"—may be possible only to printed fiction, or to the dialogue as a written genre, and not to drama or to spoken social practice. Or it may be that even unwritten social practices, like Athenian eristic debate, the Quaker meeting, the talk show, playing the dozens, or the classroom, which are repeatedly performed, are in effect pictured and enjoyed for their dialogue rules "written," or spatialized, in the minds of participants and spectators. To begin with, however, I would like to put aside the many theoretical tensions about spoken versus formal, aural (for example, I and Thou) versus visual, and spiritual versus structural models of dialogue, along with the whole current controversy about logocentricity versus writing, and along with the very complicated and various discussions of the "dialogical" to be found in the works of Buber, Bakhtin, Gadamer, Burke, Freire, Habermas, Ong, Goodman, Rorty and others.[12] These variously dialogical theorists are all, of course, important to any contemporary discussion of dialogue forms or ideas, and have not been studied enough in relation to each other. They will return later as this study continues to describe Conrad's own "dialogic." But Conrad himself ought to be considered first a dialogue craftsman, a worker in dialogue as he once called himself a "worker in prose," concerned with practical rather than metaphysical issues of represented speech; and most perplexed in any case by tough obstacles for him as a nonnative speaker trying to build good dialogue scenes—

scenes that would interest or even "arrest" readers—in the absence of easy colloquialism and dialect and other standard means of entertainment.

"The rendering of speeches gave Conrad and the writer more trouble than any department of the novel whatever," Ford Madox Ford writes in his account of their collaboration.[13] With mock solemnity he goes on to describe an "unalterable rule" that they founded for dialogue: "no speech of one character should ever answer the speech that goes before" (188). Ford insists, with heavy irony, that "this is almost invariably the case in real life where few people listen, because they are always preparing their own next speeches." Finally, Ford professes to see in these mock-realistic dialogues of mutual disregard "a profoundly significant lesson as to the self-engrossment of humanity" (190). This little scene of collaboration on a dialogue "rule" is itself an irony of production: where we might want to think that the act of collaboration itself would lead naturally to an idea of dialogue as mutual and sympathetic, their collaborative work led them to found a dialogue rule of nonconversation and noncooperation. But Ford's comments are most important for giving us major hints, if not anything like a complete story, about the ways in which Conrad himself thought about novelistic dialogue as rules and form rather than as the rendering of spontaneous or "natural" conversation governed by a principle of freedom.

Ford's unalterable rule of non sequitur, taken no further, leads to an idea of dialogue suited to pessimistic ego psychology, or to the farce of manners and unassailable egotism. Swift's *Polite Conversation*, the Shandy household, Lewis Carroll's mad tea party, as well as some of Conrad's scenes of egoistic self-engagement where each one talks to himself, are examples. Clearly this ironic "rule" could be helpful to a learning novelist if it boldly got rid of the restrictive, abstract notion that dialogue must always be thematically centered to hold the reader: energetic dialogue in individualistic fiction, on the contrary, often shows general egotism, with each character pursuing his own themes through a general nonconversation. An eloquent statement of this negative rule for the world's dialogue can be found in Leopardi's *Pensieri XXI*, which argues that since "in speaking, we feel no real or lasting pleasure unless we are allowed to speak of ourselves," it follows that the best company is that which "we have most bored," and that there are, in the universal disproportional dialogue (though this "idea of dialogue" does not shape his lyric poems), only two types of speaker, "the amiable man" who listens and the "egotistical man" who talks.[14] The satisfaction in such comic definitions of "all dialogue" is their defense against pious and humorless articulations of rules for "meaningful dialogue" that we hear too much about—not to indulge in any cheap dismissal of all those efforts.[15] This witty, pessimistic, psychological mode, where the egotist talks a great deal and the other is silent, can often be found in Conrad, of course, as when Elliot bores Whalley, or Gould listens to Holroyd, or each anarchist talks to himself at the Verlocs. But if Conrad's dialogue rested at this formal ironic rule of disproportion, one-sidedness, contactlessness, and non sequitur, we would have a Conradian dialogic which is only psychological, pessimistic, and ironic. Such a dialogic would leave us with a "model of mind" and of dialogue, which, as in Bruce Johnson's version of Conrad, makes the ego psychology of Schopenhauerian pessimism his primary concern, with politics being only a screen to reveal this mood, even in works like *Nostromo* and *Under Western Eyes*.

Even in Ford's account of their craft, however, the rigid rule of total anarchic egoism—"never answer the other"—dissolves. Ford continues with mock resignation: "Here again, compromise must necessarily come in: there must come a point in the dramatic working up of every scene in which the characters do directly answer each other, for a speech or two or for three speeches. It was in this department, as has already been pointed out, that Conrad was matchless and the writer very deficient" (191). The funny double meaning of "compromise"— does he mean the compromise of the writers, committed to portraying absolutely disconnected characters, or that of the characters themselves, forced to speak to each other?—is entirely conscious for Ford, and gives us a hint of the irony about "speech acts" which has a place in the writing of both authors. But the main point is Ford's honest emphasis on the difference between himself and Conrad. Earlier in the memoir, Ford has said that while he himself knew more about "words" (presumably English diction), Conrad knew "infinitely" more about "architectonics" (179). Thus, in Ford's account of their collaboration, Conrad becomes the one skillful at forcing otherwise isolated characters into speech with each other. Accurately or not, Ford represents himself as contributing the anarchy, while Conrad contributes the dramatic, unlikely contacts. But in regard to Conrad this alters the "unalterable" rule to such an extent that the emphasis falls on something entirely different. If Ford is correct about the difference in their powers, what he laughingly calls the "compromise" would be for a writer like Conrad the real interest of the scene, the architectonic goal of making the characters meet and speak in spite of obstacles. And, to make a final point, the radical difference here is that Ford's idea of dialogue as egocentric anarchy or chaotic freedom becomes in Conrad the nearly opposite idea of dialogue as involuntary, forceful, and productive bondage of speakers to each other.

Ford's entertaining description gives us a valuable glimpse (accurate,

I think, in spite of disparagement of Ford by some Conrad scholars)
into the prehistory of the dialogue form I will here call "forced dialogue." During the composition of "The End of the Tether," or perhaps
one step earlier, in the closing scene of "Heart of Darkness," where the
Intended compels Marlow to say the oxymoronic detonated phrase
"your name" (since "your name" is not her name), Conrad makes a
transition from preoccupation with the egotistical speakers whose desire is *to make the other listen* to a preoccupation with figures who desire *to
make the other speak*. This shift is not absolute or exclusive, but it is highly
marked, and helps us to locate a difference between early Conrad and
middle (roughly, political) Conrad. The structural format of the "forced
dialogue," at its simplest, runs as follows: there are two speakers, and
one repeatedly tries to make the other speak. For a series of exchanges
(in its most ritual form, three), we have, in quotation marks, the
speeches of the person demanding speech from the other. These are
counterpointed—or to use a visual metaphor, "striped"—to narrative
prose passages which describe mainly the silence and gestures of that
other. The prose may also describe the surrounding scene. The effect of
this is a highly stylized and ritual feeling. The reader cannot help noticing the "striping," apparently more formal than naturalistic, between
direct speech and narrative prose, as if the two were themselves in a
kind of struggle. This dynamic ends, however, with some speech or action of the heretofore silent character which amounts to an answer and
yet is at the same time a "detonation," or a loud silencing, a final non-
answer. The silent person is at last driven by combined motives and
circumstances—which Conrad tries with very exact artistry to make
clear as including the provocation by the other, the specific personalities, the background of the scene, and some inner forces—to respond in
one way or another. The answering non-answer, when Conrad is writing at his best, amounts to a great, concise "sentence upon" their relation. The whole scene works toward the production of a single
sentence, or of an action which has the status of a *sentence* in both
meanings—that of a statement and that of a punishment, often mutual.
Note here that Ford's statement of the rule for dialogue—characters
must "never answer the speech that goes before"—has been converted
from a psychological irony about selfish manners to an image of dramatic struggle which can have pronounced political implications without losing its psychological cast. The action of not answering, instead of
showing static, universal egotism, self-involvement alone, has become a
violent and conscious conflict between characters over the production
of speech. A character who consciously refuses to answer another who
is demanding speech openly is very different from the figure who talks

to himself because he is unaware of the other. Ford's merry recipe undergoes a radical conversion. The demand for speech might now generate scenes in the spirit of Cassandra's refusal to answer Clytaemnestra, Teiresias' resistance to Oedipus and his final outburst of punitive prediction, Bartleby's one-line responses under pressure to speak and participate, and so on: scenes which in their reverberations go beyond ego psychology to deal with the politics of the production of language. These scenes in Conrad's middle novels, further, usually have a marked "frame," or appear as set pieces, or "centerpieces," or even as ideas of dialogue, with their own cumulative rhythms.

Though there are many scenes of pressure to speak amid disproportion throughout the work, a set of major scenes might be mentioned in this introduction, so that the reader familiar with Conrad will note both that they are major points within their respective works, and that they are strikingly various: (1) the dialogue with the Intended in "Heart of Darkness"; (2) the central encounter between Whalley and Massy in "The End of the Tether"; (3) the plurality of inquisitorial scenes in *Nostromo*, but particularly Sotillo's torture of Hirsch and Hirsch's own earlier attempt to make Gould speak in order to sell him hides or dynamite; (4) the recurrent dialogue rhythm of the Verloc marriage, a marriage built up almost entirely of variations on the "forced dialogue" with increasingly grim closures, until she at last murders him, in Conrad's most protracted forced dialogue; (5) the confrontation between Bunter and Johns in the minor, extremely interesting problem story "The Black Mate"; (6) the great scene between Mikulin and Razumov in *Under Western Eyes*, with its complex background of allusions to other coercions to speak, both within the novel itself and within history; (7) "A Familiar Preface" to *A Personal Record*, where Conrad describes the pressure Ford put on him to write his autobiography, and makes it parallel to the scene of Conrad's master mariner's examination in that same book, in which coercion to speak seems to be presented, in contradiction to most of Conrad's work, fondly, as a wholesome educative method. These are by no means the only scenes in Conrad where there is "pumping," or where a demand for speech meets resistance to establish the dominant mood; but they are I think exemplary ones, in which we can reasonably say that Conrad makes it clear to the ordinary reader that coercion to speak is itself a main theme, not just an instrument for forwarding the action, and has its own increasingly visible, nonconversational forms. It would be nonsense, of course, to write about Conrad discussing only such scenes, and the following chapters will take up many other issues and discuss several novels in detail. But these scenes do work as extraordinary dialogical "centerpieces"—indications of Conrad's idea of dialogue—and therefore have a great deal to tell us about his fiction as a whole and about his sense of social existence.

"Forced dialogue" has to be understood in at least three larger contexts: (1) coercion to speak as a scene both in literature and in social practice; (2) recurrent dialogue form in the novel as leading to the sense that each novel has a distinctive "idea" of dialogue; (3) the development of dialogue forms over the course of Conrad's own work. Without these contexts, this scene would seem falsely isolated here, as Conrad's single, static "meaning." Before approaching Conrad's interpretation of the complex literary and social history of the scene of coercion to speak, which is the larger theme of this book, let us look first at the simplest and most formal of these issues—that of recurrent dialogue form in the novel—and then at the dialogue forms in Conrad's early work, before he concentrated on the specific problems of forced dialogue.

Robert Louis Stevenson, in "A Humble Remonstrance," quietly rejected the idea that fiction can mimic life's density, or achieve a full realism, and argued instead that the novelist as a conscious craftsman looks for formal limits, for instance the "invention (yes, invention) and preservation of a certain key in dialogue."[16] He was in this essay dissenting (humbly) from Henry James's ambitious sense of the scope of fiction, but was at the same time to a great degree sharing James's own formalism, since James himself tended to see actual social dialogue as a kind of formless chaos, passively mirrored in the "deluge of dialogue" in popular novels. James wanted to make dialogue a steady vehicle of the action.[17] To Stevenson's musical "key" and James's controlling forms, we could add that most nineteenth-century novelists, such as Austen, Balzac, Tolstoy, and Dostoevsky, have recognizable ideas of dialogue, founded on particular assumptions about what generally happens when people meet to talk. To make very quick reductions: Defoe pictures contractual negotiation, mutual exploitation that can profit both sides; this is not the same as Balzac's idea of encounter, most vividly that of elitist power struggle, often among more than two persons; this in turn differs somewhat from Dostoevsky's comic vision of gatherings as struggles to include the excluded, and of talking to oneself as fallen prayer; which in turn is different from Tolstoy's emphasis on emotive sympathy; which in turn differs from Austen's emphasis on a kind of rational sympathy. There are, that is, common themes, but also ideas specific to each about what holds one speech to the next, and what forces—erotic and eristic—combine speeches. The "idea of dialogue" must be taken, in this sense, as a clue to the author's entire notion of what links any one sentence to any following sentence: and obviously the causal connection between characters' sentences may itself be very close to the essence of a writer's social vision. The reader who learns to read the ironies and causalities of a Balzac or Austen dialogue is learning (like Rastignac in Mme. de Beauseant's drawing room) a specific social contract, and in a much more ironic sense than was meant by most political theorists. Dialogues display a kind of miniaturized, static social constitution. When repeated they become ironic (not necessarily simply representational, but rather more "liturgical") models of the novel's implicit "social contract."[18] My readings of Conrad here will try to show that he belongs roughly with those novelists (Scott being the most facile and impressive and also the most enjoyably lacking in portentous implications) who emphasize the action of coercion to speak over the various kinds of "sympathy" in the social coherence of dialogue. This is what makes his dialogue scenes alien to the high English novelistic tradition (Leavis' "great tradition"), with its vision of conversational liberation. But this major question—sympathy versus force as the main cohesive principle in dialogue—must also be put aside for now in a return to the simple technical point. In the novel, powerful and pleasurable dialogues come about not only through naturalness of speech but also through formal predictability and repetition—not only in the representation of idiolects and dialects, speech tics, characteristic habits and mannerisms of spontaneity, and digression, but also in the patent repetition of whole, strict forms of dialogue into which the characters repeatedly fall together.

The novelist, that is, often has a distinctive "idea of dialogue," made available to the reader through formal repetition, sometimes subtle, and sometimes deliberately highly outlined and visible. The reader watches for and enjoys the repetition of the strict pattern, which is in its own way analogous to socially instituted repetitions of dialogue forms, like those in religious meetings, or those in entertainment (for example the talk show) or pedagogy (Athenian eristic or the American classroom), or street play ("playing the dozens"). The novel first of all does not represent but actually shares in the cultural passion for and pleasure in formal dialogical repetition. "Conversation" itself, though we like to think of it as freedom, may be a complex form, as Austen and James knew, learnable only by an elite, an implicit set of rules of freedom, devices for appearing free. But putting aside the difficult question of whether there is a human universal of conversation or instead only a set of class and cultural devices for appearing free and intimate, at which the most skillful and accomplished conversationalists win, there is certainly a group of works that might seem at once extremely "novel," and at the same time borderline as novels by the more conservative definition, which exaggerate this formulaic quality. This is true, for instance, of *Don Quixote,* Lewis Carroll's *Alice* books, *Bouvard and Pécuchet, The Confidence-Man,* and *Catch-22,* each of which could be said in its own way to have a fixed "idea of dialogue" that recurs, that centers the pleasure of the book, and that is far from a simple spontaneous naturalism; and it is likewise true, no less fiercely though in a more subtle sense, of conversational novels like Goethe's *Elective Affinities,* Austen's *Emma,* Turgenev's *Smoke,* and James's *Awkward Age.*

In these works, against the standard wisdom that dialogue is most mimetic or enjoyable when "free" and "natural," the reader is successfully let in on dialogue as form, even as ritual, and the result is neither simply formal-aesthetic nor simply representational and historical. A sharp and pleasurable awareness of dialogue as socially repetitious formal action is closely bound up with the genre of the novel. The dramatist often fills out a unified action with as full a range of dialogue types as possible; many novels, by contrast, have a various or anarchic and wandering action which returns "home" repeatedly to a unified idea of dialogue. Such novels do not, however, exactly represent some specific socially practiced form, but instead the quality of mutual dialogical obsessiveness itself, the desire to return together to one format of relation. This return is often comic, comforting. For example, one way to define the repeated dialogue between Don Quixote and Sancho Panza: Quixote asserts absolute faith in a hallucination by citing his romances, and Sancho, less certain, objects by citing his senses. We have a dialogue— of course this is only one statement of the form—with someone who derives more certainty from his books than his servant does from his senses. Whether this image of their dialogue is acceptable or not, the point is that the audience—not entirely unlike Quixote himself in his reliance on texts—comes to rely on the way in which Quixote and Sancho (like Melville's confidence man and his rubes, or Huck and his adults, or Socrates and his students, or Bouvard and Pécuchet in their curriculum, or Emma and Mr. Knightley in their mutual teaching) will square off and return to their "home" in dialogues of interpetation of the world together. If the world of the novel is, as Lukács echoing Novalis said, "homesick," impossibly large, plural, and adventurous, nevertheless recurrent dialogue form may be its "home." To give one preliminary reading of this effect tragically reversed in Conrad: while dialogue repetition in Conrad has not received much attention, John Hagan, Jr., has argued that the unity of *The Secret Agent* comes not from the plot, which at least on a first reading is exploded and retarded like Stevie himself, but from the "recurrent interview structure."[19] Yet since the strongest of these recurrences is the formal repetition of forced dialogues in the Verloc marriage, the irony is that their "home" together in dialogue, their repeated married dialogue, sounds rather like the "forced" interviews that take place in the external, political world. And while in the drama, as among Shakespeare's lower classes or between some of his battling lovers, there is often a kind of predictability in dialogue marked as pleasure for the audience, the novel tends to objectify this repetition in a way that leads us to think of it by itself: to see something akin to a contract of dialogue in the particular social milieu being described. This in turn gives the novel a very complex representational and imaginative relation to the existence of dialogue contracts, or recurrent dialogue practices, in social groups—Quaker meetings and so on—those forms that are the subject matter of the "ethnography of dialogue."[20] To such an ethnography, the term *dialogue* itself is not universal but refers to a Greek idea of the logical division of speakers; friendly or intimate "conversation" has different rules in different places. The twentieth-century habit among thinkers of identifying oneself by one's "dialogic"—I and Thou, or deconstruction, or speech-act theory, or Harold Bloom's "agon," or Erving Goffman's "interaction," or Richard Rorty's "conversation," and so on—might itself be an ethnographic fact related to earlier religious liturgical emblems or self-identifications. If the only home in a novelistic world is a dialogue idea, such "novelistic" thinkers also make themselves known by particular dialogue signs.

For reasons particular to each, no theorist of the novel has been centrally interested in recurrent dialogue form. Bakhtin, who steers outside the usual dilemmas (formalism versus antiformalism, invention versus representation, structuralism versus historicism) for a socially vital definition of the novel, though he points to Lucianic dialogue as a major source of the novel and implies that the "dialogic" of true novelistic prose subverts the hierarchical "dialectic" of philosophy, is out to emphasize the unresolvable wildness of ideological and marketplace speech, the interference of plural consciousness and plural glossaries. It would not be in accord with this stance to spend too much time on the contractuality of dialogue in great novels like *Don Quixote* or *Moll Flanders*. Lukács, of course, would find this feature of dialogical recurrence, even where there is a "progress of dialogue" as in Bunyan or Austen, too static, marginal—perhaps a symptom of the bourgeois will to static constitution and resistance to dialectical change. In *The Rise of the Novel*, Ian Watt, discussing Richardson's epistolary form, describes just such a resistance in a class fixation on one kind of discourse, but does not in his account of the novel as "formal realism" discuss dialogue form itself as repetition. He also alludes only briefly and dismissively to the connection between the novel and the Platonic dialogue. James, though he called "the question of our speech" central, and filled his late novels with a dictated, spoken syntax that returns to the American tradition of spontaneous Protestant witness bearing—the talk show—referred, as already noted, to real speech as "deluge" and as first chaos. The essence of the world's actual dialogue is for him an almost terrifying lack of form, which the novelist works to direct, moving over the face of the waters. (Stevenson, recall, when citing the "key" of dialogue, called it invention, as *against* representation.) Mark Lambert, in an excellent book on dialogue technique in Dickens, also associates dialogue emphatically with the "fun" and "free" part of the novel, indulgence, white space. Such readers as Stanley Rosen in *The Symposium*, Kenneth Burke in *A Rhetoric of Motives*, and Gilbert Ryle in *Plato's Progress* probably come closest to mediation on recurring dialogue form as the shape of a work, but they deal with what are generally considered philosophical dialogues.[21] Strong critics and theorists of the novel, then, whether antiformalist or formalist in final perspective, have generally associated "speech" and "dialogue" as they occur in the world with freedom: the spontaneous, uncontrolled, plastic, idiomatic, digressive part of life that, to the formalists, has to be reined in, made part of the action, and to a genius of pluralism like Bakhtin represents the ultimate potential of the novel as an open genre.

Of course in practice not all dialogue is free, natural, spontaneous, informal, or lively. On the contrary, it may be true that most real dialogue is variously constrained and forced. But for some reason we usually say that the best novelistic dialogue has those qualities: the unforced movement of common, popular, or natural talk; vivid displays of low (dialect, idiolect, oaths) and high (mutually liberating) free speech. It would be shabby to dismiss all images of free dialogue as nothing but ideology, or I-Thou philosophy as just a utopian myth. But revelatory and intimate I-Thou conversation, of the kind that the greatest characters in Austen, Eliot, Lawrence, and Forster reach toward, does usually occur between those who belong to a high, even an ideal, spiritual class, who can master difficult rules; the conversational idealism of the "great tradition," with its images of autonomous but energetic intellectual intimacy, describes heroes and heroines who transcend dialogical constraints that they are alert, witty, and sensitive enough to understand. They are the "winners" in the conversational scene: an elite of sympathetic imagination, who can even overcome the flaws and limits in conventional ideas of "sympathy"; slightly below them in this world picture is a class of common people whose talk is "natural." Novelistic dialogue, however, obviously doesn't begin and end with free, natural lower-class speech and freely achieved upper-class mutual sympathy. Most real speech between classes is probably not conversational. And there is a set of great nineteenth-century *anti*-conversational, yet extremely dialogical, novels which fix on a more coercive and authoritarian dialogue regime to return it incessantly upon the reader. Scott's meditation on the varieties of dramatic forced speaking in *The Heart of Mid-Lothian* is probably the first great example. Alice's recurrent encounters with illogical, self-absorbed, and insane pedagogues is another. Melville's *The Confidence-Man* may be the most furious. Its barrage of scenes of forced selling amounts not only to a formal burden but to an attempted ethnography of American dialogue.[22] In this American Menippean satire, dialogue formalism and cultural representation meet: extreme dialogue repetition represents the scene of selling. Possibly dialogue between the classes, as opposed to "conversation" which takes place within a class, will involve more "drama," more actions like coercive inquiry, detection, selling, negotiating, blackmailing, and so on. If we can define Leavis' unstated principle in choosing most of the works of the "great tradition" as a high-conversational bias, in which moral insight and the worth of life appear through developing conversational struggle, it may be a kind of contrary, somber, critical realism, rather than an obsessive formal impulse alone, that overformalizes and even stagnates dialogue in the novel, to indicate, with necessary repetition, the rule-governed, hierarchical, fatal fixation of social and political dialogue, as Conrad oppositionally does. Here, "form" and "key" in dialogue are not just compositional or aesthetic requirements, as for Stevenson; they are, on the contrary, at the heart of the novel's critical realism.

The Conradian novel, then, as defined here—along with a small group of novels since Scott to which it belongs—has a very strong will to objectify and contemplate dialogue as constrained form, and the plurality of such dialogue forms in their social distribution. In this light, consider "Heart of Darkness" as a story about the progressive objectification of its own disproportionate and forced dialogue forms. It is, of course, easy to take Conrad's most famous story as an instance of freespoken "oral literature," in which Marlow is the skaz, yarn spinner, or ancient mariner. But the story itself has to be seen as having for one of its main actions the increasing objectification of the speaking narrator himself, so that as it proceeds, the reader has an increasingly uncanny—partly comic, partly disappointed—feeling that Marlow's longwinded yarn is proportionally and therefore somehow morally linked to the more obviously imperial and abject forms of excessive talk like Kurtz's. That is, Marlow and Kurtz, as speakers, are progressively identified with each other through a covert appeal to the reader's sense of "normal" prose masses, and of the ordinary length of a talk. We increasingly see that each does "almost all" the talking in his own dialogical context: Marlow to his audience, Kurtz to the natives and to his clownish Russian disciple.

Here is a typical short passage from "Heart of Darkness" which in its onrush might go unnoticed but which is meant to make us contemplate and "equate" three or four dialogue scenes formally. Marlow has come ashore and is listening to the young Russian, exploding with a need to talk, tell about Kurtz:

> In the next breath he advised me to keep enough steam on the boiler to blow the whistle in case of any trouble. "One good screech will do more for you than all your rifles. They are simple people," he repeated. He rattled away at such a rate he quite overwhelmed me. He seemed to be trying to make up for lots of silence, and actually hinted, laughing, that such was the case. "Don't you talk with Mr. Kurtz?" I said. "You don't talk with that man— you listen to him," he exclaimed with severe exaltation. (123)

These sentences set up a hierarchy of dialogue scenes—which the reader is invited to tear down. Lowest, apparently, are the simple natives, overwhelmed by a boat's whistle. On the next level, the Russian's talk itself, a kind of social chatter, here ironically overwhelms Marlow. At the presumed highest level is philosophical discourse like Kurtz's, aweing disciples into pious silence. Implicitly, on the fourth level, framing all this, and making its own claim to truth, is Marlow's narration to his audience, who object and grunt a few times. We might, that is, easily organize these scenes of forceful speech and disproportionate dialogue, combined so rapidly and formally that they seem to make a "dialogue fugue," into a self-congratulatory hierarchy similar to the Russian's, but with the last—ours—fiction or art, at the top, as transcendent consciousness: Marlow's ironic contemplative art, the truest frame. But just as clearly, Conrad stands behind the analogous disproportionate dialogues to suggest that all the scenes, including Marlow's art, and his writing to us, are alike: imperial assertions of "overwhelming" force. In each scene, the speaker impresses the listener by the force of sound. If the jungle's "darkness" and civilization's "light" will nearly be "welded together without a joint" (45) by the story, the same fusion applies to our preconceived images of some dialogues as civilized and some as uncivilized. The natives overwhelmed by the ship's whistle resemble the Russian himself (their narrator and explainer) being overwhelmed by the force of Kurtz's altruistic oratory. Less clear, but most important, Marlow's silent audience (representing ourselves) falls—at least potentially—into this field. But whether we accept or refuse this last irony, this passage shows *how* Conrad asks the reader to think about dialogue as formal and proportional rather than simply expressive: by seeing and hearing the parallel ratios so as to find startling affinities among apparently discrete dialogue scenes.

Note, in terms of the history of readings of "Heart of Darkness," that Marlow's portentous, forceful repetition of adjectives can be understood somewhat differently. Leavis' conversational idealism rejects some of Marlow's incessant rhetoric as hot air—which of course it is. But in this reading, Marlow's relentless insistences, his own excess of verbal steam (even the mist that pervades the landscape is an image of rhetoric), is part of the conscious imagery of the story, and of the dialogical mood of imperialism, of "overwhelming the other" by misty imperial words. The scene of "overwhelming" noise is the common denominator of the story's main theme—imperialism—and what Conrad called its "secondary" theme, Marlow's obsession with the image of Kurtz speaking. The "dialogic" here welds together the two themes "without a joint." The proportional resemblance of all dialogue scenes is both tragic and comic, even oddly hilarious, and appears as an irrationally temporal, rather than simply atemporal, simultaneity: Marlow the young man, we could say—if we break with rational time sequence—became obsessed with his image of Kurtz talking "because" Kurtz talks to his disciples in the same disproportion which Marlow the older man and narrator *now* has vis-à-vis his audience. Young Marlow was obsessed by the image of Kurtz speaking, which was itself the metaphoric and predictive image of older Marlow narrating. The "cause" of Marlow's inexplicable obsession with Kurtz's talk is his own "later" identity with its proportions during the time of the story's actual telling. From a perspective of speech production, of course, this is all rational, because the older Marlow's production of the story for his audience *is* the "origin" of the story. There is, then, a simple repetition of dialogue form in time (Kurtz's overwhelming verbosity generates Marlow's overwhelming verbosity about him), but also a simultaneity or "knot" of dialogue scenes, which has to do with the production of the story itself. Marlow's original obsession with Kurtz—which Conrad has to impose on the reader partly by fiat or pure force of insistence—has its strongest but most irrational explanation in his predestined identity with Kurtz as the current talkative narrator before us (almost in the way that Oedipus' rational power to conduct judicial inquiries and force speech from his witnesses is inherited from the Sphinx's earlier grosser power—which he dissolved and inherited—to demand the answer to the riddle, to force replies).

The fusion of categories such as "psychological" and "political" in and by dialogue form can be seen clearly here. While Marlow's resemblance to Kurtz can be read psychologically, so that each is the other's son and father in speech disproportion, and the two are "insanely" identified as willful speakers (Marlow of course trying but failing to eradicate this will to power in himself), there should be no question that this resemblance presents itself to us first as a historical and political idea. Disproportion and coercion in the speech scene become the constants because, as Conrad writes in one essay, "man is a conquering animal," [23] and history is imperialist. The famous "horror" at the end of the story is partly a joke, said twice, narcissistically, by self-echoing Kurtz, and partly a non-answer, punch line, or "detonation" coming at the close of what we could call a "shaggy dog story" (the entire action of "Heart of Darkness" is more defiantly funny than most critics have argued); but it is lastly the identification of art and politics as imperial speech. The first sentence of the story describes how the ship "swings to" (describes a forced circle about) its anchor until it rests. The secondary action of the story is the "swing to" that Marlow's own freer telling makes toward Kurtz's compulsive talk, becoming slowly and inevitably linked to it in moral and political status. In this gradual parallelism, a universal "dialogic" is being contemplated and objectified: by the end of the story the "swing to" has implicitly united philosophical dialogue (Kurtz as mock Socrates), fictive narration (or the dialogue between writer and audience), and imperialist cant into a single scene of dialogue, and Conrad has assigned himself and the reader to the same unavoidable intention of conquest and the same imperial scene. Artistic force, the desire to make the reader see, hear, or feel, is a sublimation at most of the other desires to conquer. It "must" participate in the general dialogue form.

In *Don Quixote* the repeated dialogue, in addition to its comedy, mimicked a typical debate of the age, between biblical authority and sense experience; it was then also used in the second part for baroque paradoxes, in which the *Quixote* became a new profane Bible, a book determining reality. Conrad constructs "Heart of Darkness" on similar lines, to make a baroque "knot," a "mirror" of dialogues reflecting each other out onto the audience, so as to define the typical dialogue scene of his time. As *Quixote* mimics a typical dialogue of the age, Conrad brings contemporary imperialism home in his forced dialogues. The point is that the proportions of imperialism are everywhere in an imperial age—even in stories told on yawls on the Thames, or in our reading of the novella. What bothered Leavis—Marlow's incessant, insistent, domineering, adjectival style—was meant to bother. The story could not exist without an excess of fiat. The disproportions in Kurtz's speech, in Marlow's telling, and in Conrad's representation of Marlow's telling, resemble each other; from different angles each could be said to come first and "cause" the others. Conrad "repeats" the scene of dialogue abstractly, not merely in the story of the characters but from level to level of the story's production, until we finally see Conrad, or the author, in a dialogical relation to us that resembles, in its desire for conquest, all the others. What Conrad called the "secondary" plot of "Heart of Darkness," in this reading, is this gradual identification of all dialogue relations as disproportionate and imperial.[24]

Parenthetically, it is worth adding that this process is not primarily "deconstructive" despite some apparent resemblances. "Deconstruction," from the standpoint being developed here, is another philosophical sublimation of the Oedipal drama of forced inquiry: text, language, writing oversees its own intentional disintegration. The "text" plays the role of Oedipus, undoing itself for a general sacrificial peace; though it can be argued in reverse that Oedipus' inquisitorial self-eradication is a dramatic version of what in fact writing does. But in any case all deconstructions, as Derrida writing about force half-indicates, have eristic elements, and, though "playful," are shaded by inquisition. To "make" the other's text decenter by a reading of disjunctive metaphors reenacts Socrates' forcing of the other into logical self-contradiction—elenchus. But when Kurtz scribbles "exterminate the brutes" at the bottom of his enlightening canticle, or when Marlow closes with the evasive lie "your name," or when Conrad himself uses various methods to call attention to the forced conditions of his own writing, there is certainly a drama *like* that of deconstruction, a change of intonation violent enough to be a "detonation," but the stress falls not on self-contradiction, or on endless linguistic difference and reinterpretation, but on the idea that all dialogue, even dialogue with the self, involves coercive disproportion. Kurtz's relation to himself, when he repudiates himself, remains imperial. Implicitly, nobody quarrels even with himself as an equal. Conrad is not as interested, then, in the tropes and actions we call deconstruction—which make the text itself the sublime Oedipal actor—as in outlining the inescapably disproportionate forces at work in any dialogue, including storytelling, lyrical quarrel with the self, and philosophical critique.

The power to abstract and objectify dialogue forms, then, gives fiction the force of "comparative dialogic." The novel can make startling juxtapositions of dialogues in broadly different scenes. Comparative dialogic makes it possible to move among discrete institutions of dialogue—social, religious, literary, pedagogical—to compare them formally. For example, let us isolate a dialogue pattern found in the *Oedipus Tyrannus*, that of the punishment of the speech-forcer, the discovery of the guilt of the coercive interrogator himself. We might then put aside, at least temporarily, distinctions between literary genres, between psychology and politics, or between literature and reality, and ask if we find this dialogue form anywhere else. It could be posited that this form is inscribed in the unconscious as "Oedipal"—in a sense of the term which combines Sophoclean and Freudian insights to supplement each other. It is the scene in which the father figure initiates a coercive dialogue and is surprisingly and "thrillingly" annihilated by the answers he forces from those he interrogates. In this scene the father is punished by the examination or catechism he appears to institute, but of which he is in fact the predestined victim. This dream of vengeance upon the father by the surprising but inevitable "boomerang" of catechism could be regarded either psychoanalytically or politically. And it would not be surprising to find variants of this scene both in literature and in ongoing public ritual: in the opening of *Lear*, in Dostoevsky's "Grand Inquisitor," in the resolution of the McCarthy hearings, in a popular television show of journalistic inquisition like *60 Minutes*, or in Foucault's vision (an unconsciously Oedipal vision by this account) of the world as all examination without real subjects. Wherever the democratic punishment of the speech-forcer, or the idea that inquiring power might be undone, or undo itself, by its own inquiry, is attended by feelings of fear and gratification, we might see an Oedipal dialogue process.

Likewise, a simpler idea of dialogue, the notion of necessary disproportion between speakers which I have been exploring here—the picture of one speaking a great deal and one very little—can itself be applied expressively to diverse worldviews. For Leopardi, dissymmetry is the expression of a pessimistic psychology: for Valéry, dissymmetry is the essence of all dialogue, an aesthetic-mathematical universal;[25] for Richard Ohmann, disproportion is a sign of class domination in sociological interviews.[26] My thesis is that Conrad was, if anything, a dialogist conscious of these plural possibilities, and that he used the stark universal of dialogue disproportion, sometimes adding to it the more complex Oedipal dynamic of the punishment of the speech-forcer, to "fuse" categories like the psychological, the poetic, and the political. Teaching this idea to a class, one might draw a long line and a short line on the blackboard, representing the speaker who speaks a great deal and the speaker who speaks very little, and then show how this simple, radical disproportion ironically covers diverse dialogue scenes in Conrad's works (marriage, inquisition, storytelling, selling, hiring, courtship, séance), and might incidentally be applied to other well-known scenes such as psychoanalytic dialogue. In each case the one doing most of the speaking, or the one doing very little, may be the forcer, and there are many other specific variables. The power of this formal objectification is precisely that it allows him to cut across conventional categories, putting aside any one rational standpoint—psychology, aesthetics, politics—to merge all of these into a deeply disturbing dialogical constant. Just as the interrogation of Joan of Arc in Carl Dreyer's film can't be said to be singly political, religious, or sexual but all of these fused, so strategies of reading Conrad which make him out as primarily a psychologist, a metaphysician, or a political thinker have tended to ignore his dialogical understanding. He is the novelist who most consciously understands the classical action of coercion to speak as a sometimes explicit and sometimes sublimated unifying motif. The implicit ground of poetics itself becomes the scene of coercion to speak, and genre and tone become responses to this ground.

Theories about dialogue are relatively common, but theories about the historical development and change of dialogue forms are scarce. There have been many practical comments on the uses of philosophical dialogue for pluralistic exposition by Hume, Herder, Diderot, Landor, and others; and many theories, for instance in Plato criticism from Schleiermacher to Gadamer, or in the modern line of dialogical polemics that runs from Buber to Bakhtin, give the term *dialogue* a very high place. Rudolf Hirzel's *Der Dialog* is the one major scholarly study of the development of the dialogue as a genre; but it does not really apply to the novel. It is Gilbert Ryle who has in a searching and jovial way written the one modern study of Plato, skeptical and formal, which takes changes in dialogue form not as the transcendental sign of the interpersonal as the true but as an indication of someone's actual changing social milieu. It is of course daring and ironic to apply this strategy to Plato. Looking at changes in the dialogue forms, Ryle argues—iconoclastically, entertainingly, not very believably—that Plato in the end was moving away from the theory of Ideas toward a sort of Aristotelian naturalism. He hints at an ironic novel—the book is called *Plato's Progress*[27]—in which the hero finally forsakes Ideal Forms. Plato is (by the present definition) novelized—that is, made into a dialogical progress in a historical setting. We see him first practicing eristic dialogue forms in Athens, then moving toward his Forms when politically cut off from real educational encounter, and then finally coming back to a different, less transcendental notion of form itself. Recognizing Ryle's joking allusion to Bunyan in the title word *progress* (Ryle seems to see the connection between English Protestantism and the search for new liturgical dialogue forms), we might take Ryle's hint, and for a moment, before going on to some specific examples of forced dialogue, consider Conrad's own early "progress" in dialogue.

There is no question that Conrad before the middle period which will be the main concern of this study was already a conscious formalist in dialogue. Each of the major early works has its own dialogue craft, partly distinct from that of the others, and selectively matched to its themes. There is time here only to sketch the development. In *An Outcast of the Islands*, Willems, allegorically named, is a crude early version of the parallel talkatives Kurtz and Marlow; Willems bullies his wife by making her the audience of his egotistical monologues. The Malays, by contrast, have a capacity for inexhaustible and free *collective* speech. They are viewed, romantically enough, as a primitive people "to whom talk is poetry and painting and music, all art, all history; their only accomplishment, their only superiority, their only amusement." [28] In this early novel there is a stark contrast between the civilized man's egocentric, one-sided, disproportional talk and the native's unforced, communal, totally "immersed" collective talk, never exhausted or decayed, and beyond representation. The phrase "their only superiority" seems purposely duplicit—this talk with its continuity and force (it is not represented as dialogue, because the Greek word now implies formal division of the speakers) gives them their only superiority to animals, or nature, but likewise their only superiority to civilization. The idea of a purely continuous and generative speech is probably high romantic, as expressed most convincingly in Wordsworth or Hölderlin.[29] With *The Nigger of the "Narcissus,"* certainly a technical breakthrough for Conrad in many ways, this idea undergoes plastic revision and modernization. Perhaps taking a hint from Stephen Crane,[30] Conrad amasses forecastle talk into paragraphs containing many short speeches, many of which are oaths, more "force of sound" than "meaning." He abandons the convention of speeches individuated into separate paragraphs (rejecting the image of talk as an individual act, or "dialogue") in order to suggest that forecastle "we" speech is immersed in its collectivity. The talk clusters, partly because he doesn't discard quotation marks, look radically different from the earlier idealized image of Malay talk as pure collective genius: pointillistic, lonely, isolated, the forecastle's amassed speeches are at once orchestral and anomic. This conscious break with the conventions of dialogue paragraphing to represent forecastle speech as pointillistic solidarity is one of the clearest instances in early Conrad of the association of speech and labor; it could be seen as patronizing. In a very different formal mode, *Lord Jim* collects a sort of international symposium of responses or commentaries—French, German, English—around the hero. The philosophical symposium, with its verdict of uncertainty, is reemployed here, with strong traces of Menippean satire, or attack on the presumptions of intellectual understanding.

After this, we have the highly conscious temporal arrangement of dialogue forms in "Heart of Darkness," just discussed. It criticizes the romantic ideal of a historically prophetic speech that itself has continuity and force but is innocent of evil. Tentatively, the story decides that the modern storyteller cannot get back to Malay ideal talk but rather has to be only another imperial speaker, conscious at best, "immersed" in coercion to speak rather than in a community of free speakers. The story's closure, the dialogue with the Intended, predicts Conrad's increasing turn toward dialogues of force: the turn away from romantic ideas of lyrical speech toward an objectification of tragic forced dialogue. The heart of darkness reached at the end of the story is partly the realization that fiction cannot be lyrically and narratively produced as an "only superiority," a pure lyrical freedom outside historical force, but is itself the product of coercion. The fact is that the Intended, however "horrible" and grotesquely melodramatic the scene, rescues Marlow from the idea of a sublime internal compulsion to speak out by showing him external compulsion. Partly liberated by this scene from the romantic idea that his own writing should be inner compulsion, Conrad himself can go on to become a more "objective" dramatist (whether it is a loss or gain is not the point), who makes the scene of forced speech take place between the characters rather than inside a character. This is precisely what "The End of the Tether" begins to study. In that story there is a rich distribution of dialogue forms, intended to be seen and compared by the reader, but the forced dialogue (as I will try to show in Chapter III) now occupies the central place, rather than the place of ironic closure. That is, with "The End of the Tether" we come to the middle period of Conrad's work, in which the forced dialogue now gives the central organization to Conrad's dialogues; and this will remain the case until the completion of *Under Western Eyes* in 1912, the book in which Conrad raises to its highest pitch, analyzes, and perhaps also has done with, his interest in coercion to speak, after which he will go on to write a series of romances of "interference," *Chance, Victory,* and *The Rescue.*

Since one of the main powers of the forced dialogue comes from its provocative reuse in the political novels to compare and equate what seem to be different relations and institutions (marriage, selling, inquisition, and so on), the scene chosen here as a first example of the form will have to bias us temporarily toward the clearly political use of the scene for the extortion of information. Nevertheless Sotillo's interrogation of Hirsch, with its highly "striped" counterpoints between speech and silence, dialogue and narration, made obvious on the page, and its nearly unanalyzable tension between force and farce, makes the best starting place. Placed near the end of *Nostromo*, it is the novel's most detailed, foregrounded, physical description of the interrogatory torture which is in the background of every character's consciousness—not only Monygham's—as *the* definitive scene in the culture. Hirsch suffers the "estrapade"—his arms are tied behind his back and then lifted, so that his shoulders dislocate, and he hangs by a rope (as do some other main characters in the novel, more figuratively). The attempted speech-extortion here takes the form of a primary distortion of the body, or torture. The body of the prose, the stark alternation of narrative and dialogue, is also clearly "striped," sadistic, dislocating.

Sotillo looked at him in silence. "Will you depart from your obstinacy, you rogue?" he asked. Already a rope, whose one end was fastened to Señor Hirsch's wrists, had been thrown over a beam, and three soldiers held the other end, waiting. He made no answer. His heavy lower lip hung stupidly. Sotillo made a sign. Hirsch was jerked up off his feet, and a yell of despair and agony burst out in the room, filled the passage of the great buildings, rent the air outside, caused every soldier of the camp along the shore to look up at the windows, started some of the officers in the hall babbling excitedly, with shining eyes; others, setting their lips, looked gloomily at the floor . . .

The sun had set when he went in once more. A soldier carried in two lighted candles and slunk out, shutting the door without noise.

"Speak, thou Jewish child of the devil! The silver! The silver, I say! Where is it? Where have you foreign rogues hidden it? Confess or—"

A slight quiver passed up the taut rope from the racked limbs, but the body of Señor Hirsch, enterprising businessman from Esmeralda, hung under the heavy beam perpendicular and silent, facing the colonel awfully. The inflow of the night air, cooled by the snows of the Sierra, spread gradually a delicious freshness through the close heat of the room.

"Speak—thief—scoundrel—picaro—or—"

Sotillo had seized the riding-whip, and stood with his arm lifted up. For a word, for one little word, he felt he would have knelt, cringed, grovelled on the floor before the drowsy, conscious stare of those fixed eyeballs starting out of the grimy, dishevelled head that drooped very still with his mouth closed askew. The colonel ground his teeth with rage and struck. The rope vibrated leisurely to the blow, like the long string of a pendulum starting from a rest. But no swinging motion was imparted to the body of Señor Hirsch, the well-known hide merchant on the coast. With a convulsive effort of the twisted arms it leaped up a few inches, curling upon itself like a fish on the end of a line. Señor Hirsch's head was flung back on his straining throat; his chin trembled. For a moment the rattle of his chattering teeth pervaded the vast, shadowy room, where the candles made a patch of light round the two flames burning side by side. And as Sotillo, staying his raised hand, waited for him to speak, with the sudden flash of a grin and a straining forward of the wrenched shoulders, he spat violently into his face.

The uplifted whip fell, and the colonel sprang back with a low cry of dismay, as if aspersed by a jet of deadly venom. Quick as thought he snatched up his revolver, and fired twice. The report and the concussion seemed to throw him at once from ungovernable rage into idiotic stupor. He stood with drooping jaw and stony eyes. (447–449)

This scene is one of Conrad's dialogue "sonnets," or formal meditations on the nature of dialogue. It has the characteristic rhythm, in which demanding speeches alternate liturgically with silences until a final explosion which is a "detonation" or loud silence. Scenes with this rhythm, though less violent, appear in many places throughout Conrad's work, and, in a large sense, the lives of Stevie, Winnie, and Verloc, of Razumov, of Whalley, of Nostromo, of Heyst have this rhythm: they are cornered people who finally "detonate," resolving themselves atonally. The physical triad rest, unrest, arrest, which governs much of Conrad's sense of motion, is at work here: the tension between rest (silence) and unrest (demand for speech) culminates in an arrest. Specific to this passage is the equation of speaking and spitting: Sotillo's demand, "Speak," retroactively sounds like the spitting it provokes. It is a spitter's duet. But if we try to get past this kind of observation about rhythms to deal with themes, we immediately confront a large field of possibilities open to facile commentary but in fact extremely resistant to any conclusions. Some major themes seem to be: the stupidity of Jew-baiting and anti-Semitism, without, as others have noted, its being clear where Conrad stands; formal sadism, easily psychoanalyzed; the picaresque and the "low" novel; motion and immobility; crude desublimation of Spinoza's "of human bondage"; and the violent integration of narrative to dialogue. Each of these could lead to lengthy commentary. But note only two small, strange, and related gestures in the above dialogue poem. Sotillo identifies Hirsch as picaro (the word appears in Spanish and italicized as *pícaro* in some later editions), and so calls up the whole relation between the picaresque and Spanish Jewry, suggesting that Conrad knew the social history of the genre accurately enough to allow him to revive it in a serious historical picture of the formality of persecution. From another angle, however, the word *pícaro* seems to appear here itself only as a kind of acoustic point in the series of spat words: *picar* means "to puncture," "to pick at," "to sting," "to stab." Sotillo, the inquirer wrong about everything, does not realize that Hirsch is no picaro, but a terrified decoy who like himself knows nothing; the picaresque as a genre knows nothing, and seems to have been turned inside out in a scene of absolutely ignorant inquiry. A second anomalous but intentional detail is the weather report. In bizarre contrast to Sotillo's speech-forcing ignorance (he tries to get the details from Hirsch), the "omniscient" narrator—not simply Conrad—has a peculiar and punctilious sadism, which appears as the desire to inform the reader about all details. This desire seems most clearly ridiculous in the information about the "delicious" cool air drifting into the room from the mountain peaks. The sentence seems ludicrously misplaced, since neither character can enjoy the weather. The narrator, by this reading, has a tone decadently transcendent, seeing fit to notice an irrelevant "appreciated" natural deliciousness, as if nature were cuisine. It seems one of the many startling parodies of omniscient information in *Nostromo*. Yet, significantly, the mountain air may also be one of Conrad's many parodies of romantic "inspiration," or the *cause* of speech: it is what revives Hirsch enough to spit. And the term *delicious*, in its inappropriateness to nature, which is not culinary, has an oblique sadistic reference to the scene of coercion to speak itself as a kind of cooking. Some slang metaphors for coercion to speak imply that it is acculturation as cooking, in a Lévi-Straussian way (to grill, to roast); others are theatrical (the heat, the spotlight). Conrad's usual early metaphor had been mechanical and ejaculatory: to "pump" someone. The scene of coercion to speak—as violent acculturation—has many optional metaphors, low and high, which can be employed at will for various desublimating ironies.

But put aside these details to consider this scene in the light of the tradition of such scenes. Mikhail Bakhtin tried to revive the New Testament Greek term *anacrisis* for the scene of making the other speak.[31]

For him it referred to the whole field of devices, mostly *subtle*, for getting the other to talk. Socrates is the archetypal high master of subtle, ironic anacrisis. But Oedipus and Lear—Bakhtin does not say this—are examples of a more blunt coercion. Bakhtin necessarily, in studying Dostoevsky, used the term to mean the ingenious strategies of verbal pressure to speak, but the dictionaries remind us that in its origins it refers more often to examination by extreme physical torture. Whatever Bakhtin's reasons for tacitly underplaying the physical violence of anacrisis, and emphasizing instead what he calls "the provocation of the word by the word," Conrad's scene above is a deliberately regressive, historically acute, violent, low, physical anacrisis, strangely worked up into high formal shape. It is not Bakhtinian. Arguably, it is more radical and critical, and less innocent, than Bakhtin. Taken as a whole field, anacrisis, verbal *and* violent, is a crux or foundation of dramatic imagination for many reasons. To mention only one: it amounts to a common ground between (1) being a dramatic author oneself (finding convincing ways to "make" one's characters speak the truth); (2) being a strong, directive, main character (who commands the action, stages plays within plays, or conducts inquiries); and (3) being one of the real social authorities entitled to force speech (judges, teachers, police, detectives). If, however, we look through the high English novel, and even the Russian, though we will of course necessarily find pressure to speak, we will not find direct and formal torture as in the Hirsch scene. Where then does this low and regressive dialogue poem come from? Conrad took it from his readings in history, and from adventure novels, perhaps. But even if we look to those other traditions of history, romance, and adventure, as Conrad knew them, we won't find much that is simultaneously brutal and formal in this way. There are many scenes of harsh legal examination in Scott; but Scott holds off from the reductive and insane brutality witnessed above, since his whole point is to defend the ultimate need for legal institutions. In Marryat's description of the Inquisition at Goa, which Stevenson admired, or even in Marryat's father-son coercions to speak in a boy's book called *The Little Savage*, there is nothing like this sadistic ritual of speech extortion;[32] and in the atmosphere of universal legalism in *Bleak House* or even in Kafka's *Trial* and *Amerika*, low violence and bizarrely stylized speech coercion are not combined. In Conrad's poetics above, not the skin of the victim but the prose itself becomes "striped." Unjust whippings abound in nautical protest literature, but not in connection with coercion to speak as a ritual of knowledge. As a result, Conrad's formal anacrisis here combines the supposedly "lowest" and most "popular" types of melodramatic fiction—to be anachronistic, scenes like those in Mickey

Spillane[33]—with a classical, virtually epistemological sense of interrogation, to make a new kind of prose poem about the dramatic dialogue of inquiry.

Conrad's scene, then, manages to fuse the extremely low and the extremely formal in a study of anacrisis. The focus on the scene is the theme of making the other *speak* (as it is not, for example, in Sade). The result is a formal architecture which implies that this scene describes something essential to information and communication: that what we are seeing is something like the "primal scene" of inquiry. In *Nostromo*, as will be discussed in Chapter III, the above is not just bizarre, idiotic cruelty, though it is that. Instead it seems the desublimated norm of human dialogue, the worst example of a general condition, in which coercion to speak, the will to make the other speak, which seems an even more general desire than that of "conquest," is the pattern of most (if not all) dialogue relations—including some that could be regarded as partly good.

A more sublimated, but equally formal and disturbing, variant of this dialogue poem appears in the balladic coda to chapter 3 of *The Secret Agent*. The entire marriage of the Verlocs is a set of contrapuntally alternating forced dialogues: sometimes she wants him to talk, sometimes he her. In the following scene, Verloc wants to tell Winnie about his forced mission to blow up Greenwich Observatory, but cannot, because she is too engrossed in lamenting Stevie's exposure to anarchist rhetoric in their home. She sticks to her favorite subject, the victimization of her brother.

"He isn't fit to hear what's said here. He believes it's all true. He knows no better. He gets into his passions over it."

Mr. Verloc made no comment.

"He glared at me, as if he didn't know who I was, when I went downstairs. His heart was going like a hammer. He can't help being excitable. I woke mother up, and asked her to sit with him till he went to sleep. It isn't his fault. He's no trouble when he's left alone."

Mr. Verloc made no comment.

"I wish he had never been to school," Mrs. Verloc began again, brusquely. "He's always taking away those newspapers from the window to read. He gets a red face poring over them. We don't get rid of a dozen numbers in a month. They only take up room in the front window. And Mr. Ossipon brings every week a pile of these F.P. tracts to sell at a halfpenny each. I wouldn't give a halfpenny for the whole lot. It's silly reading—that's what it is. There's no sale for it. The other day Stevie got hold of one, and there was a story in it of a German soldier officer tearing half-off the ear of a recruit, and nothing was done to him for it. The brute! I couldn't do anything with Stevie that afternoon. The story was enough, too, to make one's blood boil. But what's the use of printing things like that? We aren't German slaves here, thank God. It's not our business—is it?"

Mr. Verloc made no reply.

"I had to take the carving knife from the boy," Mrs. Verloc continued, a little sleepily now. "He was shouting and stamping and sobbing. He can't stand the notion of any cruelty. He would have stuck that officer like a pig if he had seen him then. It's true, too. Some people don't deserve much mercy." Mrs. Verloc's voice ceased, and the expression of her motionless eyes became more and more contemplative and veiled during the long pause. "Comfortable, dear?" she asked in a faint, far-away voice. "Shall I put out the light now?"

The dreary conviction that there was no sleep for him held Mr. Verloc mute and hopelessly inert in his fear of darkness. He made a great effort.

"Yes. Put it out," he said at last in a hollow tone. (59–60)

This grimly funny scene amounts to another attempt, like the interrogation of Hirsch, to picture the extreme formal antithesis of conversation. The repetition of the phrase "Mr. Verloc made no comment" makes the reader aware of an extreme and even ludicrous anti-conversational formality on the page. Nevertheless it would be misleading to say that because this is not conversation it is simply "monologue." Mrs. Verloc makes her husband her listener, while he in turn flatly beseeches her to hear about his forced mission. Obliquely they answer each other, and are aware of each other as mutual censors. Her implicit answer to him is that she does not want to hear. She responds to his attempt to start a conversation by becoming a masturbatory narrator; the entire drift of her reverie answers his weak hint that he is in bad shape by telling him that Stevie—who represents herself—cannot stand to hear of, to "overhear," any contingent violence. Information is too much for them—it is *over*hearing in the sense of amplified forced listening—and it overexcites. Winnie's speech describes a paradoxical crescendo against crescendo, a steady raising of her voice in indignation against raised voices. A voice against itself is Shakespearean, as is the bathetic joke about Othello ("put out the light"), predicting murder as marital closure; but the most authentically Shakespearean touch in the scene is the anecdote about the ear torn *"half-off,"* which drives her into a frenzy of indignation. Winnie's other comments show that she wants deafness: to tear an ear only half off is to tease the wish to be deaf at the core of her imagery. She hates the officer for not causing complete deafness. The climax of the scene oddly gratifies this wish, when Verloc, forced to answer her little question, gives her his "detonation"—his "hollow tone" of putting out. He *is* her husband. What Conrad tries to formalize here is not monologue or soliloquy, and not even double monologue, but subdued "forced dialogue."

The use of the overall pattern of forced dialogue in this case—and the murder scene will of course bring this constant relation between them into open violence, with Verloc trying to get her to talk until she kills him—has several other strong reverberations. For one thing, the pattern emphasizes the political character of their marriage. That Mr. and Mrs. Verloc talk together in the same rhythmic form in which Sotillo and Hirsch engage in the earlier novel may not seem a valid comparison, as it leaps from one novel to another. But the rhythm always has some political component, and here it recalls the more obviously political grillings in *The Secret Agent* itself. The Verlocs have a "political" marriage: each has entered into it partly out of unstated politic motives, and till now has profited from the other's predictably businesslike, silent habits. Winnie's strategic silences governed their courtship. In the bedroom now, Verloc's "no comments," as the narrator indicates them, resemble the traditional silences of interrogated politicians. Strikingly, Winnie is a kind of reverse Emma Bovary or Quixote: she tries to reject the fantasy literature of romantic politics, the "rousing" anarchist tracts, and to connect only to what seems to be reality; but her life is destroyed by the hallucinated political world anyway. She must participate.

Most abstractly, the rhythm of this scene unfolds and deadens the structure of jokes because of the way in which the three statements followed by three non-answers are left unresolved in the detonating, deliberately unfunny "punch line," "Put it out." The reader waits through three "no replies" to be finally given this hollow forced answer. The technique here is to "dialogize" the monological structure of jokes in an unsatisfying way. If usually one person tells and controls a joke up to its funny resolution, here two minimal characters are forced to participate unconsciously in a lifeless joke, so that the laughter and release of tension associated with punch lines is withdrawn. The punch line of a real joke or riddle liberates. This couple—there sometimes seems to have been a competition among English novelists to invent the worst marriage—seems to be "immersed" involuntarily together in a bad joke that doesn't work. All that they get, and all that we get at the end, is a "detonation," a willed defeat of the freeing effect of punch lines themselves. Bakhtin referred to a buried quality in ostensibly serious literature which he called *rire resorbé*, "reabsorbed laughter," the muffled presence in a serious work of its carnival, comic, popular origins—as tragedy has traces of the satyr plays or Dostoevsky of Menippean satire.[34] But in Conrad one often feels a strange, conscious desire to expose, prolong, and defeat the conventional structures of laughter, to take the formally condensed parts of the joke, decondense them, and redistribute them back among the characters for a grim anticomic effect. Here is the joke that it takes two to make, and that is no longer funny: history as forced form. Yet force *between* persons is not the evil at this moment. In this marriage-bed scene we see a fact of dialogue that is like a fact of life: for dialogue to happen, someone must initiate it. The Hirsch interrogation is all the lowest and stupidest form of coercion to speak; but if Verloc at this moment did act more aggressively to "make" her come out of her reverie to talk with him, Stevie wouldn't die; Winnie's lonely "sympathy," though in some ways admirable, destroys the family as much as his cowardice. The implication is that some more open force in any relation on both sides might sometimes make marriage possible. Obviously the scene is too static and ritualized, the people too minimal, or tragicomically puppetlike, for any such Lawrencian thesis. Conrad's point is, on the contrary, against the grain of the "great tradition": the extreme facts of dialogue, for certain people, are beyond repair, and beyond the sentimentality of saying that they lack "communication."

The gross rhythmic resemblance between the scene in the Costaguana torture room and the scene in the Verloc bedroom implies an unusual objectification of modern dialogue into one recurrent format. The repetition of this format in not one but many of Conrad's works leads to a feeling of the politically contractual—the same social contract, or formal dialogue relation, at work over a wide social horizon. In social practice, repeated dialogue rituals as diverse as the Quaker meeting, the talk show, and "playing the dozens" can be said to enact a symbolic constitution for the group: dialogue "liturgies," they enact how persons belonging to this group speak together: this is our dialogical symbol, our first idea of relation. In literature, whenever dialogue scenes appear with high and prolonged stylization, they also constitute a (conscious or unconscious) first scene of dialogue, a picture of the social covenant. Genesis 22, for example, with Abraham's dialogized repetition of the words "Here I am"—to God and then to Isaac—a concise repetition indicating the dilemma of absolute obligation to both—is the best-known formal scene of covenant, a dialogical crisis that finds a dialogical resolution. In Conrad, who sometimes formalizes dialogue with almost biblical intensity, the first idea of social covenant leads away from the dialogic of "sympathy" toward a critical, antiromantic idea of the necessity of some initiating force and action. If there is to be "dialogue," someone must make it happen. This idea does not lead to passive determinism, since it requires agency between persons; at the same time it rejects a definition of "dialogue" or "communication" as simple interpersonal freedom, or as something inherently "mutual," "sympathetic," or "good." We are on the verge of an idea of dialogue that is in fact unexpected and difficult to identify comfortably; on the one hand this idea seems potentially authoritarian and on the other intellectually freeing. This tension is itself part of the question being asked by the novels.

A hostile critic might argue that Conrad's shift to coercive dialogue was the result of a purely personal defect. This is a charge which he in fact addressed, quietly. In the prose meditation titled "A Familiar Preface," which begins his autobiographical *A Personal Record*, Conrad apologizes at one point for attempting there a "familiar" style: "I fear that in trying to be conversational I have only managed to be unduly discursive. I have never been very well acquainted with the art of conversation—that art which, I understand, is supposed to be lost now" (xxii). Like many of his apparently simple sentences, these sentences gesture ironically, yet somehow manage to register a dislike of their own irony. Conrad writes first that he is not himself "well acquainted" with, or on close speaking terms with, conversation—the joke is like something in Beckett—and this dangerous admission for a novelist might lead us to become biographical critics who peck the wound, reviewing family memoirs and portraits of him for hints about his social ineptness. But the reports are too various for a single picture of his social self, or of the personal meanings he gave to speech and silence. We know, for example, that his father at least once remained silent under interrogation,[35] and that family and friends alternately represent him as an excellent conversationalist and as taciturn.[36] George Gissing's first, romantic response to Conrad's work was to see the "soul of the world" in Conrad's expressive silences[37]—that is, to find in the silences not withdrawal but contact. A reader of the family memoirs can find, if he wants to, a disturbing, teasing distance toward Conrad that sometimes seems nasty. They seem to have treated him not as a foreigner but as an individual eccentric. But perhaps this was a way of Anglicizing him, warmly enough: in their inability to understand his manners they sometimes made him out the old bird, the Victorian papa, whose authority was worn as ornate eccentricity. It's probably not useful to judge or summarize.

Conrad's foreignness itself, however, may be important if we want to speculate about experiences that might have shaped his sense of dialogue. A sailor and then an exile is perhaps not likely to develop a dialogical art like Austen's, Balzac's, or Tolstoy's, tracing very local signals of trust or power. No one comes away from Conrad's dialogue remembering it for witty repartee, or for lyrical shading like Turgenev's. But in his context one is more likely to become alert to something else: the larger, governing shapes which make dialogue happen or not happen at all. For all his embarrassment about minor mistakes in diction or idiom or syntax, the foreigner may actually be particularly alert to major catastrophes: he may be positioned wrongly in space, or aware of the courage required to start talk at all. While from the letters it is clear that Conrad had a gift for criticism in flattery, for getting by with people if not exactly along with them, his fictional dialogues are often about a more stark near impossibility; and his real gift is for creating a remarkable variety of dialogues that happen on the brink of not happening at all, and which someone, as an agent, has to initiate or desperately cause. His dialogues do not, as in a comfortable society, simply or playfully happen; they have to be made to happen by someone, and this "making" is the main source of their variety.

But all this might sound too much like an assertion that his work is about "lack of communication," a bad contemporary cliché which, as later parts of this study will try to show, is not to the point. The theme in his work is not "lack of communication" but the recognition that communication itself is by nature more coercive and disproportionate than we think when we sentimentalize terms like *dialogue* and *communication*. In fact, there is in Conrad's work probably more communication—relay of information across a political fabric—than in most English novels. But he sees it as being effected by aggression, or conquering force, and as a result often sinister—as in international relations, for example, if communication is coercive and disproportionate in its installment, an increase in communication becomes an increase in domination and violence. The telegraph lines being built across the mountains in *Nostromo* are installed by force. When the state communicates into the family in *The Secret Agent*, it is no savior. At the same time, silence, as a reaction to communication as force, is not romanticized as always heroic, smart, or even decent; it is often mere withdrawal, and is not to be glamorized as Silence. Conrad's sense of these issues is ex-

tremely thoughtful, skeptical, complicated, and I hope that one effect of
these studies will be to increase the sense of the plurality of meanings
both of silences and of coercions to speak in Conrad, rather than to try
to affix static values to them. Notably, in thinking this scene through, he
manages in some extraordinary moments to trace the conflict between
coercion to speak and silence back to the scene of tragic inquiry in
which Oedipus coerces witnesses only to be destroyed by the answers:
that is, he seems to grasp at some "Oedipal"—in Sophocles' sense—dialogue archetype. This gives the final sense that the "Oedipus complex," translated into politics, becomes the risk of inquiry; that when
we think of "dialogue" in general terms we must not sentimentally ignore force and danger; and that there is such a thing as an "Oedipus
dialogue complex" in literature and in reality which has been overlooked.

Return for a moment to "A Familiar Preface." Conversation is the
"art which, I understand, is supposed to be lost now." The ironic representation of himself as a discursive rather than conversational man,
who has only hearsay, and no direct experience, of the death of conversation, is a very typical self-deprecating joke. The world has become
discursive rather than conversational—so they say. But this elusively
ironic statement itself is made within the real enough dramatic context
of the Preface, which tells how the autobiography came about, how it
was "forced" as a production. The Preface starts by telling how an un-
named friend—in fact, Ford Madox Hueffer—told Conrad genially that
he must write his autobiography. About this injunction Conrad, mocking English tone, says: "I consented at once. If one must! . . ." This is the
beginning. The same friend reappears, however, at the end of the Preface in effect to betray Conrad by criticizing the work produced as not
directly confessional enough, too oblique, and not clear enough in its
revelation of personal facts. Conrad answers this charge by imagining a
close reader as a "friend" who will understand the "accords" in his
prose without his having to be confessional. The reader who has come
to know Conrad's work is meant to recognize that in the title, the word
familiar is being used in an ironic echo of its dramatic meaning in the
history of the Inquisition.[38] The English Hueffer acts at the start of the
Preface as a modern, genteel version of the "familiar," a person who
both supplied and betrayed the accused in the Inquisition, and acted as
the intermediary of confession. The ironically inquisitorial nuance in
the word *familiar* in the title has a typically Conradian suggestion of the
coercive dialogical past framing a now seemingly innocent word. To
complicate this problem, however, *A Personal Record* itself is shot through
with pictures of his relations to different parent surrogates, who, in his
orphanhood and relative isolation, had been concerned enough to force

him to talk and to force some advice on him. Their "sentences" on him ring through the book. They, too, in the absence of family, were familiars—but, in this case, good ones. His quiet, even tragic, confession to his own defects of conversational existence, then, if we are ready to listen attentively, has an extraordinary impact of personal depth and history, and establishes an alternative, noninquisitorial, nonconfessional familiarity with the reader about painful questions. The circumstances of his life may well have caused him to be sensitive to what is both good and bad in forced dialogue, but we ought to be somewhat skeptical about biographical analysis, or about oversimplification in descriptions of him.

There are other writers for whom coercion to speak is a major device or theme, but Conrad is unique in his ability to contemplate it formally, relentlessly, calmly, and without resort to final closures of liberation. If we take three major anacritical novels for comparison—Scott's *Heart of Mid-Lothian*, Dostoevsky's *Crime and Punishment*, and Gissing's *New Grub Street*—we will see how Conrad stands persistently apart. In each of these there is considerable attention to coercion to produce language, confession, or witness; but each makes a final ecstatic association of the act of speaking with inward freedom, spontaneous delight, or moral initiative. Scott certainly has a genius for legal anacrisis, in multiple scenes where people are coaxed, induced, and excited to speak by interrogative subtlety.[39] He is, like Dostoevsky, brilliant about examinatory tactics. Yet the great moral events of the novel are Jeanie Deans's free refusal to bear false witness for her sister, despite all the pressures on her, and her consequent success in approaching the Queen, gaining a hearing, speaking passionately and ordinarily, and winning her case, against all odds. Jeanie thereby transforms the universal fact of coercion to speak into liberation. Dostoevsky's Porfiry, of course, is a master of anacrisis, subtle examinatory manipulation, yet Dostoevsky's point is that Raskolnikov's confession at last comes spontaneously from within, not from Porfiry's Socratic, rational teasing, and is liberating; as we shall see in *Under Western Eyes*, itself a "forced dialogue" with Dostoevsky, one of Conrad's masterstrokes there is to detonate Dostoevskian free confession and to describe confession less optimally. Gissing's *New Grub Street* studies the dismal lives of Victorian hack novelists: the novelist himself is only the victim, not the transcendental author, of anacrisis, of being forced to produce language. But into this Balzacian atmosphere of coercion to write (see, for example, *Lost Illusions*), Gissing, who wrote the book in about six weeks, introduces very readable, witty, fast-moving long dialogues. At one point Gissing himself suggests that dialogue is the novel's filler, the easiest part to write and to read.[40] We don't have to decide who is right—Ford or Gissing—

about dialogue as easier or harder to write than narrative, to see the contrast. For Gissing's miserable novelists, the times when they can meet and talk together, even when both are starving, are times of joy. The reader also experiences a letup from the relentless naturalistic misery. In a book about coercion to write, dialogue remains the potential place of release and freedom. This is almost never the case in Conrad.

Conrad's scene of forced speech is part of a larger field of coercive—though not deterministic—relations in all his writing. His characteristic trope, whether in diction, sentence structure, dialogue form, the fusion of dialogue to narrative, or plotting, is to take a form or idea usually thought of as free, and to find a surprising coercive gist or past to it. Sentences, meanings in words, and human relations are "rebound," so as to remind the English audience of coercions. Even the apparently self-liberating choice to write in English was in reality an act of self-binding, self-obligation, a forced dialogue with a difficult alien language. The condition of creative production is for him constraint. Relations usually thought of as free are reconceived as coercive mutuality. For example, sympathy, which is most often seen as freely given, becomes instead a kind of involuntary emotional servitude, the result of being "impressed"; music, often understood as the freest, purest, most abstract art, is pictured as a forced "stringing up" which creates different tones; autobiography, often seen as the personal, freely selective memoir, playful and lying, becomes something which other people press us to write; names—in comic writing the expression of individual motion and eccentricity and vice, Dickensian "twists" and freedoms and "swerves" from the norm—become the indices of having been named under violent contract; the senses themselves seem to be "impressions" as forceful contingencies; the artist becomes someone who carefully applies sublimated force to his audience. Literary allusion—implicit dialogue with an earlier text—becomes in Conrad's middle period shaded as forced dialogue, as in the refutation of Dostoevsky in *Under Western Eyes;* he steals and reworks the plots and styles of those he admires (Crane, Cunninghame Graham, Euripides, Turgenev, and Dickens, as we'll see) by scoring out freedoms and spontaneities. This study, then, will have to consider many different elements—diction, syntax, and allusion, as well as dialogue form and the fusion of dialogue to narrative—in order to reveal his idea of relation, and to reach the point where we can grasp his idea of forced dialogue as the repressed origin of our other, more appealing, egalitarian, and conversational ideas of dialogue.

II
Dialogue and Labor

Chimes

The critical method used, as everyone knows, largely predetermines the meanings found in any work, and this applies to Conrad's work as much as anyone's. Symbolic psychology, for example, has sometimes trumpeted Conrad's guilt over leaving Poland, so that this guilt has become one of the most debated topics in the literature. But symbolic scenes in Conrad are often what he in his own terms calls "arrests"—pathetic, forced stases, both political and aesthetic. As a result, a symbolic reading emphasizing high sculptural moments biases itself toward themes of paralysis, guilt, and pathos. These feelings are there, and strongly, but are not everything. Approaches that single out "arresting" high moments, static moments of pathos like Kurtz's "the horror" or Razumov's spy writing under the statue of Rousseau, tend to emphasize feelings of final isolation and stoppage over the movements and events (the "unrests" and "rests") that lead up to them. It is important, then, not to ignore such scenes of final tragic "arrest," but to consider them in the context of Conrad's whole sense of motion—in physics, in work, and in human relations; and it would be useful to approach Conrad's imagery, at least for a while, not mainly as a symbolism or impressionism but as something like a "kinetic formalism." His sense of motion, particularly in human labor, is intricate, but one main pattern is suggested by the triad of terms that underlies the Preface to *The Nigger of the "Narcissus"*: rest, unrest, arrest. These three terms often structure his scenes. Typically, they don't so much organize the Preface as "chime" through it, making for a common ground between the rhythms of "physics" and of human work in a way that is not simply a pathetic fallacy. His prose poetic has undersongs, rhymes, and off rhymes, which link one paragraph or scene to the next by musical rather than logical transition. These chimes themselves "force" the reader to work differently, paying a new kind of attention to prose motion, and to the "force" of sounds, an attention which is both aesthetic and political.

By contrast to ordinary symbolism, then, a method that responds to this "politics of motion"—rest, unrest, arrest—and looks at its transformations in the syntax, action, dialogue, and even naming, will find that in his work not guilt but the impossibility of independence, and the reality of forced interdependence, are the key themes. In dealing with the biographical "guilt," for example, this approach would end by highlighting instead of guilt the contradiction between his exhilaration and feeling of locomotor release at having left Poland, and his knowledge that this escape was no simple liberation but the somewhat forced acceptance of other social bargains and contracts. That is, as guilty as he may have felt for leaving, he was also asserting his own band of realistic Polish independence—what we might call an unfree autonomy—by leaving.

In this chapter I want to do a kind of close reading of some of Conrad's "complex" words and phrases—not entirely unlike the complex words which Empson found in Shakespeare—so as to rehear how he "overheard" the English language. Some words in Conrad's work, like *detonation* and *unrest*, acquire specific kinds of dramatic plurality of meaning, particularly in ways that graft aesthetic to political ideas. The difficult but exhilarating job is to try to understand the reuses to which he put fairly ordinary English words. He had a special gift for taking charged public terms—not necessarily the most highbrow, but among the most current—for reuse, reconsideration, and dramatic unfolding. Consider, for instance, *impressionism*, long a problem term in Conrad criticism. A method that takes Conrad for some type of "impressionist," or at least a primarily visual writer working with evanescence, haze, fleeting images, will probably also arrive at a finally "deconstructive" or simply "mysterious" or "uncertain" Conrad, who plays surface oppositions against each other until they dissolve their own ground. There is of course some truth here. But a method that recognizes in the verb *impress* a complex aesthetic, philosophical, and nautical history, which Conrad "overheard" and dramatized, will see the surface play of impressions as only one dimension of a larger "forced dialogical" poetic.

In the discussions that follow in this chapter, I will try to use a method which I think reveals Conrad's prose poetic, and derives as much as possible from the work itself. This seems like a contradiction: I opened by saying that methods impose their views on the text, and am now claiming to try to read Conrad for his own method. But Conrad is one instance of the kind of writer—Blake, Milton, and James are others—who teaches the reader to approach English in a slightly new way, establishes rules for interpretation that are to some degree his own, and also dramatizes an original "dialogic," or view of what happens when persons meet. Specifically, Conrad worked as what I call an *"over*hearer" of English in several senses: though he tries to some extent to be accessible and popular, and though it is commonly thought that irregularities in his diction are a foreigner's mistakes, the truth is that he often defies ordinary English usage intentionally, and, along with this, dramatizes scenes of international "overhearing" and forced dialogue as the central dialogues of modern experience; that is, he himself *"over*hears," "rereads," quietly distorts the English language by amplifying some of its most familiar and simple terms. He was interested dramatically in scenes of overhearing, and he also presented English diction at times as "overheard." Conrad approached English, as he had to, with a studied alertness to its terms and its polysemy; but it was also one of his gifts to be able to "dramatize" polysemy and polyglossia unsentimentally. In this approach, the goal of criticism is not to apply old terms or ideologies to his work, or to fit him into one or another sociological or philosophical tradition. The goal is to try to "overhear" and discover his own reading of English and of common journalistic and political terms, his own new concepts, which give new shadings to familiar English words. In the prose poetic, as will become clear, Conrad's "ideas" often appear as strange and riveting "chimes," or prose off rhymes, that serve to renew old concepts.

Return, as a key example, to the term *impressionism*, to look a little more closely, and, though Watt and others have already discussed some of its history, reconsider it from the angle of forced dialogue. For his contemporaries, *impressionism*, a vague term, originally pejorative, is generally associated with the play of light in the open world—with something like sensory freedom, exhilaration, and liberation from outline. Further back, there is the psychology of forcible "impression": to Hume, "impressions" are mental events more forceful than "ideas," [1] and ordinary usage also implies that "making an impression" is the manipulation of other people's fears, sympathies, and images. (The Professor in *The Secret Agent*, who claims more power to impress other people than they have to impress him, discusses forceful impression in depth; the word appears in coercive relations in *Nostromo*, as well as in the discussion of the "force" of words in "A Familiar Preface"; and Jimmy Wait, in his theatrical manipulation of the forecastle's feelings, is a kind of splendid histrionic "impressionist.") Last, and most historically in English nautical history, of course, the term refers to the arrest of seamen for naval service—pure coercion or enslavement—and the problem of "impressment" in this sense is a theme for sea writers as late as Conrad's favorite, Captain Marryat. Notably, Conrad probably took the name Donkin from Elizabeth Gaskell's *Sylvia's Lovers*, a strong historical novel about impressment circa 1800 which would have interested Conrad for several reasons.[2] This older meaning of the verb *impress* remains a major theme in *The Nigger of the "Narcissus,"* though it appears as a subtle set of demands and obligations, "desired unrests," necessities in the scene of work. One great theme of the story is that human relations, whether political or aesthetic, are more a matter of force than aesthetic "impressionism" is ordinarily able to grasp. As the term recedes into the past, from aesthetics to psychology to labor history, its openly coercive connotations increase. The story, though taking place in a consistent present, dramatizes these different epochs and connotations of impression together, and so "dialogizes"—though awkward, it is the best term—the word itself. This in turn makes us feel that there are different contemporary "classes" of the verb *impress.* These several classes of "impression" coexist in the narrative present of the story. In the opening paragraphs, Conrad chimes (and we will see again and again how important unexpected prose rhymes are to his work) the word *must,* which is one of his favorite simple English words, the element of the imperative mood, to the word *muster.* The story begins, then, not exactly as archaic "impressment" but as a modernization and "civilization" of that mood, a "muster" which is also a "must," that is, a sublimated, even "musical" variant of the deep, archaic, always still present scene of "impression" as forced labor. *The Nigger of the "Narcissus"* proceeds from the first scene to become a story in which the three orders of "impression" (the aesthetic, the psychological, and the political) are dramatized together, so that the coercive form of relations is progressively recalled, and the aesthetic illusion of impression as freedom is called into question. Aesthetic performances themselves have more coercion in their impression than is usually recognized. It is only in this richly overheard sense (the words *muster* and *impression* in English having been "overheard" and "overdetermined" by Conrad in a plurality of meanings) that *The Nigger of the "Narcissus"* can be called an "impressionist" tale.

Conrad does not use the term *impression* overmuch in the story. But in Stephen Crane's *Red Badge of Courage,* written by the man whom Conrad called *"the only* impressionist and *only* an impressionist," the youth voluntarily joins up, and then after a setback proves himself in the war. Some critics, like Jocelyn Baines, reject any link to Crane's work, fearing to suggest that Conrad's story could have been "influenced" by Crane;[3] others, like Berryman, make what they see as Crane's obvious influence into a point of Crane's implicit superiority.[4] But denying any influence or conceding inferiority are obviously not the only alternatives. While we cannot know whether Conrad had read Crane's story before he wrote *"Narcissus,"* it is arguable that he was influenced (as later by works as various as Grahams' *Mogreb-el-Acksa,* Dickens' *Bleak House,* Euripides' *Bacchae,* and Dostoevsky's *Crime and Punishment*) to dialogue with it by altering it: he was often inspired to reply by making a similar tale of his own in a more compulsory mode. His sailors do not really seem to enlist freely, but neither are they simply impressed; they appear on board in the "must-muster," a median condition of forced work which is neither overt slave labor nor free participation. That condition falls in a very complex middle ground of necessity—which is why the chime "must-muster" is not arbitrary play but an attempt to draw a very specific idea of work as necessity by exploiting the resources of English. The forecastle drama proceeds to pit the style of sensory impressionism against Wait's impressive hypochondriac rhetoric, which enthralls the crew's feelings, and finally against the impulse to strike, and the issues raised by Donkin, who brings up the theme of "impressment" in the oldest sense. The effect of the entire story, then, is to correct, to supplement, to historicize—not to ignore—what is *"only* impressionism." Conrad balances the surface style of outdoor natural "impressionism" ironically against a theme of "impressment" as intractable coercion to labor in human relations. Throughout his work we will come back repeatedly to scenes of hiring that involve coercion, self-compromise, and humiliation. In the Preface he pointedly calls himself a "worker in prose," while at the same time exploring the awkwardness of conceiving of artistic relations as simply like work relations. But the story, like the Preface, to some extent delivers a blunt message to his leisure-class readers: cut off from the facts of coercion to work, you think that impressionism is freedom; I will show you that art itself is another variant of forceful dialogue in human relations.

This is not to say that the critical unfolding of the concept of impression is *the* meaning of the story, but instead to suggest how Conrad's stories achieve unity by formal parallels among kinds of coercion, here in a dramatic critique of what is *only* impressionism. Theatrical and nautical force both, in distinct ways, "impress." Jimmy's performance—his power to "impress" the crew—enlists their piteous sympathy by forcibly exploiting the fear of dying. "Sympathy" itself is exposed as the covertly forced "contract" between art and its audience, and is shown to come from the primary narcissistic force of fear. But this study of histrionic pathos as psychological impression runs parallel to the idea of the simpler and older power of the sea to "impress" laborers. The confused forecastle hate and love their condition of forced labor at sea, and half legitimately long for what Conrad presents as a utopian and indefinite alternative. They implicitly want some pure "sympathy" to replace the "force" of working existence—sympathetic art to replace work and nature. But the prose itself, which at first seems to promise the reader free and sublime "impressions" of the sea, progressively displays nature instead as force so impressive that it almost destroys the perceivers. In this context, the strongest single gesture of the tale is the storm's sudden verticalization of the *Narcissus*'s deck, up to that time presented to us as a "stage." It is to some extent as if we were in a theater where the stage unexpectedly tilted to become absolutely perpendicular to its original plane—to the natural horizon—so that the actors now cling to it, depend from it, and experience a total forced arrest. One reading of this verticalization of the deck, which is a characteristic kinetic gesture of Conrad's, would see it paradoxically as an aesthetic device to assert the inadequacy of the aesthetic itself (the "staged"), and the inadequacy of the dramatic, at least as they were understood in his time. The stage alone is too horizontal and lazy; it must be verticalized to become real; otherwise it is an insufficient plane for understanding the forced "verticality" of existence, and allows too little understanding of physical work, force, and violence in nature and in labor relations. This extreme verticality is of course in keeping with the hierarchical passion of the whole tale.

The principle—or force—that holds narrative to dialogue in fiction, like the principle or force that holds speeches together within any one dialogue scene, can either be taken for granted and overlooked, as by convention, or can become a focus of stylistic concern. From the opening sentences of *Almayer's Folly*, and with increasing frequency as Conrad's powers increase, there is a highly conscious use of kinetic and physical verbs, particularly what are called "phrasal verbs" (verbs with prepositions, such as swing to, give up, go up toward, push back) and verb-infinitive compounds (to make see, to help to know), to hold sentences together.[5] There is in keeping with this a whole Conradian approach to syntax as "bondage" or "tethering" by verbs. The opening sentence of "Heart of Darkness" is a virtual declaration of this idea in its carefully controlled motion: "The *Nellie*, a cruising yawl, swung to her anchor without a flutter of the sails, and was at rest." This is a scene of anchorage as tethering, and the sentence likewise is tethered forcefully by the somewhat unfamiliar nautical phrasal verb *swung to.* The phrasal verb can "anchor" a sentence. The well-known image of the sky and the sea "welded together without a joint" also makes continuity something accomplished by instrumental force. The "must-muster" chime in the opening of *"Narcissus"* belongs to a verbal style which "rivets" together two words forcefully. "Rivets" themselves, Marlow's obsession at one point in "Heart of Darkness," like "Invoice" and "Ivory," which are key words chimed together in the story, are principles of forceful connection. In Conrad's style, then, we have riveting and bonding insruments on a physical plane; "muster," or the sense of compulsory community on a social plane; and phrasal and compound verbs on the grammatical plane. An ideal of unforced lyrical continuity, which was at work to a great extent in the earliest work, is now replaced by connective agencies: tethers, rivets, ropes, musters, involuntary sympathies, coercions, weldings, directive prepositions. Though the earliest works may be somewhat underrated, it is true that *The Nigger of the "Narcissus"* marks a sudden major breakthrough into this social-aesthetic theme.

In keeping with this, the stories themselves, like the relations between their dialogues and narratives, are often about unusually forceful bonds, rivets, and interferences. This is obvious in "Heart of Darkness," in which, as already discussed, the compulsive telling of the story increasingly becomes the story's theme. But there is much more in other pieces less often discussed. *The Rescue,* which Conrad did not finish for twenty years, may well have been delayed because it almost too clearly spells out the major themes of his lifework. Rescue itself, which is the problem of the novel, is conceived of here as "interference."[6] Hassim and his sister Immada have "a life calling to" Lingard "distinctly for interference" (88), and Lingard seeks to reestablish their sovereignty in their own country after they have been overthrown. The name Lingard means, to Conrad's overhearing of English, lingering guardianship, colonial interference which protects but also temporizes and retards those it governs. No matter that the name was real: Conrad gives it an allegorically contractual meaning: colonialism is lingering guardianship. Lingard professes his commitment to his Malay allies in these terms that make a temporal paradox of intention: "I must have meant something when I interfered, whether I knew it or not. I meant it then—and did not know it. Very well. I mean it now—and do know it"(102). As the novel progresses it becomes an intricate discussion of life as "interference/rescue" itself, and resembles many of the strongest scenes in Conrad's work, in which fostering and destruction are uneasily mixed. The specific action of *The Rescue* begins when Lingard's interference in Malay political sovereignty itself suffers an unexpected interference from the presence of the stranded Europeans on their yacht, whose presence botches his grand plan. At this point, Lingard has to try to perform two simultaneous rescues—two interferences—and fails. The result is a story of the "interference of interferences," in many ways the typical Conradian plot both for its poetic paradox and its idea of history. Even while we feel the "music" or "polyphony" of the plot, it is also clear that the plot is an allegory of the growth of colonialism as the "interference of interferences" that leads to disaster.

There is no need to list any more scenes of "interference" or "impression." The point is that forms of forceful and problematic connection—of which interference is only one example—rather than isolation and "alienation," should be stressed as Conrad's major themes. Probably the most common emphasis in Conrad criticism has been on the loneliness of his people. Though often real enough, this can be overstated to the exclusion of his forceful sense of relation. Take a slightly oblique example. So canny a writer as V. S. Pritchett puts this powerful metaphor over on us in suggesting that Conrad is "flat": "His people are morally and physically stamped like medallions, and he himself referred to his desire for an effect of sculpture."[7] (Pritchett probably takes the reference to sculpture from the Preface to *The Nigger of the "Narcissus."*) Pritchett's conjunctive sentence implies, through its "and," that medallion-making and sculpture are nearly identical; that is, he unfairly cites Conrad against himself, as if the juxtaposition of masses in sculpture and the movements of the audience around it were simply equivalent to the medallion's flat epideictic reliefs of heroes. Sculpture certainly may "arrest" motion to seize on relations between "rest" and "unrest," but the action of Conrad's work, for instance the circular "swing to" in the opening sentence, is not two dimensional, processional, or tableauistic. Moments of static high relief exist in Conrad, as in the portrait of Mrs. Neale in *The Secret Agent*, deliberately executed that way because she is like a classical slave; but they are not his only art. The attention just given to Pritchett's syntax as being a little tricky in its own movement of comparison is exactly the kind of moral and physical attention Conrad wanted for his sentences from his readers. Working within the tradition of E. M. Forster's classical statement about flatness and roundness in characterization, Pritchett is really using a powerful metaphor to imply that Conrad's characters don't change. Obviously I am being unfair to Pritchett by focusing so closely on one *and*, but I do so because his comment represents a set of standard English friendly disparagements of Conrad's art. In fact, some of Conrad's characters change, with difficulty and suffering, but sometimes when they don't change or learn, as with Winnie Verloc, their inability to change is more surprising and terrible than change in other novelists. There is more force involved in the change, and less psychological freedom or transcendence. Lastly, it would be fair to say that it is not in fact Conrad's characters who are isolated—on the contrary, many of them, like Mrs. Gould, Winnie, Razumov, Heyst, and Nostromo, seem *too* rounded out or ground smooth by the social demands put on them, as if overinterrogated and overdetermined by political circumstance—but that many of his most gifted English critics, unconsciously shocked by his art, have sought to distance his characters by overemphasizing their isolation, in order effectively to deny the highly disturbing things Conrad has to say not only about loneliness but about contractuality, impression, interference, forced relation, and so on. Such critics choose to see the isolation over the "destructive immersion," the forced secular baptism. All the studies here will be in part attempts to shift attention away from isolation onto the vision of the whole variety of forced connections. These must appear not only in the narrative and in the dialogic, but in the surprising forced bonds *between* the narrative and the dialogic.

The best place to start for this is where most interpretation starts, at the Preface to *The Nigger of the "Narcissus,"* but with a shift of emphasis from his theory of art and the senses to his picture of the coercive relation, however sublimated, between the artist and the audience. From the present standpoint, the Preface is not one aesthetic doctrine; it addresses the disproportion between the writer's labor and the audience's. What can "the worker in prose" expect or exact by way of work from his readers? "One writes only half the book: the other half is with the reader," Conrad wrote to Graham about this time,[8] and though this may be one of those platitudes for which he made fun of himself,[9] it is a serious enough statement that resembles a passionate attack on the philosophical "know thyself" in an early letter to his aunt: "One quickly gets to know oneself. The difficulty lies in knowing others."[10] The Preface is exceedingly polite—and politic—and has to be, for the little-known Conrad at this time, but at least one of its themes is the same as that of its story, the relation between art and work. The problem arises that in the contemporary world, according to Conrad's rather simple picture, there are two classes: the resting and the unresting, the leisure class and the working class. Just as the story itself brings those who labor and those who malinger or scrimshank into juxtaposition and collision, Conrad also pictures, toward the end of the Preface, a peculiarly double audience, *two* kinds of readers. There are, on the one hand, "restful" or leisure-class people, who seem to constitute the first idea of his readership. Within the story this is represented by Jimmy's own laziness: one oddity of the tale is that Jimmy at times seems less the nineteenth-century type of the "lazy nigger" than the type of the decadent white artist, so that both types look odd in the fusion, and become a strange picture of "the reader." [11] Conrad pictures this sort of restful reader as someone stretched "at ease in the shade of a roadside tree" and watching "the motion of a labourer in a distant field" (xv). After a time, Conrad writes, probably using the *we* with heavy irony, "We begin to wonder languidly as to what the fellow may be at." The tone, offensively "polite," suggests that Conrad's writing, which works so hard, might ultimately exact some careful attention to the work from one of these languid voyeurs. But then, after this tableau of reading as laziness, and with no indication of the transition, Conrad suddenly in the last paragraph makes a transition to a second, entirely different idea of the audience: "To arrest, for the space of a breath, the hands busy about the work of the earth, and compel men entranced by the sight of distant goals to glance for a moment at the surrounding vision of form and color" (xvi). Here the audience has undergone a clear change. The prose is now much more utopian and breathless, as indicated by the infinitive mood, and the projected audience is now made up of workers, the unrestful, too busy for art. But these also, in another way, would need to be compelled, forced, arrested into attention to Conrad's sort of difficult writing. The worker Singleton, as the story itself tells us, reads Bulwer Lytton's *Pelham,* a sort of high-fashion literature as remote as possible from his own work life. Thus in Conrad's picture the leisure-class figure looks from a distance at workers and half wonders, while the working-class figure reads about doings among the aristocracy. The act of reading is generally an act of distant, phantasmal contemplation of the other class. Each one reads, as the text of the story tells us, for "Mystery!" and this dialogical fact is itself a kind of Mystery. It is the mystery of reading as a class rite, and Conrad's odd position in this, as "serious" artist, is to try to wake both sides from the dream: art is forced to compel.

We see, then, what in this world of rest and unrest the specific dilemma for the writer is. There are two classes: the restful and the unrestful. The prose must dialogically "arrest," "compel"—"make" both kinds of reader interested in art about work. The worker Singleton is not likely to ship out with a story like *"Narcissus,"* because he has little time to read, and when he does it is not "mysterious" or classy enough for his leisure hours; the leisure-class reader will have a hard time grasping the physical reality of work which is the story's force and theme. The almost obsessively repeated word *make*, then, in the famous sentence "My task which I am trying to achieve is, by the power of the word to make you hear, to make you feel—it is, before all, to make you see" has the dramatic character of forcing or compelling. This is a sentence, once again, about the imperative mood in human relations, in this case in the relation of art. Make you hear, make you feel, make you see: the governing verb here, *make*, is at least as important as the sensory verbs, and is almost desperate. The writer is forced to use a kind of force, and has doubts about this. If he resorts to "impressing" his audience in the age of impressionism, he may be exploiting his audience's indolence and inattention by a kind of hyperbole. As Conrad writes elsewhere, the artist is like an actor raising his voice "above the pitch of natural conversation." [12] To write, then, is to alternate between raising the voice and quieting it, and good writing will involve a constant modulation between rests and unrests, silences and raised voices, to achieve "arrests," or conscious attention to the divided process.

Ian Watt, who briefly calls attention to the word *make* but doesn't emphasize it further, remarks that the sentence has been breathily intoned too often and has become an idol.[13] He is right. But it is a great sentence, and for reasons that have not usually been noticed. It is great not only because of the insistence on the importance of the senses to reading but because of the specific paradoxical order in which the senses appear. At this point in his work Conrad was laboring over the forms of sentences at great length.[14] What makes this sentence strong is the dramatized paradoxical syntax: the actual sequence of senses opposes the finally stated priority among them. Hearing is placed first, but seeing, we learn at the end, is "before all." This amounts to something other than the rhetoric of the periodic sentence, saving its strongest points for last, or the technique of crescendo. The technique that Watt calls "anachrony" (quoting Gérard Genette, who is echoing Lukács) in Conrad's plotting appears here in the construction of a sentence. Instead of a sensory synesthesia, as in symbolist work, or an egalitarian procession of the senses as in Whitman's poetry, or a mythical genesis of the sensorium as in Blake, here there is a chiastic and dramatic ordering of the senses into (1) a temporal sequence in which hearing is first and (2) an order in which seeing is the telos. The sentence is a sailor's knot, in which hearing and seeing are in conflict for priority: narrative versus intellectual. Feeling stands between them. It should be obvious to any reader of Conrad that the organization of events in the sentences resembles the plots of many of his works, in which some *over*hearing, some intense aural idea or obsession, comes first—hearsay, legends, the image of talk, frightening information—and tempts the character into a seemingly compulsive participation. In a deeper sense—though this will seem absolutely unacceptable and recondite to many readers—the organization of the senses here repeats the action of recognition in the drama of Oedipus, in which the hero moves toward seeing through a complex process of vague but coercive overhearing and of feeling. As in Oedipal tragedy, the success of the effort to underline *seeing,* to make it assume a final power over the other "vaguer" senses, to give "enlightenment" the highest and final place, is left intentionally in doubt.[15] Critics who have taken Conrad's sentence for its stated meaning only, and ignored this syntactical knottiness, have usually accepted the notion that his work is primarily visual; in fact it is "primarily"—that is, in its greatest force and in temporal sequence— aural, overheard, powerful about experiences of sound and silence, with the visual being more careful, deliberate, and (sometimes unconvincingly) underlined.

Even if some of the details of this analysis—particularly the notion, on which I would insist, that the sentence is Oedipal, which is an unconscious source of its power and of the idolatry it receives—seem unacceptable, two points should be reasonably clear: the word *make* is repeated with something like desperation in the artist's desire to reach his audience, and it defines a relation between artist and audience shaded by that forcefulness and coerciveness which we have already seen in other ways between Sotillo and Hirsch, between the senators and the *Titanic* witnesses, between Marlow and his audience on the Thames. Artistic storytelling is one of a group of dialogues of force; it is not conversation, or if it is, then conversation itself ought to be understood differently, with more emphasis upon the ways in which it also includes corralling and grilling.

The phrase "to make you hear," then, must be seen in its entirety, not for its sense theory alone. For one last point, consider it as verbal action. The compounding of infinitive verbs (to make to hear) itself expresses by linked verbs what Conrad later called "continuity and force." To link verbs is to make a continuity of force. But this is completed by the introduction of the second-person pronoun, so that the entire phrase means that sense experience in art is a dialogical relation involving force. If the artist is a "maker," then, it is not primarily, if we are to take Conrad at his word, in regard to an object. Conrad does not say that his task is to make a beautiful piece, which is then simply available to the free perception of the audience; but rather that the art of art is to "make" a "you" perceive something. By itself, the notion of making someone perceive or feel something is not unusual; but in the phrase "to make you see"—or, as in this study, "speak"—there is the problem that the two faculties, sight and speech, to different degrees, are usually considered relatively autonomous or free. "Seeing" is often thought of as the archetypal faculty of independence: idiomatically, "see for yourself." It is slightly unusual to speak of teaching another to see, and nearly violent or visionary to speak of making another see. It is, we might say, not typically "English" in spirit. It's a bit much. Speaking is, likewise, an action that in democratic or parliamentary communities is generally thought of as being initiated by the speaker. Even in Todorov's analysis of Homer, "to speak is to risk"; that is, speech is a free action within an assembly, an act of courage, and of standing up for oneself—"speaking out." [16] Being forced to speak, particularly in liberal theory, tends to get less attention than being censored or forced into silence; the tyrant most often shows up as the one who makes us silent by forbidding us to "speak out"—as the censor, not as the speech-forcer. Thus Conrad's sensibility might be seen—the famous knotty sentence is one example—as having an idea about the senses and about dialogue relations which is in emphasis "illiberal." It shifts our attention in all dialogue scenes away from the desire to speak out and toward the forcing of speech, and therefore has a different "politics." In this one might say that Conrad resembles Foucault; but that would be anachronistic, and Foucault is not the only figure in the twentieth century or earlier to make the shift from the problem of censorship to the problem of speech-forcing his ground. From the present standpoint, the critically illuminating fact is that Conrad experiences this (for him involuntary) shift from parliamentary conversation to speech-forcing not as Foucauldian but as classical. He is reviving a classical scene that has been partly lost. The topos of this classical scene may be the moment of stichomythia between Oedipus and Teiresias, when on hearing Teiresias' first accusation Oedipus scoffs: "Who has taught you truth? Not your profession surely?" and Teiresias answers, "You have taught me, for you have made me speak against my will." [17]

I am trying to defamiliarize the famous sentence by seeing it as a rule of violence and coercion sublimated into aesthetics, and by seeing the paradoxical order of the senses in it as related to Conrad's feeling for the forced structure of "recognition." Let us take a minor, accessible, typical, and entertaining example from *The Nigger of the "Narcissus"* itself, to see how the attentive reader will be "made" to organize hearing, feeling, and seeing. There are many symmetries and contrasts in the story's characterization, and at one point it might become clear to any reader that Baker's working grunt, signifying his dutifulness, and written out as a comic "ough ough," stands in relation to Jimmy's repetitious, melodramatic, and penetrating "cough" which horrifies the sympathetic crew.[18] Baker, that is, goes around "oughing" and working while Jimmy lies around "coughing" and complaining. The moral implication is pretty clear. Each man has his own "ough" to live out; and "ough" lies between silent breath on the one hand and words on the other. It is the simplest sound of breathing as force overcoming resistance without quite being voice. Both sound distinctly mortal. But Baker harnesses his "ough" for labor, while Jimmy exploits his as an image of mortality. The one uses his "ough" for work, the other for histrionic self-pity and a chance to malinger. Note here how the three senses work in relation to each other. The visual sign is the same—*ough* being a graphic unit that can have many sounds. The two sounds are implicitly different in character, and we are led to "overhear" the difference in their primary tones. The reader who notices this at all is one who likes to both hear and see words, to work orthography against sound. But once this is done, the reader is supposed to grasp the whole process as a contrast of "feeling," even "moral feeling," not only as an aesthetic contrast. Each being interprets his own "ough," or feels his own body's motion (the story, after all, takes place on the *Narcissus* and is partly about different responses to bodily mortality) in his own way. So the mortal "ough" of each man is both a written object and a sound, a universal contract and a personal tonality. But this relation between print uniformity and sound difference is used by Conrad not just for an aesthetic game but for the nearly Wordsworthian purposes first of making the senses correct each other so that no one sense tyrannizes, and second of making us see subtle differences among nearly inarticulable feelings about life, by placing them in an understated dialogical relation to each other.[19] Of course there are other parallels like this in the story. When, for example, Captain Allistoun shouts "No!" to prevent the cutting of the mast, he in fact says his strongest "yes," insisting that the ship will survive intact; and this is to be compared to the "no's" of Donkin, which Conrad wants us to despise. The two men are in other ways similar—both small, stubborn, and virtually without beliefs. Each is mainly a variant of the force of "no" (if life is a forced dialogue, the quality of the "no" will define the quality of the person), but one "no" is authority's and one rebellion's. As there are different ough's there are different no's. This is very elemental and, in Conrad, early "physics of dialogue" bound up with feelings about work and resistance. Another obvious physical disproportion: Donkin throws a heavy belaying pin at Allistoun and fails to faze him, but later throws a biscuit at the dying Jimmy and virtually kills him. The sense of physical disproportion, grounded in physical perceptions like those of weight, mass, and self-motion, also governs sounds like coughs, outcries, whistles, and grunts, which Conrad so often uses in "physical dialogue" in this period.

The juxtaposition of Baker's dutiful "ough" to Jimmy's pitiful cough is part of the technique of "chiming" recurrent in Conrad's prose. In this case, feeling stands between seeing and hearing in a virtually Wordsworthian way—the way in which seeing and hearing are integrated is determined by our "feeling" for life—but we will see many complex uses of such echoes or chimes. In this particular instance, anyone who has taught early reading or English as a second language will recognize immediately that "ough" is the exemplary freak or emblem of difficulty in English orthography. Because of its multiple pronunciations it is often used to remind the native English speaker how difficult it is for foreigners to learn English spelling. The play on "ough" and "cough," I believe, is obvious by itself. But since it is so effectively used for poetic characterization, it is interesting to find that in Conrad's brief interview with Megroz, he focuses on just these issues: the plural meanings of strong physical verbs like *punch*, and the difficulty of orthography. "Can you wonder that I experienced enormous difficulty in learning the English language? Look at the words pronounced alike and meaning different things—words ending in 'ough' for instance. The phonetics of English is indeed a dismal thing for foreigners."[20] We can see here one little example of how Conrad works with language, and experiences writing in a foreign languge itself as an act of force, or of overcoming resistance. He takes a difficulty, an obstacle, the difficult elementary plurality of "ough," itself also the elementary sound of breath meeting resistance (voice itself as the application of force to resistance, or a variant of forced dialogue), and distributes it dialogically among the characters. For some this resistance is work, for others illness. (Conrad drew on himself for both these "oughs," of course, as both a hypochondriac and a hard worker.) The variety of "ough," an orthographical constant with different sounds, becomes for him a dramatic metaphor for the variety in similarity of human temperaments as "practical inspiration." Conrad *uses* his own difficulty with English dialogically.

I bring this up not to segregate Conrad as a foreigner writing English but to show how he handled "overheard" materials in the language in ways not available to a native speaker. His work shows neither simple awkwardness of diction, nor simple astounding mastery of English, but dramatic reuse of the difficulties of English. He wants the reader to perceive his "forced dialogue" with it. In this sense, Conrad is neither a writer of conventional English prose nor simply a "poet." The kind of prose action which consists in meeting and handling interferences, and in exploiting unexpected obstacles in the language ordinarily forgotten by a native speaker, is best called "dialogical," though the word is clumsy. The debate as to whether Conrad should be approached as a prosaic novelist or a poet has no simple answer, then, but the term *dialogist* solves the problem partly. He dramatizes the difficulties of "languages in contact." [21] If he can turn the elementary problem of seeing and hearing written "ough" into an allegory about diverse moral intonations, it is because of his struggle with English—which he exploits and shares—rather than because of any mystifying mastery of it. The reader who accepts this middle ground will get the most from the prose.

Forceful overhearing is the condition in which Conrad places himself toward English, the condition in which he wants to place the reader vis-à-vis his writing, and the condition in which he often situates his most convincing characters. To make an incomplete list of Conrad's overhearers as dramatic figures: Stevie, the reduced Pentheus in *The Secret Agent*, overhears polemical talk and overreacts, while his overprotective sister, Winnie, herself participates as overreactive overhearer, as has already been discussed. Razumov in *Under Western Eyes*, in many respects the climactic figure in the development of the theme of overhearing in Conrad's work, stands as the world's overhearer. Once Haldin has made him his involuntary confessor, Razumov goes on to become an unwilling listening spy among Geneva's utopian revolutionaries. Marlow overhears savage yells and describes himself as being almost seduced by them; he also overhears telegraphic conspiratorial talk and becomes obsessed with Kurtz as a voice. In a strong scene early in *Lord Jim*, the friendship of Jim and Marlow starts when Jim overreacts to the phrase "wretched cur," which he mistakenly thinks was spoken by Marlow about him; Jim's overreacting pride and amplification of the phrase make him accessible and extremely likable for perhaps the first time in the book. Davidson in the bitterly entitled "Because of the Dollars" is overheard by the thieves, who use the information to rob Laughing Anne, whose murder he later overhears helplessly in the darkness; overhearing is both cause and effect in that story. Heyst in *Victory* renounces his "taste for silence" when he is drawn, very strangely for him, to a noisy concert at Schomberg's, where Lena's voice seduces him. Navigating blind, Whalley in "The End of the Tether" can be said to be overhearing the sea in his last months, steering by overhearing and by talk with his Serang. Amy Foster is an "overhearer," an exaggerater of noises, whose hypersensitivity amplifies cries for help to the degree that she cannot stand them and runs away. "Sympathy" in that portrait becomes ironically identified with *"overhearing"*: the ability to be "sensitive" to cries is at the same time the cause of flight, which is why sympathy as a faculty, identified with the pathos of overhearing (as it is also for Winnie) is inactive and self-contradictory. Many of Conrad's ships seem designed as spaces of unavoidable overhearing. Hirsch dies for the disproportion between what he has and has not overheard. Marlow, Razumov, Stevie, Winnie, Heyst, Hirsch—among others—overhear the world involuntarily, amplifying, hearing one-sidedly and distortedly, so that moments in which they are "made to hear" define them and obligate them against their will; an overhearing is one of the determining and catastrophic events in their lives.[22]

As this list should suggest, the scene of forced overhearing in Conrad is often marked by overreaction, and this kind of *over*hearing is not merely a device in his work but, like coercion to speak, is a theme. The literary background for this meaning of the scene of hypersensitive overhearing lies also in the tragic tradition, as when Greek choruses are passively horrified by cries from the household, or most saliently, as when Polonius overreacts to the quarrel between Hamlet and Gertrude. Whatever real violence there is between the mother and the son, Polonius is an instance of hyperbole by the eavesdropper, indicated as the likely result of the position of overhearing. Shakespeare of course not infrequently seems to go almost inadvertently to the heart of a particular dialogue form while apparently exploiting it only for the action; in the arras scene he manages to suggest that the essence of the scene of overhearing is unstable amplification, and that this is a political fact. Polonius crying out expresses the ignorance and overreaction inherent in the overhearer's position, which flattens the sense of relation and context felt by the speakers themselves, and thereby, oddly enough, unrealistically amplifies the force of what they say.

Mikhail Bakhtin, in a sketch of "the history of laughter," argues that the scene of overhearing—without the double meaning I have just given it—lies at the heart of bourgeois chamber comedy, and is linked to middle-class architecture and privacy: "Seventeenth century literature with its dialogue was a preparation to the 'alcove realism' of private life, a realism of eavesdropping and peeping which reached its climax in the nineteenth century."[23] But in considering Conrad's new overhearers, Shakespeare's poetics of overhearing as amplification and Bakhtin's historical treatment of middle-class chamber comedy overhearing can serve only as first steps in placing his historical revision and interpretation of the scene. He makes it a new pathos. The overhearer in Conrad, often the central figure, does not listen in or spy intentionally, but is forced to hear, situated as the overhearer against his own will. Winnie, Stevie, Razumov, and Heyst may be the most powerful examples of this kind of victim of undesired information. As with the structure of coercion to speak, the structure of forcible overhearing appears on all levels: in Conrad's way of hearing words, in his picture of his own audience as made up of unwilling overhearers, and in his representations of modern persons as besieged by information.

"I doubt the heroism of the hearers," Conrad wrote in his essay on James,[24] implying through one of his small prose chimes that audiences in general cannot be expected to make heroic efforts to understand difficult novels, such as James's late work. The same chime (hero-hearer) applies to some of Conrad's own characters. His hearers, his heroes and heroines, have a heroism which is not absent, or simply negated, but rather continually "in doubt." We might take a fall from the high idea of the tragic overreacher, and say that in Conrad we have the tragic overhearer—like Winnie or Razumov—a character offered as typical of the modern era of disproportioning colonial relations, languages in contact, and forced information. This figure is neither as degraded as Polonius nor as safely situated in the alcove as Bakhtin's middle-class overhearer in farces and melodramas.

When, for example, Marlow in "Heart of Darkness" travels upriver, he finds himself in scenes of forced dialogue and involuntary overhearing. These are, in a disturbing way, both outdoor and indoor, international and domestic. They recreate what used to appear in tragic overhearings—a disturbing fusion of public and private for something beyond snooping and intrigue. At first, for example, when at the beginning of part 2 he hears the manager talk and conspire about Kurtz, we feel it may be only part of an "adventure"; but the main point soon becomes that everything in the closeness of the central station brings Marlow into moral proximity with them. His situation of overhearing them is not incidental but thematic. As in tragedy, it sustains the sense that overhearing is bound up with evil and with being "overwhelmed." This is part of the dialogue that he overhears:

> "Anything since then?" asked the other hoarsely. "Ivory," jerked the nephew: "lots of it—prime sort—lots—most annoying, from him." "And with that?" questioned the heavy rumble. "Invoice," was the reply fired out, so to speak. Then silence. They had been talking about Kurtz. (89–90)

This is the moment in which two key terms, *Ivory*—the narrative fetish—and *Invoice*—a poetic name for Marlow's growing obsession with Kurtz's voice and his sense of obligation and debt vaguely associated with Kurtz—are brought together into an overheard and overdeter-

mined chiming parallelism. The polysemous word *Invoice* here means
something roughly equivalent to "inscape" in Hopkins, but the force is
more political and moral. Marlow from this point onward goes mad
with "Invoice" as the world is mad with "Ivory." The scene goes beyond the "realism of eavesdropping and peeping" described by Bakhtin
to suggest that moments of overhearing—here called moments of "Invoice"—in the context of modern colonialism, are no longer funny, as
in chamber comedy, or thrilling, but intolerable, maddening, nauseat-
ing. The overhearer is not primarily a spy but a victim of what he
hears. The setting thus is one of overhearing as conspiratorial colonial
drama; and the diction calls for the reader also to "overhear" an odd
prose chime, to be aurally hyperacute.

Having established that conspiratorial overhearing has an unusual
force to rob the immersed listener of his moral autonomy ("Invoice"),
Conrad goes on to objectify overhearing further in "Heart of Darkness." In a later scene, Marlow and the "pilgrims" find themselves
blinded with a dense opaque mist, and suddenly overhear native threat/
lamentations. Overhearing, in both senses, now dramatizes not domestic space, and not conspiracy, but simply and starkly the relation between alien peoples. This is reinforced by the way in which the wall is
not architectural but natural, a wall of mist. This stark relation is not
one of "Invoice" of the moral sort, personal obligation or obsession, but
an objective wall, which seems to Marlow's aural imagination itself to
speak about its own existence. "To me it seemed as though the mist itself had screamed" (102), Marlow says. The wall of mist, as a white
darkness, or a "blind whiteness," obviously and deliberately comprises
the moral blindness of the white race, and also combines the two
"races," white and black, light and darkness, into a single whole, as will
the action of the story: a case in which Conrad might fairly be said to be
undoing the simplistic opposition between the races by a natural image.
This white darkness itself seems to cry out, even while it is itself the
barrier and the protective wall between the peoples. Conrad here tries,
in another example of fusion, to turn the "comic" and "scheming" conventions of overhearing inside out. The wall itself speaks. To Marlow's
hypersensitive imagination, it presents itself as a natural barrier that
"objects to" itself: that is, it points out its own objectivity at the same
time that it protests against its own existence. This occurs only ten
pages after the more conspiratorial scene of overhearing at the start of
part 2. The scene of overhearing here is theme, not device; its structure
is violently foregrounded, and it is given a shifting historical meaning.
Overhearing now speaks out overloudly against itself. The amplification of overhearing becomes the emblematic condition of languages in

contact and peoples in contact. The scene is *not* what might be called romantic bathos; on the contrary, it is an attempt to undo that bathos—the poetry of the desperate cry—by resetting it historically. "Romanticism," for Conrad, is the literary expression of imperialism in its dialogical disproportions. Its "overheardnesses," its half dialogues, its longings, cries, ambiguous speech acts, and prophecies, even its sense of adventure, grow out of the dramatic conditions of colonialism. The scene of the absolute mist that seems itself to scream is an attempt to picture the historical self-contradictions of romanticism objectively.

Let us go back for a moment and consider the glossary of Conrad's poetic terms I have been accumulating slowly here: "detonation" as a pun that "explodes" the dialectic of sound and silence; "impression" as historically polysemous and reminding us of force in dialogue; Lingard as lingering guardianship, or the temporizing of colonialism; the physical but also social triad rest, unrest, arrest, whose importance to the construction of Conrad's scenes I have only suggested; Invoice-Ivory as one of the points of welding between dialogic obsession and narrative fetish in "Heart of Darkness"; must-muster as the modern scene of hiring; hero-hearer; ough-cough. Each of these is deployed, in the readings I have given, for the creation of dramatic and representational ideas. What may be difficult for most readers now to accept is that the device of prose rhyme here, which we are accustomed to think of as only hermetic or abstract, is put in the service of his moral and historical imagination, and in all seriousness. I would go so far as to say that Conrad at many high points in his work *thinks in* what he would probably call either "chimes" or "accords" (we would be likely to call them prose rhymes or prose off rhymes). These are among his most important ideas, and they are generated as a response to the historical and personal condition of being an overhearer of English. He invents a poetics of overhearing which comprises both diction and scene construction. Author, readers, and characters are united in a condition of overhearing, which generates a different kind of vocabulary. This in turn is part of his most characteristic idiosyncrasy as a fiction writer, which is to create unexpected "poetic" fusions between the narrative and the dialogical structures with which he works. For example, Ivory, which is the colonial fetish, chimes jarringly with Invoice, which is one term for Marlow's moral obsession with Kurtz's voice. The general effect of this kind of structure is to insist that dialogue forms are inseparably and forcefully fused to narrative events. The two—dialogue and narrative—do not so much alternate or support one another as "fuse" violently and try to take each other over. Chimes or accords are among the instruments, or "rivets," by which Conrad holds our idea of the narrative action of any story to the idea of the dialogic of that story. As a result, the argument as to whether Conrad is a literalist or a deconstructionist becomes itself somewhat shallow. What he is is a writer who fuses dialogue and narrative in such a way that each seems to seek domination over the other. This is not deconstruction but the presentation of a world of force, in which even those abstract ingredients, dialogue and narrative, try to force each other into subordination, try to conquer each other, like imperial powers; and this amounts to a bizarre subversion of the hybrid nature of the novel itself, which usually either seeks to blend dialogue to narrative harmoniously or to joke in various entertaining ways about their disharmony and mutual interruption.

The sense of a delicate balance of forces between persons can also be felt throughout his letters. Commentary on the letters has paid attention mainly to his ideas or to data about his life. I would like here to pay some attention to his epistolary ways of saying "you." If there is a key-note phrase for "Heart of Darkness," from this standpoint, it is not "the horror!" but the phrase "you,—even you!" which appears in a famous letter to Robert Cunninghame Graham. Graham had just highly praised part 1 of the story. Conrad's long answer to this praise is written in alternating French and English stripes. He quarrels with Graham's socialist optimism and pacifism, describes society as organized criminality, and condemns everything Russian. Though later passages are more often quoted, for present purposes the opening of the letter is especially interesting:

> I am simply in seventh heaven to find you like the "H. of D." so far. You bless me indeed. Mind you don't curse me by and bye for the very same thing. There are two more instalments in which the idea is so wrapped up in secondary notions that you,—even you!—may miss it. And also you must remember that I don't start with an abstract notion. I start with definite images and as their rendering is true some little effect is produced. So far the note struck chimes in with your convictions,—*mais après?* There is an *après.* But I think that if you look a little into the episodes, you will find in them the right intention, though I fear nothing that is practically effective.
>
> *Somme toute, c'est une bête d'histoire qui aurait pu être quelque chose de très bien si j'avais su l'écrire.*
>
> The thing on West. Gar. is excellent, excellent. I am most interested in your plans of work and travel. I don't know in which most. *Nous allons causer de tout cela.*[25]

The striping of French and English goes on in other letters, of course. It has an odd quality that might be variously called affectation, sheer frustration with language, split personality, Polishness, or dialogism. Consider the last possibility. The two languages here correspond to two slightly different attitudes toward dialogue. The French Conrad— throughout the rest of the well-known letter too long to quote here— articulates a Balzacian theory of society as organized crime, and paints a Vautrin-like picture of universal criminality; it leads him to imply that all order is therefore arbitrary, not just, and that anyone who affirms order must not try to affirm it as natural. The English Conrad is more personal and less bitter. He relies on direct address of his friend, and on a play of richly allusive "speech acts"—a primary English mannerism long before Austin analyzed it—to continually achieve social "touch." He sounds less skeptical, more local and communal. "You bless me . . . mind you don't curse me by and bye." In French he calls chat *causerie*, a word which derives from the legal pleading of causes, which as in *Bleak House* goes on endlessly: "Nous allons causer de tout cela." Thus, in French, "conversation," chatting, is oddly if obliquely and gently linked to causality, ideology, and legal debate. But English leads Conrad to make his dialogue with Graham a sympathetic musical connection, less legalistic, more irrational, and at the same time more modest, a villager's model: "So far the note struck*chimes in with your convictions." The common but not clichéd phrasal verb "chimes in with" is highly characteristic of Conrad's English at this period. It is arguably more vivid and local than the French equivalent, *accord*. In keeping with the metaphor of chiming, which is one of Conrad's key metaphors for relations between persons, the strongest chime in the letter itself is the chiming phrase "you,—even you!" While this seems to be flattery— even someone as attentive and sympathetic to me as you will have trouble with my increasingly dark story—the ultimate burden of the whole letter, addressed in aggressive critical friendship to Graham, is unflattering and critical. It is, we'd have to say, a letter of I and You. Graham himself—even Graham—is one of us criminal animals with a capricious will to destroy—a *frondeur* Conrad calls him—and the world is a place of *bêtise*. "Heart of Darkness" itself is *une bête d'histoire*, a stupid story, and the clearest "secondary" message of the story will not be "the horror!" but a feeling of universal *bêtise*: "you,—even you!" addressed to Marlow, to Graham as liberal socialist, and to the reader. If we want to feel Conrad's linguistic precision here, his exploitation of the gaps between languages, we can point not only to the gap between *accord* in French (which is rational-harmonic) and "chimes in with" (which is local, idiomatic, and perhaps Dickensian) but also to the gap between *une bête d'histoire* and "a beastly story."

It seems willful to make "you,—even you!" a keynote for "Heart of

Darkness," when the phrase occurs not in the story but in a letter to Graham. Yet in fact a good case can be made that the writing down of the Congo experience was catalyzed precisely by Conrad's reading of *Mogreb-el-Acksa*, Graham's account of his travels in Morocco, and that to some degree Conrad's famous story was a reply to, a dialogue with, and finally a refutation of his flamboyant friend. The characteristic sentence of *Mogreb-el-Acksa*, much like its plot, travels freely, through a combination of events, folklore, and philosophical reflections, to end up nowhere; it is long, apparently semidirectionless, but stylistically alert, full of commas, Byronic, with a little more meander than punch. A frontispiece map to the travelogue shows the main plot, the failed attempt to reach the mysterious city of Tarudant, so that the journey's dotted line loops back onto itself to make a big lasso to the north of the goal. Graham's writing is singularly entertaining, and Conrad, just before he probably began work on "Heart of Darkness"—written rapidly—praised it with real and unforced enthusiasm in letters to both Graham and Graham's mother.[26] One can see why. Yet Graham's vivid and appealing style is antithetical to Conrad's own. Marlow is a kind of Graham stunned into afterthought and tragic direction. The plot of Conrad's story, in spite of Conrad's insistence (to Graham, whose work he was stealing and refuting) in the letter above that "I don't start with an abstract notion" in fact does abstract—though on the basis of real experience—the journey of Graham's free loop. Marlow is confined to a river. The strong linearity of his trip abstracts the freer, less narrow journey of the freebooter Graham, just as everything in Conrad's style in the story *swings to*, that is, has a compelled or tethered directionality. Graham's swashbuckling, freebooting, filibustering style of travel and writing masterfully combines vanity and diffidence and Shavian moralizing; he becomes, in Conrad's brutally addressive story, Marlow, "you,—even you!" the domineering but likable yarn spinner made to hear his own flowing periods as compulsivity rather than freedom. Having read and probably loved the zany folklorist voice of *Mogreb-el-Acksa*, Conrad used his own radically more involuntary political experience to steal and correct Graham's "plot," in which the hero, almost happily, never reaches the dark goal of his travels. Conrad's story takes the key prepositional mood, "to," which is the force of both stories, and makes it a matter of compulsion more than roving will; in addition, he makes it forcefully interpersonal and addressive. The effect is to become his main organizational gesture: that of turning someone else's apparently "free" text into a more coerced action, all within the hidden dialogue of answering someone else's deludedly free account of events.

There was no demonic bitterness in this. Conrad seems personally to have taken real pleasure in the freedoms of other people's styles. But in his writing he always found himself critically reconstructing those freedoms to make stories which display—gracefully—a more coercive reality: not so much a determining Nature as persons coercing other persons in a plurality of ways. This was no narrow impulse to see slavery everywhere but the result of historical experiences he could not alter. His personal good humor can be seen at times in the letters. A small sentence from one of them is worth looking at, though perhaps no other critic would. Edward Garnett had been dangerously ill and was recovering. He had some of the manuscript of the book then called *The Rescuer;* Conrad expressed joy about the recovery, and then wrote, "Don't you read the *Resc.;* read nothing but Rabelais, if you must read." [27] The sentence is in a mock-imperative mood, exuberant, friendly, and playful. His advice to read Rabelais may not seem like one of the key moments in the letters, but is startling if we want to dwell on his grimness rather than his dialogism. He implies here that his own work would be less healthy for a convalescent than Rabelais. And he jokes, typically and colloquially, that reading is experienced in the mood of "must." But most interesting is the spontaneous transformation of sounds in the first phrase. The potentially plain, self-conscious, and stern sentence "Don't read *The Rescuer*" is transformed into the energetically dialogized "Don't you read the *Resc.*" Unconsciously, naturally, he abbreviates, contracts, foreshortens the title of his own work, dropping the sound "you" in that word to transpose it to the idiomatic and friendly "Don't you read." The gesture, entirely unconscious, entirely sincere, is therefore that of erasing his own command of the "you" in "rescue." His own "rescuer" powers in the melancholy book *The Rescuer* are disavowed: *The Rescuer* would not rescue you now in your convalescence: Rabelais would be healthier stuff. "Rescue" is given back to "you." The little sentence is not mainly a condemnation of his own work as morbid; it implies instead a sane perspective on himself, and on the effects of his writing on others. The modest sentence in its friendly, transposed "you" sound is one unaffected and spontaneous example of his feeling for the dialogical placement of echoes in prose. When Kurtz says, "The horror!" twice, it's narcissism: even in his most "curt" moment, he can't stop the histrionic self-chiming. At the moment of last resort, he falls into selfishly penitential repetition. It is, probably, a final joke about his egoism. Conrad, unlike Kurtz, whom he was afraid he resembled, and despite limits and tautnesses, had the strongest possible dramatic awareness of the presence and absence of the "you" in acts of "rescue."

"The End of the Tether"

The working title of "The End of the Tether" was "The End of the Song." [28] Even the ship's name, *Sofala*, three syllables of the singer's scale, indicates that, as on the *Narcissus*, one theme will be the rudiments of voice and dialogue. Though both title words—*song* and *tether*—may seem to be clichés, and alike, Conrad's decision to change the title reinforces two points already made: that music and tethering, the aural and the compulsory, are for him linked, and that now when revising he will choose to emphasize a compulsory over a lyrical idea. The anchor that in the opening line of "Heart of Darkness" sets both the yawl and the yarn within a circular "swing to" here becomes the earthly tether. An anchor is a vertical tether to the sea bottom that causes horizontal circling on the sea surface. Each story, then, starts with the image of a rope limiting the arc of action; but "The End of the Tether" takes up the themes implicit in this image (forced labor, contractual relations, man as a work animal, *bêtise*, and force in dialogue forms) in a much more "horizontal," quiet, objective mode than any of Conrad's earlier works. Though it sounds portentous to say so, while "Heart of Darkness" is anchored in something like the unconscious, vertically downward, and traces a circular returning action caused by unconscious forces, and while Hirsch's torture later will take place as a melodramatic verticalized bondage, ironically transcendental and humanizing, Whalley's story, as the title indicates, is about a man "horizontally"—that is, ordinarily—tethered to an earthly and social horizon of labor. He has neither a significant unconscious obsession nor significant transcendental needs; he runs on self-esteem, duty, contractual obligation, love for a daughter. His sort of tether makes an ordinary "horizon"; it is not a "deep" anchor, and not a suspensory rope for horrific crucifying torture of the political animal. Whalley is, in some sense, like a noble work animal, operating in a "blind" but worldly horizon. In keeping with this spirit of horizontality and contractual ordinariness, the many controlled dialogue scenes in "The End of the Tether," unlike those in "Heart of Darkness," are sequential, rather than interfused for effects of verticality, polyphony, or "invoice." We have to read the dialogues by comparing them one after the other, horizontally, instead of seeing them as violent interferences.

A large section of the story accidentally burned up on Conrad's desk in June 1902 and had to be rewritten. Conrad finally made it part of a "three ages of man" triptych, with "Youth" and "Heart of Darkness." Responses to it vary: one reader calls it "tepid," [29] another "a moving,

well-told story" in which Conrad effectively builds suspense.[30] Both
have a case. The first time through the reader will probably be held
largely by Whalley's obscure actions as captain, which make sense
once his blindness is revealed. The story has no great theme approaching the scale of Kurtz's corruption or Jim's shame. But just for this reason, it can address dialogical relations in the ordinary context of labor
and production, and is in its own way as unforgettable as the tours de
force. Conrad obviously labored over the story carefully, and the destruction of part of the manuscript and subsequent rewriting may have
added to the restrained mood, the combination of suspense and luke-
warmness. These qualities of care and median stature allow us to see
how Conrad works on dialogue when he has no grand theme—how he
"builds" a story as a progress of dialogues. The habits of future objective narratives are also being articulated. Because of this transition to
third-person narration, one dialogue form does not explicitly and vertically control the others, to be then usurped by them, as when Marlow
speaks. But the "forced dialogue" does emerge, slowly, as the central
idea.

A plot summary will be useful. Captain Whalley is a modest, stuffier
Lingard, a locally famous explorer with a territory named after him.
"Whalley" indicates a little too totemically his individualist, at-large
independence, but becomes more interesting in its relation to his antag-
onist's name, Massy. Till now, his old age, he has been able to hold
himself stolidly aloof from the modern nautical bureaucracy. He has
one vulnerable ruling passion, though: a low-key Goriot, he is devoted
to an affectionate but indifferent daughter a thousand miles away, who
has mismarried. At the outset of the story, fearful that she will be de-
classed and reduced to "running a boarding-house," he has been forced
to sell his beloved ship, *The Fair Maid*, to send her money.

Having kept some capital for himself, Whalley is now looking for
work. He runs into an old acquaintance and rival, Captain Eliott, one of
the pat egotists who do all the talking. In the past—when Whalley
might have done something similar—Eliott chose to quit the sea and
become the port's Master Attendant, and so is now the secure old bu-
reaucrat. In their casual conversation, Eliott assumes that his famous
adventurer friend is likewise economically secure; he doesn't guess that
Whalley might need work. He gossips at random about the port, and
then contemptuously brings up Massy, owner and engineer of the *Sofala*. Massy once won the lottery (the game of the masses) and so had
the capital to buy the *Sofala*, a mail boat which he mismanages disas-
trously; paranoid and petty, always trying to find the numerological
code to a new lottery win, he has fired a succession of captains; broke,

he needs a partner. Whalley listens to this as if it were another drab yarn meaningless to him, but in fact is interested without telling Eliott.

This mundane conversation between Whalley and Eliott is by Conrad's own account the beginning of Whalley's decline, and I will return to it in a moment. To sketch the story from this point on: Whalley becomes Massy's partner, and most of the tale takes place toward the end of their contractual term. At this point Whalley is hiding his almost total blindness to protect his investment under the terms of the contract. Working with his Serang, he manages to steer the ship, in detailed navigation scenes, by dialogue, overhearing, memory, and a tactile sense of place. But there is a near grounding of the ship at one point (the new reader supposedly hasn't guessed Whalley's blindness, and is puzzled and intrigued by the mystery of the bad navigation). It takes place while Massy demands a second contract, steadily badgering Whalley, who wants to withdraw from the partnership, to renew and reinvest. Massy interprets the near wreck as part of a game of chicken. This contractual struggle takes the form of a forced dialogue, Massy pushing for negotiation while Whalley remains cryptically mute, saying nothing for long stretches. Other characters participate in the dialogical action: Sterne, an ambitious first mate and eavesdropper, catches on to Whalley's secret blindness and tries to force Massy into a dialogue so that he can tell him, but fails; Van Wyk, a civilized hermit who lives along their mail route, holds philosophical dialogues with Whalley about optimism and pessimism, and finally hears Whalley's confession of blindness; and Jack, a second engineer who spends most of his time in absolute silence, but then gets drunk and raves, in his overheard ravings gives Massy the idea (which he has not had by himself) to sink the ship for the insurance money. With Jack as his muse, Massy hangs scraps of iron in a jacket pocket near the compass on a cloudy day; the ship goes off course and sinks with Whalley still aboard. This final gesture, usually a heroic closure of a captain's life, is here determined by his understanding that should he survive, his blindness would be discovered, he would be blamed for the wreck, and would forfeit the capital and insurance meant for his daughter.

"The pathos for me is in this that the concealment of his extremity is as it were forced upon him," Conrad wrote to David Meldrum about Whalley. Pathos—involuntary or passive suffering—is defined as a consequence of the construction: forced silence. The specific concealment Conrad is referring to is not the prolonged concealment of his blindness, or the mock-heroic death aboard ship, but the first very slight and understandable lapse from frankness and openness at the early moment when Whalley fails to let Eliott know that he has a personal interest in the gossip about the *Sofala*. Eliott's story, in the process of its telling, ceases to be a yarn and becomes useful job information. And this is Conrad's strict, though not exactly harsh judgment on the moment: "A character like Whalley's cannot cease to be frank with impunity. He is not frank with his old friend—such as the old friend is. For, if Eliott had been a geniune sort of man Whalley's secrecy would have been that of an intolerable fool. The pathos for me is in this that the concealment of his extremity is as it were forced upon him. Nevertheless it is weakness, it is deterioration."[31] Putting aside a crucial moral ambiguity here—does Conrad rigidly judge Whalley for lack of frankness, or does he mean that Whalley's rigid sense of self cannot handle the first concealment?—what Conrad tells us is that he constructs a scene to impose silence on a character, but regards that silence as the pathos of deterioration, not as simple taciturn strength.

This judgment is extremely important; it gives us a precise instance where Conrad describes taciturnity or silence as weakness, not as stoical virtue. It should check the tendency to see silence in Conrad's work always as dignified transcendence.[32] Nothing in fact could be more damaging to a real reading of the politics and sense of dialogue in Conrad than an oversimplified gloss of his silences. A good part of his dialogical craft consists in the work-up of specific silences, each of which is particular to persons and contexts, and none of which is simply valorized as Silence. Conrad began by telling Meldrum: "The Eliott episode has a fundamental significance insofar that it exhibits the first weakening of old Whalley's character before the assault of poverty."[33] This is Conrad's very precise judgment and moral calculation, in which a first very slight "weakening" is the onset of a progressive deterioration: a minor devious silence indicates a total disease. Against Conrad's scrutiny of his own hero, we might try to trust the tale, and argue that Whalley's lack of frankness with Eliott is no lapse at all; that common sense would prevent him from describing his interest in the *Sofala* to a rival, an egoist, and a port gossip before approaching Massy himself, since if the deal did not work out, he would be doubly humiliated. But Conrad is not miscalculating his character; and the corruption, traced in that encounter, of a dignified, sad silence into a utilitarian, slightly devious one, can stand for his method of dialogue, and also his notion of how people find work through forced dialogue that compromises the personality.

Consider the scene in detail. Having just sold *The Fair Maid*, Whalley walks anxiously through the port. The commercial history of the port during his life is brought into retrospect, and then Whalley runs into Eliott, a man with "a conceited and tyrannical disposition" (195). Eliott filibusters and poortalks, and while Whalley stays largely silent, "changes"—the word is ironic—the conversation "from his pension, his daughters, and his poverty back again to the only other topic in the world—the Marine Office, the men and ships of the port" (202). His topic is his own world—as is everyone's—but the proportion here is carefully made out to be the one we saw in Leopardi's model of the dialogue of the egotist and the amiable man, with Whalley the subdued listener. But "silences have their character," the narrator will tell us nine years later in *Under Western Eyes*—one of the most signal abstract assertions in all Conrad's work—and the character of Whalley's silence against the changing but unchanging talk of Eliott is the symmetrical opposite: his silence appears to be unchanging but in fact changes. Whalley's silence, though it looks the same throughout, unfolds and develops against the chatter of the other, and this is done with exacting skill. At first, we are told, nothing prevents Whalley from "saying goodnight and walking away" (202) except his tiredness. The initial silence, then, is that of exhaustion. He has just sold the boat and is depressed and depleted. But this silence in the course of listening takes on a slightly different character: it soon appears to be shot through with the new "idleness" Whalley feels. There will be more of this, a useless cronyism, from now on. The silence also includes some wariness: Eliott, though a friend, was always "a bit of a humbug" (203), and Whalley's new state makes him cautious. So Conrad through a series of comments paints the particular prolonged and varying silence of a newly unemployed man. In this we are not very far from Strindberg's method in *The Stronger*, where the single protracted silence of a listener becomes a plurality of silences; here there are shifts from exhaustion to idleness to alert distrust.

The crux of the scene, however, is the transition from an unemployed to an employed silence. The reader's attention is transferred from Whalley's mood to his search for work. With the story of Massy, Whalley's silence becomes active, fully politic, no longer psychological, and the reader also participates in the unsaid, understanding the interest of the gossip. Whalley becomes one of the most quiet forcers of dialogue while saying almost nothing. He ceases to be disinterested, and moves without moving from the status of listener to that of overhearer. This is the Conradian opening scene, the first take: getting work, or being hired, with some degree of humiliation, coercion, compromise, involuntary action, degrading connection, "muster," or "tethering." In his other fiction, looking for work in morally shady conditions is often the semicomical "beginning"—the contract—in a very different spirit from the coy, scary scenes of hiring in some gothic novels, or even in

James where innocents find mysterious jobs with uncanny employers. Marlow, a little amazed at himself in "Heart of Darkness" for relying on his aunt to get him the Congo gig, protests that looking for work is "the hardest work on earth" (52). The entire section of the brilliant first part of *Under Western Eyes* is from one angle the story of Razumov's hiring as a spy—of how one gets a job inside autocracy. And there is also the opening to *The Secret Agent*, when Vladimir pushes Verloc to stop shirking and deliver some bona fide chaos; the first part of *The Shadow-Line*; Lord Jim's long search for work after his trial; and the great searches for labor in *Nostromo*, whose foreman hero beats dock workers into working. In Conrad, the hardest job is finding a job; the next hardest is making others work. Each involves forced relation, people pushing themselves and others. He is particularly concerned with the humiliation or self-compromise involved when "friendship" or "conversation" becomes a "job interview" or part of the search for work. Conrad does not show simple job interviews but typically creates "other" scenes that turn out, obliquely, to have been hirings all along, though they looked like something else.

The forced silence in the meeting of Whalley and Eliott starts the progress of the story's meanings, to show how Whalley, the freebooter, becomes increasingly unfree in his social relations. What begins as "conversation" with his inferior Eliott turns into a search for work. When Whalley crosses the line from conversation to purposive overhearing, he forfeits—this is not too strong—his status as "conversational" and therefore as free man. The essence of the scene we call the job interview, and one reason it interests Conrad so much, is that it harnesses a conversational surface to social production, and in a contradictory and painful way. The subject is supposed to be personable and pleasant and equal but also to seek employment. This leads to an atmosphere of "forced dialogue" in both senses: the participant is forced to appear unforced, forced to pretend to conversation. When the comically literal-minded MacWhirr in *Typhoon*, while being interviewed for master, says almost nothing except to notice that a door handle is broken, a rich young relative of the ship's owner is astounded and offended by his social density; MacWhirr is, as his own father says, an "ass." But this scene *is* one example of triumphant silence, if unintentional: MacWhirr has not put his personality on display—he has none—in order to be hired, and so has avoided a forced fusion of socializing with work. But the portrait of MacWhirr has great limits. Most people, by contrast, do have both private personalities and needs for work, and are aware of making uneasy combinations of the two in order to get and keep work. Novelists themselves, insofar as they exploit their private lives as a public task, could be thought of as being in a similar position; fiction itself is an appearance of private conversation that is actually discursive self-exploitation. The scene between Whalley and Eliott lies uneasily on the border between friendly talk and the search for labor; it seems to suggest that many more conversations are stages of hiring than we allow; it also carefully traces the gradual process by which a supposedly free conversation turns to use. Whalley, because he suffers the shift consciously, becomes the major representative figure of the fall out of the illusion of conversation into dialogue as labor.

From this point onward the story becomes a "musical meditation" on dialogue and labor in forms arranged horizontally. The horizontality, already mentioned, is programmatic—as if Conrad were trying to make himself write an anti–tour de force in the wake of his more powerful novellas. The rhetoric of *The Nigger* had been vertical and violent—the verticalization of the deck of the *Narcissus* accompanied studies of vertical hierarchy; the rhetoric of "Heart of Darkness" had been a spatial tour de force relying on a compulsory drive inward along a river, an almost insane exaggeration of the sense of direction as the colonial drive to internalize, as if the imperialist drive toward conquest were being punished by being overdone in its "must." But "The End of the Tether" seeks to illustrate a completely different orientation in space—neither inwardness nor verticality but a horizontal ordinariness which has its own small sad vertigo, the vertigo that accompanies even the flattest and most mundane life. At one point, when Whalley after talking with Van Wyk stands up to walk back blind to his own ship, he becomes dizzy—and that ordinary moment is in a muted way as powerful as Conrad's more violent spatial gestures in the other tales. Whalley now finds even the ordinary verticality of existence difficult.

Along with this horizontality, social relations, working relations, and even names in the story suggest a world of democratic equality as a set of quiet contradictions. The Massy and Whalley partnership is a democratic comedy of names quietly resembling puppet duos like Punch and Judy or Bouvard and Pécuchet or Dickens' battling Smallweeds. "Mass" and "Whale" both connote "big," but the *y* ending for each is diminutive. Thus Massy and Whalley are a pair: a little big man, Whalley, and a big little man, Massy. Their names are dialogized to each other. To say it in the most forbidding way, for Conrad here, as often in his work, onomastic is dialogic: that is, names are given in relation to other names, as social contracts, rather than solely as the proper characterization of the named one. A name is a relation. In keeping with these names, the relative status of the two men on board has been carefully and contractually arranged into a contradictory democracy. Massy is the original owner of the ship, and in that sense Whalley's superior; Whalley is the captain, so that Massy is his functional subordinate as engineer; but they are finally nominal partners under contract. This is a little cartoon of a bad democracy, or a "mass" constitution, which cannot make up its mind about the distribution of powers. The story is by no means—it would be plainly stupid to say so—an allegory of democracy, and Conrad was not exactly an opponent of democracy; but the ship does have a ludicrously self-contradictory social contract, and we are meant to pay attention to its disproportion and formal disorder. The strong, vertical, hierarchical order aboard the *Narcissus* here becomes the weak, paradoxical structure of democratic powers aboard the *Sofala*; and in its own muted way, this latter order is more originally conceived.

The central chapters of the story can be read as a progress of dialogues which make the reader "see and hear and also feel" the *forms* of dialogue aboard ship. This formal progress in the dialogues of labor is as important as their contribution to the action or plot. In Whalley's talk with his Serang while Massy overhears, for example, exactly what Whalley says to the Serang is not as important as the shaping and staging of the scene triadically. The two talk in a Malayan language which Massy, overhearing, cannot interpret and so exaggerates and resents. We see, both pictorially and in the simple syllables of their speech, a successful collaboration in disproportion between Whalley and the Serang, resented by an outsider. Physical disproportion between Whalley and the Serang ("giant" and "pigmy") is reconciled by their musical ability to harmonize in instrumental talk and in navigation. Since *serang* means captain, and since Whalley's blindness makes him dependent on the Serang, we have another contractual democracy of powers, this time harmonic. The formal qualities—symmetrical disproportions, overhearing—and the emotion produced—resentment—take the foreground, rather than the content of conversations. We are made to "see" a dialogue and an overhearing as formal facts which will recur in other scenes. Throughout the rest of the story, with the possible exception of the dialogue about pessimism and optimism between Van Wyk and Whalley (though this should also be included, because "philosophical conversation" here is displayed as only another class proportion, one practiced between two vaguely escapist gentlemen—it is implicitly not the main condition of human speech whatever its appeal), scenes of speech all call attention to their own forms, shapes, and proportions, rather than only to their content.

The portrait of Jack the second engineer in chapter 7 is the story's greatest set piece in this mode. Proportionally, Jack is to Massy as the Serang is to Whalley: the subordinate in an instrumental dialogue of "sounds." He makes his first appearance as a musical tone—"a short hoot on which it would be impossible to put any interpretation" (222)—the sound of his voice answering Massy from the engine room below. Jack—the work animal, the jackass—is then described as "wrapped up in such a taciturn concern for his engines that he seemed to have lost the use of speech. When addressed directly his only answer would be a grunt or a hoot, according to the distance." His tones are determined quantitatively: the sound *accords to* the distance between the speakers. His talk is limited by practical necessity, responding only to the needs of labor, and excluding even greetings; yet this oddly is what makes it "musical," or by a pun, "instrumental."

This description of Jack's instrumental working hoots to his boss Massy doesn't stand by itself. In the tale it has a clear, formal relation, as a "picture of dialogue," to other scenes of speech. One is that of Whalley and the Serang talking. The comparison shows a marked social and political irony: where Whalley and the Serang, white captain and Malay captain, in fact achieve a practical and even sublime instrumental communication—which the reader can translate by a little close attention to the ongoing work they do while they talk—reduced or bestial dialogue occurs between a laborer and a degrading employer (Jack and Massy) within the same society. Whalley's dialogue with an Oriental, a Serang, has more harmony and meaning than Massy's with his worker, though the last two are white and speak the same native language. The logic is clear: class is a greater obstacle in dialogue than linguistic difference. But the study of Jack's reduced worker's language doesn't end there. A turnabout makes for the most important critical insight. Not only an idiot or beast of burden, Jack twice a year reverses the usual proportions of his talk to go on ingenious narrative binges. An extreme and abstract contrast, it resembles Kurtz's reversal of his long, altruistic rants by short sentences passed on himself. Jack, the otherwise wordless laborer, gets drunk twice a year and locks himself in his cabin to argue, whine, and chronicle in "an amazing variety of tones" (223). This scene is framed and given lengthy deserved attention as a vignette within the larger tale. Jack discovers himself to be a prodigy of language as hoarded resentment, naming the names of everyone on board. The boat's philippic historian, he comments "upon them all with an extraordinary and ingenious venom of scandalous inventions."

Jack is a later, harsher variant of Marlow, with less sentimentality about the ineffable sources of compulsive talk; the portrait suggests that Conrad's idea of involuntary storytelling has changed. Kurtz and Marlow, the two speakers for high fidelity in "Heart of Darkness," were trapped in romantic asymmetries of production, long-windednesses capped by short self-refutations: "the horror," and "your name." By direct contrast, the worker Jack here says almost nothing most of the time, but bursts out periodically into vindictive harangues. We might want to rush to a familiar moralization of these patterns, to say that idealistic imperialist rant of Kurtz's type is evil and has to refute itself; and that working-class outburst is all "ressentiment" and malign fiction. These are easy and limited readings: they take each monological self-contradiction by itself and adjust the meaning to ideologies not exactly Conrad's own. What is actually going on here is the application of a dialogical universal, the disproportion appearing even in monological structures like "quarrels with the self" (all monologues are partly dialogized, or determined by forceful relations to the outside world), to a study of class speech as measure, not emotion or dialect. The discovered measures are formally realistic, and proportionally relate upper-class and lower-class monologue to each other. Elite or imperial persons talk at length, to later recant, self-repudiate, deconstruct, in brief apparent elenchi that are less authentic than they seem, since they continue to express conquering will. Lower-class people, in an equally compulsive and unsatisfying disproportion, maintain long silences periodically broken by violent, bitter loquacity. These two speech patterns are inversely symmetrical (chiastic) as upper class and lower class. In neither case is the *content* of the reversal itself simply the "truth" or simply a "lie," though each (for example, Kurtz's "horror" at himself and Jack's inventory of rage from the hold) may be surprising and dramatic and have truths to tell. What is "true" or dialogically accurate in a larger sense is the parallel compulsive disproportion—the strange chiastic symmetry in the dialogical compulsions of the two classes. Highly stylized and formalized this may be, but it is not static, or dialogically "flat." It has wisdom that might still be useful for us in understanding our dialogical myths and their relation to class proportions in speech. If we think clearly, and forget the usual ranking of Conrad's works, Jack's self-reversal to become the *Sofala*'s Céline may be more mature and startling in its impact than Kurtz's recantation or Marlow's admission of his ultimate lie. At the very least, the portrait of Jack complements those reversals significantly. If we accept the possibility of comparing scenes between stories, what Conrad approaches here through the two studies of disproportionate and surprising self-reversal—Kurtz and Jack—is a picture of the real conditions under which the disproportionate speech of different classes is produced. Among the elite, social conditions coax the production of lengthy discourse, which then meets its comeuppance in brief self-refutation, in turn *not* really a higher truth but only temporary closure that generates more long discourse; among the lowest, social conditions lead to protracted silences periodically interrupted by haranguing rage, outbursts themselves reused by the social order for its own purposes. These two lonely and pathetic asymmetries of monological speech production are themselves dialogized to each other by chiastic symmetry: people talk, for some reason, within these narrowly ironic class formats. And in each case what appear to be "monologues" are in fact determined in their solitary disproportions by external conditions.

The last irony in the picture of Jack, however, depends on the action, not on formal comparison alone: the irony that his raving is in effect not monologue but a usable product. As he shows by locking the door, Jack knows that others listen and that his tirades have a forced audience. He wants to be heard and—we could say—to negatively entertain, like Jimmy Wait. The relation between him and Massy has the rhythm of all forced dialogue. He goes on raving until Massy, though in fact relishing the description of himself as an evil mastermind, screams at him to shut up, scolding to save face before the crew. That is, where Jack appears to "talk to himself" in drunken privacy, he in fact enjoys making others overhear, and where Massy appears to scold Jack bitterly, his motive is to prove to the crew his indifference to Jack's "flattery." But within this field of covertly other-directed speeches aboard ship, the main narrative yield of Jack's pseudomonologue, as already noted, is to give Massy the idea to sink the boat for profit. In this, it appears as the last and strongest irony that Jack, however he speaks, can do nothing to avoid the status of producer for Massy (and perhaps even for Conrad the writer). His violent semiprivate ravings, themselves reusable and profitable, bound to the continuity and force of overhearing aboard, work up, unintentionally "engineer," supply the raw fuel of the story's closure. The subtle truth about Jack is that even his "freest" outbursts of historical rage become output instrumentally profitable to the boss. To take Marx's most ironic term out of context—Conrad has many ideas that run parallel to Marx's, even though he rejects Marx's conclusions—Jack's raving has a surplus value unknown to him.

Of all the characters, Jack is the hardest to place morally. Massy's mean villainy as the "little man," the lottery man, the envious mass man; Whalley's pathos as the old whale, the sea's heavy bourgeois hunted down; Sterne's backhanded malevolence; Van Wyk's feebly elegant, pessimistic gentility—all those are easy to grasp if subtly drawn. But Jack, though a clear instance of instrumental "bestiality," or *bêtise*, is in his own minor way impossible to locate, partly because the status of the human work animal is one of Conrad's most uneasy concerns. On the lowest rung in the ship's hierarchy, Jack does not, as in Trilling's phrase for Flaubert's simpletons, have "sanctified stupidity," but is much more dismally inscribed into the tale as the forced producer on all levels. His alternate ravings and silences seem to have absorbed the conflcts of all the relations above him into their contradictory structure. He is one of the abject figures—others are Donkin and the Professor—to be seen either as hateful anomalies in their social contexts or as the dialogical expression of everything that presses on them from above.

Together, Jack and Whalley show how "free" speech forms are put to forced use: "conversational" existence for Whalley is reused for employment; Jack's wild fantasy raving is converted to profit and closure. This and other scenes set in place a dialogical "force field." The scene at the story's center and turning point is an explicit forced dialogue, the struggle in chapter 8 in which Massy, after incessant nagging, provokes Whalley into a surprising reply. Whalley has just missed grounding the ship, and Massy has read this as a threat. He approaches Whalley accusingly, and drones on in a "dogmatic, reproachful whine" for several pages, his speeches alternating with descriptions of Whalley's uneasy silences and shufflings. Whalley is miserably trying to hide his blindness, so that what looks to Massy like a disdainful aristocratic taciturnity and commerical ruthlessness is the silence of the interrogated afraid to slip up.

Recall for a moment again how Conrad has fixed their relationship as a crisscross of authority. Contracted as a business equal, Whalley nevertheless is the captain and Massy his engineer; but Massy is the original owner. The structure of authority-interferences replicates paradoxes of authority in "mass democracy." The *Sofala* is a bit of the modern world. The subtly preposterous chiming of the two names, Massy-Whalley, also leads to a feeling of "dialogue-doggerel," Tweedledum and Tweedledee. But before jumping to the conclusion that Conrad here simply ridicules and laments democratic contractuality by showing how it forces a grand Whalley to answer to a cheap little Massy, we should note how strangely close the scene is to the dilemmas of authority in Greek tragedy. Specifically, the Massy-Whalley confrontation, though in a very muted, "low," and contractual way, unmistakably recasts the forced dialogue of Oedipus and Teiresias in Sophocles' play. The same visual irony pertains: one figure is physically blind and the other figurally blind (ignorant). The figurally blind man tries to force the other to speak. There is symmetry. Massy is "blind" in that, among other things, he can't see Whalley's obvious blindness. The result is, likewise, a finally provoked answer that boomerangs on the questioner and seems to stun him. Conrad—I will return to this point repeatedly—seems to have understood the figure of Oedipus not primarily as the incestuous parricide son but as a contractual man engaged in coercive inquiry, the answers to which shatter him and the contract. This was at least his conscious interest in the drama. It shouldn't be any more surprising here to note traces in Whalley of Oedipus than of Lear or Goriot: major works in a tradition in which this story is a deliberately minor or "ordinary" example. But what should be felt by the reader is that Massy and Whalley are now engaged in a strangely "ritual" dialogue that unfolds the dramatic character of their contract itself. To quote only the resolution of the scene:

> "It's like dealing with the devil," he said. "Why don't you speak? At first you were so high and mighty with me I hardly dared to creep about my own deck. Now I can't get a word from you. You don't seem to see me at all. What does it mean? Upon my soul, you terrify me with this deaf and dumb trick. What's going on in that head of yours? What are you plotting against me there so hard that you can't say a word? You will never make me believe that you—you—don't know where to lay your hands on a couple of hundred. You have made me curse the day I was born . . ."
>
> "Mr. Massy," said Captain Whalley, suddenly, without stirring.
>
> The engineer started violently.
>
> "If that is so I can only beg you to forgive me."
>
> "Starboard," muttered the Serang to the helmsman; and the *Sofala* began to swing round the bend into the second reach. (233–234)

This is, morally and as dialogue form, the "peripety," or turning point, of the story, as Conrad emphasizes by the "swing round" of the ship. A great deal is said here quietly. We have been prepared and, like Massy, comically unprepared for Whalley's surprise gesture as an aloof, undemonstrative beggar for forgiveness. The musical structure of the previous chapter ended in Massy's outcry to Jack—"Shut up, you fool"—preparing us for the closure of any long, nagging rant by another speaker's sudden brief interference. But Whalley's unexpected speech after long silence—"If that is so I can only beg you to forgive me"—reinforced by the turning of the ship, seems now to have been the goal of that earlier rhythm. Whalley is now, after all, forced to relive, as a perpetual little hell, his lack of frankness with Eliott, but with a much more degrading interlocutor. As he initially practiced a somewhat devious silence with Eliott, "forced" to keep silent, here he is forced into silence and then into final speech, which is itself a "detonation," or an exquisitely mannered half-truth. Pious and naive, honest and snobbish, in this single speech "begging" forgiveness he resorts to a patronizing tone, but at the same time comes as close as he can to the abject and frank admission he wants to make. It is a new example of that "honesty in dishonesty" which Dickens in *Hard Times* and Hardy in *The Mayor of Casterbridge* had studied as the paradox of capitalist manners.[34] The split here between aloofness and beggary also displays Whalley's literary ancestry: he has become, by this point in the story, an aloof beggar, Lear without howls, Goriot without any great last speech.

But the critical image of forced speech here is stronger than the pathos of silence. Put directly, unforgivingly, the meaning is that Whalley forfeited his freedom in speech, his status as a conversational being, when the conversation with Eliott "turned" into an exploitation. From that moment, Whalley began to "contract"—to lose his right to conversational existence along with his status as "freebooter"—and fell into the common worldly condition of forced dialogue. At the same moment he became, in the modern sense, "human," which in Conrad, irregularly enough, means contractually forced in the language scene, and at the same time fantasizing some freedom beyond it. The portrait discloses this tension. Whalley would like to remain a free speaker, above forced contractuality. He feels that he has contracted with Massy to run the ship, to be an economic partner, even to listen to Massy's harangues, but that he draws a line, and has not agreed to speak when constrained. The hero doesn't do that. The ultimate indignity and debasement into the common world is to be made to speak by someone else, especially a moral inferior. But the whole scene suggests, quietly enough, that this value system falsifies reality, and that Whalley can't sustain it. He belongs to the same world Jack inhabits, where speech operates according to the productive laws of labor, not of ideal conversation.

This is what makes his answer powerful. Conrad moves here toward the notion that when forced to speak, a person defines his real contradictions, whereas when speaking "freely" in conversation, as in Whalley's philosophical discussions about pessimism and optimism with his new friend Van Wyk, he will only rehearse his preferred ideology. "Truth"—or what indicates it—is unfortunately more likely to be generated by forced dialogue between persons of different classes than by free conversation between persons of the same class. This is, for Conrad, a harsh and narrow, not a witty idea. He doesn't relish it as a masterly irony. Part of the force of such scenes is that the writing seems to resist, not melodramatically flaunt, what it suggests about forced dialogue as truth. Here, the confrontation between Massy and Whalley brings each to a self-definitive "sentence" upon himself. Ridiculous as it is for the self-pitying Massy to make himself a Job, his histrionic biblical phrase, "You have made me curse the day I was born," accurately sums up his existence. His "speech act" metaphor—the "cursed" life— is a paranoid projection onto Whalley of the forced dialogue he himself initiates: *you* have made *me* curse, he says, implying that Whalley makes *him* speak. This melodramatic projection of the fact of life—making the other speak—in turn provokes Whalley into speech by arousing his guilt. Because "beg," like "curse," is histrionic in context, the more moderate term *forgive*, the last speech act in the series, is all the more convincing. Whalley of course does want and need forgiveness, if on his own terms. The use of "speech acts," with all their indications of sublimated and ritualized force between persons, has a specific function here. This kind of causal diction (made me curse, can only beg) is used because it is appropriate to a scene in which Whalley has been pressed out of the world of spontaneous conversation into the world in which speech is bound up with contractual obligation and necessity.

Superficially, the friendly philosophical discussions between Van Wyk and Whalley seem to oppose this thesis, and to introduce the alternative value of intimate colloquium. Their friendship rescues each of them from scenes of forced dialogue, and gives the reader some relief from the steady disproportion, overhearing, and coercion. But what they have to say freely about optimism and pessimism is in fact boring and a little pretentious. And the portrait of Van Wyk himself also subtly reconfirms the universality of forced dialogue and forced speech. Here is a long paragraph about his manners with the old Sultan who has made him welcome and has given him land:

All this prosperity was not yet; and Mr. Van Wyk prospered alone on the left bank on his deep clearing carved out of the forest, which came down above and below to the water's edge. His lonely bungalow faced across the river the houses of the Sultan: a restless and melancholy old ruler who had done with love and war, for whom life no longer held any savour (except of evil forebodings) and time never had any value. He was afraid of death, and hoped he would die before the white men were ready to take his country from him. He crossed the river frequently (with never less than ten boats crammed full of people), in the wistful hope of extracting some information on the subject from his own white man. There was a certain chair on the verandah he always took: the dignitaries of the court squatted on the rugs and skins between the furniture: the inferior people remained below on the grass-plot between the house and the river in rows three or four deep all along the front. Not seldom the visit began at daybreak. Mr. Van Wyk tolerated these inroads. He would nod out of his bedroom window, tooth-brush or razor in hand, or pass through the throng of courtiers in his bathing robe. He appeared and disappeared humming a tune, polished his nails with attention, rubbed his shaved face with eau-de-cologne, drank his early tea, went out to see his coolies at work; returned, looked through some papers on his desk, read a page or two in a book or sat before his cottage piano leaning back on the stool, his arms extended, fingers on the keys, his body swaying slightly from side to side. When absolutely forced to speak he gave evasive, vaguely soothing answers out of pure compassion: the same feeling perhaps made him so lavishly hospitable with the aerated drinks that more than once he left himself without soda-water for a whole week. That old man had granted him as much land as he cared to have cleared: it was neither more nor less than a fortune. (277–278)

This scene is a pathetic comedy of forced "information." It all has Conrad's seal: a colonial setting and a semiwithdrawn character who has tried to get away from the social demands of civilization, only to find himself thrown into another forced dialogue, the whole world's lit-any. The habits of Van Wyk on the "left bank" amount to a nearly Ra-belaisian catalogue of genteel evasions (tea, shaving, nail polishing, applying cologne, piano playing) of social and political pressure to speak. He uses "arts" to avoid the scene of real historical communica-tion—which is the forcible extraction of information. But like Whalley, Van Wyk finally has to meet his contract, pay for wealth and comfort by participating in some real forced dialogue; the contract implicitly includes an obligation to speak. In the historical scene the Sultan is try-ing to exchange *some* of his land for information about the coming tragic and inevitable appropriation of *all* of his land. This has more pathos than the Whalley-Massy contract, and the Sultan is both more pitiful and more admirable than Massy, but the idea of contractual relation is nearly identical. A contract gives one the chance to try to make the other speak about the darker forced relations that lie beyond the con-tract itself. We go through a whole whimsical repertoire of evasive arty "activities" to arrive at the end at forced dialogue. Forced dialogue shapes most human historical contacts of any interest, even "compas-sionate" and genteel ones. The climactic sentence, from a logical perspective, is a deliberate contradiction: "When absolutely forced to speak he gave evasive, vaguely soothing answers out of pure compassion." Why does he speak? Out of compassion, or because forced? The two causes here—coercion and compassion—do not really mix, except by implication in Van Wyk's soft consciousness, and Conrad projects this duplicity intentionally and ironically, as the vagueness of a scene in which both causes are present, but coercion outweighs compassion as the first cause of speech.

Van Wyk participates in forced language in one other way: as a forcer. Though he thinks himself detached, he has been annoyed, before Whalley's captaincy, whenever the *Sofala* arrived late with his European journals. A "left bank" type, he wants newspapers. He meets Whalley because he terminates his contract with the *Sofala* just as Whalley becomes captain. Whalley goes to see him to solicit—really to beg—his continued faith in the *Sofala* to deliver *The Times*, the *Rotterdam Courant*, and the *Graphic*. Thrown together by this scene of demand for newsprint they then become conversational friends. Further, Whalley's conversational style is what proves his reliability and wins back the client. Their philosophical and conversational friendship, then, starts as a mutually forcing business deal, defined as Van Wyk's need to get information from the mails and Whalley's need for a paying customer. All of it is genteel, but that's the point: even genteel relations, like demanding your overseas newspaper, have a forced dialogical quality. One reading would insist that Conrad still rejects forced dialogue, or information extraction, as debased, and, like Van Wyk, tolerates its reality but laments its necessity; free conversational friendship, the higher reality, somehow transcends forced circumstance. But the tale seems skeptical: Van Wyk and Whalley know each other through "polite" contractual coercion, so that their friendship is originated in and dramatically shaded by it. Attempts to deny this causal priority are a little vain in both senses. The Sultan, Whalley, and Van Wyk are all three historical subjects forced to speak and forced to subtly extort information. Van Wyk demands the news: his place in this type of relation shows most clearly who he is. We are approaching the idea that "civilized man," as a historical and psychological subject, is coercion to speak.

Bêtise

This entire chapter has been proposing that dialogue becomes a sort of labor in Conrad's prose to a degree unusual for English fiction, in which dialogue takes place most often as freedom from work. Even Melville's

Bartleby, in American literature's strongest forced disproportional dialogue, asserts some kind of freedom from labor when he says, "I prefer not to." His talk, however minimal and suicidal, opposes the scrivener's servitude, at the tragicomic point zero of freedom, away from the scene of language production. A complete nonparticipation like this never happens in Conrad; to talk is to take part in production. The conversational memoir *A Personal Record* begins by invoking pressure from a friend to write; Conrad is not being simply ironic when he suggests that an external and not only an internal "must" moved him to write his autobiography. Both "Heart of Darkness" and "The End of the Tether" represent the hero's speech as increasingly yoked, in a dialogical progress, to the domains of labor and compulsory language production.

Before going on to *Nostromo*, it would be useful to suggest the integration of this theme of forced speech to Conrad's imagery by looking briefly at some of his images of the work animal. Since Aristophanes at least, and from Lucian's satires to the emblem of the Democratic party, the donkey, the ass, the mule, the *bête,* have been standard, if not always fully conscious, popular and journalistic emblems of the laboring or producing class, and in supposed keeping with this, of skeptical realism and hard work, but also of their contraries, stubbornness, back-kicking and "striking": resistance to forced productivity. Not exactly a symbol, not exactly a cliché, the donkey is a public figure. Critics have often noted that, instead of inventing private symbols, Conrad most often takes the givens of public discourse and reworks them disconcertingly. In the terms of this study, he "dialogizes" journalistic imagery. Kinetically, the donkey's typical rhythms suit his art because they can be contained by the triad rest, unrest, arrest; popularly, when it won't budge, the donkey is the animal that goes on strike. As the animal of "low arrest," laziness, toil, and resistance, it becomes at times in Conrad the unexpected totem of the rhythm of history: *bêtise.*

The theft and reuse of the term *unrest* in *The Nigger of the "Narcissus,"* in connection with the feelings Donkin arouses, is one extremely clear instance of Conrad's technique. As in the Victorian phrase "the Great Unrest," [35] the word in journalism connotes strikes, riots, and mutinies, but is also a euphemism, a vaguely psychological and aesthetic cover term for class violence. Conrad here contrives to make "unrest" mean antithetically the condition of "work" itself. After the storm has shown the forecastle the misery of being forced by nature *not* to work, in extreme immobility, he calls the restorative labor that follows their "desired unrest." The crew are punished for (political) unrest by a forced rest (an arrest) in nature, and then are reprieved, and allowed to work again, in a new "desired unrest": work itself. "Unrest," with its melancholy and self-pitying implication that "rest" or "death" is the ground of being, is twisted to mean the pleasure of life as work, so that Conrad can teach a lesson, making it a term ironically surveying the whole "condition of labor." To live, the story argues polemically, is to be in a state of "unrest" one way or the other, whether working or striking: choose. "Unrest" is fatalistically doubled; depending on one's bias, one might consider this reuse of the word either ingenious or an insidious regression from dialectical reason to make motion itself a paradoxically static universal.

Clearly, a Freudian reading would identify Conrad's image of the donkey or ass (*l'âne* in French) an anality, outraged stubbornness, a complex of resistances to productivity; a Marxist reading in a different, more typical light; a Bakhtinian reading in a third light, as a kind of stifled carnivalization. In fact, all three have some application to Conrad's uses, because the beast of burden is a topic of enormous contradictions for him. Personally, there is his own temperamental contradiction between the ethic of dutiful labor and the feeling of hatred for work. In a larger sense, the donkey is the image of the working class as at once loved and despised. When the mule kicks the biscuit tin that represents the *Titanic*, for example, it is clear that Conrad obliquely makes a common laborer backswipe commercial privilege, and takes pleasure in the kick of vengeance, but that this is possible only because the worker has first been reduced to an animal that seems not revolutionary but *bête*. But it is clear that Conrad himself was sometimes consciously *bête* in his own productive work rhythms and in his "genius." Besides kicking, one typical gesture of the donkey—stalling, retardation, not going on, withholding—is after all identical in its form and energy to the narrative gesture or rhythm which is usually considered Conrad's most salient contribution to narrative technique: his elaborate ways of stalling, delaying, and withholding information in the plot, as if the reader were trying to force him to say something, and he were, not only for suspense or for tact or as an impressionist strategy but from some more primary motive, refusing to tell. In his letters he frequently calls himself *bête*; laziness—though it hardly looks like it from the productivity of his life—seems to have been one main cause of conscious guilt for him. The retardations of the novels, then, are not only "brilliant" and "ingenious" devices; they are also sometimes intentional *bêtises*, or outrageous stubbornnesses and withholdings. If *The Secret Agent*, for example, is analyzed only for its ingenious strategies of narrative "retardation," without any sense of irony about them, then the reader overlooks the structural joke—that its central figure, Stevie, is what we would call now "mentally retarded," as is the plotting of the book, which seeks continually to retard or temporize or just slow the mind of the reader. This may seem like a nasty joke, but the fact is that Conrad's major works often have an element of sadistic *bêtise* and willfully stupid comedy in their globally delayed structures.

To study *bêtise*, we can start with common curse words, move on to naming and characterization, and then discuss the pivotal place of the beast of burden as the image of the low prime mover, the "base" of higher social and aesthetic themes such as sympathy. For those who agree with Bakhtin that Rabelais and Menippean satire are major sources of the novelistic in the larger sense, onomastic gestures like Balzac's *Peau de chagrin,* James's "Fanny Assingham," Zola's *Bête humaine,* or Conrad's Donkin signal that middle-class fiction is touching on carnival and approaching themes of work and sexuality that seem past its own reach. The slang meanings of the English word *ass* are obvious, but the word *also* imagines the work animal as the energetic pivot of bodily motion, sexual *or* working: that is, physical agency itself. In the upper-class literature—Flaubert and James, among others—in which Conrad was only partly immersed, this agency is considered "fundamental," but is also somewhat distanced and despised. Even Bakhtin, at least in translation, calls this a little bit archly and hierarchically the "bodily lowest strata." That is, *agency* itself, regarded as necessary to all plot and dialogue, can be imaged as the "low" animality of motion, and then be made remote from "us." While James has a kind of repressed, even sticky-eerie fascination with the necessity of physical agency and its sublimations, which appears partly in his habit of putting slang phrasal verbs into quotation marks, Conrad's representations of pivotal motion are stronger and much more directly vital. He is able to describe motion; and able, for example, against his audience's training, to create scenes of beating violence not simply charged with piteous sadism but more with a kind of unexpected locomotor vitality. When Donkin is beaten into cooperation, when Stevie pities the whipped cab horse, or when Razumov beats Ziemianitch but fails to budge him, Conrad clearly parodies the double message—the pitying sadism—in nineteenth-century scenes about beaten animals as symbols of the oppressed, by focusing back on life as necessarily forceful motion and away from the "emotions" in "us"; we read jests about sentimental manipulation of the audience's "fundamental" feelings. At the same time it is clear that Conrad can't decide that this primal scene of nineteenth-century interclass social pathos is just nonsense. On one level he asks the reader to contemplate and laugh at the "motion" as a socialist literary cliché, but on the other to be "moved," and to feel that this injustice may in fact be the "base" of social life. The scene itself, then, is *bête,* and meant to make "us" feel *bête*—that is, stupid toward reality.

Bête and *bêtise* are probably the most important curses or imprecations in Conrad's early letters. As with any curse, the force is both bodily and social, and not easy to define, although the standard definition tells us that as a noun *bête* means "beast" and as an adjective "stupid." *Bêtise* is one of the key words in Sartre's long reading of Flaubert;[36] we might also think of *Ulysses'* Buck Mulligan, the pseudocarnal, cerebral mocker who wounds Stephen: "O, it's only Dedalus whose mother is beastly dead." The word functions as something like a lapsed Catholic aesthete's wafer: a word of gross consubstantiation. *Bêtise* is bodily communion without redemption. Conrad was no believer: as he wrote to Mme. Poradowska, "Once upon a time I was a Christian." [37] But his sense of *bêtise* is not identical to that of Flaubert or Joyce, though it has a similar pathos. For Conrad, *bêtise* is more the name of history than of social idiocy; and though not used outside the letters (except in Decoud's slogan *Gran' bestia!* itself a *bêtise*), it recalls the "stupid tragedy" which pervades the political novels, as Eloise Knapp Hay has emphasized, from the tragic farce in the Congo to the scattering of Stevie's body. Conrad concludes a letter to Graham about the Boer War with this self-arrest: *Assez de ces bêtises!*[38] Typically, this exclamatory sentence (like Kurtz's sentences on himself at the end of long discourses) passes judgment not only on the "appalling fatuity" of the war, not only on Kipling's "war undertaken for the cause of democracy," but also upon Conrad's own preceding platitudes in the letter. He dismisses his own political *bêtises*, ideological claptrap, along with that of the others. Elsewhere he refers to the respectable bourgeois *bêtise* he sees on his own face in a photograph, implies that the genius of photography is to disclose the *bêtise* in everyone, and seems strangely pleased to see it in himself, as if it were the proof of his knack of survival, a healthy baseness.[39] Finally, during the time when still making the transition between the sea and writing, despairing of his chances as a writer, and thinking of returning to sea, he writes to Graham: *Quelle bête de vie! Nom de nom, quelle bête de vie!*[40]

Name of name, chime of chimes: *bête* serves him as the common denominator, the "base" of imprecation, of language as force. What matters most is that Conrad, unlike Decoud, includes himself unhesitatingly when invoking the *Gran' bestia* as the totality of society. Unlike Sartre's Flaubert, for whom there are two *bêtises*—that of the stupid bourgeoisie on the one hand and on the other that of certain sanctified idiots like Charles Bovary or *un coeur simple*—for Conrad there is one general *bêtise*, of which he is a part. "No, I belong to the wretched gang. We all belong to it," he sermonizes at Graham with a lot of grim satisfaction in the protest.[41] Conrad would probably have rejected this comparison of himself to Flaubert as itself *bête*, since Flaubert is the greater writer, and would have argued that he learned the theme and technique of immersion in *bêtise* from Flaubert: that would be fair. There is a protest of this kind against a critic who compared a hack story of his, "Gaspar Ruiz," to a masterpiece by Turgenev.[42] But it is fair to say that if Conrad's personal and literary notions of *bêtise* come largely from Flaubert, he implicates himself more historically. If the most ingenious new plotting strategies in his novels—the most abstract devices of his craft—share the rhythms of *bêtise,* and are Menippean expressions of his own and the reader's resistance to work, reaction against work, which is at the same time Conrad's stated gripe with the Donkins of the world in the early stories, then the *bête* is indeed the "base" in Conrad, the locus of the conflict. He will increasingly relent toward resistance to work as his work matures. One of the themes of the political novels is the omnipresence of *bêtise* (as rest, unrest, arrest; going on strike; not wanting to be budged; stubbornness), not only in the characters and the action but also in the apparently fancy and sometimes overdone techniques with which these are narrated. The narrator participates in the *bêtise* of the characters through the pervasive *bêtise* of stubbornly jerky narrations, themselves "jerking" forward with the forced rhythm of history.[43] As a producer of historical novels, the author, beyond the narrator, is himself a kind of work animal, and the rhythm of the forced production of masses of historical langue is re-produced in the narration. This is a "dialogical" rhythm becaue it indi-cates the author's immersed status as forced and self-forcing producer and "worker in prose."

The most violent early instance of the Donkey image appears in a letter in French to his distant relation (whom he calls "aunt") Mme. Poradowska. She has obviously gotten to him by labeling him a mis-anthrope like Hamlet. He answers defiantly, in a complicated soliloquy about "others." This is, with all its mannerisms, a crucial moment in the early letters:

> You are making a little fun of your nephew in comparing him to the late Hamlet (who was mad, I believe). Nevertheless I permit myself to think that apart from his madness he was an entirely worthy person. I am therefore not offended by the comparison. I don't know where you found any indication of my contempt for mankind. This persuades me that, to make a generalization, one may say that even those who know us best know us very little. The philosopher who said "know thyself" was, I believe probably tipsy (having supped with Greek damsels—which was one of the philo-sophical customs of the time), since I cannot admit him to have

been stupid. A philosopher cannot be stupid, can he? One quickly gets to know oneself. The difficulty lies in knowing others. I hasten to assure you before my departure (which will occur on the twenty-fifth of this month) that I love humanity doubtless as much as you do, but perhaps in a different fashion. Still, you know, a lot humanity cares! I despise no one, for I don't wish to have the feeling requited. I am not philosophical enough to bear (calmly) the contempt of those not my peers. And note well that the kicks of a donkey's hoof hurt very badly. One of the constant studies of my life has been to avoid them. Please take cognizance by this writing that I respect the Donkey (with a capital D). I seize this occasion to make my profession of faith. Long ears are eternal, the beginning and the end of all things; I find my rest, my life, and my consolation in the melodious braying of my master! There you are; what else can you expect? One must live when one has had the misfortune to be born.

Next Wednesday will see me on the blue (more or less) sea.[44]

Putting aside the wounded self-pity—anyway not despicable unless we think ourselves past dramatic resentment and self-pity—the striking thing here is the vigorous and sharp meditation Conrad at this time already undertakes on the difference between "philosophy," defined prejudicially as monologue and solipsism, and his own sense of the world, dramatic and critical. He accepts at the start the comparison to soliloquizing, self-dramatizing Hamlet, but parries by playing the part fully, even in the rhythm of metaphors. In the process he rejects philosophy as without dialogue: "One quickly gets to know oneself. The difficulty lies in knowing others." Mme. Poradowska, he implies, does not know him, and has misread *Hamlet.* What she mistakes for misanthropy in him is the acumen that comes from working with people as well as from his early loss of his parents to politics. She idealizes human relations, and is in that way more in flight from them than he is. His departure to the "blue (more or less) sea"—that is, the sea both as ideal and as real—is on the one hand a flight from the Donkey, an avoidance, but on the other a participation in the work life of the world more immersed than hers. Clearly he has decided that he has a right to his "contractual" (that is, withdrawn and specific) character— what contemporary lingo would call his "defenses"—of some aloofness and aristocratic tautness, which in fact allow him to participate. He does not—as he will later hint Graham does—fancy himself a socialist while being a royal snob. The philosopher, who is "tipsy" (*gris,* or "gray" in French—dull or lacking dialogical contrast), can bear the contempt of other people stoically only because he effectively denies their reality. But Conrad's past, implicitly what he feels was the political murder of his parents, makes such a rationalization impossible. Thus he will neither whitewash "otherness" nor deny it. After this, the histrionic, Quixotic dream of the Donkey appears—*l'âne (avec un grand Â)*—droll and bitter, in which Conrad represents himself doubly, as on the one hand avoiding the Donkey and on the other hand being its votary and slave. He is, we might even say, the Donkey's donkey, by the end. The proverbial long ears here, though a tired, snobbish cliché for stupidity, become a kind of canopy, or shade, under which he can rest—as if the Donkey's stupidity were the Tree of Life. Conrad will later define the source of good novels as "a conviction of our fellow-men's existence strong enough to take upon itself a form of imagined life."[45] He closes with a strong question to his aunt about the limits of her idealism: *Voilà! Que voulez-vous?*[46]

The Donkey, then, is the emblem of the condition of forced participation. That condition is the letter *A*, the beginning of knowledge. Several years later, of course, when Conrad alters the capitalized, general *Âne* in the bitter letter into the individual man Donkin, the same dilemma is at work. Conrad at this point still hates this figure, but now the representational art makes Donkin a great question mark: to what extent does the story make Donkin the *bête* of the community, the "butt" of the community, or the "base" of the community? Is he the outsider or the lowest but most precise common denominator? The answer, if we read fairly, is hard to give, and this testifies to the achieved objectivity of Conrad's art, in spite of an obvious loathing for Donkin. Ian Watt's rich discussion of *Gemeinschaft* and *Gesellschaft* as the sociological background of the story is helpful here, but also can present some obstacles.[47] Watt draws a clear distinction between the ship as "community," archaic tangible order, and the outside world as "society," the anomic bureaucracy that appears grotesquely at the end to despise Singleton and reward Donkin. But the claims of each of these two modes of organization *on each other* are somewhat stronger in the story than this division suggests. For one thing, we have to recall that the ship itself is named *Narcissus* not only because its people are all "singletons" (one-tone monadic individuals chiming in with each other in a kind of pointillist chorus) and also "allistouns" (tones all merged together at the highest level of duty into one collective working tone); and not only because the ship itself at the crisis leans over into the mirror of the sea, as if considering a Narcissus-like plunge, and then rights itself at the last moment. The ship also has this name because as a whole it represents an avoidance of the outside world, a social space turned away from the world. The title, and some comments in the story, imply a criticism of the ship as a childish *Gemeinschaft,* not only an old-fashioned organic community. In some sense this ship is a "kindergarten," and partakes of a long tradition of adult kindergartens, in fact a major tradition in novelistic fiction. In this light, Donkin's force is not easy to fix. He can be seen as the satanic, *lumpen* foil to the others, or as the embodiment of the universal motive "no" which makes him analogous even to the "all-tone" of Allistoun.

Can he be both? Obviously novels often project a hierarchy among characters, as they represent accepted and rejected parts of a relatively unified psychology. Though the novelistic, as many theorists have suggested, may be a variety of radical disunities, we often find in highly formalized novels what may be called "base" characters who represent what the novelist considers the "basest" of human drives but also the necessary passion which must be sublimated by the others. This can even be the first character to appear, as if to define the novel. Oblonsky's painfully funny adulterous scrapes initiate a compact between Tolstoy and the reader: we are getting ready to take Anna more seriously. In Austen's *Emma*, the riotously funny hypochondria of the father in the opening scenes introduces the question of "harmless" selfishness, legitimates Emma's fancifulness as his unguided daughter, and initiates Emma's development from fanciful selfishness into a consciousness which can look at others with some rational sympathy. Austen, through introductory hilarity about Woodhouse, has us laugh aloud at him so that we can proceed not to reject infantile selfishness itself but to recognize it as the "base" of Emma's development as well, which, though also comic, is more serious. There is of course another kind of "base" character, like Edmund in *Lear*, or Balzac's Vautrin, who proclaims himself the "base," the *bête*, and declares frankly that he represents what really drives everyone else. Such a figure is too declarative to be truly antisocial; in fact the author has covertly constructed the villain to desire above all to "belong" to collective meaning, to define himself in the hierarchy. By contrast, no one in Flaubert cares enough about the community to become its villain, or its explanatory base. Conrad's art is not Flaubertian in this respect. He never really tries to imitate Flaubert's scrupulous effort to eliminate the character system. Where Woodhouse represents something like "primary narcissism" as the hilarious base of life, which can be sublimated into rational sympathy, where Oblonsky has lust, Vautrin the will to power, Donkin represents Conrad's much more unusual idea of the "base": a primal stubbornness, even more contracted and implosive than anything in Defoe's alleged "individualism" (Defoe was acutally a genius of contractual dialogical relation in his own way). The shock in Donkin is not in the conventional use of the "base" figure who is a low version of the "high" figures—we realize that Donkin and Allistoun are mirror images, for example—but that for Conrad the primary human drive is not an eros or a will to power or even a narcissism but a petulant nay saying and spiteful resistance. This is not to be confused with Dostoevsky's cosmic "spite." It is something more ordinary, like an intensification of the various stages in which children say no. Intellectualization might be put in the way of seeing this negative stubbornness in all its force: it can be argued that Donkin is ressentiment, or that he is egoistic selfishness, or a thwarted will to power. But these terms screen the really fascinated energy in the characterization of Donkin. Unlike Vautrin, Oblonsky, Woodhouse, or even Conrad's own later Professor, Donkin's negativity seems to have been deliberately and scrupulously constructed *not* to amuse, to entertain, to be easily placed and included. It is half-consciously admired as well as feared. Conrad may want us to detest him, but he stands in the story as the force of "base" identity itself, as "what is," not as what can be easily placed by laughter. No other English writer, not even Defoe or Lawrence, has such a strong involuntary pleasure in plain spite and reaction. Conrad the moralist may want to despise it, but Conrad the artist is in love with it. For him, this defiance is not reducible to other energies, and is not a function of some will to power or eros.

I point this out emphatically because it goes against the grain of contemporary argument. We often say that what makes a character great or strong is lack of boundary, unpredictability of desire, inner deconstructedness.[48] This is of course true of many great figures. But some figures, after all, acquire force not from being wildly scattered but from extreme contraction. Conrad's work is often energized not by wildness, not even by the usual boundaries of "character," but by something ferally narrower than "character." We might say that whereas our mythology posits character as stifling inner expansive drives, in Conrad character often seems to mask a force of even greater contraction and defiance than itself; character prevents not expansion but total implosion. This whole dynamic of stubbornness and resistance of course invites a dismissal as anal retentiveness. Maybe photos of Conrad support that conclusion: he looks taut and stiff. But this tautness, unusual among modern writers of his stature, and strange in relation to his social and historical scope, may in fact have as much to tell us about social reality and history as do more erotic or power-haunted rhetorics. He writes about a taut world, in which "character" controls the self's desire to be even *less* expanded, even more petty, than it is. Modern psychological and public jargon uses unconsciously anal phrases like *bind* and *dropping out*, when discussing some of these very themes of forced labor and forced participation. If the "base" of the human world is not a positive drive of the glamorous or fashionable kind, a splendid desire or a will to power, but a petty will to negative boundary, a universal petulance, if the Donkey's divided rhythm is the world, then the primary rhythm arrived at must be, as we will see in *Nostromo*, "jerky." One main rhythm of history will be that of the Donkey. In *Nostromo* the society—what Decoud calls as a totality the *Gran' bestia*—produces, balks, starts up again. It undergoes periodic alternations of rest (stability), unrest (revolution), and arrest (new constitutions intended to halt the dialectic between unrest and rest). If some of the main rhythms of history are "anally" determined, stupid, and sadistic, then the great rhetoricians like Nietzsche and Lawrence are flattering—in spite of all their apparent criticisms—their readers by locating the main drives as eros and power. Conrad, in his own "jerky" work portraits, refuses to do that.

Reading Conrad's historical or political novels is then partly unpleasant, but it shows another rhythm, less immediately flattering and appealing than that in historical works which make the main historical drives love, power, or capital accumulation. Of course Conrad includes these drives, but it is a matter of emphasis: he puts an unusual emphasis on forced production as it modifies these other relations. To accept this general forced productivity as a theme is, however, paradoxically to relent toward it, if not exactly to forgive. In *Nostromo* the rhythm of jerkiness is less narrowly located. *Nostromo* may be as great as it is, taken as a whole, because it is the book in which Conrad identifies most fully with resistance rather than reaction. Reaction closes the world out stiffly; resistance confronts the world to gain independence; but the two are more alike, even more indistinguishable, than it first seems, and Conrad likes to write about the penumbra where they merge. *Nostromo* has a lot to do with that inability to differentiate reaction from resistance. For all its relentless critique of the resulting human misery in the land where resistance and reaction may be the same, Conrad relents here toward individual workers and rebels, who no longer take primary blame, and who are almost, as in the case of Hernandez, celebrated. We can move from the early letter, where the Donkey was generalized, hated, and worshipped, to the *Narcissus*, where the Donkey was individuated and despised and secretly validated, to the beginning of *Nostromo*, where we find a real, lower-case mule, not at first apparently an allegory, carrying the deposed Ribiera over the mountains. "Poor Señor Ribiera (such was the dictator's name) had come pelting eighty miles over mountain tracks after the lost battle of Socorro, in the hope of outdistancing the fatal news—which, of course, he could not manage to do on a lame mule. The animal, moreover, expired under him at the end of the alameda, where the military band sometimes plays in the evenings between the revolutions" (11). The fully burlesque character of this running description is at first lost in the forestalled release of facts in the novel: at the close of part 1 we will learn that Ribiera is one of Conrad's many grotesquely obese politicos—one of the fatsos recurring in his work who are comically pitied by others for massive immobility. The disproportionate weight of ruler on dying mule here, straight out of Aristophanes, lets us know that the attitude toward the working class in this book will no longer be that of the antisocialist scold.

Even more significantly, careful reading shows that during the long and ironic "search for labor," the childless Mrs. Gould is transformed from a woman capable of childbirth as creative "labor," which is what Conrad implies she wants, to a beast of burden:

> She bore a whole two months of wandering very well; she had that power of resistance to fatigue which one discovers here and there in some quite frail-looking women with surprise—like a state of possession by a remarkably stubborn spirit. Don Pépé— the old Costaguana major—after much display of solicitude for the delicate lady, had ended by conferring upon her the name of the "Never-tired Señora." Mrs. Gould was indeed becoming a Costaguanera. Having acquired in southern Europe a knowledge of true peasantry, she was able to appreciate the great worth of the people. She saw the man under the silent, sad-eyed beast of burden. (88–89)

This can easily be read as solemn elegiac prose, praising her capacities and sympathies, but it is also an extended irony, and the point is harsh. She has undergone a process of enforced substitution, to become a Costaguanera—citizen of the "coast of bird droppings," which replace children. In this melancholy, productive, laborious context, she shows stubborn spirit, inexhaustibility, and relentlessness—qualities usually attributed to women in labor—during a long, forced "search for labor." When she sees through the beast of burden in the peasant to his humanity—and of course she's admirable for that—the unforgiving, objective irony is that she doesn't see the way in which she herself has been translated from a woman into a beast of burden. If we put aside our possibly narrow objection to the assumptions about women, we will see that the main point is a tragic reading of the action of mental "sympathy." It all depends, as usual, on laborious puns, purposely too "basic" to an English speaker: bore, burden; labor, labor. Mrs. Gould denies her identity as a beast of burden, immersed with the other beasts, by humanizing them. Conrad describes even the best kind of "sympathy," then, as an action partly motivated by a desire to deny one's threatening animal identity with the object of pity. One sympathizes in order to convince oneself that one is detached from common bestial reuse. (We will see a similar analysis of sympathy in Winnie's statements about Mrs. Neale.) In this immersive dialogic, everyone in Costaguana, even Emilia Gould—however admired—is *bête*, and sympathy, however admirable, is a mental defense *against* the functional identity of all the beasts of burden.

A last set piece, from *The Rescue*, shows how Conrad sounds when he fantasizes escape from coercive relation into free and easy physical cooperation. Lingard, the twice-burdened hero, has a small personal boat which gives him his only moments of freedom. They are, in the physics of dialogue, equals: she carries him on the water, and he carries her on the land. They are erotically mutual pleasurable burdens, the contrary of imperialist mutual interference:

> In that little boat Lingard was accustomed to traverse the Shallows alone. She had a short mast and a lug-sail, carried two easily, floated in a few inches of water. In her he was independent of crew . . . when he wished to land he could pull her up a beach, striding ahead, painter in hand, like a giant child dragging a toy boat . . . Once, when caught up by a sudden freshening of the sea-breeze, he had waded up a shelving bank carrying her on his head and for two days they had rested together on the sand, while around them the shallow waters raged lividly . . . Her behaviour had a stout trustworthiness about it, and she reminded one of a sure-footed mountain-pony carrying over difficult ground a rider much bigger than himself. (196–197)

This "dinghy," as the framing implies, is the ideal seagoing "donkey," and the whole scene is childish, sweet, and slightly mawkish. Lingard's boy's-story "nutshell" is like an idyllic girlfriend, ideal for lightness and mutual portability. As opposed to the elephantine Ribiera on his mule, Lingard is mobile, active, and has got right at least one practical relation in the world: with her. This is as close as Lingard comes anywhere to a successful match. Conrad may want the romantic prose to reflect Lingard's limited consciousness; but in any case this picture, though sentimental, works well in the allegorical context, where Lingard is overburdened by forced responsibility for two other heavy and arrested ships—the yacht stuck on the sandbar with its cargo of stick-in-the-mud hypercivilized tourists, and the *Emma*, with its magazine of weapons that will finally detonate. The prose poetry here is obviously not Conrad's strong suit; but it attempts to show that Lingard, like the genre in which he is presented, may only be happy regressively, as a kind of boy with a "nutshell." The scene should reemphasize Conrad's usual idea of forced and unequal relation; when he tries to represent the romance of unforced relation he sounds a little foolish.

The variety in this field of work animal images should be helpful in seeing how he "dialogizes" a common term. I use "dialogism" only for want of a better word: not to be set up as *the* word for his approach, but to counter notions about his impressionism, romanticism, alienation, and so on. Here he begins with a simple public image—the donkey—deploys it to allow the reader to understand the general topic—necessary labor and its rhythms—but also to disrupt accepted ideas, and in the course of his writing reworks the term considerably. In the private early letter, the Donkey is purely allegorical for humanity as brutal and stupid; in Donkin, an individual naming, there is scorn, combined with an involuntary penchant for Donkin's "basic" spite opposed to the "general will"; Ribiera riding the mule is an Aristophanic allegory of class relations; the ironic scene where Mrs. Gould "sees through" the beast of burden to the human being demonstrates that even the highest sympathetic idealism is partly motivated by a desire to deny that we are working animals; in the scene about the "dinghy," the word is peculiarly and with deliberate infantilism "chimed" or "echoed," dialogized from land to sea by the change of a vowel; and when the mule kicks a biscuit tin that is analogous to the *Titanic,* we have a scene of simple proportional "physics" with a moral and political edge, as we do in Donkin's relations to Allistoun, in the picture of Lingard on the dinghy, and in the weight of Ribiera on the mule. In all these scenes, the common denominator is dramatized disproportion and force in relations.

The flexibly various use of the Donkey might seem to show a kind of plastic freedom in language: comically, the emblem of slave labor can be put to work: for universal allegory, personal allegory, ironic realism, a hint about the subjugation of a high idealistic character, a device for an illustration in physics, a strangely forceful but childish "chime." We might want to see a kind of liberating progress in these uses, from the letter, almost hysterical about the Donkey, to *Nostromo,* where the understanding of the themes emblematized by the lower-case donkey has become arguably more complex, forgiving, and self-forgiving, to the dinghy, a fantasy of romantic freedom in relation. There seems however to be a principle of "forceful variety" rather than of freedom in Conrad's aesthetic reuses. The intellectual variety in the use of the image generates something like a "fugue," or forced polyphony, as does the variety of scenes of coercion to speak. This effect of a plurality of coercions is not "free," but it cancels any association of the theme of coercion with narrative one-dimensionality, causal flatness, or determinism. The multiplicity in the image of the donkey is an example of his work's variety. Like this image, the scene of coercion to speak is not a monody. In the political novels, the "same" common theme of coercion to speak is elaborated with such conscious variety that it seems, paradoxically, almost a "liberation" from the conversational format to face the polyphony of forced dialogues in reality. His characters, caught inside the format of "civilization," force each other to speak and respond to that force in so many different ways that they seem, if not free, at least alive in their mutual agencies.

III

Silver and Silence:
Dependent Currencies in *Nostromo*

NOSTROMO is a smaller giant novel, an oxymoron of scale, and not
simply a work of vast historical scope. Rhythmic obstacles—jer-
kinesses and breaks that interrupt the expansive prose—force the
reader to share a feeling of historical disproportion with the characters,
as well as tensions between force and farce. The novel establishes a
rhythm of contraction against expansion. A historical understanding
of this contradictory rhythm governing the sometimes vast and sometimes Lilliputian Sulaco can free us at least in part from Leavis' split
evaluation of the novel as great but finally "hollow." [1] His judgment anticipates many other strong but slightly unfair statements about Conrad
as elusive, cold, stilted. These complaints are reasonable—anybody can
see the source of them—but they come in part from a desire to set his
work tonally inside the framework of the English "sympathetic" moral
imagination and against the background of the great nineteenth-
century historical novel. These standards don't apply, or aren't entirely
applicable, because Conrad has an ironic relation to these traditions.
Canonization has led to overemphasis of his historical range and blindness to his other side—his stubborn, even Menippean dislike of greatness. *Nostromo* isn't exactly meant to have the inclusive sympathetic
force of *War and Peace, Bleak House, Middlemarch,* or even *Waverly,* but
reads partly like an ironic attack on historical scope, a contracted scale
model of "the great novel"—like the model ships Conrad encouraged
his son John to build. His well-known comment, in the Note to *The Secret
Agent,* that *Nostromo* had been his "largest canvas" stands more in relation to his own fiction than to that of other writers. His largest canvas
may still be less grandiose than a historical novel by, for example,

Henryk Sienkiewicz. The word *canvas* itself, beneath the obvious metaphor, may even connote sailing, the grandest sailing ship being small
compared to a modern steamer.

Close reading will show that Conrad did not want to write a great
national novel or even a great ironic provincial novel. Though Avrom
Fleishman has accurately deflated what he calls "the Polish myth"
about Conrad by sketching ethnic and social relations in the part of the
Ukraine where he grew up,[2] there is no doubt that Conrad saw himself
as Polish. Where major works by Tolstoy, Melville, and Dickens, whatever their melancholy about scale, try to achieve a great rhythm appropriate to their great nations or cities, and where provincial novels
enlarge small communities, Conrad insists on an a priori confusion
about scale itself, paying attention to a large community that is at the
same time small, half inside and half outside a "great world" that is
somehow trivial. In *Nostromo*, paltriness and greatness often show up
undecidably fused in the same person or incident. Nostromo's adventure on the lighter, for instance, is pettily grand. In the central political
action, when Sulaco secedes, does secession amount to becoming larger
or smaller? Is secession success? Is the newly condensed nation made
practicably small (as Rousseau suggested Poland should contract to
preserve freedom[3]), or is it in fact only enslaved to a greater empire?
Stylistically *Nostromo* mocks "greatness," and has a consistent strain of
anti-imperial puns, dialogical fusions, and noise. It jeers at and violently contracts the scope of the great novel. Edward Said, one of
the novel's most serious readers, takes up this question (for different
reasons, since he argues that Conrad's motive for narrative disorder is
to break with authorial intention), and writes about standard comparisons to *War and Peace:* "In sheer size, of course, the two novels are similar; but beyond that, comparing them is not valuable."[4] Yet the two
books are not similar in sheer size. He then goes on—as if looking for
justification by another standard of immensity—to compare the book's
epically clumsy quality to that of *Moby-Dick*. The comparison is strong,
but again *Nostromo* has a much more skeptically confined idiom of
space—sometimes like that on a chessboard—than Melville's epic.

Politically the main theme of *Nostromo* may be the impossibility of
real secession—the forced dialogue of Sulaco with the outside world.
Sulaco wins independence through separation, but this effects inclusion
in a larger empire. The story of *Nostromo*, then, is partly that of the attempt of one smaller but vast "place"—not clearly defined as a nation
or a province—to contract for autonomy within an expansionist setting.
"If the country of Poland was, curiously," Fernand Braudel writes of the
sixteenth century, "a kind of free-trade area or rather an area of free

passage with a minimum of duties or tolls, it was also a vast expanse, 'twice as big as France.' " [5] As with historical Poland, we are left uncertain as to geographical and commercial status. The center of attention here is colonial dependency, in dialogue form, in imagery, and in spatialization. The snakes, the ropes and threads from which characters are suspended, the rocking chair on which Avellanos sits, the silences, the silver, the recurrent forced dialogues—images and relations are organized around the idea of forced dependency. And if we want to understand the dialogical force of *Nostromo*, both in its own form and in its relation to other writings, we have to point toward the special poetics of this ironic project, which led Conrad to reject, more than Scott, the historical novel's dialectic of inclusion, and to insist upon the falsity of any historical "dialectic" that disguises or ignores the reality of the coercive dialogic.

When Dickens begins *Bleak House,* the grim chime name "London," to make an understatement, locates the novel for his audience, and foretells the chiming prose to follow. Dickens, of course, doesn't have to supply a London map. Sulaco, by contrast, not unlike a place in Swift, is mapped for the reader in the first chapters: the shape of the harbor, the islands, the circumscribing mountain chain or cordillera, the position of the mine, the alameda. But it is done so as to implicate the reader in a problem of scale. On the one hand it is alien, a very limited stage, as was the deck of the *Narcissus;* at the other extreme, and not only to avoid making this place too small or too much like a stage for reductive satire, Sulaco is also "vast" and almost equivalent to all of nature. This is a deliberate proportional anomaly in the opening chapters. Conrad builds us not a stage but what has to be called a problem geography, in the way that we speak of Shakespeare's "problem plays," making the reader work on a dilemma of scale. The geographical question of Sulaco—a country, a province, vast, small, part of Costaguana, part of the sea—is imposed at the outset on the reader by the opening descriptions long before Decoud's secessionist plan appears.

Lawrence Graver has argued that Conrad's "shorter fictions," the novellas or long stories, are his most perfect works, but that he tended to lose his way in his novels.[6] Graver speaks of the "longer short" pieces as the most perfect. This thesis is right to consider scale the agony of Conrad's prose, but a little too simple. Aesthetic and political proportion are not for Conrad separable issues. In his image of the world, Russia is largeness, Poland relative smallness, Napoleonic Europe largeness, England a bleakly brilliant compromise, contract, or bargain, like his own life, between smallness and largeness. A novella might be successful in aesthetic scale, and achieve aesthetic unity, but fail to take on real quandaries of scale in the political world: its perfection is its limitation. Conrad in fact deliberately writes novellas that go on too long and large novels which are somehow abrupt, and this is a kind of historical wit. In the Author's Note to *Nostromo* Conrad describes himself as returning to his family from obsessive work on the book "somewhat in the style of Captain Gulliver" (x)—who was of course caught up in a bathos of scale, between megalomania and insignificance—and also gives the book a carnivalesque source in José Avellanos' neverpublished *Fifty Years of Misrule*. These burlesques of the book's in fact agonized production remind us that for all its immensity and seriousness, it has many stops and dwarfing ironies, offered with a good deal of Bakhtin's *rire resorbé*—hints of other more comic genres, and of what the narrator calls "mock solemnity" (105)—and is indebted to Swift, perhaps even to Rabelais, for a sense of joking about its own proportions. Conrad's well-known preference for Turgenev over Dostoevsky and Tolstoy is partly a matter of scale.

Stealing Graver's phrase to travesty it, then, we could say that even *Nostromo* is one of Conrad's "shorter fictions." Graver may be right that Conrad worked best scaling down, but he fails to see how this happens most effectively and absorbingly not in the novellas, where compression is formally typical, but in his political novels, *Nostromo, The Secret Agent,* and *Under Western Eyes,* all three of which put the scope of larger historical novels under an idiosyncratic and surprising contractual pressure. Some of this pressure, I will try to show, appears in the Menippean device of organizing its own information as the result of "forced dialogue." That is, pressing people to speak, inquisitorial process, yields a kind of truth, whose origin itself is in question. The result of this process, which shows the prose that we read as "forced" in its forcefulness, is a contraction of romantic prose energy. "Expansion" and "contraction," which are the problems of imperialism, are also the problems of prose form in historical narration. This conflict is simultaneously political (having to do with the reining in of the expansive rhetoric of imperialism), aesthetic (having to do with the dramatic relation of prose masses to each other as presented to the reader), and dialogical (having to do with the amount each person speaks in a dialogue).

Nostromo is in fact a dialogue with a number of energetic works usually not mentioned. Cunninghame Graham's *Mogreb-el-Acksa,* with its picture of a "sub-European" Morocco in which Muslims, Jews, and Christians are brought together into continual uneasy contact, and its mobile, traveling sentences, had a complex influence on Conrad in this period—though partly because he quarreled with its simple linguistic flamboyance and the nature of its assumptions about polyglossia.[7] The

"Italian" element in *Nostromo*—the Garibaldian politics and melodramatically "operatic" pitch[8]—recalls the more general use of Italian settings in English tradition, from Shakespeare to Browning, to mean anarchic, Machiavellian, and therefore dramatically interesting politics, but of a kind that doesn't hit satirically home. The strongest and most similar text among all *Nostromo*'s ancestors may be *The Pelopponesian Wars*, and not the later histories which Conrad used for documentation. Conrad arguably had wide classical reading,[9] and the counterpoint in *Nostromo* between dense realpolitik and scenes of ironically framed set speeches resembles Thucydides' version of the classical irony about speech and action. Thucydides' most famous problem scene is itself a colonial "forced dialogue," the Dialogue at Melos. *Nostromo* recalls Thucydides also in its intricate and demanding sentence style based on phrasal verbs; and in its historical context, that of a colonial world of "force" and dismal dependency, in which political speech conceals its unfreedom by rhetorical flourish. Finally, what *Nostromo* may owe to Swift is that prose masses on the page sometimes appear in visibly excessive, even scatological *dis*proportion, as a part of the satirical and political meaning. Even if we exclude the element of popular romance full of various "types" who will capture an audience, *Nostromo* has an intention which is at least double: first as a realistic, even vast, history, but second as an ingenious satiric "miniature" of the disproportions in relations that occur under imperialism. This complex intention must be held together, but *not* "unified," by a general sense of forced relation. As in the other political novels, Conrad here seems to burlesque his own unusual powers of international synthesis. He does not mean, as does Pound in the *Cantos*, to bring international variety into a unity of civilized feeling. On the contrary, he shows us, intentionally, a variegate hodgepodge, held together only by his own openly arbitrary force as a novelist, as the characters also force each other into relation.

A first sense of force as disproportion appears in the portrait of the banker Holroyd—the first figure in *Nostromo* whose speech as proportion receives specific comment. He believes expansively that he can hold the world together as one coherent empire. Holroyd's personal rhythms express the historical period *Nostromo* seeks to capture. The key word for him would be *filibuster*; though Conrad does not himself use the word, Cunninghame Graham does, again in *Mogreb-el-Acksa*, to refer to his own reputation as a rover,[10] and Conrad later calls Peyrol a "freebooter," from which the more cynical and politically shady modern term derives. The word *freebooter*, which also appears in Scott, applies, though at a historical slant, to a whole class of Conradian postromantic heroes, from Lingard to Whalley to Nostromo to Peyrol. In each case, however, the story shows how specific historical or political "tethers" bind and contract the figure of the freebooter, so that this type of Conradian hero is another trope of coercion, the "unfree freebooter," whose gift for roving and "free piracy" is now politically under "contract." Politicized freebooting is "filibuster." The "unfree freebooter" in Conrad—the filibuster or hired man of force—acts in the field of coercive contractual politics and usually fails in some way. Nostromo himself is this figure on a ledge between the two conditions.

But *filibuster* as a dual and historically dialogized term—like *impression*—is a good metaphor for the entire novel *Nostromo* because it also links disproportion in action to disproportion in oratory. These are, the novel shows, parallel problems in a colonial setting. We should remember that as a noun *filibuster* means, first of all, "an American who in the mid-19th century took part in fomenting revolutions and insurrections in a Latin-American country"; [11] nineteenth-century slang only secondarily and figurally makes it the pirating of parliamentary time by a minority or dependent group. By bringing up this word, which Conrad does not use—as by bringing up Graham, Thucydides, and Swift—I am trying to reinforce our sense of the age in which Conrad and his readers felt immersed, and which he was both criticizing and representing, when he created his own narrative methods of plural filibuster. As speech, filibuster is a kind of morosely politicized sailor's yarn; the Spanish idiom *hablar de la mar* means "endless speech." A filibuster, as a personal noun, is a politicized freebooter; but as a parliamentary speech act it resembles that "temporizing," stalling, monologuing delay which has always been recognized as a key to Conrad's narrative technique, yet which has never been fully grasped as a political, as well as poetic, rhythm.

The genius of *Nostromo* in its prose rhythms is to render the emergence of filibuster as both action and speech on all sides of the colonial relation: those in power and those who are powerless all filibuster. The San Franciscan, Holroyd, for example, foments his own Latin American revolution by directive investment; visiting Gould he talks in egotistical, expansive monologues—seen on the page—about his expansionist religion in a way that Gould rejects but can't openly criticize. The representation of talkative people is an old comic device, but here we have something different from Austen's Miss Bates or Scott's pedants. The equation made on the page is clear: his talk expands to take over as his politics does. By contrast and resemblance, many other characters indigenous to Sulaco, and weaker, filibuster more secretly and pathetically, insofar as each is forced to work at his own incongruous revolution, and to make his own monologue about it. Certainly the ancestor of José Avellanos might be found in Walter Scott's loquacious old Scotsman, whose lengthy jargon, sometimes nearly unreadable, often indicates the historical pathos of speaking at length in a "dead" language, and who talks so much because he is a living encyclopedia of a group about to disappear. But Conrad's gesture, though it grows out of this tradition, seems more abstract and planned: the historical period which *Nostromo* seeks to give us via prose rhythm is one in which romantic expansive "freebooting" has turned into "filibustering," both in action and in speech—that is, in which the romantic piratical free agent, and the expansively hopeful monologuing self, are in process of losing their glamour, and have come under contraction and contract. Parliamentary coherence in aggressive debate threatens to degenerate into a "concatenation" (Eloise Knapp Hay's word) of pathetically forceful monologues. Romantic poetry, expansive about the joyous self, now seems a function of expansionism in politics. Romanticism is expansionism: that was the pivot of Marlow's self-recognition. In this context, if there were no forced dialogue to hold speech together, speech in *Nostromo* would be only anarchic pathos. Instead, "masses of words" are dramatized as imperial, not romantically free, energies.

To read *Nostromo*, then, is to have our idea of the "field" of dialogue, in both politics and aesthetics, forcibly changed, and to move out of a world of parliamentary dialogue into one of general filibuster. In both its meanings, the dialogical world of "filibuster" opposes, or subverts, the liberal parliamentary idea that energetic public speech, for all its conflict and egoism, can cohere positively, and lead to collective action. Parliaments work in nations, not for empires or colonies. "A lot of words" here is often synonymous not with parliamentary spirit but with hopelessness and the inability to be heard. Individuals act diversely to foment each his own revolution in the Americas; dilatory, powerless talk has become the self-caricaturing *essence* of an ineffective parliament. Decoud's skepticism may often be a pose, but there is no doubt that his ridicule of Parliament as a *Gran' bestia* (191) is partly endorsed.[12] In the true parliamentary idea of dialogue—to be found from Milton to early Dickens at the core of "English" energy—everyone heatedly but addressively tries to exert as much power over public dialogue as he can. Dickens caught this brilliantly in what are in some sense the "first" pages of his work, the description of the mutual insults of the Pickwick Club, which hilariously transform themselves into praise. There may be shouting down, interference, and denunciation, but even at its most brutal and dilatory the parliamentary image optimistically implies some communal action, and the assumption by all the speakers that they address someone and belong. "Filibuster" appears because parliamentary form collapses under the weight of imperialist and colonial disproportions. The technique of filibuster was first

Silver and Silence

used in the British parliament as the strategy of the nearest colony, Ireland[13] (think of Swift again and *A Tale of a Tub*), and in the United States the filibuster is of course the exemplary speech act of the defeated South. Personal filibuster might be one way to describe the great power of Faulkner's style in *Absalom! Absalom!* and other works. The pathos of filibuster begins as a conscious tactical subversion of the dialogue of parliament—which implies that everyone belongs—by overdoing the right to be heard to the point where the principle annihilates itself. Intead of leaving the scene, the outnumbered minority speaker, to protest a lack of actual power, gains a futile, temporary "grieving" monopoly on talk which in no way hides his powerlessness in reality or his marginality in history. Filibuster then appears as a grievance against parliamentary order itself. This creates a new image of dialogue and speech in the novel. Faulkner's liking for Conrad can be traced partly to their shared intuition of the emergence of filibuster to replace the Dickensian exuberance of the parliament. The more language the speaker produces (including the writers themselves) the more they seem defeated, "taken over" by the force of history, dependent, Faulkner as Southern, Conrad as Polish.

Nostromo tries to capture this paradoxical rhythm of colonial talk in a prose of self-defeating rhythms. Verbal "expansion" and accumulation lack expansive romantic joy. This is one reason for the book's unpopularity in spite of its virtuoso cast of romantic characters, clearly a bid to attract an audience: Conrad here makes the very technique of romantic expansiveness which he seems to be practicing deliberately joyless. This contracted expansiveness in prose style may be typical of a certain kind of poetic novel, in which condensation is ill at ease with narrative momentum. But here it "refers" rhythmically to the historical problem of expansion itself. As in the difficult prose rhythm, in politics neither contraction nor expansion is shown to be the simple answer.

As often in Conrad's best work, the alert characters are painfully conscious of the problems of speech proportion and discuss them openly, but are unable to alter them. The Goulds, for example, confront together the fact that both Holroyd and Avellanos talk a lot, and find themselves suddenly disagreeing:

> They had stopped near the cage. The parrot, catching the sound of a word belonging to his vocabulary, was moved to interfere. Parrots are very human.
> "Viva Costaguana!" he shrieked, with intense self-assertion, and, instantly ruffling up his feathers, assumed an air of puffed-up somnolence behind the glittering wires.

"And do you believe that, Charley?" Mrs. Gould asked. "This seems to me most awful materialism, and—"

"My dear, it's nothing to me," interrupted her husband, in a reasonable tone. "I make use of what I see. What's it to me whether his talk is the voice of destiny or simply a bit of claptrap eloquence? There's a good deal of eloquence of one sort or another produced in both Americas. The air of the New World seems favourable to the art of declamation. Have you forgotten how dear Avellanos can hold forth for hours here—?"

"Oh, but that's different," protested Mrs. Gould, almost shocked. The allusion was not to the point. Don José was a dear good man, who talked very well, and was enthusiastic about the greatness of the San Tomé mine. "How can you compare them, Charles?" she exclaimed, reproachfully. "He has suffered—and yet he hopes."

The working competence of men—which she never questioned—was very surprising to Mrs. Gould, because upon so many obvious issues they showed themselves strangely muddleheaded.

Charles Gould, with a careworn calmness which secured for him at once his wife's anxious sympathy, assured her that he was not comparing. (82–83)

Here the Goulds between them divide up the meaning of those masses of words that challenge the reader's sense of rhythm on encountering the difficult opening movement of the novel. What are we to think of the production of "major force" by cumulative language? Is this force aesthetic or political? Is it force or farce? Is Avellanos' force the same as Holroyd's, or ethically different? Before siding too quickly with one of the speakers, we should recognize the intended dialogism: the equal case made for each side. The scene itself is framed and emblematized by the deceptively banal parrot, who screams out (in translation), "Long live the coast of bird-droppings," one instance of Swiftian satire partly hidden from the English audience by polyglossia. The slogan that comes out of a bird's mouth—its *bêtise*—will celebrate whatever comes out of its rectum or "mine." That is, the parrot is an emblem of ideological speech itself. The name Costaguana is typical of Conrad's punning—onomastic jokes being themselves allegorical coercions which the reader with an urge for freedom will usually want to resist.[14] But that is the point: the parrot is not just the emblem of mechanically produced speech but a representative of language as not free but materially "caused." This is what Charles, the materialist, believes. Language is matter, and a lot coming from one mouth is the same as a lot coming from another. Language must be judged as pure extension, even as mass. Emilia, for once "almost shocked" by an idea of Charles's, insists on a self-evident ethical distinction between the two men: the wordy constitutionalist Avellanos articulates a social ethic that cannot be equated by plain word count to claptrap like Holroyd's material evangelism. But while obviously her critical idealism pervades the entire novel, she is not coextensive with its dramatic meaning. When Charles as a producer sees words only as mass and extension, he resembles Conrad's own working conditions, as a producer of many words for a living, more than does Emilia.

These two positions regarding amassed language—the ethical, which holds that the altruistic content of verbal expansiveness can be real, and the materialist, which dismisses all expansiveness as the same sublimation of imperial force in "inclusive" prose rhythms—are irreconcilable and at the heart of the novel's tortured prose, of Conrad's quarrel with cumulative effect in the historical novel, and even with his own evolved techniques of *progression d'effet*, as described a little too preciously by Ford. Conrad often criticizes or mocks his own techniques for creating aesthetic "force." So the reader is meant to feel the amassing of prose in this novel itself, not simply as sublime energy, and not simply as historical "shit" (or excrementitious burden), but as the conflict between these. The prose-poetic question that the novel poses is: how are we to feel about the accumulation of language in any "great" historical or social novel whose physical mass as a big book is a weighty metaphor for populousness, even a demographic gesture? Is it potentially "beautiful," ethically high and sublime, socially inclusive, like a great constitution, potentially democratic and compassionate, as to Emilia and José; or is it always, even more violently than in the bleakness of late Dickens, some unconscious brand of "nationalist shit," the sublimated image of national greatness in the great massive novel? Thus when we scan *Nostromo* visually, or its amassed long paragraphs, and recall its temporal rhythms, we are presented with a question regarding massiveness itself.

Prose as the laborious production of masses of words is a recurrent theme in Conrad's letters, in which he often counts words in units of ten thousand, parentally scolding or praising himself for the month's yield.[15] The parrot may come from Flaubert on banality, or may recall Melville's despair at writing as scrivening in his forced dialogue *Bartleby*—but it is also just a crude joke. Conrad's picture of himself as being compelled to write a lot, and his ability to register this strain and make it a prose rhythm, combine with his complex Polish sense of scale, and his very harsh sense of humor, to redefine the rhythmic ambition of the historical novel. To ignore his sadly "solemn mockery" of the ethical figures in the novel—even Emilia Gould, when she attends a birth of warm, fecal silver from the mine (107)—is to sentimentalize his real case for them as persons with hopeful ideas. Leavis and Berthoud, who write brilliantly about the book in the tradition of moral criticism, nevertheless are a little too oblique or silent about this grosser laughter that has a different impact from high "irony." Consider this description of José Avellanos talking: "Then giving up the empty cup into his young friend's hand, extended with a smile, he continued to expatiate upon the patriotic nature of the San Tomé mine for the simple pleasure of talking fluently, it seemed, while his reclining body jerked backwards and forwards in a rocking-chair of the sort imported from the United States (51)." This sentence imports the jerky physics of the rocking chair into its own syntax and shrieking rhymes in order to comment on Avellanos' dependent politics. The rhythmic form mocks the stated theme of fluency. The four *at*'s (expatiate, patriotic, nature) at the outset are monotonous, mechanical; the "it seemed" interrupts at just the wrong moment, after "fluently," for an effect of gross rhythmic farce; the image of the talking body of Avellanos sitting on a jerky machine indicates that he remains unconscious of the material base of his own eloquence; rest, unrest, arrest come together in false unison in the key motion of jerking;[16] and the rocking-chair rhythm of the phrase "sort exported" shows us that Avellanos has an imported rhythm (rocking chairs being at this time a piece of furniture particularly associated with New England): his own rhetorical continuity and force are dependent. This is not to say that Conrad regards all parliamentary talk as just "superstructure"; but he does present most historical and political discourse as "jerkily" disconnected from historical reality. This "jerking" rhythm, with affectionate, almost Homeric satire about the tremors of the old, is associated throughout the novel with the speech and movements of Mitchell, Monygham, and Giorgio; it signifies both their broken physical courage and their various incomplete relations to the forced dialogues of social history. Avellanos, no matter how admirable in having survived torture, is a leisure-class figure in a rocking chair, somewhat cut off from material and social reality, whose speech, like the parrot's, derives from his "bottom," base, or seat.

Among other things, what Avellanos, like Mitchell, omits in his jerkiness is that labor is impressed, forced to work, imported, even enslaved. Impressment at the docks is left to Nostromo; he impresses laborers visually by his silver displays, and acts as a one-man press gang toward them, beating them to make them work (96). Such impressive "force" makes labor continuous. In discussing the "patriotic nature" of the mine, Avellanos also omits—as immediately afterward we are told Mrs. Gould knows—that "whole tribes of Indians had perished in the exploitation" (52). Again, in this view of its supposed "nature," he omits the great joke, that Charles Gould himself owns the mine because it was originally *forced* on his father at a time when it was nonproductive; the mine itself has its origins in a grimly funny forced dialogue between the state and the Gould family. In all this the point is that Avellanos uses an unconscious oxymoron when he refers to "patriotic nature," just as Holroyd does more blatantly when he refers to the coming time for "proper interference" (78) by North America in Sulaco. For Avellanos, the "deliciousness" of the rhetorical figure "patriotic nature" lies not only in its euphony but in its sublime combination of father and mother, patriotism and nature. But this is meant here to be an irrational synthesis: mines do not have patriotic natures, as interference cannot be proper, since it violates identity. Speaking about property and nature, the two fall into similar contradictions. The argument that Conrad had a bad ear for English, and was himself trying to capture euphoniously the rhythms of the rocking chair, would, I think, be nonsense. His sense of the English verb is acute; *jerk* is the key verb for going on without achieved continuity throughout the novel. At the very least, the contrast between Avellanos' alleged fluency and the rhythms of the imported chair gives some credence to Charles's materialistic reduction of him. At the most, it implies that Avellanos, however sympathetic, is as much of a historical fool, out of touch with the real "continuity and force" of history, and of class relations, as is the more obviously ludicrous historian Mitchell. Avellanos is materially dependent on the United States for his rhythms; his speech is jerky because dependent systems of thought are by nature full of gaps.

To summarize what has to be a set of indicators rather than a complete description of this part of the novel's prose poetic: (1) *Nostromo* is a small big novel because its play with scale calls into question the spirit of amassing which it creates. It continually "contracts" the noisiness and expansiveness it also renders. (2) It can be helpful to understand the organization of the whole novel, as history and as the aesthetics of dialogue, by the term *filibuster*. The multiple dependent speakers threaten the parliamentary image of collective speech as much as the multiple fomenters of different revolutions in action in Latin America. (3) The issues of amassed prose and of proportion in dialogue are inextricably fused as both aesthetic and political in Conrad's work.

One main unstudied question about the poetics of *Nostromo* deserves close attention: the chime beween the economy of "silver" in the narrative and the economy of "silence" in the dialogues. In a singularly precise way (whose significance for the novel as a structural hybrid of dialogue and narrative I will look at later) the whole of *Nostromo* works to demonstrate that the two economies run parallel in any society, and that in this particular one "silence is silver," not golden. Silence, the reserve of dialogical power, resembles silver, the reserve of political power, and both appear, when looked at closely, to be dependent, secondary currencies. They fluctuate in value in response to other currencies. Silver, for all its sometimes overworked visual recurrence in the book, has been carefully chosen by Conrad to displace gold as the "typical symbol" of value because it is less stable, and more dependent. In addition, as the lesser of the two "major" currencies, the smaller standard of value, silver had various meanings in the Americas at the turn of the century, and also, as we will see in a moment, makes a possible symbolic reference to Poland as a dependent nation. Silences likewise (at least the local silences in human dialogue, if not the natural silence of places like the Golfo Placido) are the lesser and more fluctuating part of social language; though sometimes silence in Conrad seems to be at the base of all dialogue, a reserve from which meaning is drawn, at least as often it seems by contrast dependent on and determined by the speeches surrounding it. He does not have a theory but a practice: his ability to exploit both these possibilities leads to much of the dramatic complexity of his writing. Throughout *Nostromo*, silver and silence become the linked defensive "possessions" of the various characters. The two elements are more meaningful together than alone: they indicate ironically that dependent persons who try to achieve autonomy have to do so through dependent, not absolute, means. This may be the most original feature of *Nostromo*, an extraordinary idea of linkage between the political economy and the dialogue economy that colonial people are forced to practice, formally registered by a polyphony between the dialogical and narrative forms of the novel. But to follow this prose chime—even to convince the reader that it is forcibly there—I will have to backtrack and discuss the way in which words are offered in the novel.

The geographical Sulaco, defended from the profane outside world, appears at the start as a natural temple of silence. The narrative, however, quickly dissolves this legendary, "dumb show" atmosphere (including the story of the gringos' silent death) to give a portrait of the progressive modernization of the country as "noise"—much as Decoud will later suggest, annoying Avellanos and Antonia by his own loud insistence, that colonial history is a progress of increasing noise. Though the opening folk tale about gringos and their ghostly fate has often been taken to foreshadow the action, it is also one of those legends frequently found in Conrad, whose silent simplicity is at odds with novelistic realism. The dumb show is a legend of silence; the novel is a history of both silence and noise. Especially during the riot, part 1 sets up a contrast between nature as silence and history as noise. Between the absolute silence of the Golfo Placido and the total noise of anarchic riot, however, there is also music, which is here a kind of forced, or "strung-up," order, and characters here are implicitly orchestrated as different political instruments. Mrs. Viola, for example, takes her name from her sonorous, perhaps pseudoprophetic "contralto," which has an ambiguous effect on Nostromo's future; and less clearly, Decoud's name suggests "unstrung" or "unthreaded," so that it is, as will be clear further on, part of an entire system of "musical bondage" and the political instrumentalization of persons—derived from the forcible tuning of strings—in the imagery.

For an understanding of the use of words, names, and noises, however, the companion book to the first part of *Nostromo* is probably again Cunninghame Graham's *Mogreb-el-Acksa*. That book is sprinkled with foreign words, and has a random exuberance of polyglossia or languages in contact. Graham presents himself as an ethnographer of speech, a collector of folk proverbs, and a *bête noire* to his contemporaries, reversing their moralisms into antimoralisms of his own. In his witty protests he seems full of himself, where Conrad often seems, in direct contrast, empty of himself. As a result, what seems to be the common ground between them—ironic, detached criticism of a polyglot imperial world—is in fact the radical difference, because Graham finds it to be full, Conrad empty. Graham, for example, gives a waggish portrait of a vagabond as someone who "spoke almost every language in the world" and was therefore a "knave" (22). Thus he seems to be debunking polyglossia. But at the same time Graham lets us know that he himself is the knave, the vagabond trickster, filling his book with clever insights. The book is filled with Spanish proverbs, jokes about the pretensions of philologists, and the entertainment of the mixed races of Morocco. Graham speaks in these heavily witty tones about naming: "How much there is in names; fancy a deity, accustomed to be prayed to as Allah by Arabs, suddenly addressed by an Armenian as Es Stuatz, it would be almost pitiable enough to make him turn an atheist upon himself." (The artfully assumed run-on speaking character of this syntax typified Graham's mobile style in the whole book.) "I feel convinced a rose by any other name does not smell sweet; and the word Allah is responsible for much of the reverence and the faith of those who worship him" (73). He jokes, but he believes in the fullness of names. In spite of his apparent mockery of name superstition, as a stylist he creates a roving, rich, and exotic text full of interesting words and scenes. The book is a true travelogue.

Nostromo at first looks similar to *Mogreb-el-Acksa*. It presents us an American nation positioned roughly where Morocco is vis-à-vis Europe—"below"—and likewise "filled" with plural races. We get a medley of Italian, English, Spanish, American, American Indian, and Jewish figures. One impulse Conrad had in contructing the book was no doubt to fill it with these so that it would sell. The modern reader who sees Conrad as gloomy forgets to what extent the work had to be sold as full of swashbucklers and dark women.[17] But of course at the same time he does subvert his own romance with bitterness and skepticism, and gives, unlike Graham, a feeling of contraction. The names that speckle his text in various languages are mostly empty, lacking in appropriateness, in property. They are not romantic but contractual, deliberately hollow, and often oxymoronic. Mrs. Viola, with her operatic faith in the force of speech, scoffs at Nostromo that his name is only a fool's contract: "He would take a name that is properly no word from them" (23). But Nostromo's name, "taken from them," is a contract much like "Joseph Conrad," a contraction, and the word *proper* resonates emptily throughout the novel, most bitterly when Holroyd says his oxymoron, already quoted, about "the time for proper interference on our part." The littlest and ugliest of the islands is improperly named Hermosa—"beautiful"; the Rio Seco is the obvious oxymoronic place for Montero's great victory; the ubiquitous military guards are "serenos." From the beginning, steamship names from the Roman pantheon are inappropriate: "The *Juno* was known only for her comfortable cabin amidships, the *Saturn* for the geniality of her captain" (9), and so on. What interests Conrad here is not the old boy's lament that words are losing their meaning. Conrad has a much larger intelligence of the transience of language and names in history. Though there is an obvious joke in the discrepancy between the Roman gods' attributes and the individual boats and captains, Rome *itself* is appropriate to this context of modern imperial sailing. What interests him is that figures like Mrs. Viola, who believe "profoundly" in the individual propriety of names miss the larger force and continuity within changing language and history. A name that is improper for the individual, and that lacks appropriateness to his first character or being, may by that very emptiness be true to the force of history. "Nostromo," the name as renamed, as renown (compare the French *renommé*) is "taken from them" because fame necessarily has the structure of being renamed for others. Józef Korzeniowski himself altered his name so that it would have English currency. There is accurate comedy in the fact that the new *Saturn* is known for geniality. The fact that the original tones of names are "detonated" or "unthreaded" by history does not fill Conrad with conservative horror, or with the desire, like Graham, to be a wag. Names of historical persons *are* contracts. Mrs. Viola has a case when she points out that Nostromo is paid in words but is not even allowed his own name; but the fact that it is someone named Mrs. Viola who says this should lead us to suspect the sonority of the criticism as much as anything else.

Just as Decoud hears history in the changing noises of Sulaco, the reader is meant to hear the many little noises, splutters, and renamings in the prose, and to organize them skeptically as signs of colonial history. Though it is risky to posit a "global" sense of names and words, it would be helpful to emphasize the frequent contractual emptiness of naming here. This is a kind of polyphony which is not "fullness" and not historical or social "plenitude." In Bakhtin's concept of novelistic diction as "heteroglossia" or "polyglossia" (plurality of dialects, languages, and ideologies), the novel in its truest generic examples shows forth the irreconcilable languages of different groups—classes, nationalities, and professions. These give the novel its unique sense of plenitude as surfeit, and its special powers to present a variety of consciousnesses. Bakhtin's work is great; yet the crude criticism could be leveled that, in spite of his desire to affirm "otherness," his work adds up, surprisingly enough, to an encomium on expansive nationalism.[18] The novel, in all its exuberance, equals the various, large, cacophonous, tolerant, multivoiced nation—and the favorite examples will be national geniuses like Dickens and Dostoevsky—whose robust dialogics Bakhtin advocated partly as a protest against his own political situation. The relation of *Nostromo* to this pluralism of the historical novel is unusual to the point of being bizarrely antithetical. Conrad equally apprehends, but does not equally celebrate, what Bakhtin sees. The "heteroglossia" here, the polyphony of ideas, the diverse, irreconcilable languages have no exuberant flavor. Conrad imagined a more forced and negative "polyglossia," not exactly Babel, but a world in which the plurality of languages and ideas does not amount to a new plenitude. It only exists, marked by ironies, emptinesses, contractions, and contractualities of its own, rather than by glorious worldliness and freedom. That is, Conrad created, from his Polish-English contractual standpoint, a deliberately hollow and coercive international polyphony.

It is in this strangely ironic, oxymoronic, contractual, historically emptying context of naming in *Nostromo* that we have to ask the question, Why is the Gould mine a silver mine? Why choose silver as the ore and then name the owning family Gould? The false easy answers are two. One is that gold and silver are functionally identical here; the Gould family name indicates its position as source of value in Sulaco.[19] The contrary, slightly less oversimplified reading would argue that this naming is a harsh oxymoron, almost on the order of Orwellian satire, which points mockingly to the relative instability and worthlessness of the novel's actual fetish of silver, as opposed to the family's illusory idealism in its search for a stable and perfect standard of value and of politics for Costaguana.

Neither reading is precise. Instead, silver in the novel has to be understood both in its relation to the book's dialogue forms and in its historical connotations. "Heart of Darkness," as we saw, "chimed" Ivory to Invoice, the economic standard of value to Marlow's obsession with an "in-voice," a powerful, idealist, standard-giving Kurtz. In that story the two fetishes equally required critique, but Marlow's effort to liberate himself from his idea of Kurtz's voice was a more difficult and prolonged "secondary" struggle, ending in the realization that forced dialogue, not freedom, is the form of Intention. *Nostromo* carries on, but in a more subtle and unforgettable way, this project of a chiming or parallelism between an economic currency—in Sulaco silver—and an illusory, pseudoliberating dialogical currency—in Sulaco no longer voice but silence. As often in Conrad, the alteration of a commonplace, as if both to rivet and revise the thinking of a large audience, is being undertaken without Flaubert's contempt or hilarity. According to convention, of course, "silence is golden." In the structure of *Nostromo*, "silence is silver." That is, both are secondary or dependent currencies, relatively unstable in comparison to the main currencies, language and gold.

Put the poetics of the parallelism between silence and silver aside for a moment, and consider the historical theme of silver. In the Americas at the time Conrad describes, bimetallism was a major popular issue; silver symbolized the increased distribution of wealth downward without forsaking the standards of capitalism. In the *Titanic* essays eight years later Conrad refers ironically to "nasty, cheap silver" (241), parodying the voice of the superrich who might have to use it on a sea journey. One need not connect Charles Gould to William Jennings Bryan to see that Gould uses the idea of "cheap" silver as the more democratic and politicized of the two standards of value to half convince Emilia that his is an idealist capitalism, ultimately good for "the people." Silver will spread the wealth; when it is appropriated by Nostromo, the man of the people, as a secret hoard to which he is also in some sense entitled (actively and in dialogue, because no one has asked him about it), the political connotations are intentional: Nostromo has taken by covert silent force a form of popular wealth that was patronizingly given him before. And just as silver has a dependent but varying relation to gold—a restless relation—in its value, so silence, in any major work by Conrad, has exact but restless relations to what is being said. This restless shifting in the meanings of silences, as I indicated in the reading of "The End of The Tether," was noticed by some of Conrad's earliest readers as an essential part of his ironic mastery and his involvement of the reader.

Thus we have broad historical and poetic uses of "silver" in this novel. Silver is (1) a secondary currency, raising the issue of dependence; (2) the currency in the Americas which theoretically, if not in fact, might open the field of wealth out from the aristocracy and oligarchy toward the people; (3) an analogy to silence itself, not only as the "natural reserve" but because it is secondary and dependent. Silver is the only weapon of Sulaco against the outside world; silence is the only weapon of dependent persons who are being made to speak. By this technique of chiming or parallelism between the political economy and the dialogue economy of resistance, Conrad can give form to his precise insight that dialogue forms are not the "free" part of social life, *or* of the novel, but complex expressions of other working relations and currencies. And he does this not in an abstract way but by showing how each of the major characters makes a *distinctive* personal synthesis of the two Sulacan defenses, silver and silence, in the struggle to achieve some kind of autonomy. The limit of these varied attempts to achieve independence via dependent means is the desperate plural story of the different persons in the novel.

Conrad would later write about the structure of *A Personal Record*: "In the purposely mingled resonance of this double strain a friend here and there will perhaps detect a subtle accord (xxiii). "Silver and silence" is another subtle accord, giving a strange new unity to a work. One of the major actions of *Nostromo*—if by action we mean with Francis Fergusson the way the poetic writing leads the mind of the reader to make conscious connections among previously segregated categories of experience—is the play between dependent dialogical manners and dependent monetary currency. Through this action *Nostromo* departs significantly from Conrad's earlier sense of dialogue as primarily a "physics" toward the sense that dialogue is primarily a "political economy" practiced by dependent persons. Though here too there is a great deal of attention to the physical force of noise, to physically amassed language, to dialogue as a meeting of weights, the more economic and historical action of "silver as silence" allows Conrad to offer a representation of the linguistic economies of colonized persons, in which they discover parallel ways of using money and silence together.

The central compounder of silence and silver is of course Charles Gould. He prizes silver as the key to Costaguana's redemption from restless politics; he maintains various aloof silences with Holroyd, with the local bureaucrats, and with Hirsch (who wants to sell him dynamite and hides, but has trouble getting him to talk at all). Gould takes part in such "degrading" marketplace dialogue as little as possible. His stolid "character" *is* this resistive alloy of silver and silence; but his imperial stance eventually extends to the dialogue of his marriage, which had been intimate, or at least tender, at first. "It was," we are told in a scene clarifying that the marriage is dead, "as if the inspiration of their early years had left her heart to turn into a wall of silver bricks, erected by the silent work of evil spirits, between her and her husband" (221–222). There is no question that in the portrait of Charles Gould, taciturnity is a fetish as recurrent and as crucial as silver, or that Conrad does whatever he can to make us hear the near-silent chime, even at the risk of seeming grossly allegorical. As in *The Secret Agent*, there seems to be no way for political people to draw a line between the dialogue economy with which they meet the world and the dialogue of their marriages. To simplify somewhat, the reader is meant to reason in this way: in the context of this whole inquisitorial society, silence is the most common mode of defense, from the Indios to Monygham. Gould—hence his name—seems to personify the proverb, or cliché, that silence is golden, but the whole effect is vaguely ridiculous, and in reality, he is in possession of silence and silver, a more ambiguous, less absolute, more comically mechanical power.

That the Gould-silver irony is being emphasized throughout the novel to point to a general condition of dependency is clear enough within the novel itself, but can perhaps be reinforced by a look at Adam Mickiewicz. Here is Napoleon in *Pan Tadeusz*: "Such were the amusements and disputes of those days in the quiet Lithuanian village, where the rest of the world was swimming in tears and blood, and while that man, the god of war, surrounded by a cloud of regiments, armed with a thousand cannon, harnessing in his chariot golden eagles besides those of silver, was flying from the deserts of Libya to the lofty Alps, casting thunderbolt on thunderbolt, at the Pyramids, at Tabor, Matengo, Ulm, and Austerlitz. Victory and Conquest ran before and after him." For our purposes, the footnote to the same translation is useful when it informs us that "the reference is *of course* [my italics] to the golden eagles of Napoleon joined with the silver eagles of Poland."[20] Of course? Probably not for most of Conrad's audience, but probably for Conrad himself. Here a little effort can help us become "familiar" with—that is, factitiously informed about—his non-English historical perspective. Charles Gould has, in relation to Sulaco, and then to Holroyd, a paradoxical *imperium in imperio,* an empire within an empire. During the Napoleonic era, the emblematic alliance between gold and silver gave brief hope that Poland might repel the Russian empire by a French alliance. There is no space here to survey nineteenth-century Franco-Polish relations, but only to note that by the 1890s, they had fallen somewhat into the shadow of a new French taste for things and novels Russian, which may be one reason why Conrad—unlike Mickiewicz and Juljusz Słowacki—chose England as his haven. The important point here is that gold and silver (Gould's silver mine) may be taken as an emblem of the unstable, unreliable, and often in the end disappointing alliance between a dependent nation and a great modernizing empire. Gould's silver alliance with the American golden boy Holroyd has *some* analogies to Poland's alliance with the golden power of Napoleon and its new world capitalism. It is not of course transparent symbolism— *Nostromo* is by no means "about" Poland's desire to secede from Russia—but the analogy helps us to feel Conrad's sense of "silver" as an ambiguous social force touched with dependency, weakness, and secondariness. The figure relies again on the reader's grasp of an uncertain "measure" and "disproportion" between two elements.

Silver has two nonmonetary meanings in the novel: it means "lesser" (like Poland) and it means "silence"; these together in turn mean the condition of dependency. To remain in Poland would have been to remain silent, or to have had to practice the arts of silent resistance. Mickiewicz, in the patriotic drama *Forefathers' Eve,* celebrates a Polish martyr who was messianically silent under interrogation but then was unable, after his release, to stop being silent with his friends and family.[21] Conrad echoes this tragic fable when he shows how the necessary political silence invades and destroys the Gould marriage. But he was also skeptical of messianic or ineffable ideas of resistive silence in the first place. For him, silence, though sometimes admirable, is only *part* of the forced dialogue, not romantically transcendent. The misreading of Conrad that takes taciturnity in his work as a sign of transcendence must be critically dispelled.[22] Only the early sea stories have something of this character, and even there not without irony. We might almost go to the opposite extreme and say that a major theme in the novels from *Nostromo* to *Victory* is a near-systematic critique of his own and his reader's "taste for silence" to show that it is often dangerously impractical and sadly deceived. Gould's English taciturnity, his practical English version of Polish messianic silence, is one of numerous examples: a strong political reserve, praised and admired to a degree, but also exposed as personally destructive. It kills his marriage, and is perhaps also a partial delusion of independence in the political realm: "Charles Gould assumed that if the appearance of listening to deplorable balderdash must form part of the price he had to pay for being left unmolested, the obligation of uttering balderdash personally was by no means included in the bargain. He drew the line there" (92). His gentlemanly rule in dialogue is not unlike Whalley's: he will suffer cant politely but not lower himself to actually speak it. But in the perpetual stream of critical irony the sentence that ends with the emphatic word *there* sounds like mockery of his arbitary choice as one made from vanity, snobbism, and class safety, not from real dignity or truth. It is of extreme importance that with Holroyd, Gould does relent, does not draw the line. Even his silences with Holroyd have less dignity, and are more compromised, than those he practices with bureaucrats or merchants; they mean that he suppresses frankness to keep the backing. In all this, the silence and silver of Charles Gould add up to a "strong character" not nearly as autonomous or regal as it seems. Gould cannot make himself the Golfo Placido incarnate; his silences are human and dialogized, not natural and infinite, however successfully he seems to transcend.

Gould's character and consciousness are outlined in three ironically related meanings of the word *mine:* (1) the personal pronoun—possession as silent self-possession; (2) the quarry itself—possession as material wealth, with emphasis on ore as buried and secret; (3) the final threat to detonate the mine, turning it into a "mine" in the third sense, found particularly in the nautical lexicon: a hidden explosive sometimes set off by acoustic force. At least some of this forced polysemy is implied when Decoud scoffs bitterly: "He and his mine" (182); "he has his mine in his head" (239). It is a negative progress of meanings which needs no paraphrase. The simplest, even most childish English word for the owning self is being redefined within the mode we are learning to recognize as forced dialogue. Ego is ultimately a property one can't refuse to have been given, and may be forced to define itself by a threat of self-destruction. This is why Charles Gould is not so much a great character as a great image of the tragic illusion in the idea that character is self-possession. "Mine" claims a self through an external object; this leads, logically, to the claim to the right to destroy the object. As in many places in Conrad's glossary, a word acquires its full meaning only when we perceive that identity has the unlikely structure of forced dialogue, involuntary relation. In addition, the polysemy of a word is not that of a "free" variety but of a dramatically conditioned forced relation. Gould's consciousness—the feeling throughout the novel that he em-

Silver and Silence

bodies the ideas of "the mine," of strong secular identity as a logic of self-destructive pathos—implies that private identity paradoxically makes a last stand at the threat of self-destruction. Where Dickens ridicules the Coketown barons' threat to hurl their factories into the sea if the state intrudes, Gould's threat to detonate "his" mine, in a vast act of grotesque historical spite, though no less critically displayed as the logic of possessive identity, is no absurd bluff. And his attempt to make silence and silver the adequate sources of a locally strong personality is more than just stuffiness and archness. He expresses, through the logic of his class, one of the main themes of the novel—that the means, such as "property," by which dependent people must seek to establish independence are themselves dependent, and can become illusions of self-sufficiency, because all relation is in essence dependency, "destructive immersion." Only dependent instruments and compromising, coercive contracts are available.

The history of the Gould mine, called ironically a "Concession," and itself told as a forced dialogue, is one of the wittiest accounts of the origin of property in the English novel. "Concession" is a contractual speech act term used ironically here, since it was Gould Senior who conceded when he was forced by a political enemy to take on the mine as a tax burden, an unwanted, useless property. To own, for the Gould family, was originally to concede; property was not freedom but a forced relation. Later, Nostromo will become a more ambiguously forced owner of silver and silence in a similar concession of his best self to property. But the original outrage committed against Gould Senior, to *make him own* something, is very funny, with a sort of Balzacian acerbity about the idea that ownership is in essence free. The origin of this great family's wealth is a great crime against the family. English tradition usually associates ownership, like speech, with free choice. But here, to speak and to own are forced actions in which one must find a personality by choosing an answer from among limited options. This is how I would question, with more emphasis on circumstance and mutual force, Edward Said's thesis that Conrad's work in principle rejects "beginnings," and is concerned with tentative intentions rather than with origins. While this makes some sense in regard to Conrad's skepticism about authorship itself (though as already suggested he sometimes saw his writing as a forced contract), over and over, it seems to me, Conrad does present a clear notion of the forced origins of his various characters' lives in specific contracts they can't avoid. *Nostromo* as an action begins, comically, robustly, and primevally, when ownership of a useless mine is forced on Gould Senior; *The Secret Agent* begins when Verloc is forced, in dialogue with Vladimir, to produce terror; *Under Western Eyes* begins when Razumov is forced to talk with and shelter Haldin. Charles Gould's life, including his early study of mine engineering, is determined by the existence of the original Concession. He lives to reverse the status of the covenant that defeated his father, but though he then tries to forget the original involuntary character of the "mine" ownership, his life in fact has been defined by that coercion. Victory in forced dialogue is not the same as transcendence of its form.

This idea of ownership as forced possession, something inherited against one's will, like existence itself, both resembles and diverges from Harold Bloom's concept of poetic "influence." In *The Prelude* Wordsworth uses the term *inquisition* to describe his examination of himself for possible themes. As in Borges' reference to literature as "other inquisitions," the irony is infinite. Conrad, as his own work progressed, seems however to have turned, or to have tried to turn, partly away from the infinite ironic romance of self-inquisition (represented by the romantically compelled speaker Marlow) toward the representation, during the period of the political novels, of limited, external, crude forced dialogues in the world. There is the hint of a suspicion that it might be a bad defense, a bad infinity, to always internalize the format of coercion to speak as poetic will. Poetics, in Bloomian romanticism, may be the denial, by internalization, of the Oedipal order of forced dialogue in the outside world—the translation of inquisition into an inner feeling of compulsion to quarrel with a forebear or with oneself. In any case, Conrad turned from infinite self-inquisition to emphasize "objective" political scenes in which the enslaved, colonized, or dependent individual is made to speak, to own, to respond. In Bloom's signally moving personal terms, Gould's inheritance of the silver mine from his defeated father symbolizes Conrad's inheritance, from his own father and his "fathers," of Polish poetic dependency, Polish tragic "silence," Polish poetic minority in the greater world. And this is, to say the least, a viable reading. But Conrad's description of historical struggles for independence via dependent means is certainly also meant as a representation of actual political struggle by colonials against outside influences. This is one of the self-critical questions Conrad's later political novels direct, not always successfully, against his early work. He becomes convinced that the compulsion to speak does not always come from within, and that the political aspect of coercion to speak is at times disguised by inner agony.

Characterization in *Nostromo* is at its most original and goes deepest when describing the individual as a distinctive response to the common immersion in forced dialogue. How a character deals with the common condition—that of forcing others to speak and being forced to speak oneself—tells more than anything else. This method of characterization is neither simply psychological nor simply political. Gould's rigid sense of himself, for example, as a fixed locus of strength and value derives from his largely successful illusion, political and personal, that he rises above the general forced dialogue; except for Decoud, the others largely accept this notion of him because they want such a "king," outside social coercion, to exist. Yet in the implicit irony of the novel, he seems like the relatively arrested chess king, immobilized, fixed at his mine, as the other figures in the novel sometimes seem to move chesslike around him, each confined to one or two types of action in space and society. Monygham is the knight of indirection; Emilia Gould moves among the classes like a chess queen, apparently mobile but in fact strictly confined. Gould's "fixed freedom" sets the *false* but desired standard of autonomy against which the various modes of realistically restricted action practiced by the other characters can be measured. All the main characters in the novel, with the possible exception of Emilia Gould, are understandable as personal defenses, combining silence and silver, against the condition of forced dialogue. In the resolution, each becomes a particular kind of tragic proprietor (the genius lies in the variety here) of silence and silver; each also becomes a distinctive variant of life in the form of, and in response to, coercion to speak.

Dr. Monygham, for example—even onomastically Gould's negative—is the novel's figure of experience: he was once forced to speak and to betray his friends under torture. This is the fact of his existence. Innocence here is not to know forced dialogue; experience is to have known it. Implicitly the past of having been made to speak has wounded him into a knowledge that Conrad locates as Oedipal wisdom: "Both his ankles had been seriously damaged" (370), and he limps. Conrad aligns Monygham's jerky walk with Oedipus not in a Freudian but in a Sophoclean sense, one difficult for us to grasp now because of the strength of Freud's image. Conrad consciously locates Oedipus as the figure who has been forced to speak by the Sphinx, and has won, but only to become later forced to force others to speak, and to be annihilated in the process. An Oedipal format of historical cycles of increasingly rationalized coercions to speak could be called the punishment of the speech forcer; it is very close to the pattern of forced dialogue which Conrad intuits as the dramatic constant of history. The comparison is intuitive, not exact, but it is nonetheless unavoidably there: Oedipus is any figure whose identity has been first created and then tragically re-formed by forced inquisitorial processes. Just as, by pursuing inquiry to its end, but also by being forced himself to force others to speak, Oedipus becomes the defiled and blessed mediator at Colonus, Monygham, whose limp is repeatedly noticed, is the man who "knows" identity itself as the end product of forced inquiry. With this one-sidedly pessimistic attitude, making forced dialogue into everything (as Conrad does not, but almost does), he stigmatizes himself by repulsive dress, a foil to the military plumage of many others in the novel; but when he visits Mrs. Gould he agrees to wear a plain white jacket, as if accepting her redeemed version of him as a finally innocent man who goes too far in self-reproach. We are not supposed to feel that Monygham knows all, and are made to see the negative result of his vision—for Hirsch, obviously; but we are supposed to feel that he knows the given procedure of Costaguana. His role as doctor (also as midwife of the novel's action) reinforces this sense of him as a mundane knower. Intensifying the cliché that the physician should heal himself, this physician has suffered the inquisitorial order. In Monygham, Conrad gives us one of his strongest pictures of tragic knowledge from coercion to speak. This measure of knowledge creates depth of characterization without being in the usual sense psychological; male character in particular is the result of each person's distinctive response to and assimilation of the historical situation of coercion to speak, and is therefore Oedipal. The general inquisition in *Nostromo*, for all its historical reality and documentary background, is from one angle a political psychology, or dialogical economy, of character. Perhaps, Conrad's work teaches us to see, political speech is itself Oedipal—a continual cycle of riddling coercions to speak and punishments of the coercer, the central figure who "makes speech happen" and is alternately cursed and blessed for that agency.

The three other middlemen, those together on the lighter in the great central scene—Decoud, Nostromo, and Hirsch—all partake during the journey on the lighter of a kind of baptism or communion of silence and silver; the outcome for each is an end to the forced dialogue in a "detonation" of the self. Decoud, stranded alone with the silver and silence, goes mad, and engages in a peculiar effort to force silence itself to make a sound, or speak to him. When it doesn't he shoots himself to evoke a noise, attempting to "make the cord of silence snap," suicide here being a forced dialogue with nothing. Hirsch, tortured, has to be "silent about the silver" simply because he knows nothing about it, and finally "detonates" by spitting. Nostromo, to revive the chess analogy, reaches the last square like a pawn to become a new little *rey* or petty king of silver and silence, but, contrary to Mrs. Viola's operatic deathbed prophecy, does not win autonomy. Instead, partly because these currencies are modes of dependency, not freedom, Nostromo, who was earlier "our man," a hero under contract, dependent on payment in words but also the possessor of some splendid tone, forfeits that first contract to these illusory means of independence. Formally, the transfer of Gould's "silence and silver" to Nostromo's "silence about silver" is the great central and tragic moment of the novel, holding it together from beginning to end. There is a major shift: while Gould aristocratically resists degrading attempts to make him speak, Nostromo, in the last movement of the book, falls into a dialogical vacuum, in which no one tries to make him tell his story. He sees with contempt that no one inquires about his adventure or after the silver—that among the civilized, noninquisitorial patrons who assigned him to risk his life there is now an absence of any forceful questioning as simple interest in what happened. To oversimplify slightly, Nostromo is allegorically from "the people," the agent of history about whom no one knows how to inquire.

The group of three middlemen aboard the lighter—the intellectual journalist Decoud, the labor foreman Nostromo, the salesman Hirsch—a tableau that may allude negatively to Géricault's painting of revolutionary longing for freedom *Le Radeau de la Méduse*—has been carefully constructed to be an extreme antithesis of solidarity. Nostromo and Decoud distrust each other and don't want to act together, but start to make some oblique sense to one another in talk. But then the surprise appearance of Hirsch—himself the most abjectly isolated entrepreneur, a Jewish salesman of hides and dynamite, and therefore a "base" reminder of their status as used men or go-betweens—startlingly reconfirms the feeling that the other two have been accidentally forced on each other in an entrepreneurial venture. The oxymoron here is that such agents, when thrown together, oddly belong together through their shared lack of community. The silences of this scene, natural and social, are as a result plural and bitter. On the one hand it is true that when Hirsch whimpers, it endangers them, so that their silence is heroic; at the same time, the simpler point is that they have nothing to say to each other. The epic silences of the gulf and of night adventure are counterpointed to the empty silences of alienated middlemen. On the Golfo Placido each of them is baptized in "silence and silver." From this point they become, figurally, fatal alloys of these two elements, and musically, three "bells," who toll for themselves but "chime in with" the other two by dying in related "detonations." This variety in unity, or tripartite harmony in alienation, is worth examining in detail, because it becomes the poetic structure of the novel in its last half.

The torture of Hirsch, though the most extreme scene of *bêtise* in the novel, the nadir toward which many subtler scenes of forced speech progress, has for a deliberately problematic analogy the prior scene, in which Hirsch tries to sell Gould dynamite. Selling, that scene indicates, has itself the form of forced dialogue: as everybody knows, the salesman's toughest job is to "get his foot in the door," to start dialogue. A grotesque moral question is now raised and not answered by the representation of Hirsch's death: does Hirsch "deserve" to be tortured to death in a context of inquisitorial forced dialogue because his own life, as in the earlier scene, took shape as mercantile forced dialogue, the selling of dynamite, a morally neutral commodity usable either for mining or for war? The formal resemblance between Hirsch's conduct with Gould and Sotillo's conduct with Hirsch—both forced dialogues that end in little explosive detonations—raises this bizarre, perhaps extremely anti-Semitic question. In part, the scene whitewashes the anti-Semitism in the previous image of Hirsch as a vile little coward by making him spit courageously at Sotillo. Also, it could be said, the events argue allegorically that Jews do not have the central place in political economy, or the information which fools like Sotillo attribute to them by hysterical projection of their own greed. The Jew, then, is carefully pictured as the accidental victim or decoy of historical actions in which he has, in fact, no major role. He is also associated with the crucified (as if only crucifixion could legitimize him). So we would half vindicate Conrad of the racial nastiness that marks the portrait by pointing to the contextual action. And this allegory has in fact clearly been worked into the story, along with some sudden respect for Hirsch's melodramatic defiance. But this part of the meaning does not eliminate the more original, detached, and insidious formal analogy between Hirsch and his torturer as initiators of forced dialogue. Hirsch has practiced commercial forced dialogue to sell dynamite for profit; Sotillo practices political forced dialogue to get hold of a treasure. The dialogical isomorphism is the reality behind the scene. The reader is forced to recall that, much earlier, nagging Gould for a reply, Hirsch finally provoked the explosive boast: "I have enough dynamite stored up at the mountain to send it down crashing into the valley" (204). This is the only moment in the book when Gould, usually so restrained, raises his voice to "detonate" his customary silence. But the reversal of character here is rhythmically and formally identical to that in which Hirsch, usually so fearful, courageously explodes to spit in Sotillo's face, "detonating" his own life. In fact, Hirsch does what Gould only threatens to do: he explodes defiantly. We can dismiss the rhythm here as a crude device for making otherwise flat characters apocalyptically round; or we can admire it. But the parallelism itself undermines the apparent moral distinction between the ordinary middle-class forced dialogue of selling and the extraordinary forced dialogue of inquisition. As a result, the implication is that forced dialogue is the common denominator of political and commercial life. Hirsch long before his capture by Sotillo has been living his ordinary life in this form, and so his scene with Sotillo is "the death of a salesman": he dies in an intensification of the scene of forcing the other to talk in which he has conventionally lived. The reader is, I think, intended to feel a kind of objectifying nausea: selling and inquisition cannot be morally equivalent, but look phenomenally the same as dialogue. But because this is an objective structural isomorphism on which Conrad does not comment, the reader is drawn to feel on the one hand that the punishment is disproportionate, totally undeserved, an insane symmetry, and on the other that it is symmetrically apt. Conrad does not say: the dialogical analogy itself, whether we like it or not, is the riddle.

The action of Hirsch's torture centers ritually on the uses of rope. "Already a rope, whose one end was fastened to Señor Hirsch's wrists, had been thrown over a beam, and three soldiers held the other end, waiting. He made no answer. His heavy lower lip hung stupidly. Sotillo made a sign. Hirsch was jerked up off his feet, and a yell of despair and agony burst out in the room, filled the passage of the great buildings, rent the air outside, caused every soldier of the camp along the shore to look up at the windows" (447). The three soldiers pulling the rope require no explanation as a biblical allusion. More subtly, Conrad delivers the information here so that many readers will be made to look back to the beginning of the previous paragraph, read more closely, and notice that Hirsch's wrists have been tied behind his back. This rereading will explain why he now screams. Strange as it sounds, this is kinetic identification: the reader is to be "forced back" also in the "tortured" and "strained" prose work. But the rope itself as an icon of communal bondage also deserves attention. The discovery of "symbols" in Conrad may often mislead us when it calls attention away from the action and dialogue, but the suspensory rope, which "vibrates leisurely," "like the long string of a pendulum" when Sotillo hits Hirsch, is the symbol of dialogue itself, and is at the center of the novel's imagery of human dependency.

There are many tethers in the earlier works. Ships are tethered to the sea bottom by anchors which make them "swing to"; animals are tethered horizontally; to be human by ironic definition is to be vertically tethered. But the "large canvas" of *Nostromo* has a more elaborate rigging of symbolic ropes and threads than any earlier work. They recur at many moments of crisis, and are used for torture, rescue, work, bells (music), and even geographical description. They represent human connection to others as neither inherently good nor inherently evil but forceful rather than sympathetic. Hirsch catches hold of the anchor when the steamer and the lighter collide (293), so that rope is the instrument of both his rescue and his torture. Mitchell lowers ousted ruling-class friends by rope out of "a hole in the wall" at the back of the O.S.N. Company's office so that they can escape the mob, a comic rescue in the Menippean mood of part 1 (10). More subtly, Giorgio Viola's icon, the colored lithograph of Garibaldi, is "cut perpendicularly" by "a thread of strong sunshine" (21). If Emilia's idealism and Charles's materialism seem to be the main ideologies at war here, there is actually a third principle—"force"—not identical to either Emilia's ethical or Charles's material principle, which competes for the reader's regard as the principle of community. The picture of Garibaldi's face cut in half by a thin thread of sunlight implies that Giorgio's republicanism is a fragile, weak enlightenment, disconnected in particular from the continuity and force of "the people," and working people in particular. His idealism is not a rope or bond but a thread of light, and so he seems incapable of dialogue, especially with Nostromo, "the man of the people," and of course ends his life ironically stranded at the Lighthouse, a symbol of abstract or remote liberty which Conrad is not simply praising. The cordillera, or mountain cord, functions as the land horizon of the province. Decoud complains to Antonia, "You seem satisfied to see my life hang on a thread" (180), and when he goes mad imagines (in an image to be discussed shortly) that he hangs from "the cord of silence" (498–501). Finally, when the three bells indicating Pedrito's triumphal entry sound out near the beginning of part 3 (paralleling the three Isabels, and tolling for the three suspended deaths of Hirsch, Decoud, and Nostromo), the women scream, "Misericordia!" (382) in what is another pun on chords and sounds.

In his personal letters Conrad uses this same image with the same emphasis on dependency, tautness, hypersensitivity, and forced connection. Possibly echoing Kleist on the marionette theater,[23] he writes: "Marionettes are beautiful,—especially those of the old kind with wires, thick as my little finger, coming out of the top of the head. Their impassibility in love, in crime, in mirth, in sorrow,—is heroic, superhuman, fascinating. Their rigid violence when they fall upon one another to embrace or to fight is simply a joy to behold."[24] There are other, less well known and somewhat more trite and personal examples of this image: "Life . . . would pass like a dream were it not that the nerves are stretched like fiddle strings."[25] "I am like a tight-rope dancer who, in the midst of his performance, should suddenly discover that he knows nothing about tight-rope dancing. He may appear ridiculous to the spectators, but a broken neck is the result of such untimely wisdom." [26] In the same manner of self-deprecation as a writer: *"Il y a trop de tirage* from novel writing to the command of a ship, I fear." [27] And finally, in the most important example of all for this purpose, some advice to Helen Sanderson about her prose style: "I would say that your prose, full of merits as it is, wants 'stringing up.' " [28] This is potentially Rabelaisian if in the metaphor we hear the polite hint that her prose is so bad it deserves hanging.

One use of such English phrasal verbs, as Conrad knew, whether or not he intended the duplicity here, is exemplified in the way "stringing up" can mean either instrumental fine tuning or summary execution. The accorded images of Hirsch hanging from a thick rope that vibrates below the threshold of sound, and of Decoud hanging from a "tense, thin cord" above the threshold of sound, are simultaneously "political," "musical," and "religious." Hanging from a thread or a rope, they make a music of political execution: they are their own tolling bells. By the third part of *Nostromo,* having come all the way from the first scattered, Menippean movement, and then through the adventurous, kinetically serious action of the second part, we now have a closure in which the three middlemen, having been baptized by the silent Golfo Placido, are fatally "strung up" at different pitches to society *and* to its absence, a "musical" vision of politics and of character as taut dependency. The Aristotelian notion that man is the political animal here translates into the profoundly bitter anti-idealist idea that man is the animal who is tethered vertically. The thickness of rope by which each happens to be tethered determines his "note" in the world. Pater's famous "all art aspires to the condition of music"—which Conrad echoed in the Preface to *"Narcissus"*—has been politicized without losing aesthetic force. Through the imagery Conrad fuses Aristotle's statement to Pater's, though our bad habit of segregating the "musical" from the "political" would leave us unable to describe an action like this. The individual in *Nostromo,* like the prose itself, is tautly and forcibly "strung up," or attuned to the social world, just as the strings of an instrument take their pitch from relative tautness and thickness. This entire image, then, is intuitively linked to the image of forced dialogue, the image of tones as relations created by tenuous force. In the strange music of political dependency that closes this novel, each suspended figure, like a bell, tolls for himself but "chimes in with" the others. Hirsch's low mercantile relation to community is a thick rope that vibrates submusically, making no sound; Decoud's skepticism is a thread so "fine" that it comes to equal the fantasy of the highest note just below silence; Nostromo's death, in between theirs, represents the silent truth about the historical agency of the people passing again into oblivion. (Even Pedrito's mocking comment on Costaguana as "the paradise of snakes" probably belongs as much with the rope images as with biblical symbolism.[29] The snake here is an emblem not of evil but of resistive independence, as in the American revolutionary slogan "Don't tread on me." Sulaco is a "paradise of snakes" because kinetically snakes suggest the fiercest contradiction between an extreme independence of motion and an equally extreme forced connection to the ground.)

Martin Decoud (*coudre* means "to sew," and *décousu*, which means "unthreaded," "unstitched," can be applied to an incoherent discourse) appears not only through his mode of thought—analytical pessimism which reads colonialism as noise and conquest—and not simply through ideological comparison with other characters, but most subtly through the way he approaches women. That is, not only his philosophy and his dismissive jokes but the various tactics by which he forces himself upon women to insist with them delineate his character. It is too easy to reduce him to "the Frenchman," a stereotype who talks about "evil flowers" and who enacts, perhaps, Conrad's own resentment against France's late nineteenth-century turn toward Russian "nihilistic" ideas and novels. Conrad leaves the portrait open to this oversimplification—but equally to its opposite, that Decoud is a Jamesian observer, whose skepticism about the other characters is nearly Conrad's own and makes them clear. Neither view is enough, and the dialectic of these, and of his involvement, is his story. But the most unusual thing about Decoud is his approach to women through ideological insistence. No other man in the novel, and no other man in Conrad's work, has just this obliquely forcing, ideological relation to women.

In part 2, chapters 5, 6, and 7, the chapters preceding the scene on the lighter, Decoud approaches three women in succession, one in each chapter, making for a subtle dialogical progress. In the first scene (168–169), after having angered Antonia by his Caesarist talk in front of Scarfe and José (one of the strongest dialogues in the book, which there is no room to discuss), he demands forgiveness with a sort of chivalrous aggression, standing behind her back and doing most of the talking. When he finally manages, by referring to his own possible death, to make her say, "Martin, you will make me cry," he is "overwhelmed by a sort of awed happiness" (181). He has made her say something; lovemaking here takes the form of a gently insistent forced dialogue. But she herself does *not* cry; she only says she might cry, as Marlow with the Intended, forced to speak, says "your name," but does not say her name. Forced dialogue generates civilized substitutions. In this whole scene, there is a recollection of James's *Bostonians,* in which the attempt to convert a young woman from her father's politics is the surface theme of lovemaking. But the relation between Conrad's pair is more symmetrical. Decoud is much less arch than Ransom, and Antonia herself breaks with convention to stand alone with him on the typically romantic balcony and shock the old ladies. What is even more important in this symmetry of iconoclastic energy between them—in the creation of that "amorousness" between them that isn't quite love—is the play on the word *press* that governs their whole relation. During a crucial earlier scene, Antonia subtly "forces" Decoud to stay in Sulaco and become a journalist. Having come to Sulaco for a short visit to observe the revolution with his usual ironic detachment, he is met by "the pressure of Antonia's hand" (157). This pressure keeps him there. The noun *pressure* of course would mean nothing if its value were not repeated in the next paragraphs through a series of plain puns. Her father, Don José, engages in "pressing entreaties to take the direction of a newspaper"; and we are told, to make this deliberately crude chime of English words of physical force and journalism as clear as possible, that the matter of acquiring a journalist for the parliamentarians "was now becoming pressing; some organ was absolutely needed to counteract the effect of the lies disseminated by the Monterist Press" (158). After this, Decoud declares to Mrs. Gould, with studied irony, that he now has found his "vocation"; and the chapter ends painting the new committed Decoud as "the Journalist of Sulaco going to and fro on the business of his august calling" (159). "Calling," which usually suggests an *inner* compulsion, is of course put last with heavy irony.

Again a job—journalism, like selling—takes form in and through forced dialogue. To be a journalist in this case is to have been pressed into writing forceful slogans for the press: as Conrad says later about his agreement to write *A Personal Record,* "I consented at once. If one must . . ." Decoud has been impressed, in both senses of the word, into becoming a man of the Press. This scene of amorous coercion, a genteel parallel to Nostromo's work with "forced labor," is nonetheless fatal; Decoud will now, as he tells Mrs. Gould in ironic extensions of this kinetic metaphor of pressure or weight, have more "gravity," and no longer be "an idle cumberer of the earth" (157). When he with conscious irony calls his new involuntary hackwork a "vocation," the action subverts a familiar word—*vocation,* one of George Eliot's great terms of developmental freedom—to emphasize that here it is a variety of forced dialogue, a response to external "pressure," instead of a spontaneous belief or drive. But Decoud's irony about "vocation" is also introduced as indirect speech (not in quotation marks), so that the irony seems to be seconded or shared by the narrator. In the story of Decoud and Antonia, both lovemaking and journalistic commitment have been framed to a great extent as scenes of pressure to produce language. He makes her say, "You will make me cry"; she makes him write slogans. They are conjoined. And Conrad becomes verbally and metaphorically most inspired—so that the prose deepens into forced, "expressive" puns—when he represents the scene of being hired to write, or made to produce language (we will see this again in Bunter's forced ghost story and in Razumov's forced spy reports) under circumstantial coercion. Even desire is shaded this way.

Decoud's second insistence is with Mrs. Gould in the next chapter. He comes to her house pretending to look for Antonia's fan and, without meeting much resistance, makes her listen to his plan for an independent Sulaco. Their frank and intimate dialogue is meant to be "French," in that it replaces and fills the tragic English silence which has just been shown to fall between the Goulds in their desperately taciturn marriage. Decoud appears in the house, then, as a very oblique and romantic sublimation of the adulterous lover. They talk politics as love. He offers his French, woman-centered, romantic blend of dependence and independence, eros and theory: " 'Your idea, of course, is separation,' she said. 'Separation, of course,' declared Martin, 'Yes; separation of the whole Occidental province from the rest of the unquiet body. But my true idea, the only one I care for, is not to be separated from Antonia' " (215). That is, his idea of separation in history is disjunctive with his idea of forceful relation in private life. This superficially silly exchange is also powerful because of the background of separation in the Gould marriage about which Mrs. Gould here remains, of course, painfully silent. The whole movement of the book will finally hand over the "silence about silver" into Mrs. Gould's keeping; and if we think that the last scene, in which she takes on herself Nostromo's confession and in which the whole burden of silence and silver "stops" with her, frees anyone, we have missed the bitterness of it entirely.

Decoud's third insistence—the long and somewhat *décousu* or incoherent letter to his sister (itself finally pressed into Mrs. Gould's hands in the closure of this whole movement of journalism as pressure)—explains by a strange prose chime the goal of this progression of three approaches to women. Decoud, though separated from his sister by the ocean, believes that no one else can "understand him so well" (230). This scene closes the progression, and Decoud becomes a realized character for the second time—not the bohemian or nihilist, but the romantic man; his way of dialogue is "insistence" with "sisters." We thought we had been going through a decrescendo of analogous dialogues: that

Decoud feels most strongly for Antonia, whom he approaches aggressively; then breaks into the silent marriage of Mrs. Gould, for whom he cares less; and then finally writes some of the narrative for Conrad in a sort of letters-from-abroad magazine piece to his distant sister. But in fact, the progress is also that of a crescendo of another kind of romantic insistence. The speeches to Mrs. Gould—when he insists on his idea of separation—are less studied than his talk with Antonia; and when he writes his semi-incoherent, direct letter about the incoherent events to his sister—while surrounded in a dreamy, emblematic way by the two frightened Viola sisters—the form of his romantic attachment to the Sister as an idea suddenly becomes apparent in a binding chime:

> Decoud turned half round in his chair, and asked, "Is there any bread here?"
> Linda's dark head was shaken negatively in response, above the fair head of her sister nestling on her breast.
> "You couldn't get me some bread?" insisted Decoud. The child did not move.

The romance of insistence with women which is Decoud's existence reaches its strangely beautiful closure here. It may seem arbitrary to excerpt this apparently minor moment of dreamlike interruption in the long letter-writing scene to consider an "accidental" echo between "sister" and "insisted" which many would interpret as a sign of sloppy writing, not craft; yet this exchange is not at all minor, and the chime is no more sloppy than that between "must" and "muster" in the opening lines of *"Narcissus."* This is the moment, in Conrad's poetic of "chimes," or subtle prose rhymes introduced for the reader "here and there" who likes to listen to "accords" (a method historically derived from Milton and then Dickens as a "thing unattempted yet in prose or rhyme"—that is, a political prose poetic in which narrative prose is spiked with rhymes forcefully appearing in unexpected places to create nodal ideas) when we finally perceive Decoud's dialogue romance as stronger than his nihilism or dismissiveness. There may well be two Decouds, not entirely coherent with each other. The first is drawn by the objective narrator, the second shown in dialogues of oblique force. The omniscient narrator tells us convincingly about his shallowness, and shows us his at times embarrassingly stupid cynicism; but Decoud in action after all loses his life, determined, however ironically, by pressure from Antonia, after having created the plot of independence. Decoud has been pictured doubly, on the one hand by casually dismissive descriptions of his casual dismissiveness, but on the other by passionate descriptions of his passionate dialogues with women as sexually desired sisters. He talks with them in scenes that lie outside the opera bouffe of male politics. We might recall that Decoud grew up with Antonia, and that in English romantic poetry sister-brother attachments recur, possibly as a longing for but fear of some sort of total immersion, as with Wordsworth's delayed apostrophe to Dorothy in "Tintern Abbey." The man of insistence with the deprived sister is a romantic, not a nihilist, and Decoud is this kind of romantic. He jeers at this part of himself, but at the same time it seems, in action, stronger. He turns the Oedipal inquisition not toward women as wives and daughters, as Shakespeare had done, but more specifically toward sisters. Insistence with the sister is an attempt to make a higher music. (Like silver and silence, the terms *sister* and *insist* here fuse into a "speech-act image" in a way also characteristic of romantic political poetics.[30]) It is still barely possible, however, after pointing to this irrationally compelling element in the portrait, to suggest how this makes Decoud a great lively figure within the novel's grim emphasis on the force-farce of politics. Decoud's isolatedly "higher" attunement to the possibility of lively political bonds between men and women, in which both show energy and initiative, makes him the most alert figure in the book, but it also strands him outside Oedipal politics as given.

Like his relations to women, his suicide takes the form of trying to force "a high note," an answer within a scene where an answer is nearly impossible. Suicide must be expressed as paradox, self-contradiction, or oxymoron in the poetic tradition which includes Canto XIII of the *Inferno* and Hamlet's soliloquy. The set piece about Decoud's suicide takes the form of an insistent "dialogue with silence." The oxymoron governing the scene is that of the "cord of silence." In keeping with this, the narrator of this scene has an omniscience which is, I believe, a deliberate gesture of epistemological impossibility.[31] This narrator informs us about psychic events of Decoud's last moments which are probably unknowable even to the suicide himself, and in any case certainly "unreportable." They belong in the class not just of unknowability to the narrator but of unknowability to *anyone*, including the person who commits suicide. Having gone mad with protracted solitude, Decoud as anti-Crusoe hallucinates that the silence of the gulf is "a tense, thin cord to which he hung suspended by both hands . . . Only toward the evening . . . he began to wish that the cord would snap. He imagined it snapping with a report as of a pistol—a sharp, full crack" (498–499). Decoud has previously made contemptuous statements about all history as "noise." Now we see him wanting noise at any cost. The likeness between the punishment and the lifelong sin of detachment from community is almost Dantean. The man who despised the noise of history is being punished by finding out, on the Golfo Placido, that silence is the worst. As the high-strung and imaginative man, he has figured heretofore as the highest string of the social instrument, looking down with contempt on the baseness of the others. Left alone, he begins, in a careful study of self-protective fantasy, to imagine that "silence" it-self—the only sound more attenuated and higher than his own—can be made a companionable sound.

When he shoots himself, the omniscient narrator tells us, "The stiff-ness of the fingers relaxed, and the lover of Antonia Avellanos rolled overboard without having heard the cord of silence snap in the Placid Gulf" (501). Putting aside the sexual language (Decoud dies without, figuratively, violating the virginity, forcing the silence, of the Gulf or of Antonia), the phrase "without having heard" is probably the most neg-ative "report" in the entire novel: a "detonation" and probably a mockery of information itself. How do we know whether a dead man heard the "report" of the gun with which he killed himself? Conrad has directed the scene intentionally against the epistemology of self-knowl-edge, to displace it by a critical epistemology of dialogue. There is no way to learn from Decoud what he experienced, and therefore there is no "report." Since Decoud "did not hear," and we as readers can't know—can't make him tell us any more than he can make the cord of silence snap—the impossibly omniscient voice dialogizes the reader's forced ignorance to Decoud's forced last silence. Knowledge can only take place between persons. The dialogue of inquiry which cannot take place about his death is the point: Conrad assumes a "false," impossible omniscience to underscore the act of suicide as a forced dialogue with nothing. If the reader objects that the information is impossible, the art is beginning to work. Decoud's death is a portrait of philosophy left alone with itself as self-knowledge, a silent self-"report."

To some extent, this image may arise from Conrad's own early sui-cide attempt or duel: the biographers, not being omniscient either, still don't know with certainty why he was shot. Decoud's death may sug-gest that Conrad recalled the event as a paradox of hearing and was surprised, after surviving, that he could not recall the shot—which, had he died, would have been his last experience. The whole idea is of course not solemn but Menippean, like a problem out of *Bouvard and Pécuchet*. It shows the limits of logical inquiry. Within the development of Conrad's poetic language, however, the dramatic, illogical structure will later condense into the concept of "detonation"—the oxymoronic term of closure of forced dialogue, which Conrad uses, as I have al-ready said, to mean several things at once: "explosion" (loud noise), si-lence (de-toning), and self-destruction. In the Professor's perfect detonator, Gould's threat to explode his mine, and the detonation of Razumov's eardrums, detonation appears as the futile closure of the reality of unfree relations. Decoud's suicide takes one metaphysical form of this ironically "perfect" detonation. We might say that in suicide, since bullets travel faster than sound, the only potential audience of the "report," the suicide himself, is already dead at the time the report reaches him. "Detonation" is the sound which would (not) be heard by a man shooting himself in the head. It is the "end" of history. He does not hear the bullet that kills him, because hearing, like music and history, is an aftervibration. Note how even to think this through is to be *bête*. Anything that can be known must be known dialogically and in time, this scene seems to say. But Decoud's death is desperate, not punitive, because Conrad has *not* drawn him simply as contented isolation; he has, on the contrary, already shown how insistently Decoud the separationist talks with others.

We have just seen how the relations we call property, selling, journalism, courtship, and suicide fall within the expressive form of compelling the other to respond, so that Gould, Hirsch, Sotillo, and Decoud live in a common relational world. The portrait of Nostromo, though often thought to lack subtlety, uses the same notion to make us think in a new way about praise, irony, fostership, and historical narration. To begin with, Nostromo is a man who lives for praise, reputation, recognition. But these are represented as a kind of naively forceful dialogue: his personal force, his charity, and his bravery force recognition out of other people. This picture of praise as the recognition we make others give us has a beauty and honesty which Conrad makes into Nostromo's early, if sometimes naive and ridiculous, grandeur. When he lives to display his force, Nostromo may be naive, but he is much less ridiculous than the "magnificent" Barrios, his foil, whose one-eyed piratical demeanor *"extorted* the acclamations of the populace" (143, my italics). Barrios is one of Conrad's lively caricatures of the impressive. The cheers of the crowd for the splendid military clown have the same tonal quality as the "extorted" confessions of people being tortured. Both public praise and inquisitorial confessions have the same final form: they are "forced" outcries. But Nostromo, for all his showy popping of silver buttons, has a charitable force that is congenial and popular. If praise here is the compelled recognition in words of someone else's force, that structure is not, as in Mrs. Viola's repeated false metaphor, simply identical to a *payment* "in words" (253, 257). It is, on the contrary, the oldest form of community as mutual recognition.

The story of Nostromo, however, addresses not only the issue of linguistic versus monetary recognition, with Nostromo making the shift from the one to the other. Nostromo makes a transition from being paid in words to paying himself in stolen silver; but he also makes the transition from naivety to irony. When Conrad seeks to show the destruction of Nostromo, he turns his life from one of naive praise and fame— which lacks any sense of "irony"—into a life that defines itself by irony. Nostromo acquires, absorbs, and becomes the "irony," the silence and the silver, of the novel, and it is out of character for him to change in this way. He tries to do what Charles Gould does: to make a life of reserve, a defense of what other people do not know.

Here we come to an extremely difficult concept that is nevertheless at the core of the book and its unique power. What is most hard to prove, but most important to suggest, is that the inquisitorial, sadistic forced dialogue scenes in the novel seek to unfold, lay bare, and radically question the structure of civilized, literary, and Socratic irony, at which Conrad is of course gifted. The book suggests that coercion to speak is the underlying structure of irony. This is one reason why the tone of the scene between Hirsch and Sotillo is unsettling: it is an attack on irony itself. The obsessive return to the "base" of forced dialogue in the most brutal scenes suggests that irony itself is a "fancy" sublimation and condensation of this power relation: the *eiron*, whether philosopher, novelist, dramatist, or grand inquisitor, is the one who sophisticatedly makes another, "weaker" voice speak for him. Everyone wants to seize the language of the other person; the inquisitor does it in a "crude," violent way, the ironist in a subtle way, the naive epic man, out for praise, in an open, childlike way. The reader enjoys literary irony because it gives appropriative power over a very large field of "others'" words: they mean what *we* know they mean, not what they themselves believe they mean. Where the naive hero like the early Nostromo openly seeks the words of others, and makes them cheer, the philosophical *eiron* more covertly forces others to mean what he means, despite their intentions; the inquisitor like Sotillo represents the basic will of all persons in dialogue, but brought low into "farce"; and the novelist, seeing all this with irony, himself appropriates their dialogues for our contempt, pity, and laughter. Everyone is trying not to speak well himself but to own the language of the other. Dramatic irony is the most civilized form of this struggle. Open scenes of coercion to speak seem crude and low, then, because they are true—or we want to dismiss them as low because they expose this will.

To force dialogue in a civilized way for one's own purposes is the strategy of the *eiron*, whether philosopher or dramatist, and this is in part what Monygham knows how to do with Sotillo. He exploits the forced dialogue that Sotillo imposes for his own purposes, and defeats

Sotillo. This is "civilization": not an escape from forced dialogue, not conversation, but the conversion of forced dialogue to one's own subtle reuses. Nostromo is presented at first as the man who lives "below" this web of crude coercions to speak and subtle ironies. He simply wants the forcing of the other to speak to be positive—to be praise, recognition. He is "subironic" at first.[32] And the novel itself, in its bare, "atonal," hard-to-grasp forced dialogues, often seems anti-ironic, for all its irony. *Nostromo*, we might say, hates, rather than rejoices in, its own achieved ironies. It seeks by dialogical formalism to expose irony itself, even Conrad's own irony, as a mode of seizure. Ironists are *rey zamuros*, king vultures. To come into his own irony, his own silence about silver, destroys Nostromo, the man of the people and of earned praise, because irony for all its sophistication is the most cowardly way of getting the other's words to be your own. Conrad certainly seems to detest one of his own greatest gifts here. When Nostromo learns irony, and becomes a secret appropriator of personal worth, enacting the "ironic" Balzacian crime of possession that ought to make him the founder of a great new family, he is instead destroyed. The project of characterization here seems to be an exposure of the limits of irony itself as an instrument; it argues, perhaps even against Henry James, that for some of the best human beings, to come into possession of the controlling irony is a defeat, not a transcendence. Nostromo has ceased to be, in another language, a hero of "use value" in society, and become a master of "exchange value." He has ceased to value his own open usefulness and begun to value a means of exchange which is also secretive. That, Conrad indicates, is inevitable, but it is not an improvement. The irony of irony is that it is a subtly demeaning form of forced dialogue.

The question of force in dialogue also gives substance and moral complexity to Nostromo's relations with his parent figures. Among the three figures who stand as parents toward him—Captain Mitchell, Giorgio Viola, and Teresa Viola—no one but Mrs. Viola cares enough about him to force him to speak; Mitchell patronizes and uses him, but shows his indifference to the man himself by not inquiring; and Giorgio talks to himself.

Consider Mitchell first. "Proud of his experience, penetrated by the sense of the historical importance of men, events, and buildings, he talked pompously in jerky periods" (475). What are these jerky periods? How does Conrad let us know what Mitchell lacks? He thinks that history is his own easy memory, and has no inkling that real history would have to be gleaned by a forceful break out of his own class, information derived from forcing others, who are reluctant, to tell us what they know. In this case, of course, the other is Nostromo. Mitchell believes in conversational history, pleasant yarning, and so he is imaginatively inadequate as a historian. He does not know that in historical events there is much forcing of information, and that "history" as narration, to approach the truth, would have to acquire much of its information violently. As he leaves to Nostromo the job of coercing labor, and fails to ask Nostromo what happened on the Gulf, he is also astounded when Sotillo dares to put a free Englishman like himself under interrogation. When he fails to grasp Monygham's strategy of deception in dialogue with Sotillo, all our mixed feelings about strategic irony itself are brought to the fore, and we simultaneously like him and despise him. Mitchell's comical ignorance of forced dialogue (when he hears Hirsch screaming he blanches—that is, he shows his innocence—and does nothing) and his failure to inquire forcefully about Nostromo's adventure on the lighter lead to one of the novel's central theses: that a conversational history is not possible. To oversimplify, historical fact can be presented in one of two forms: either it is coerced information from the "other" class, whichever that is, in which case it has the distortion attendant upon all forced answers, but also the tragic truth of visibly forced information; or it is a lyrical story, unforced, like Mitchell's, in which case it is naive and innocent of its own context: it leaves out the kind of truth known only in and through forced dialogue as a central process.

Nostromo's largest effect is to assert that "history" to be accurate must have the rhythm of forced dialogue, not of information. Historical discourse must have the rhythmic relation to its content and its people that the inquisitor has to the silent interrogated: it is jerky; it asks, waits, gets no response, starts up again. It is a complex of scenes of coercion to speak, of filibuster, of egoistic talk, of parliamentary discussion, and of lyrical legend making fused together not as a happy and plentiful "polyphony" but as a field of disproportions and coercions. The pluralism here is not that of optimistic plenitude but of *bêtise,* and rest, unrest, arrest. This forced complexity stands in a critical relation to the positive idea of the polyphonic novel to which Bakhtin has given the fullest expression. Conrad's historical novel not only presents the plurality of discourses but dramatizes the unequal and "jerky" relations among them.

In this spirit, by contrast to Mitchell or Giorgio (who talks to himself), Teresa Viola's claim on Nostromo becomes apparent. She at least demands, makes him attend her, asks who he is, and this is a kind of care, however selfish and imperative. Like the surrogate parent figures in *A Personal Record* who try to get through to young Conrad with insistent statements about his directionlessness, she tries to "make" him respond; and in spite of the fact that she is partly wrong—just like some of the surrogate parents in that autobiography—Conrad pays homage to them and to her for trying, for insisting, for raising the voice "above the pitch of natural conversation."[33]

At the same time, of course, nothing could be more ambiguous than this foster parenting, this complex relation between two relatively simple persons, and nothing more clearly analogous to the danger of colonial interference. The analogy between foster parenting and destructive colonization is one of the great themes of Conrad's work. It is lingering guardianship, the "Lingard" motif. It retards and delays even while it seems to foster, like Conrad's plots themselves, which are not mere ingenious devices but represent in their confusing temporality the combined retardation and precocity of the colonial relation. Colonial "parents," both as individuals and as states, force the child ahead yet also keep him back. These confusions of precocity and retardation, anticipation and withholding, the immersion in the world that is "too much with us, late and soon," reenacted in relation to the reader, are for Conrad not just a novelistic technique but the apposite technique for the colonial world of interference. The lingering guardianship appears again and again in Conrad as the disturbed romantic relation: Winnie's obsessive guardianship over Stevie; Amy Foster's marriage to Yanko, which fails to combine love and fostering into a single whole, as her name indicates; Heyst's fostering of the woman he inaccurately names Lena, that is, "leaner," or innocent, dependent; Stein's and Marlow's insidious rescue of Jim; Mikulin's sympathetic hovering over Razumov till he makes him a spy; Lingard's fostering destruction of Hassim; Nostromo's hovering over his annexed treasure.

Teresa's sonorously "sound" advice to Nostromo—to earn money instead of old-fashioned praise—is one instance of destructive fostering love. Technically correct, it happens to be entirely wrong, given the nature of the man advised. The foster parent does not have the same "nature" as the child, and therefore the advice, even if realistic and aggressively loving, is off key. She represents the mixed values and dangers of foster parenting, dangers which are to Conrad parallel to the bad interference of all selfish-altruistic colonialism. What she advises Nostromo, a primitive man, and the people to do, is to "grow up," to modernize, to become petit bourgeois. Nostromo won't thrive as the contracted ironist among ironists, the bourgeois with a secret hoard of meanings. Nostromo, crucially and in one of the novel's most difficult ideas, acquires his silver as a function of the absence of forced dialogue, and therefore of community itself. His new treasure is not the praise of the others but their silent indifference. The silver is given him by their silence as well as by his own. Out of English tact, or reticence, no one asks him what happened—partly also out of shame for having used him, and out of faith in that reputation for honesty which he has indeed earned. But all this silence—the coming into property under the conditions of the negation of forced dialogue—is not personal freedom. Though Nostromo changes, by his own account, from a childish man who wanted praise into a mature, secretive, silent man in possession of the only real wealth, he is even more lost than he was as an orphan addicted to recognition. When he had social worth—when he forced praise out of others—he was habitually poor; now that he has silver, he is socially alone and secretive. Nostromo, then, lives out two antithetical forms of the forced dialogue: first, direct initiation of it as the public hero provoking praise; second, its complete absence when no one else demands that he tell his history. But to live in the absence of forced dialogue—of anyone asking you forcefully what has happened to you—is not freedom or power, and is not to escape the Oedipal field of inquiry. On the contrary: to repress forced dialogue so as to make it seem merely absent (we are now free men of property at the Lighthouse and do not force each other to speak, since that would be ungentlemanly and irrational) is only to invite the most simple reenactment of the Oedipal scene. Giorgio, his foster "father," kills Nostromo without knowing whom he kills. Forced dialogue may often seem to be the very process of evil, but it is also the process whereby we know each other. To repress it is to risk eradicating all mutuality. Perhaps to give up trying to know each other would be for many writers freedom, but this is not Conrad's idea. It would seem, then, that *Nostromo* calls not for liberation from coercion to speak and write, but for a steady recognition that it is necessary and inevitable in human relations. This is not a playful idea, but it is Conrad's.

In *Nostromo*, as just described, the narrative historical action is complemented by a sense that many "free" personal relations are in fact forced dialogues. Selling, praise, journalism, property, suicide, courtship, fostering, irony, and historical narration itself, in addition to the explicit scenes of inquisitorial torture, are organized, with remarkable subtlety and variety, by disproportion and pressure in the scene of speech. From the moment the Gould family is forced to own the mine, the contractual terms of the novel are set. Actions usually categorized as "free" take on a different color. In selling we usually emphasize the quality of free-market activity; in critical journalism the work of the free press; in irony the masterful free play of language; in property free ownership; in romantic courtship free rebellion against parental will; in fostership voluntary parenting; even in suicide an individual and free act. These actions as a result become peculiarly interesting when represented, surprisingly, through the slant of forced dialogue. A "free" journalist has been pressed into journalism, a suicide takes place in the form of a compulsive desire to force the other to speak, the cheers of the people are "extorted," and so on. An analysis like this, however, has to highlight the recurrence of the form somewhat out of context, and therefore belie the critical complexity of the novel, which steeps the reader in this field of relations subtly, and so questions its own rhetorical "force" in the discovery of the pattern. Clearly *Nostromo* has other themes, and would not work if it were a mechanistic, force-worshipping book, in a Prussian or protofascist mode; on the contrary, the unusual formal style manages to make the late nineteenth-century concept of "force" itself over into an object of contemplation. To translate "force" into a study of coercions in dialogue is to be interested in consciousness, not in the unconscious and uncritical myth and metaphors of "power" and realpolitik in the usual sense.

However, even if we grant that *Nostromo*—though not the type of comic novel, like *Alice in Wonderland* or *Bouvard and Pécuchet*, which broadly shows us the same dialogue obviously recurring—builds a formal dialogue picture meant to be seen and felt as its greatest meaning, we are still left with one major question about this meaning itself: is *Nostromo* mainly a "historical novel" which illuminates and criticizes an inquisitorial society by showing that all relations in such a society necessarily become forced dialogues, or is it a dialogical novel, with Sulaco only the instance of the "essential" human condition as that of forced dialogue? In the first reading, for example, Decoud's courtship of Antonia becomes tinged by coercion to speak because they are talking together in a historically inquisitorial state. One would then try to show how the conditions that surround them force them to force each other in speech. In the second reading, Decoud and Antonia talk love as sublimated forced dialogue because forced dialogue—the fact that someone must make someone else talk—is the forgotten essence or ground of all dialogue.

That *Nostromo* is a historical novel about an inquisitorial society, yet with a vaguely universal bearing, is implied, though not fully elaborated, by Eloise Knapp Hay, who begins her powerful chapter on the novel: "Like other modern intellectuals, Conrad is haunted by the ghost of the Inquisition and ideological warfare in general. Like the others, whether he will or no, he inherits the premises of the Inquisition: that ideas distinguish and objectify good and evil in history, and there can be no escape from or muddling through the ideological issues."[34] This opening statement does not make it completely clear whether the novel's inquisitorial mode is universal or local, and Hay does not return pointedly to the theme of inquisition as form in the rest of her chapter. But to paraphrase and slightly alter what her sentence suggests: according to this view, *Nostromo* belongs in the tradition that runs from Dickens' late novels, to Dostoevsky on the "Grand Inquisition," to Weber's studies in examinatory bureaucracy, to Kafka, and finally to Foucault. These works are slightly vague on the question of the universality versus the historical specificity of examinatory inquisition, but they variously represent the *modern* social complex as a sort of pan-inquisition. At the same time, in some sense, they give in to its "premise," which is that language must be produced and that character expresses itself most clearly as ideology. In this field, Hay's Conrad figures as part of this representational dilemma, using and accepting inquisition *himself* to force out the definitive ideas of his characters. Inquisition is, consequently, the author's device more than his theme. Such an author, as Hay implies, "must" be immersed as one inquisitor in a world where cognition has this form; he immerses himself in the destructive element. To Hay, however, what interests him most is the set of ideas finally provoked, not the analysis of the forced form in which they must be provoked.

In Hay's sentences, Conrad's novel resembles the Dostoevskian ideological novel as Bakhtin and others describe it. The author makes plural ideologies voice their plurality. His negative capability objectifies, represents, and concatenates. Different modes of consciousness—Nostromo's ideal of personal pride, Decoud's sense of farce, Emilia's ethics, Charles's materialism, Monygham's bitterness, Hernandez's populism—are presented so as to throw the reader into that consciousness. The writer interrogates dramatically, creating a backdrop of grand inquisition, to bring everybody's position to light. *But* if, as I have suggested, Conrad organizes much of the novel's diversity formally and cognitively around forced dialogue and its metaphoric images of silver and silence, then it does not have exactly the kind of antisystematic free energy Bakhtin likes, nor does it simply "inherit" and exploit the premises of the Inquisition. On the contrary, it is an imaginative reconsideration of both inheritances, that of free polyphony and that of inquisitorial drama. It is blatantly tethered or held in, with a great deal of contractual strain, by a unified "poetic" vision of dialogical contraction and constraint itself, of the kind which would be nearly anathema to Bakhtin; and at the same time it uses this stylistic constraint to examine and analyze the forms of constraint themselves. The fact that love, praise, property, selling, and writing are held together by a single poetic or formal vision of coercion to speak would be a strong indication for Bakhtin of "monological" or "poetic" thinking: enforced unity, alien to the open freedom of the true novel. Most readers, I think, would recognize that for all its diversity *Nostromo* is taut. It has a poetics of dialogue form, as well as what Bakhtin calls a "dialogic." It is as much a prose poem about dialogue as what Bakhtin means by a "dialogical" novel.

In the most abstract reading, the inquisitorial scenes, such as Father Berón's torture of Monygham, or Sotillo's grillings of Monygham and Mitchell and his murder of Hirsch, are not primarily intended to show us the violence of a particular historical place but appear as historical reminders and clarifications of the deeper reality of dialogue itself as Conrad intuits it. Conrad wrote in his essay on James: "Fiction is history, human history, or it is nothing. But it is also more than that; it stands on firmer ground, being based on the reality of forms and the observation of social phenomena, whereas history is based on documents, and the reading of print and handwriting—on second-hand impression. Thus fiction is nearer truth."[35] This formalism and "truth" might please almost no one today. But it is Conrad's language, and though it does not allow a simple choice between formalism and historical representation, it emphasizes a final depiction of "forms" of human relation over a specific documentation—and he must mean by form the forms of encounter and conflict. The South American inquisitions are of interest because they are a vivid formal example, suspended between force and farce, of what most dialogue *is*. To contemplate this formal truth is the purpose of the dialogue craft. This truth Conrad probably found also in classical writers like Aeschylus, Sophocles, and Thucydides and reapplied to the modern world of increasingly international and colonizing "communication." As other writers, for instance Balzac in *Le Père Goriot,* import elements of tragedy into the novel, Conrad in his political novel imported this singularly unromantic dialogue form to interpret colonial relations. But the forced dialogue is not at home in the middle-class novel, which looks for entertaining conversation; and so the "hollow" ring of *Nostromo* in its picture of human encounters is deliberate. Free conversation is not going to rescue or absolve us from the truth of colonial dialogue.

Beyond this first point, Conrad's other formal aim is to fuse the dialogue in the novel to the narrative, and to the other forms of exchange, so as to show, even more directly and starkly than James, that dialogue is not free from action; it will not even serve as a tentative "relief" from other kinds of relation or exchange. To do this he has to effect his original forced "rhyme" between silver and silence. "Although the points would seem to be obvious," Karl Kroeber has written, "no critic to my knowledge has considered, first, that interaction between narrative and dialogue in large measure defines 'fiction' in its broadest sense as a literary type . . . and second, that interaction between narrative and dialogue occurs at every level of fiction."[36] Kroeber takes this "simple" definition of fiction as the technical integration of narrative to dialogue heuristically, leading only to modest assertions, for instance that "dialogue sentences are usually shorter and more fragmentary than narrative ones" in the novelists he considers.[37] Kroeber's word *interaction* is itself, however, worth questioning. The word often works to hide what are really enormous disagreements among us about dialogue itself—what it is and what it can or cannot be. It merges scientific and religious connotations uncritically. To talk about "interaction" is sometimes to avoid taking a stance. One ought to take a risk and assert that Conrad's way of joining dialogue to narrative in *Nostromo*, by forcibly "rhyming" silence and silver throughout, is no neutral "interaction" but makes a major statement, telling us that in any society the economy of "dialogue" is bound up with the other economies of exchange.

Mark Lambert has written about the "tags" in Dickens, and the narrator's way of interrupting characters to make mocking asides about them, as a sign of Dickens' Regency dandyism, and of his envy of the popularity which his characters stole from him as their author.[38] But Lambert, though absolutely right to focus on "tags" as junctures between dialogue and narrative which stylistically reveal the power structure and social mood of a novel, is, I believe, being a little too narrowly shrewd in emphasizing only Dickens' will to power, and ignoring the equally obvious participatory and comically parliamentary character of his intrusions. That is, Dickens joins in pushily, but most of his characters do also. Some of the "tags" or interruptions Lambert quotes even "rhyme," or "off rhyme," with speeches they tag, for the usual symphonic effects found in Dickensian prose. Bakhtin, though some Dickensians simply reject his readings, describes similar Dickensian voice interferences positively; recall also how Esther Summerson talks about her part in the pages of *Bleak House,* as if she knew of the book's existence. This is one example of Dickens giving uncanny power to a character. Dickens' parliamentary model of dialogue, from which Conrad was forced historically to dissent by introducing his "filibustering" model of the proportion and masses of dialogue, shares with Conrad the sense that narrative and dialogue "rhyme," or can sing together in a complex proportion. But where Dickens took this to a final sense of regenerating integration, in Conrad the "riveting" of dialogue to narrative, so that they interfuse, expresses forced dependence, not charitable community. In the silver-silence echo that "rivets" the narrative to the dialogic in *Nostromo,* as Invoice-Ivory does for "Heart of Darkness," Conrad had conceived the novel's "simple" structural dualism—dialogue and narrative—as a relation of riveted "dependence." Dialogue tries to take over narrative, and vice versa. We can't know which to put first. Dialogue and narrative are locked, in Conrad's work, in a sort of death struggle with each other. This in turn expresses the conflicted dependence of action and words upon each other; of currencies and languages upon each other; of colonial conquest. Probably in conscious opposition to Marx, Conrad conceives of languages and currencies themselves, drawn from nature, as failing to become the transcendent modes of pure exchange, self-governing systems, which are the ground of Marx's analysis of capitalism as both dehumanizing and potentially a stage of liberation. Currencies in Conrad do not and cannot transcend nature as modes of exchange. Thus Conrad is simultaneously anti-Marxist and anticapitalist; his concern is to represent the failure of each of the two ideologies to achieve the transcendence it claims.

This explains why Conrad's syntax, sentence combination, and paragraphing throughout the book are highly charged by a difficult, strained "continuity and force," which is at the same time distinctly *not* free or dialectical. As the forced polysemy (the chimes which some readers may find repugnant) is part of the forced dialogic, the forced syntax also creates a sense of violent physical and social interdependence, without a sense of dialectical progress or resolution. Sentences that are kinetic and phrasal but not periodic are right for this. The nineteenth-century dialectical sentence, a complex action of plural dependent clauses with periodic suspension of verbal resolution—even in James—is being skeptically returned from its metaphysical movement. While Conrad wants "continuity and force" (512), he does not want resolved complexity. The jerkiness, in addition, is *not* the discontinuity we associate with freeing modernist juxtaposition and collage, or the love of a propositional and discontinuous philosophy of discrete, luminous, but skeptical images, in which the world has become a "ladder" whose gaps are at least as important as its rungs. To see Conrad clearly, we have to ignore momentarily either nineteenth-century dialectical rhythms or twentieth-century propositional ladders. He does not exactly want either. That is not why *Nostromo* is both "jerky" and "continuous" in rhythm. Conrad holds polysemous words, sentences, dialogues, and novels together by a (to us) alien sense of working "force," practical necessity, "ough," and "rivets," without a necessarily assigned telos. He has, in relation to this, an unmistakably strained style, and is paradoxically often most inspired when most practically forced.

At the same time, we have to steer away from the sense that his work is a paean to "force" in the bad sense. There is no fascist hypostasis of force here. His kind of work (his strain has something in common with Virginia Woolf and Henry Green) is enjoyable—if it is—because the writer makes us overwork with him and achieve a subtle reassessment of "work" itself, not play, but living "forces." This is one reason why all the forms of breathing sounds—whispers, whistles, coughs, grunts, and so on—take on the meaning of a new, nonromantic imagery of "inspiration" as work. He blocks sentences together under duress, and this is enjoyable, but as work in itself, not play in itself, is enjoyable. This style is a social idea, strained to match the strain between classes, and between the writer and audience. This strain itself becomes a subject of contemplation. If Conrad at times can seem vaguely pre-"fascist"—a Dühring or Spencer—believing in force only,[39] in fact for the most part he admires only a kind of ordinary force that works hard and achieves little; and he is of course well aware of political "force worship," despises it, and associates it with his autocratic bogeys, Russia and Germany. His satire very often is meant to train our attention away from personifications of physical force to a conscious contemplation of forces in dialogical relation. Here, for example, in forceful but farcical sentences, is his "dialogical materialism," in a description of the dictator Guzmán Bento, who in rare moments of political security holds compulsory mass meetings to exalt himself, Kurtzlike:

At such times he would impulsively *command the celebration of* a solemn Mass of thanksgiving which would be *sung in great pomp in* the cathedral of Sta. Marta by the trembling, subservient Archbishop of his creation. He *heard it sitting in* a gilt armchair *placed before* the high altar, *surrounded by* the civil and military heads of the Government. The unofficial world of Sta. Marta *would crowd into* the cathedral, for it was not quite safe for anybody of mark *to stay away from* these manifestations of presidential piety. Having thus acknowledged the only power he was at all disposed *to recognize as above* himself, he would *scatter acts* of political grace in a sardonic wantonness of clemency. There was no other way left now to enjoy his power but by seeing his crushed adversaries *crawl impotently into* the light of day *out of* the dark, noisome cells of the Collegio. Their harmlessness fed his insatiable vanity, and they could always *be got hold of* again. It was the rule for all the women of their families *to present thanks afterwards in* a special audience. The incarnation of that strange god, El Gobierno Supremo, *received them standing,* cocked hat on head, and *exhorted* them in a menacing mutter *to show* their gratitude *by bringing up* their children in fidelity to the democratic form of government, "which I have *established for* the happiness of our country." His front teeth *having been knocked out in* some accident of his former herdsman's life, his utterance was spluttering and indistinct. (139, my italics)

A Miltonic effect of mock power, funny and horrible, is effected by the parodic and purposely unusual linkage of strong phrasal verbs. The baroque assemblage of ordinary phrasal verbs in combination with more irregular and clumsy ones can be attributed either to Conrad's poor English or to deliberate artistry. They are in fact mostly intentional, and the passage ends with the pugilistic joke about the Gobierno's teeth "having been knocked out" somehow, this slang verb the intentionally *bête* anticlimax of all the other grandiose phrasals. The strongest phrase, reverberating to the rest of the novel, tells us that the Gobierno "scatters acts of political grace." This superb idea, which is not poor English but a mockery of the messianic—"to scatter acts"—is itself stylistically embodied in the scattered connection of verb to verb in the prose, which simultaneously immerses the reader in a phrasal verb continuity, gives a grotesquely clumsy feeling of fragmentation and disorder and clumsy outsizedness, and ends as usual in a comic "detonation," here of "spluttering utterance." This is a carefully considered kinetics of prose as awkwardly fragmented and then arbitrarily linked power. It belongs not with Hegelian dialectical syntax, grandly moving toward resolution, nor even with the Jamesian grandeur of multiple interruptions and psychic qualifications, but if anything with the Miltonic style that parodies infernal energy. It could be called a "mock-dialectical" style. Conrad shares with Milton not only a politicized syntax, a preoccupation with chains of forceful verbs, but also the fact that he, like Milton, imports into English a demonic inflectedness from a foreign language. Milton's was Latin, Conrad's Polish. Some of the force of inflection can be translated into English by the phrasal verb. Consider the following sentence about Hernandez's formal request to be reincluded in legitimate society: "It was *joined*, as an evidence of good faith, *to* a petition praying the Sulaco Assembly for permission to *enlist*, with all his followers, *in* the forces being *raised* in Sulaco *for* the defense of the Five-Year Mandate of regeneration" (146–147, my italics). By disjoining the verbs *joined to* and *enlist in*, so that they both unify and separate the motion of the ideas, Conrad constitutes the formal idea of the sentence itself, that of kinetic dependence, ironic separation and conjunction, by force, which is at the same time the central political and poetic idea of the entire novel. Hernandez wants to be reincluded, and is separated. The dynamic of separation and inclusion is treated with respect: Hernandez's desire to be part of society, to join and enlist, itself binds the sentence together; but the word *regeneration* at the end is obviously a bitter joke. Forceful enlistment is real enough—mandated regeneration is unlikely. Hopeful dialectic is parodied by forced dialogic: "mandate" and "regeneration" clash.

That currencies themselves are "dependent" upon the natural materials from which they are made appears to be a theme as late as the opening paragraph to *Victory,* whose working title was *Dollars:*

There is, as every schoolboy knows in this scientific age, a very close chemical relation between coal and diamonds. It is the reason, I believe, why some people allude to coal as "black diamonds." Both these commodities represent wealth: but coal is a much less portable form of property. There is, from that point of view, a deplorable lack of concentration in coal. Now, if a coal-mine could be put into one's waistcoat pocket—but it can't! At the same time, there is a fascination in coal, the supreme commodity of the age in which we are camped like bewildered travellers in a garish, unrestful hotel. And I suppose these two considerations, the practical and the mystical, prevented Heyst—Axel Heyst—from going away.

This lighthearted paragraph is about several diverse things. After a little reflection it becomes clear that, despite the casual tone, coal mines and diamonds here stand in part for the difference between raw novelistic prose and poetic condensation. The "portable coal mine" suggests something like the paradoxical portability of massive social novels like Zola's. A novel can be carried around in the pocket, as if it were the coal mine (the social reality) that is a diamond (a poetic condensation). It can "carry" a mass of raw social fact, as the Professor later carries his ridiculous detonator, the apotheosis of the novelty item, in his pocket. "But it can't." Conrad implies conventionally enough that the analogy between society and novel will only be of use if the reader can see through it, and strictly recall that society can't be grasped, and that the command of a dialectic is an illusion.

At the heart of the paragraph's metaphors, however, is a more surprising and subtle criticism of Marx's distinction between use value and exchange value. We learn first that everyone knows the theory of commodities, in which all things become equated as exchange values, just as everyone knows that the chemistry of coal and diamonds, despite appearances, is nearly the same. These scientific and economic versions of coal and diamonds both ignore the sensory, physical qualities that differentiate them, to set them into structural equation. Such inevitable equation makes people *restless* rather than free because it cancels once reliable if illusory qualitative differences. In contradistinction to Marx—who spends so much careful labor in the early pages of *Capital* proving that exchange value displaces and transcends use value in capitalist relations, but thereby demonstrates a possible and/or inevitable new freedom to make our own system in and over nature—the genial speaker here recalls attention to some still binding "natural" disproportions between things like coal and diamonds: color, mass, weight. In the coal-diamonds contrast, what would stand out for an impressionist or symbolist would be the visual black-white distinction, usable for chiaroscuro, or clichéd contrasts between good and evil. But beyond these uses are qualities—apparently more radical and inescapable—of mass and weight, presented almost as the signs of bondage to the old laws of physics and social relation. Since the thesis is actually all too serious, he uses a light tone to return us from impressionism, symbolism, or imagism to a rhetoric in which use value or practical workability, presented in terms of mass, is still the strongest criterion in imagery. And from this stance, whereby use and mass are most important, he turns to end the paragraph by—it is no accident—finally being able to *name* his central character emphatically—"Heyst—Axel Heyst"—as if this entire discussion of *economic* theory had all along been working toward the climactic *onomastic* issue of a personal naming which is itself identical to the condition of "usedness," "gravity," not being able to "go away." To be named is to be a usable person in the world. This poetics is reinforced by the fact that the name Heyst means in German "named," as Nostromo is named "our man." All this is virtually a polemic on the inescapability of use, even in the modern world of total exchangeability, and on the (predicated) natural properties of those materials which we happen to decide to turn into "currencies." Names are not free from use; currencies are not free from the materials out of which they are made, or from the forced condition of being made into currencies. While apparently half understanding Marx, Conrad takes great pains to swerve from what Marx drives at in the difficult opening section of *Capital*, and assert the continued interdependence of exchange value and use value. Neither represents freedom. The two modes of value to Conrad are still forcibly related. The point is not whether Conrad's comprehension of economics, or his critique, is right but the terms in which he makes it. Axel Heyst, who wants to "go away," is nevertheless, even in his empty name, "the named," unable to transcend nature, use, and namedness; he exists in compelled proportional relations, not in a world of free "exchange." This is an outlook compatible neither with capitalist nor with Marxist dialectics of some final freedom growing out of forced relations.

Conrad's distrust of free dialectical closure should not be underestimated. Just like *The Heart of Mid-Lothian*, the greatest earlier study of forced dialogue in English, *Nostromo* ends with a blind and melodramatic father-son murder, as if to deny the reader a historical answer, and to reassert the reality of the Oedipal scene. But at the same time it should not be used to make the novel seem more conservative than it is. There is such a thing as a dialogical left, which continually reminds us of the forms of coercion rather than promising something better. Irving

Howe in his essay on *Nostromo*, which treats the book as dialectical and not sufficiently as dialogical, ends by asserting that *"Nostromo,* like *Middlemarch,* is one of the few novels in our language which commands a whole society." [40] The novel stands in line as another version of the historical dialectic. Its art "commands" a whole society. Howe's comments on the novel's critique of capitalism should by no means be dismissed. But it is not just a quibble to say that he finds a bad rhetorical closure (the speech act *command*) for his insights into the novel by making Conrad as author too much like the Gobierno Supremo. Obviously, the fact that Conrad satirizes Guzmán Bento doesn't void the possibility that he has his own similar ambitions on the page. But *Nostromo* certainly tries to reject any faith we might have in one sufficient command over all the scattered acts. The whole spirit of *Nostromo* appeals to us to check the need to pocket the mine, and argues instead that we should go on studying the forced contractual relations in the dependent world.

When Leavis said that the book has a "hollow" reverberation, he used a metaphor which failed to note the dependent bells of human suspension ringing as deliberately hollow oxymorons through the novel's last movement, as it "tolls" for the hollowness of reading. The metaphor ignores the communal chime of "Misericordia" in the novel. Leavis' metaphor of hollowness, like Forster's of mist, shows only that he was unsatisfied—as Conrad wanted his English readers to be—because some need he had for a vision of sympathetic plenitude went unrealized. But it has not been unrealized or even withheld: it hasn't been desired to begin with. The limit of "command" is one of Conrad's themes. No one commands the structure of relation as forced dialogue in which everyone is immersed. This is the theme of the first chapter of *The Shadow-Line,* in which the young, testy hero comes into his own limited "command," but only through a complex dialogue in which a Socratic father figure, Captain Giles, by pretending to be a silly old man, knowing that the young man hates being forced into anything, in fact forcibly steers him toward his own vocation of limited command. *Nostromo* points toward a general condition of forced interdependency, and describes human beings as working, but largely failing, to assert independence through dependent means. But it is pointless to insist on even this meaning as conclusively demonstrated; the novel has to stop, or give up, before the reader who wants a historical answer has been satisfied. At the end Giorgio, who at the Lighthouse is a tragic burlesque of "the reader," continues to stare at his book after his death, slowly doing what can only be called a nosedive into the Bible. "But he never detached his eyes from the book while he swayed forward, gently, gradually, till his snow-white head rested upon the open pages" (565). This is not an image of reading as transcendent consciousness.

IV

The Fragmentation of Sympathy
in *The Secret Agent*

THE AUTHOR'S NOTE TO *The Secret Agent*, written in 1920, concludes with a remarkable passage in which Conrad describes himself as having been compelled by unspecified "circumstances" to take a second look at the novel:

> The twelve years that have elapsed since the publication of the book have not changed my attitude. I do not regret having written it. Lately, circumstances, which have nothing to do with the general tenor of this preface, have compelled me to strip this tale of the literary robe of indignant scorn it has cost me so much to fit on it decently, years ago. I have been forced, so to speak, to look upon its bare bones. I confess that it makes a grisly skeleton. But still I will submit that telling Winnie Verloc's story to its anarchistic end of utter desolation, madness and despair, and telling it as I have told it here, I have not intended to commit a gratuitous outrage on the feelings of mankind. (xiv)

Somewhat like Winnie, who suspects that "life doesn't stand much looking into" (xiii), the author here is ironically "compelled" to look back into his own earlier work; is "forced, so to speak," to confess that it is grisly; and then, in a final, complex speech act combining artistic servitude and freedom, "submits"—that is, continues to insist—that the book's outrageousness was warranted. This whole action—of forced looking, forced confession, and a last, defiantly ironic "submission"— places this anecdote within the larger frame of forced dialogue. Analogously, Conrad began the Note to *Under Western Eyes* saying that the "force" of recent "circumstances" (the Revolution) had changed that book into a "historical" novel. Rereading one's own work can be a personal yet historical variant of the forced dialogue which makes the author rethink and redefend his purposes; the genre of a text may itself be another historically forced relation, not a timeless fact.

Megroz's interview with Conrad on November 2, 1922, the first night of the play The Secret Agent, shows that the reticent word circumstances may be less mysterious or teasing than it looks. According to Megroz—who doesn't cite the parallel—Conrad that night made a comment almost identical to the Note's, except that it added an image of "flesh": "I do not enjoy writing plays. It is an exercise in ingenuity. I found the writing of The Secret Agent very trying; it meant cutting all the flesh off the book. And I realized then, as I had never done, what a gruesome story I had written." [1] Conrad then went on to repeat the metaphor in the Note: the disrobing of bare bones. We might rely totally on Megroz and say that what made Conrad see the grisly skeleton of the novel was simply his translation of it into a play.

But the word circumstances is plural, and the Author's Note, no matter how occasional, has a more "general tenor," and was aimed at a broad audience most of whom, as he knew, wouldn't recall the play. The reticence of "circumstances" seems deliberately meant to hint that historical as well as private events, without changing the text, have changed the tone of the novel. On the first page, the Note half ironically mentions Conrad's "pristine innocence of the year 1907" (vii), the year of composition. This indicates that when he now reconsiders his gruesome tragicomedy he feels forced into some new anxiety about its tone because of the more than public facts of the First World War and the mostly private fact of his own son's participation.[2] The young do in fact go out on deadly missions (though Stevie, contrary to the reader's possible first impression, is at least twenty-one when Verloc employs him to carry the bomb, he seems underage[3]); and in the interval between pristine 1907 and postwar 1920, whatever element of comedy there was in Stevie's death has soured. Conrad seems afraid that the aesthetic control of 1907 may now, paradoxically, cheapen the book. Although he finally wants to defend the novel's irony as an idiot boy's Bildungsroman, and as "Winnie's story," and to reject any simple analogy between Verloc's outrage and the novel itself, he at the same time recognizes a legitimate connection between a book's represented actions and its author. If we deny the naive analogy between an author and his themes, we risk an equally naive objectivity or positivism which cancels the power of fiction itself. (Twenty years later the bombing in Hitchcock's Sabotage, based on The Secret Agent, caused a public outcry, although the movie is less bitter than Conrad's novel.[4]) In the end, he finds the answer in a somehow servile but free relation to his outraged audience, a "submission," a tone which combines freedom and necessity by a speech act that reverses confession: he *submits* that the book was but was not an outrage. That is, the familiar reader—in the Note he refers to "those who have read so far through my work"—will hear that in the Note's last phrase the negated word is sardonically not *outrage* but *gratuitous*. *The Secret Agent* was undeniably an outrage, but that outrageousness was necessary and mimetic.

Whether we take the word *circumstances* as a narrow reference to the play or as a broad reference to 1908–1920, the concluding paragraph and the whole Note remain crucial to our understanding of Conrad's picture of the historical or political novel as coercive and violent inquiry. Consider the macabre temporal reorganization of the standard image of stripping as revelation. When writing (as opposed to the talk Megroz jotted down), he does *not* use the metaphor of "flesh." On the contrary, the jolt in the unveiling here is precisely that the flesh is missing. By stripping off a robe of literary irony, he suddenly sees not the body of truth but its skeleton. This is, I think, intentional, in keeping with "the tenor of the preface," his sense of the aims of his own kind of skeptical political drama, and his cautionary irony about creating and knowing in the whole Note. Conventionally, if we imagine inquiry as the metaphor of stripping, or laying bare, we might arrive at two different processes. The first, like a striptease, is erotic: the clothes come off to show the living body. Erotic art displays naked beauty. A second metaphorical sequence, roughly speaking analytic, pursues a relentless inquisitorial course of anatomy: after the first nakedness, the skin is flayed to show muscular anatomy, and after that, dissection goes on to the bones, and so on. Humanism, anatomy, and structuralism appear as an unstoppable sequence. The first image is that of romantically regenerative nakedness, the second that of romantic protest against scientific inquiry and anatomy. *But*—and this is the subtlety of his macabre joke in the metaphor above—as Conrad pictures the sequence of inquiry in his own despondent political novel it is, to be exact, neither of these. Instead, you remove the clothing only to come immediately to the skeleton. There is no midphase of nakedness or sacrifice, no corpus delicti at all, neither of the romantic kind nor of Conan Doyle's kind; no wholeness in the discovery, no substance in the solution to the crime in this novel, but only a sudden fragmentation or skeletalization, and the revelation of a bare causal structure that had previously been "robed."

Implicitly, this macabre joke, the omission of the most "human" or "beautiful" stage from the process of inquiry—the stage of real flesh—is the form of Conrad's novel, which is a political novel, and more exactly an empty historical novel about the recent past, a skeleton wearing clothes. But the bizarre and macabre here bring about an unexpectedly comic tone of consolation and a sense of sanity. We laugh, or are supposed to, because while the unveiling of a skeleton at first seems like a neurotic image, the lack of pretense to recreate the living body of the tragic past is in fact to a great degree sane. Conrad insists that as a political novelist he is not the sculptural flesher-out of political life but a skeleton's tailor. The novel is a skeleton covered by a careful literary robe of scorn. It takes bare events, skeletons of action, and clothes them. When this fitting process is later reversed—when Conrad rereads his own book planning to make it into a play, or, implicitly, whenever we read it—we have what might be called a "stripping enthymeme," a sequence in which the one key step of sufficient historical resurrection is missing. The reader sees through the robe of scorn, not to perceive a body or living characters or lifelike history but to perceive a skeleton; what is laid bare is only the causal underlying structure of tragic events.

In the Note, then, it is hard not to feel that both the writing of the play and the historical circumstances of the war are not mentioned because they are secondary to this theme of the limits of historical and political reading and writing. He spares us the details of *all* the "circumstances" precisely because he is getting at something even more general in "the tenor of this preface." That tenor is to deny that the political novelist of his sort can engage the reader in a recreation of life, as someone who restores the flesh of the past. Instead, the novelist's central task is to participate consciously, and make the reader conscious of, the action of forced inquiry as central to representation also. Tragic dramatic art is not primarily a kind of recreation of life but a kind of analytic interrogation into causes. The metaphor of unveiling describes not only the effect upon Conrad as forced rereader of his own work but also, and most important, what he knew—and intended—would be the depressingly gruesome effect of his novel on any reader. The idea of corpus delicti is ironically reversed: the strict point is to show the reader that the "living body" of the past is irrecoverable, and that we can only have instead a tragic idea of the causal sequence of actions.

This argument in the Note should not be overstated to mean that *The Secret Agent* itself is only a Punch and Judy show, a cool dissection, a marionette play—though Conrad said he liked marionettes.[5] On the contrary, Winnie, Stevie, and their mother are extraordinarily convincing characters, though partly because their expectations are so deadened; and the novel is a triumph of domestic detail. But for various reasons, the aim in the Note itself is to caution against the idea of the writer as "creator." He wants to remind the audience of the limited way in which art is made. Some critics have recently argued about the degree to which Conrad was a Christian. He wasn't. "Once upon a time I was a Christian," he wrote. But he thought in metaphors such as that of baptism as naming by immersion, and toward the end of his life returned slightly toward a manner of Christian piety in public statements and essays. There is a Catholic traditionalism in this macabre 1920 description of the structure of political novels as rags on bones. The writer is only a writer, not a savior or god effecting bodily resurrections of the past; he cannot give the reader living characters but only the sharp contrast between the "clothing" of a time (its illusions) and the underlying bare structure of fears and events which tragic coercive inquiry exposes. The first task is not naturalistic lifelikeness. At its most ironic, the novel is an inquiry into coercive inquiry, and shows itself as such. It shows inquiry to be the "nature" that contradicts sympathetic naturalism. Strong tragic form is not exactly lifelike, but it is marked by cognizance of the coerciveness of its own inquiry; it inquires cruelly into the cruel inquiries that destroy life. This is Conrad's feeling for the structure of recognition: the audience must be made to recognize that the doors of the home are thrown open violently by their own will to see in, to force knowledge. Without this reflection upon the audience's will to inquire, tragedy becomes sensational melodrama. Tragic form, then, for Conrad is dramatic inquiry conducted with the awareness that the act of inquiry is itself dissective and murderous. Art participates in and does not transcend the murderousness of other historical relations.

Throughout the Note there is an effort to point the reader away from the idea that the novel is a creative vision toward the idea that the novel is an artful reduction. Though the passages about his vision of an enormous town may seem to be evidence that this is Conrad's grand novel of London, in fact Conrad here is jeering at the "immense" genesis of his own "vision" at the first stages of the book's conception. He is not serious, but is parodying Genesis when he tells us how he first saw an enormous town, a vast population, universal tragedy. "It would take years to find the right way! It seemed to take years!" (xii) After more of this self-mocking bombast, he describes how the tale began to take more definite, contracted, concentrated, but still not proportional shape as Winnie's story. Then he closes the description of this vast creative process with a deliberate deflation of himself as the Creator in Genesis: "All this took about three days" (xii). If Pope is the early English master of the mock-heroic and Scott of the mock-romantic, Conrad may be the master of the mock-creative. He often parodies the creative portentousness of which he is frequently accused. The next paragraph reinforces the shift of tone from visionary scope to contractual realism of production, giving us his usual sense of the activity of writing: *"This book is that story, reduced to manageable proportions"* (xii). In other words, the novel *The Secret Agent* as we have it is the reduction of a contraction of a vision. He italicizes the deictic words to insist on the thisness and thatness, rather than the vastness, of his story.

So the Note deflates the image of the author as creator and highlights the methods of practical proportioning that allow a book to be made. The book is not about London's immensity; but it is made possible because it is about various people who dread that immensity. Conrad implies that, like some of these characters (most obviously the Professor) he may have his own immense fear-visions of the "enormous town," of "endless vistas" somewhere between terror and exultation, but that this vision for him is not the ground of the novelist's work. The specific reduction here, he goes on to say, is effected through the "absurd explosion" of Stevie, and through the final organization of the book as a set of figures grouped about "Winnie Verloc and related directly or indirectly to her tragic suspicion that 'life doesn't stand much looking into.' " Thus even as he himself can make a story only by scaling down his own chaotic vision of London's immensity, he gives us a central character who tries to do something similar, though in a more pathetic way: Winnie tries, and fails, to narrow the range of what she is forced to see, because to see more would kill her (she is right—it does). The implication is not that Winnie is not simply wrong for trying, like Jocasta, to limit and contract her range of inquiry—we have just seen that the novel itself could only come into existence as the defensive contraction of a frightening vision—but because she is not permitted to do it successfully.

This dramatization of art as a nontranscendent process of inquiry, itself caught up within other inquiries, is one of Conrad's main points in the novel. But where does this theme come from? What is the source of Winnie's simple suspicion, which Conrad indicates is the organizing idea of the book, that inquiry is dangerous, that life won't stand scrutiny? And why the intuition, more complex, that forced inquiry itself is the problem and cause of tragic form? The answers are plural. From one angle the reason is only that *The Secret Agent* is not exactly, as Ford said, a great detective novel,[6] but an involution of Conan Doyle's playful detection, showing detection as something which the characters, like Heat and the Assistant Commissioner, are forced to do, and not a voluntary pastime. Winnie's distrust of inquiry is partly sound lower-class "common sense" and fear in a world where other agents are forced to inquire. Her fear of looking comes also from the novel's family structure: her own temporal placement within the family, as the mother of her brother and the wife of a "gentleman" like Verloc, of the "fat-pig style" (13). Her refusal to look, that is, is bound up with the problem of a semi-incestuous order in the family. Behind this also, though without an exclusively psychoanalytic meaning, are the figures of Jocasta and Oedipus. Oedipus for Conrad, at least consciously, is Sophocles' forcing inquirer rather than the figure of desire that he is in Freudian thought; and Jocasta is the figure who tries to stop inquiry. We have already noted the association between Oedipus and forced interrogation in Monygham, and in Massy and Whalley, and will see this again in the life of Razumov in the next chapter. In Conrad's work Oedipus stands first for unlimited inquiry as self-destruction, and for the process in which the enlightened distinction between "reasoning" and "forcing" breaks down. In a minor book review of 1910, for example, Conrad closes by quoting a mystic who warned against taking rational inquiry to the limit: "I have attempted to tear asunder the veil you [Nature] have hung to conceal from us the pain of life, and I have been wounded by the mystery . . . Oedipus, half way to finding the word of the enigma, young Faust, regretting already the simple life, the life of the heart, I come back to you repentant, reconciled, O gentle deceiver!" [7] The mystical speaker (whom Conrad in the essay seems to endorse by giving him the last word) recommends that we abandon the quest of Oedipus halfway, before it is too late. This is of course what Jocasta recommends; and Winnie, who is partly Jocasta, and not all that remotely an image of Conrad's destroyed mother, caught up in a political scene she does not will or understand, is not simply wrong in the way she tries to ward off destruction. Jocasta and Winnie both commit suicide because they cannot in fact stop the process.

But Conrad himself, in *The Secret Agent,* as an author writing a book with a plot tragicomically analogous to his own childhood family's destruction, does not either completely take or completely reject the advice not to inquire. He conducts an inquiry into the destruction of one marginal family by politics. He says in the Note, "Man may smile and smile, but he is not an investigating animal. He loves the obvious. He shrinks from explanations. But I will go on with mine" (viii). That is, he revises a Shakespearean phrase to say that common people, people in general, like Winnie or Jocasta, shy away from inquiry. And he says it without contempt at all: on the contrary. But he then tentatively identifies himself as Oedipus. This novel, though obliquely, examines the greatest trauma of his past, the one in which he himself was psychologically blown to bits by the politically caused death of his parents. Thus if we are to reach the brilliantly self-contradictory tone of the novel at all, the ingenious way in which it plays fragmentation against unity, hilarity against depressing tragedy, and builds comic details into a tragic whole, we have to hint at the source of its strong confusion of detachment and empathy as coming from Conrad's need to handle this theme—the political annihilation of a family—objectively, and at the same time to see the dangers of his own inquiry.

The stripping enthymeme tells us that, contrary to pieties, the intelligent historical novel, the inquiry into a tragic past, if it takes on important material (here very obliquely the death of Conrad's mother and father and his own subsequent *bêtise* and fragmentation), should remain comically aware of its ambivalence about retrieving the full "life" of the past in empathic identification. The historical novel lies and flatters if it implies that the reader simply wants to know history or politics. If we can believe anthropologists, we usually want to get rid of a dead body quickly. Santayana sounds unctuous when he tells us that we can avoid repeating history by knowing it; on the contrary, knowing may sometimes cause repetition. A more honest attitude toward our real attitude toward the past translates here into the comedy of the novel. To take only one example, Stevie's instant fragmentation into a thousand-piece corpse, the central image in the book, is on one level funny because it accomplishes for the reader an instant detachment from the dead, from decay, from slow disintegration; obliteration is the work of time immediately effected. This whole act of forceful detachment from overwhelming pity continues to operate for Conrad even twelve years later, and even in so simple an act as rereading. When he tears open the veil of *The Secret Agent* to find its skeleton, he is saying, again with grim comedy, that the "living" body of the past, the persons of his family, cannot be sympathetically resurrected in the flesh, and thankfully have not been by his novel. His novel is a comical displacement of his family's history, of the "skeleton" in his past. He does not have the body of the past, or a complete and "creative" repossession of his parents' destroyed lives. And in keeping with this, the plot itself warns against the idea that a complete historical "sympathy" can comprehend and control events.

I mean this obliquely biographical discussion of the novel's sense of the nature of inquiry into the past to lead us to the complex emotional effect of the novel, particularly in regard to the pity it evokes for Winnie. *The Secret Agent* is Conrad's greatest and most unhappy study of the problem of "sympathy," which has long been recognized as one of his main themes. Winnie, if Conrad succeeds with her, will have a contradictory effect on the reader's "pity" (viii). On the one hand, she is one of his greatest characters, a lower-class figure whose pathos is not bathos, and is entirely justified by her experience. It would be snobbism to feel only what Conrad calls "scorn" for her manipulativeness, resignation, and failure to learn. At the same time, when we pity her, as events make inevitable—we're not "touched" but made to feel painful pity of an austere kind unusual in modern literature—we are reminded at the same time that her own pity for Stevie is precisely what deforms her, and that her pathetic "contract with existence" (251) is one of the most important contributory causes of Stevie's death, since it leads her to nag Verloc into spending time with Stevie and into thinking of Stevie as useful. As a result, even while the novel drives the reader to feel a stronger pity for Winnie than for most other major Conrad characters, at the same time, with ruthless casualness, it lets the reader know that pity was the destructive illusion in Winnie's life. Pity is both the effect on the reader and an unmistakable cause of the tragedy. As a result, an extreme pity is evoked but withheld as catharsis. This is one reason why *The Secret Agent* is not so much a parody as an examination of tragedy. Many excellent readings have been given of the novel, some emphasizing time, some domesticity, some the dialogue design.[8] But while referring to these, I want to focus here on the novel as a study of the problematic of sympathy. The plot asks whether "compassion" can really (as Conrad sometimes suggested it could in his political essays) replace "force" as the order of the world, and then gives a negative answer, showing almost mathematically how the destruction of the family takes place as a result of its most admirable character's pity.

Trauma, not drama or dream, is the main mood of *The Secret Agent*. Trauma is usually defined as a wound that does not heal or as the shock resulting from a force too great to absorb. The novel focuses largely, of course, on the traumatized dialogical fixation of the characters, not on any "dialectic." Beginning with a political forced dialogue, when Vladimir musters Verloc, and reaching its climax in the long marital forced dialogue in which Winnie murders Verloc, the book seems primarily intended not to expose any changing consciousness of reality, or any desire—for all Winnie's power as a figure—but rather to unfold a bureaucratically static world of forced dialogues, equally at work in the home and in politics—what John Hagan, Jr., a little too weakly called "interviews."[9] The last married dialogue, for example, which Leavis thought one of the greatest scenes in the English novel, takes dramatically delayed revenge—classically used to make a "consciousness" like Hamlet's or Ahab's visible during the delay—and makes it seem emptily ritualistic. The long delay that culminates in Winnie's stabbing of

The Fragmentation of Sympathy

Verloc does not primarily show thought or consciousness, or even, as has usually been thought, their mutual misunderstanding. Instead the Verloc marriage dialogues, in their slow prolongation and repetition, expose mainly their own disproportion, silence, and coercion, which is that of the book's "bureaucratic" civilization. Winnie, traumatized from the outset by her childhood, is not educated but only retraumatized by the main action. She learns nothing by the end of the book; she kills Verloc in the same dialogue in which she lived with him—one talking a lot, one a little, until a "detonation" at the end, whether it is putting out the lamp for the night or murder. And then, having learned nothing, she goes on to try to push Ossipon into a similar union. What we have here in the foreground is an absolute stasis in relational form, not a dream or drama.

In keeping with this general format of trauma, it would be useful here to question one standard judgment: that this is a great novel of London. As already discussed, in the Note Conrad subtly indicates that he had to cut away his sense of London's immensity to write. If we compare Dickens' London, I think we have to ask, as Fox asked about a Jacobin insurrection circa 1800 the fear of which Pitt was exploiting, "Where is it?" The world in *The Secret Agent* is to some extent also a little Jacobin insurrection that isn't there. While the parodies of the anarchists seem to stand out in a first reading of the novel, in fact the novel as a whole in its own way repeats Fox's question, suggesting that the great anarchist "revolution" is first a triviality of romantic imagination and second a reactionary ploy meant to scare liberal society into reaction. London anarchism is shown to be a gaggle of four madmen (most of whom may be provocateurs) in a Soho shop. Terror is in fact triggered by forced dialogue from right-wing autocracies abroad. This is not to say that Conrad is a leftist—which is nonsense; but the plot dismisses the danger of the anarchists to condemn Russian and German autocracy. As for the Professor, the only anarchist who does act (by supplying dynamite), his free anarchist consciousness is shown ironically to be only the most apocalyptic fantasia of "forced dialogue": he lives his life picturing an ultimate forced dialogue, in which he will be cornered, and will detonate. The city of London here, seen most sharply as the crowds and corridors of his terrified, reductive imagination, seems, in spite of what most critics have said, like a taut "model" insofar as it is there at all—a non-London. To a great degree, as the Note hints, the great commercial London is kept deliberately remote from much of the novel. The urban variety of Dickensian London is condensed into a negative set of inquisitorial routes, bureaucratic rooms, a ludicrous salon, and a pornography shop. Each class is changed from the time of Dickens: the family is pornographic, the elite classes are sentimental-socialist, the detectives are bureaucrats. The book seems itself to "give up" on trying to celebrate or denounce London's largeness, just as all the characters, from Ethelred at the top, with his fear of details, to Winnie near the bottom, feel apprehension and contraction, and have given up on seeing the whole scene.

The ingenious structure of the book is perhaps the most obvious thing about it, including the much-discussed connection between the shattered time sequence and the attempt to blow up Time, or Greenwich.[10] But this structure is itself as much a joke as a high symbolism. The excess of structural ingenuity is not finally structuralist but expressionist; it reminds us how intensely the people feel caught up in narrowing structures. The art of *The Secret Agent*, as if in grotesque mechanical sympathy with their condition, makes a drastic formal reduction of aesthetic values. Tragedy, for example, is commonly thought of as encompassing pity and terror, two different affects, which together enlarge the audience (though an argument can be made that even for Aristotle, pity and terror are not two emotions but one[11]). In *The Secret Agent*, however, these two are explicitly contracted into one "base" modern feeling: "sympathy is a form of fear" (88), the narrator tells us at one point, in a scene to which I will return. Spatially, largely through corridorization and parody, the novel makes it seem that England has become her own colony; that bureaucracy is autocolonization; and that the mirror of the sea has been turned into the city as aquarium, a national fishery, full of magnified bathetic sprats. The image of London as an aquarium amounts to a declaration that the novel willingly takes immersive "bathos" (literally "sinking") as its inescapable modern problem. The Assistant Commissioner considers his forced life in London's weather "horrible, horrible," parodying and diminishing the already parodic and diminished Kurtz.

Finally, the disorganization of time, as has not been pointed out strongly enough, takes place not only in the narrative order and the grand plan to destroy Greenwich but more powerfully in the small precocities and retardations in the Verloc family. That is, the "late and soon" of mental and family time here, a Victorian theme, should perhaps take priority over the clever mock symbolism of the attack on Greenwich. Stevie is retarded—that is, the world goes by "too fast" for him. Winnie is her retarded brother's foster mother, and for his sake has married with precocious resignation a man too old for her; their mother seems their grandmother, and leaves before her time for an old-age home. They fall into a generational blur; each one has a kind of double agedness. The best word in English for the resulting family mood is *apprehension,* which suggests a fear of time that anticipates and brings about what is feared. To focus on the structural ingenuity of the book is to ignore this other purpose: the structural and temporal are meant to lead back to such moral themes as sympathy, agency, fear of life, and family dependence. This is why Conrad was not being entirely ironic when he dubbed the book a "Simple Tale of the XIX Century" in the dedication (though "XIX" may be meant to look not so much like a number as a nihilistic-egoic scrawl). The tale's themes are in fact the basic sympathetic themes of nineteenth-century domestic fiction, drastically altered.

The approach to destructive sympathy should begin by pointing out that Stevie's explosion alludes simultaneously to two "low" tragedians whose powers to evoke pathos are among their greatest and most controversial gifts: Euripides and Dickens. The two fused ancestor scenes for Stevie's explosion are the tragic death of Pentheus in *The Bacchae* and the famous joke of "Spontaneous Combustion" at the center of *Bleak House,* the novel to which Conrad referred most often when praising Dickens.[12] Of course the tragicomic description of Stevie's death, which is the "unifying scattering" of the novel, is a tour de force. There is no need to think of other scenes to get at that primary force; on the contrary, as a tour de force, Stevie's death seems to cancel any idea of ancestry. At the same time, working beneath this first power of the novel, the double allusion seems inescapable, not really recondite at all, and necessary to the book's composition as a dramatic novel.

A great deal of work has been done on allusions and sources in Conrad,[13] but in general there has not been enough work to describe the way he alludes. As already indicated, in the political novels he often sets himself into a revoking dialogue with ancestor works, often several at a time, to alter them by adding his own almost geometrical vision of mutually coercive relations. Here, what Euripides' scene and Dickens' have in common is intoxication and anarchic freedom. They are Mysteries, tragic and comic, about the return of repressed drives. Conrad reading *Bleak House* perhaps saw Dickens as making a zany reuse of Bacchic imagery, since Krook is a drunk. But in any case, in each work the body goes to pieces because of some mysterious, compulsive, yet liberating force—Bacchus or a scientific Mystery—beyond human agency and social constraint. Whatever humanizing theories we might try to foist on these moments (for example that Bacchus is really human, as has sometimes been suggested, or that "Spontaneous Combustion" is Dickens' funniest metaphor for laughter itself), intoxication, wild release, and unreason tear Pentheus to pieces and turn Krook into slime all over the windowsills. Dickens' genius makes free with natural causality to put a freeing outburst of laughter at the center of a book about relentless Chancery determinism. But in Conrad's book the simultaneously tragic and funny explosion brings these two, Dickens and Euripides, into surprising forced conjunction for a plot in which the real causes of Stevie's death are entirely those of human agency, not of a god or of science. This is agency in both senses, in that the agents are both those who act for others and those who initiate actions. We don't have to look outside the political order for the causes of Stevie's death, but only to add together Vladimir's agency on Verloc by forced dialogue; the Professor's willingness to supply explosives as part of his sense that the whole world is a forced dialogue; Winnie's manipulative sympathy gently forcing Verloc and Stevie into alliance; and her mother's secret agency in leaving home, a "move of deep policy"(162) also intended to bond Stevie and Verloc. These are the main causes, the plural convergent "secret agencies," political and domestic and political-domestic, of Stevie's death. But the "secret agency" of charity and pity itself—even as the Christian ethic tells one to practice charity in secret—is the most important moral component. Winnie and her mother practice secret charity, and in so doing their sympathy becomes, in direct contradiction to many strands of traditional representation of kindness, the collaborative cause of disaster, with Vladimir's terrorism and Verloc's cowardice. Hence the novel is not merely a tragedy of realpolitik but a tragedy of sympathy as its secret agency.

But why should Conrad want to show the secret agency of sympathy as leading to destruction? One classical answer has long been available in the canon of Conrad criticism. This is, as any number of writers have suggested, that sympathy is disguised self-interest.[14] As with the crew of the *Narcissus*, sympathy, though perceived as a form of connection by the one who feels it, draws its energy from fear for the self, and so generates division, selfishness, and even weak mutiny. Sympathy is the "selfish," mental mode of otherness, and also the ground of theatrical effect. I don't want to quarrel with this obvious line of argument but to develop it by looking at *The Secret Agent* as the novel that most effectively subsumes sympathy within forced dialogue, the two being opposed forms of force in human relations. To do this, one must first admit a larger background for Conradian sympathy than most discussions have recognized. Changing attitudes toward social and aesthetic sympathy of course help to mark the shift from nineteenth-century literature to modernism, and Conrad seems to lie on the border, half a be liever in sympathetic art and half a "sort of" Nietzschean critic. He is not however, just a figure of transition, uncertain about sentiment, nor a timid Nietzsche, but someone with a highly advanced knowledge of

The Fragmentation of Sympathy

the nineteenth century's varieties of sympathetic representation. To see this, we have to consider a series of representations of sympathy in this novel one by one. The result will be not a simple or easy answer about Conrad's final meaning but a revelation of the book as a more complex meditation on sympathy than any earlier story.

In spite of attempts to locate the main source of Conrad's idea of sympathy in one writer—Schopenhauer, for example—the difficult truth is that Conrad drew from as many as four distinct traditions. One is, of course, that of Schopenhauer, and more generally the sympathy of German romanticism. Another, however, and probably more important to him by 1907, is the sympathy of English philosophy and fiction. Here sympathy is a mental faculty or process enabling individuals (assumed a priori to be individuals) to imagine one another by conscious rational comparisons, a kind of conscious analogue from one's own experience and class to another's (this is, for example, the rational sympathy which Knightley teaches Emma in order to become an adult, ready to marry); a human faculty which generates a set of institutions and practical actions with many different names, such as philanthropy, charity, kindness, fellow feeling, pity, forgiveness, mercy, and so on. Whether in fact *sympathy* is really the primary or most inclusive term of this set is itself an ideological and historical question. Part of the genius of the nineteenth-century English novel, as in Dickens and James, is the critical representation in dialogue of the limits of sympathy, and the contradictions of sympathetic institutions. In Dickens, obviously, kindness and philanthropy may be opposed. Mrs. Jellyby is philanthropy, John Jarndyce is kindness and charity. Max Scheler tried to write a phenomenology of these terms, but what we need more is a history of them.[15] If we indulge for a moment in Conrad's belief in "national temperament," which figures in all his novels, we could say that where the German treatment tends to be cosmic and unitary—and this remains so in Nietzsche's witty attacks on bad sympathy and even finally in Scheler's critique of Nietzsche in *The Nature of Sympathy*—the English tradition particularizes sympathy, breaking it down into plural social acts and institutions. English literature gives particular dramatic criticism of these plural actions. That is, the English novel at its strongest analyzed not the cosmic unity of sympathy but its ironic plurality, in heart and head, action and thought, and so on.

Further, it would not be an exaggeration to say that in European nineteenth-century fiction the nature of sympathy is a major problem, and that the most powerful novelists can be discriminated partly by locating the kind of sympathetic action or institution—an immense field—that obsesses each most. It would, for instance, be reasonable to say that while Dickens is concerned with kindnesses as social acts, and with the many contradictions of philanthropy and charity, he is not nearly as interested as Jane Austen or George Eliot in the philosophical or mental action of "sympathy" as a process. In Russia we might note that Dostoevsky is of course involved with Christian forgiveness and compassion (in this he resembles Blake), while Tolstoy is involved with mental and emotional "sympathy" between classes and the, for him, vexed question of whether it comes from the heart or the head. The representation of the many diverse actions which might be called, as a group, "sympathetic" lies at the core of much nineteenth-century fiction and poetry, as well as at the core of the notion of what happens to the audience. The break with bourgeois sympathy as a viable aesthetic and social value almost constitutes the definition of transitional modernist figures like Nietzsche and Brecht; but at the same time this break blinds us to the fact that in the nineteenth century sympathy itself was already broken into conflicting parts or terms. The discovery that sympathy may be many different events that are, strangely enough, in disharmony was always lying under the surface, even in the most sympathetic novelists like George Eliot. In *The Secret Agent* this fragmentation of sympathy reaches the status of a demonic proof.

But the background is still more plural and various. Though this may seem a crazy cultural mix—and the strength of Conrad's work is just that crazy at times—notions which are neither exactly like cosmic sympathy in Schopenhauer, nor English practical representation of sympathetic institutions, have to be considered also. There is the messianic spirit found in Polish poets like Mickiewicz and Słowacki,[16] and the commonplace Aristotelian theory of tragedy, pity, and terror. In *The Secret Agent* all of these strands, as much as they may seem pastiched or irreconcilable, are being reconsidered by the tragic action, though not quite systematically. Sympathy between characters, and as the key to audience response, is for Conrad the central feature of nineteenth-century representation, now dying, or exploding. It is the dramatic form of the question of community. If he may once have been largely Schopenhauerian, by now he has mastered the English language, and along with it the English syntax of dramatic criticism of sympathetic institutions. But he retains a strong feeling for Schopenhauerian and Slavic cosmic sympathies, for the messianic romantic sympathy of the Polish poets, and for tragic theory. As a result, part of the "dialogical" power of *The Secret Agent* is that, though unsystematically, it confronts all of these, and brilliantly "dialogizes" sympathy itself into its unreconciled kinds. There is an unusually passionate amalgamation: English practical representation in the novel through dialogue and action; romantic ideas about "sympathy" as a cosmic bond; "Slavic" romantic ideas of a more intense, personalized, messianic passion of mercy and forgiveness and pity; Greek tragic theory and the sense that pity connects the audience to violent events. Winnie's sisterly devotion to Stevie, for example, is finally not quite like anything else in English fiction in its exclusive intensity. Dickens' people, no matter how committed or altruistic, do not love with the kind of world-excluding devotion she has. Rather Winnie reminds us a little either of a cockney Antigone, giving up all for a brother, or of some domestic bond in Dostoevsky. Wounded love for her brother is her whole "contract with existence." This sisterly bondage is the strongest motive in the novel, and one of the strongest Conrad depicts anywhere. With these preliminary remarks, let us look now at the variety of dramatic postulates about sympathy in this novel.

The comic and crass connection between sympathetic affect, secret action, and masturbation may be easiest to see. Throughout *The Secret Agent* anarchism, masturbation, and sympathy are imagined as similar forms of solitary secret activity. Secret references to masturbation appear from the first page on in a mock-Victorian, or covertly obscene, style. The Verloc family runs what we'd call a pornography shop (in the front window bawdy novels are strung out "as if to dry") because the family itself is full of masturbatory affect. In their shop anarchists hold nonmeetings in which each talks to himself to work himself up into a frenzy of compassionate rage over images of suffering. The childless Verloc marriage takes this form, with Winnie's talk being a kind of self-inciting passion—though the sense that they also want on some level to force each other to speak makes them as a couple more likable and more pitiful. In the bar where Ossipon meets the Professor, a mechanical piano plays itself while they talk. The Professor defines himself entirely by the "ball" in his pocket, the detonator he'll press if the police try to arrest him. And Stevie, in the central expressive detail of this set, plunges his hands deep into his pockets whenever he feels pity. Anarchism, Conrad implies, contrary to popular imagery of liberation as leading to wild intercourse, leads logically to a kind of masturbation, because it is based on a principle of extreme individuation. Anarchism would be a Bacchic orgy not of lovers but of intense, "deep" masturbators.

Maybe this all makes for an obvious, conservative, thumbs-in-suspenders joke—except that in this set of images Conrad very skillfully employs the art, from Dickens to Reich, of combining sexuality and politics in personal gesture. With the image of the hands in the pockets he makes narcissistic sympathy seem like the only means of exchange for those somehow deprived of other coin. The more abstract point is that, contary to nineteenth-century aspirations, sympathy cannot be the ground of community—not because it is too weak but because it is in essence a form of isolationist activity, mental disconnection. It takes place only inside the individual. The more intense it is, the more it explodes and divides, in effect barring persons from each other without their being able to understand why, since they experience themselves as deeply emotional beings, full of feeling. Still more important, the ritual of tragic sympathetic catharsis found in art, and of course drawn up first as a sort of dramatic "contract" by Aristotle, is therefore not a communal ritual at all but an enforced imaginative anarchy. Art as pathos more or less forces eveyone to have feelings alone, to plunge hands into pockets, to coin bathetic feelings, to "feel deeply." The sense of comic disgust with this attitude that pervades the novel is unmistakable. Conrad, more mildly in *"Narcissus,"* more gruesomely here, makes aesthetic sympathy seem lurid. But he doesn't, like Nietzsche, object to sympathy as a "herd" affect; on the contrary, he objects to the lack of final collective feeling in it. The artistic relation as a sympathetic one, rather than as a revelation of group action and force, is dangerous not because it is "sentimental" and weakening, but because sympathy in fact explodes the community it pretends to create. Community can be seen not typically in dialogues of free sympathy but in the whole range of "forced dialogues," of which sympathetic secret agency is one instance. The ideology of sympathy as free exchange, in fact, is the attempt to mask and deny this more forced connection, by making it a matter of personal thought, choice, and sentiment. Conrad seems to fear this insight, and the language of "force," because of its autocratic implications if misunderstood, but he persists in it. The illusion of choosing community can have disastrous consequences as a disguised sentimental denial of the force of community.

That sympathy is divisive, and is itself a kind of covert "force," is the argument. One good place in which to see this, of course, is in syntax, in the stammering repetition that marks Stevie's speech when he feels overwhelming pity. During the cab drive, when Stevie cries out for the whipped cab horse and goes on a sort of one-boy strike, he struggles to articulate his rage at social oppression and forced labor. He says, "Bad! Bad!" and then, "Poor! Poor!" and then, in a passage that is like a grammatical pilgrim's progress, manages to forge a proposition: "He got it at last. He hung back to utter it at once. 'Bad world for poor people' " (146). Conrad probably wants a contradictory response here from the audience: to agree with Stevie, to see a universal truth in the proposition, to pity the horse with him, to pity him—but also to scorn, the scorn making the pity worse. But one main point, easily overlooked, is grammatical: while the idiot boy appears to generate an unmistakably true "sentence," it remains a sentence with no verb, or what we call a fragment. The secret agent, the absent verb, the connective force behind this world order of poverty remains inaccessible to his accurate "sympathy," which is a traumatized but true enough outcry. Whatever it is that holds persons together, giving the political world the form it has, it is not accessible to sympathy's verbless syntax.

The highest proposition which sympathy by itself can achieve, then, remains a sentence fragment. Stevie's broken outcries obviously forecast the later fragmentation of his body. An objection could be made to this reading of the scene as a grammatical study of the limits of sympathetic statement via the omission of the verb; it would argue that Conrad gives Stevie the greatest truth of the book. This is a bad world for poor people; there's no explaining it; the idiot speaks the truth; it is the static permanent horror, inarticulable; "the poor you always have with you"; the sound and the fury; and so on. While this thesis is there, and includes the usual concern for inarticulable suffering in Conrad as in Tolstoy, it belies the critical irony about this in the novel. The Assistant Commissioner's lament "Horrible, horrible!" (100) concerning the weather, and the compassionate stutters in the salon when the fashionable guests see the obese Michaelis and refer to his weight as "terrible—terrible" (108), are echoes of Stevie's stuttering, verbless sympathy; and it is no accident that both Dickens and Euripides are known for using the rhetoric of plosive repetitions and speech tics to stir the audience. As we saw in earlier chapters, Conrad is preoccupied with what he conceives to be the realistic motive force of verbs, and is self-consciously alert to the ways verbs organize the "continuity and force" of sentences. The omission of the verb from Stevie's sympathetic consciousness is intentional. In the action of the novel, Stevie himself could be said to be the involuntary, forced, or unconscious verb, made to perform an action which he does not understand, his sympathy completely reused by the forced dialogue initiated by Vladimir on one side and Winnie on the other.

The most thoughtfully constructed scene about sympathy is, however, the set piece about the charwoman, Mrs. Neale, toward the beginning of chapter 9. Albert Guerard, I think wrongly, dismisses this scene as an example of the novel's slightness. It is, he says, a "rather gratuitous horror" which fits in only because the novel itself is an entertainment more minor than Leavis thought.[17] Guerard's strong argument acknowledges the ironic detachment fully, and he decribes the whole novel as "coolly distant." But the power of the book lies in its *mock* detachment, covering forced participation even on Conrad's part. Mrs. Neale is central to this mood, falling at the center of the novel's ethical and dramatic organization, and intended to question Dickens on sympathy and servitude.

There Mrs. Neale was scrubbing the floor. At Stevie's appearance she groaned lamentably, having observed that he could be induced easily to bestow for the benefit of her infant children the shilling his sister Winnie presented him with from time to time. On all fours among the puddles, wet and begrimed, like a sort of amphibious and domestic animal living in ashbins and dirty water, she uttered the usual exordium: "It's all very well for you, keep doing nothing like a gentleman." And she followed it with the everlasting plaint of the poor, pathetically mendacious, miserably authenticated by the horrible breath of cheap rum and soap-suds. She scrubbed hard, snuffling all the time, and talking volubly. And she was sincere. And on each side of her thin red nose her bleared, misty eyes swam in tears, because she felt really the want of some sort of stimulant in the morning.

In the parlor Mrs. Verloc observed, with knowledge:

"There's Mrs. Neale at it again with her harrowing tales about her little children. They can't be all so little as she makes them out. Some of them must be big enough by now to try to do something for themselves. It only makes Stevie angry."

These words were confirmed by a thud as of a fist striking the kitchen table. In the normal evolution of his sympathy Stevie had become angry on discovering that he had no shilling in his pocket. In his inability to relieve at once Mrs. Neale's "little 'uns' " privations, he felt that somebody should be made to suffer for it. Mrs. Verloc rose, and went into the kitchen to "stop that nonsense." And she did it firmly but gently. She was well aware that directly Mrs. Neale received her money she went round the corner to drink ardent spirits in a mean and musty public-house—the unavoidable station on the *via dolorosa* of her life. Mrs. Verloc's comment on this practice had an unexpected profundity, as coming from a person disinclined to look under the surface of things. "Of course, what is she to do to keep up? If I were like Mrs. Neale I expect I wouldn't act any different." (184–185)

Except for the thud, this stylized, fairly flat scene largely withholds laughter. Instead, the dialogue with Dickens here says, "Dickens was wrong about English servitude," and this charge makes up for the absence of humor. The key to the scene—its uncompromisingly allegorical note—lies in the naming. Conrad here does everything he can, short of extreme heavy-handedness—or not short, since he himself thuds the table with this grim pun—to lead us to the pun *kneel* in the amphibious working woman's name. Unlike Dickens' exuberant, pleasurable, kinetic names and nicknames—such as Twist, Pip, Guppy, Flite, Heep— which expresses the free movement of the self by the self, to create comic identification and pleasure, Conrad's strongest names, as I have already noted, indicate relatively forced social contracts with someone else: Nostromo (our man), Tuan Jim (Lord mixed with a nickname), Lena (leaner), Heyst (named), Amy Foster, and so on. Names are dependent and contractual rather than expressively autokinetic. "Mrs. Neale," as an abstract revision of Dickensian naming, is extraordinarily precise and acute. It first looks Dickensian, because it indicates a body posture, but then the humor, if it is that, pulls away from Dickens, who in his most downtrodden people usually finds some poetic freedom of expression. The class name here refers to the plainest servitude or slavery. By creating the plain slave Mrs. Neale—much grayer and less enjoyable than her immediate forebear Sairey Gamp, who also makes up fictions but whose stories entertain—Conrad, even with the hint of sadism, is not a weak Dickens or a class snob, but he is making a deliberate and thankless and angry point. He refuses to patronize the alcoholic worker by finding her richly fanciful. The flatness and spareness are an attack on Dickensian humor.

The scene is there, however, for other reasons, which have nothing to do with Dickens' class comedy, and instead affect the organization of the novel itself. One of Winnie's recurrent assertions is that in England we "ain't slaves"; and it is in relation to Winnie's cockney pride about her freedom that Mrs. Neale becomes one of the key figures of the novel. In the scene above, Winnie interferes. She is admirable when she breaches the boundary of pity and overhearing to put a forceful stop to Mrs. Neale's manipulative begging. She puts a stop to "sympathetic art," with its rhetoric and its overhearing: all to the good. But she then turns to express apparently free sympathy for Mrs. Neale in a classical proposition: if I were like . . . then I would do the same. In this statement, Winnie echoes the common philosophical definition of sympathy but also the pious cliché "There but for . . ." The individual makes an imaginative, rational analogy from his own experience to someone else's condition. All this, the narrator tells us, is "surprisingly profound." Yet the surrounding action repudiates the profundity. Just before the interference, Winnie herself has been doing something similar to Mrs. Neale's begging: dishonestly trying to cadge Verloc's sympathy for Stevie, her own poor grown-up child. She has told Verloc that Stevie would do anything for him—even go through fire (183–184). Plainly, the very philosophical, very rational-sounding proposition "If I were like . . . then I would also . . ."—the kind of subjunctive ethical calculus we find in English moral philosophy and in the sympathetic English novel—is contextually presented to us as a gross, if understandable, lie, which Winnie tells herself by substitution of verbal mood. She *is* like Mrs. Neale, or rather, she is forced to be like her. Constrained into a horrible marriage, she plays similar beggarly tricks. In George Eliot and Virginia Woolf, subjunctives and optatives reinforce sympathetic moods; in Conrad an imperative governs the subjunctive. Winnie, who asserts that "we ain't downtrodden slaves here" (205), in the novel's recognition scene a few pages later kneels at a door in her own house to overhear the news of Stevie's death. "The door was hardly shut when Mrs. Verloc, jumping up from the chair, ran to it as if to fling it open, but instead of doing so fell on her knees, with her ear to the keyhole" (208). She hears the news, and then springs up "suddenly from her crouching position, and stopping her ears" *reels* (a verb about the effect of reality on her) "to and fro between the counter and the shelves on the wall" (210). "Kneel" and "reel" are the verb polarities of Winnie's existence, from servitude to recognition. We have seen before that forced verticalization is one of Conrad's metaphors for the violence of humanization. Winnie now tragically overhears information traumatically disproportionate to her understanding of action and cause, and experiences another completely unexpected wound to the self in a scene of absolute traumatic *over*hearing. She becomes the figure of English servitude, the allegorical grotesque "Mrs. Kneel," related to the suppliant women of Greek tragedy, forcibly identified with the woman she had earlier sought to distance herself from by sympathy. It is for this reason that after murdering Verloc, in trying to think of a friend, Winnie can only think of Mrs. Neale (221). The scene with Mrs. Neale is not a gratuitous fragment or vignette but a necessary part of the story.

But doesn't this prove Guerard's point, since "bad" puns on names are gratuitous and trivial? Why pay so much attention to one forced naming? This question goes to the heart of the problem, and is finally a matter of values, and of orientation toward naming itself. Patricia Spence has described sympathy in Adam Smith's theory as an economy within the rest of his system.[18] She argues that Smith's "sympathy" resembles money as a means of exchange between individuals that does not threaten their a priori individuality. The nineteenth-century English fiction, the function of "sympathy" is often just this, like the function of a totally nonallegorical name: to leave the person conceptually autonomous while related to others. "Sympathy" is like capital. The sympathetic hero has a great store of this capital, spent gloriously in intimate conversations and generous encounters, conspicuous displays of the great inner wealth. The more classical sense of the word *sympathy*, however, such as Milton's, takes it for involuntary sharing: "Horror on them fell, and horrid sympathy." [19] That is, classically, sympathy violates individuality; it is not a rational choice or a faculty. Winnie thinks she is acting on the first kind of free sympathy but is actually involved in a sympathy closer to that of classical symmetrical force. In the supposed decorum of the realistic novel, naming, like sympathy, should not depersonalize. It should avoid gross allegory because such allegory seems to us to depersonalize, making the individual "only" a dependent meaning within a system, not a free agent. Separate individuals have personal names and can sympathize with one another freely. This individual decorum of naming and feeling can never be totally obeyed, of course, and almost every novelist classifies characters in some onomastic order. Conrad at his strongest does not want to obey the purely individualist decorum; nor does he want to give us some uncanny sense of "depersonalization," as in Dickens and Kafka. He assumes more classically that names and sympathies occur as processes of forceful community rather than of individual freedom: that the person is by definition not exactly an individual. Persons are identified with each other by something other than sympathy, money, or other free transaction. But this is where criticism has always had a tremendous difficulty defining Conrad and his "politics," his "ideas." What is this force of identification? What is his sense of community? There is no one-word answer. He does not define the bond but demonstrates it dramatically. Here, between Winnie and the implicit archetype "Mrs. Kneel," the enslaved wife, the indication of this more forceful identification can be made by giving names which quietly subvert the sense of individuation. Even if the murder scene is funny and parodies Ibsen, the scene with Mrs. Neale demonstrates with demonic compassion how a free, subjunctive, sympathetic speech might conceal a more coercive reality of class identity. Both Winnie and her serving woman are tragically the same woman, not individuals; representation has to dialogize them to each other by forceful *naming* itself—that is, by breaking the rule of individualism implicit in personal naming. This in turn reintroduces an element of the first importance in reading almost all of Conrad, what must be called the "onomastic plot." There is often in Conrad, as in some other novelists, a compellingly irrational field of yoked names (in *Under Western Eyes* we find Rousseau, Razumov, Reason, Russia, and *roseau*, and one might recall Goethe's quadrangle, Otto-Eduard, Otto, Ottilie, and Charlotte, in *Elective Affinities*) which works with the plot and the dialogue to hint at some prior bond among the persons, deeper than anything they elect. What Conrad has to say about Winnie and Mrs. Neale is best said by indicating that they share identity through the binding form of the low pun. Finally, the pun also forces the reader into an uncomfortable "overhearing" by traumatizing the decorum of prose in the novel. Such auditory effects have a secret agency of their own.

The two passages just considered study parallel expressions of "sympathy" by Stevie and Winnie. Stevie's stuttering, a spontaneous animal feeling of connection in suffering, and Winnie's articulate proposition, a fully realized subjunctive sentence, are allied in the same way that she is allied to him—as precocious sister of a retarded brother. Hers is the highest, most rationalized, precocious, and calculated formulation of Stevie's outcry. As the verb is missing from Stevie's outcry, the agency of her more real and more forceful connection to Mrs. Neale is hidden from Winnie.

The main action of the novel—compassion leading to a "frenzy" of destruction—is not however fully explained by these two scenes about sympathy. At the close of the first chapter Conrad gives us the Bacchic plot of the entire novel when he tells us how, at his first job, Stevie touched off fireworks on the staircase, "angry catherine-wheels, loudly exploding squibs." The cause is simple: "two other office-boys in the building had worked upon his feeling by tales of injustice and oppression till they had wrought his compassion to the pitch of that frenzy" (9–10). But why or how does compassion cause destruction? The theme of this novel—and Conrad, despite his conservatism, has much more feeling for this than is commonly recognized—is not the sentimental passion of the men of the *Narcissus* but a more "Bacchic" feeling of collective rage at injustice, which unintentionally compounds the suffering. If, as he tells us in the Note, *The Secret Agent* "can be traced to a period of mental and emotional reaction" (vii), it was a reaction in part against the social vision in *Nostromo*, which almost brought him to a socialist position in spite of himself. Conrad here reacts against that in himself—takes the social rage he himself was always on the verge of feeling, and which comes out in various bitter tirades, to make it criticize itself. The book sets out to *prove* that sympathies can be destructive, and the plot is a demonstration.

The scene that comes closest to explaining how sympathy can destroy is the harsh satire on Heat's apocalyptic vision of the moment of death:

> The Chief Inspector, stooping guardedly over the table, fought down the unpleasant sensation in his throat. The shattering violence of destruction which had made of that body a heap of name-

less fragments affected his feelings with a sense of ruthless cruelty, though his reason told him the effect must have been as swift as a flash of lightning. The man, whoever he was, had died instantaneously; and yet it seemed impossible to believe that a human body could have reached that state of disintegration without passing through the pangs of inconceivable agony. No physiologist, and still less of a metaphysician, Chief Inspector Heat rose by the force of sympathy, which is a form of fear, above the vulgar conception of time. Instantaneous! He remembered all he had ever read in popular publications of long and terrifying dreams dreamed in the instant of waking; of the whole past life lived with frightful intensity by a drowning man as his doomed head bobs up, streaming, for the last time. The inexplicable mysteries of conscious existence beset Chief Inspector Heat till he evolved a horrible notion that ages of atrocious pain and mental torture could be contained between successive winks of an eye. (87–88)

This parody of apocalyptic imagination falls at the center of the novel. Heat, partly named for throwing more heat than light on most of the mysteries he confronts, here becomes an example of the psychology of apocalyptic thought. The scene itself holds together as a mad pastiche, or even a literary Molotov cocktail, of allusions to famous sympathetic scenes, and a crude joke showing what happens when one idiot contemplates the death of another. For the allusions: Stevie is like Pentheus; Heat is a Dickensian, Victorian policeman; the idea that sympathy is fear reduces Aristotelian tragic emotion into one selfish panic; there is a Flaubertian style of banality to the whole organization of Heat's thoughts; and *The Idiot*, not coincidentally, has in its opening pages a similar compassionate meditation by Prince Myshkin on the instant of death by guillotining.[20] Against this network of allusions, there is the organizing temporal joke: Stevie was "slow," retarded, and Heat now, not too quick himself, looking at the fragments of the corpse, imagines a slowing up of mental time until it becomes hell. The prose slows up idiotically—"popular publications," "dreams dreamed," "life lived"—for a crescendo of journalese melodrama. If chimes elsewhere in Conrad are mostly subtle, here they are strange idiot chimes. Conrad seems to be parodying the "horror" of his own earlier style. He seems to ridicule his own power to fuse so much allusion into a concentrated satire on apocalyptic imagination.

Even if all this ridicule of the visionary imagination seems obvious or heavy-handed, the matter-of-fact reductive announcement, in a little subordinate clause, that "the force of sympathy . . . is a form of fear" should still come as a jolt. The announcement would first of all be less jolting if the word were *pity*. To reduce sympathy to fear is to attack the whole field of actions and processes, and not just one emotion, pity, which can be dismissed as primitive or singular. Sympathy—that is, all of sympathy—is only formalized fear. In the context of the novel this reductive statement is problematic. The objective narrator, as we have seen, later intrudes to say that Winnie was profound to sympathize with Mrs. Neale, but here intrudes to say that sympathy is fear. We immediately see that, irony and reliability aside, this objective judge does not have a logically consistent notion. He, whoever or whatever he is or represents in his judgments, cannot make up his mind about sympathy; sometimes he thinks it is fear, sometimes profundity. About this, he is divided. Nevertheless, it would be hard to overestimate the importance of this bitter definition to the entire novel. Even if we read the scene as being deliberately written from inside Heat's overheated consciousness, and even if we recall that "physiological" reductions of the soul may be the target of satire in this novel, the cynical assertion stands out precisely because it is tossed off in a matter-of-fact dependent clause. If sympathy has no independent station of its own in the psyche, in spite of what many philosophers and artists have wanted to believe, but is only "a form of fear," it becomes much clearer how in direct contradiction to the ethical and aesthetic inclinations of the greatest nineteenth-century English novelists sympathy could in a simply causal way generate catastrophe. This is indeed "a simple tale of the XIX century," since its causality is reductive. The Dickensian ethic that sympathy, kindness, and charity can rescue, in some cases at least, is in fact not simply qualified (as Dickens himself qualified it, worrying that these are too weak to defeat other forces) but directly reversed. Increase in sympathy is increase in fearful action and therefore increase in destruction. This makes for a kind of tragic wit rather than tragicomedy.

Among all these explorations of problematic sympathy, Conrad's most original dramatic ideas show up when he implicitly breaks sympathy down into its component sensory metaphors—imagination, overhearing, and tact—and notices ironically that these do not harmonize, or coincide, but sometimes work against each other. To his dramatic sense, sympathy must be understood not only according to the visual metaphor or "imagination" but also as overhearing. I have already suggested that Winnie, like other Conrad characters, like Conrad himself vis-à-vis languages, and like the reader he posits, is an *"over-hearer"*—that is, someone hyperreactive to sound and to information, who feels overwhelmed by it. Stevie, likewise, except for the cab horse, has his strongest sympathetic overreactions to stories heard rather than things actually seen. If sympathy in the nineteenth century was most often consciously linked to "imagination," Conrad seems more interested in those moments when sympathy takes the form of *"overhearing"*—that is, of trauma to listening. The forced overhearer as the exemplary sympathizer stands outside the context of actual events, but at the same time, and perhaps as a result, amplifies, exaggerates, and overreacts.

Conrad's scenes of sympathy as forced overhearing combine the Greek tragic scene and the romantic feeling for the power of sound into one discerning and critical moment. They simultaneously represent and criticize sympathy as intolerable aural amplification. In classical tragedy there are many scenes of a relatively passive overhearing leading to panic or fragmentation;[21] throughout the nineteenth century there had been an association between the "crowd," the symphonic, and intolerable noise in the historical novel; while from Schopenhauer to Nietzsche there was of course a connection between the "power of music" topos and ideas about the masses and sympathy. The sense that all this is to be understood skeptically and dramatically as a poetics and politics of "overhearing" is Conrad's own. The forced overhearer as the figure at the center of the dilemma of sympathy is one of Conrad's most original conceptions. This difficult idea can perhaps be understood best by a look at "Amy Foster," whose heroine is a weak forebear of Winnie Verloc. That early study (1903) sketches out the contradiction between two kinds of sympathy—imagination and overhearing—in its portrait of an ordinary, even imbecile peasant woman. The narrator, Kennedy, describes Amy:

I don't know what induced me to notice her at all. There are faces that call your attention by a curious want of definiteness in their whole aspect, as, walking in a mist, you peer attentively at a vague shape which, after all, may be nothing more curious or strange than a signpost. The only peculiarity I perceived in her was a slight hesitation in her utterance, a sort of preliminary stammer which passes away with the first word. When sharply spoken to, she was apt to lose her head at once; but her heart was of the kindest. She had never been heard to express a dislike for a single human being, and she was tender to every living creature. She was devoted to Mrs. Smith, to Mr. Smith, to their dogs, cats, canaries; and as to Mrs. Smith's grey parrot, its peculiarities exercised upon her a positive fascination. Nevertheless, when that outlandish bird, attacked by the cat, shrieked for help in human accents, she ran out into the yard stopping her ears, and did not prevent the crime. For Mrs. Smith this was another evidence of her stupidity; on the other hand, her want of charm, in view of Smith's well-known frivolousness, was a great recommendation. Her short-sighted eyes would swim with pity for a poor mouse in a trap, and she had been seen once by some boys on her knees in the wet grass helping a toad in difficulties. If it's true, as some German fellow has said, that without phosphorus there is no thought, it is still more true that there is no kindness of heart without a certain amount of imagination. She had some. She had even more than is necessary to understand suffering and be moved by pity. (108–109)

One half of this description emphasizes sympathy as imagination, the other half sympathy as overhearing. Amy here has been taken, in broad outline, from Flaubert's "Un Coeur simple." Visually, she lacks facial definition. In this she resembles Razumov, and James's Miss Birdseye, who has been eroded down to near facelessness by a life of abstract political sympathies.[22] But the name Birdseye pictures bad sympathy as *far*-sightedness, in the line of Dickens' telescopic philanthropy.[23] Amy's pathetic sympathy, by contrast, is near-sightedness. That is, sympathy as an optical metaphor runs up against extremes of nearness and farness, as in George Eliot. Amy's eyes see not a false philanthropic vista but a close, idiot blur, the domestic sort of "imaginative" fellow feeling indistinguishable from the tears which fill and blur the eyes. Her sympathy resembles Winnie's feeling for Stevie, which obviates the rest of the world. Kennedy closes this study of the optics of "fostering" sympathy with some familiar pieties about the "imagination" as the source of sympathy, a formula which of course Conrad did not himself originate, and which sounds slightly out of place for the character we have in fact just seen. What stands out as more pertinent, terrible, and funny in the paragraph, by contrast, is the alternate strand: how Amy hears. She is phobic about strong sound, cannot stand the brute force in ordinary life's dialogue, and even has trouble starting to speak, stammering at first as if terrified even of her own vocal force. At the only moment of action that matters—when the parrot shrieks for help from the cat—she runs away. This comic nonsense is of course put in by Conrad because it predicts the story's crisis: married to Yanko, she becomes increasingly disturbed by his foreign talk and song, and finally runs away from his calls for help while he dies. Amy's failures imply that if sympathetic sight brings us close enough to establish a quaint, blurry intimacy, what we do when we are then *made to hear* is the dilemma of sympathy. Sympathy as imagination is active; sympathy as overhearing is passive; response to the latter decides real action for the former. Sympathy in the metaphors of literary philosophy may be primarily "imagination," but in drama, and in the structure of information in the world, it is overhearing. As a result, "sympathy," understood in fiction both as imagination and overhearing, may become a contradiction between two senses, or two faculties. Further, sympathy as overhearing contradicts itself; the sensitivity of sympathetic natures makes them unable to act sympathetically.

Sympathy as imagination contradicts itself as nearness and farness; sympathy as overhearing contradicts itself as compassion and terror; and the two, imagination and overhearing, are themselves in disaccord. One is mental, the other is dramatic. There is, however, a third sense, ideally supposed to mediate these disorders of sympathetic proportion: "tact." [24] As in the series "to make you hear, to make you feel—before all, to make you see," touch seems to occupy the mediating or middle position between the violently discordant claims for priority of seeing and hearing. Tact ought to be the sense of sympathy as coherence. If feeling could do this, then we would have a *careful* romanticism of sensible feeling. This is, predictably enough, where a certain kind of congenial, tactful narrator should come in. Tact is the ideal organizational force of Kennedy's speech, of the older Marlow's speeches in *Chance*, and of the English narrator's speech in *Under Western Eyes*. Such narrators, ideally, have divided imaginations, and suffer intolerable overhearings, but manage to come out not on top but in the human, organizing middle by tact. It is sometimes Conrad's object in his later works—reputedly sentimental but deservedly popular—to represent narrative sympathy as a principle of postponing tact. The idea of tact itself is a function of forced dialogue in part; often by tact in social conversation we mean knowing the skill of not obviously forcing either oneself or the other in speech and yet making it happen. Tact is the navigation of the reality of forced dialogue somewhere between bad "familiarity" and confessionalism on the one hand and complete silence on the other. Tact, suspense, delay in telling the reader everything, and modification of the forced dialogue are therefore part of the same idea. We see here where time and forced dialogue may meet in the postponing structures of Conrad's novels. But all of this is an idealism. The later Conrad tries to give "tact" a narrative structure of its own, and to turn time ingenuities into graceful modes of tactful postponement. He tries to teach us that suspense itself should become a variety of tact—of not forcing the truth out too quickly. But none of this applies to *The Secret Agent*, which is, and must be, not so much a "detached" work as a necessarily tactless and outrageous work about contactless people. Tragedy is of course the least tactful, most invasive form of drama, given over by its very structure to violent interference and breaches of privacy, the genre with the least concern for touch, or for "touching" the reader's feelings. Whatever else it is, a comic amusement to some or a real tragedy to others, no one would say that *The Se-*

cret Agent is "touching." But *Chance,* and perhaps also *Victory,* try to be touching, and that is probably the main reason for their place in Conrad's works both as his first best sellers and as books his "serious" critics tend to dismiss. The dismissal is not always fair—touch is not the strong suit of modern criticism—and Conrad's own motives in later life for softening his powers of tragic inquiry into caressive tact are understandable efforts at a late romance. But it has to be admitted that when he makes tact the central question he sometimes becomes silly. Conrad even tells us in the odd preface to *Victory* that Lena had her genesis when in the South of France he saw a girl being cruelly pinched (xvii). But the pinched Lena and the destroyed Winnie have something in common: Conrad hates the tactless structure of inquiry itself which he at the same time identifies with telling.

This reading has just described the fragmentation of sympathy into three different sensory metaphors. The important point in Conrad's own sensibility is that these three do not simply or easily integrate. They are not "organically" part of a unified whole. Tact may be opposed to imagination, imagination to overhearing, and so on. They are at most *dramatically* integrated by the principle of conscious force in human relations: "to make you hear, to make you feel—before all, to make you see." Conrad's tragic critical inquiry into the fragments of sympathy reveals that even the three types of sympathy are out of sympathy with, and in competition with, each other, not in accord. "Sympathy," then, as one of the complex words of *The Secret Agent,* is not one thing but many different functions which can and must be considered, represented, criticized separately. In this way also the book tends to show that sympathy is fragmentation. If sympathy cannot even hold itself together, how can it be expected to hold the world together? Or is it necessary that sympathy be as broken as its object? As in Conrad's famous sentence, what binds or makes for solidarity is not sympathy but some kind of "making" as "contractual force," like that which shows up in the scene of coercive dialogue. Sympathy itself is ontologically anarchic, an appealing principle of fragmentation, not wholeness. But the world in fact is "organized" not as sympathy but as a temporal series of forced contracts and forced dialogues. What Hagan called the "design" of *The Secret Agent* as a series of political and marital interviews is in fact this final idea. Forced dialogue—coercive inquiry, not sympathy—is the effective agency of personal relations, political relations, and dramatic construction—the not entirely secret spring of dramatic events.

In *Bleak House* benevolent sympathy opposes the fragmenting powers of the Chancery state. Domestic kindness is partly defeated, partly victorious. Throughout, Dickens sustains a conflict between the inquisitorial-legal Chancery and sympathetic family efforts to ameliorate that system. Particularly through Richard's death, Dickens seems to conclude that benevolence often can do nothing against the state. Jarndyce as Richard's foster parent can't finally protect him from the destructive effects of the Chancery system, but the novel doesn't conclude that Jarndyce's benevolence and kindness are secret agents of that system, or that his fostership and charity themselves help to destroy Richard.

Conrad read *Bleak House*—the book that *The Secret Agent* rewrites and modernizes along with *The Bacchae*—repeatedly. This was not only because of its greatness as a novel but for the personal reason that Jarndyce's fostership of Richard, who wavers among careers while hoping for his inheritance, and finally dies "of" Chancery, has some strong parallels to Conrad's early, difficult relation to his uncle, Tadeusz Bobrowski. There is as a result a strong autobiographical allusion when Conrad brings in *Bleak House* near the end of *A Personal Record*—a book largely about himself as an orphan with some baffled but caring advisers. In Conrad's life, however, the choice made to rebel against Bobrowski's direction and go to sea led, after nearly fatal scrapes, to success. He chose to abandon Poland and, to a large extent, his uncle's advice, and it worked. In one way, then, the experience of Conrad's youth affirms *Bleak House*'s stock verdict: choose a career and stay with it. But in another more important way it refutes *Bleak House* on the issue of fostership. In Dickens, tragic young Richard "should have" listened to Jarndyce, though of course Dickens makes it clear why he does not. The contrary verdict of Conrad's experience was that his uncle's fostership, no matter how well meant, was limited, off key, or even dangerous to his temperament. In his own life, then, Conrad acted successfully against sympathetic fostership. By killing Richard, Dickens shows that a foster parent can see clearly; by killing Stevie, Conrad shows how even the most near and familiar fostership—Winnie's sisterly sympathy—can be fatal.

Conrad does this through a very specific use of Euripides, and of tragic condensation, *against* Dickens. He abstracts and condenses the long Dickensian novel down to the length and form of the Euripidean tragic drama, focused, like much of Euripides, on "pity." In keeping with this he fills the novel, as we've seen, with the most elementary speech repetitions as indications of bathos: repetitious stutters of compassion, a device both these forebears drew on as part of the craft of mimetic tragedy. But Conrad then uses the Euripidean plot against Dickens' conclusions, by sharpening the sense of causality, to realize the idea that sympathy itself causes the tragedy: it is the effective cause and not only the permeating affect. As maenads of pity and charity,

Winnie and her mother involuntarily help to kill Stevie, driven not by intoxication but by pity. Winnie's mother leaves a vacuum in the home through her politic withdrawal, and Winnie carefully brings Stevie and Verloc together. Moved to secret action by pity Winnie gently "forces" Stevie and Verloc into a father-son relation: their companionship is her work. She persists in pushing them into a dialogue with each other.

If we can't decide whether the Verlocs are comic or tragic, it's partly because Conrad has deliberately violated and fused the rules of forced dialogue as they relate to tragedy and comedy. In tragedy, the state has a final right to inquire violently into families—to throw open the doors. If that remains an invasion, not an innocent act, nevertheless the violation of family privacy by the state is justified, because the family has in fact broken taboos or laws. By contrast, in one type of comedy at least, the family or group may be zany, may appear to be in violation of taboos, but in fact is not. It is merely outrageous or bizarre or confused or, in modern American lingo, "weird." In a typical closure to the comedy of the grotesque or zany group, an authority figure enters, after the audience has witnessed a complication, and tries to inquire, to find out what has happened in his absence, and why. The audience is made to feel with pleasure that it understands, but that the interrogator will never untangle the order of private events just seen, and that it's none of his business anyway. Comedy, from this angle, is the genre that fends off the state's forced examination of the family or group, which despite all appearances is in fact innocent. The social point in this kind of comedy is that a family or group, by its very status, has a right to a great degree of irregularity, of idiosyncrasy, of inviolable private language, defended against forced dialogue. The family resists superfluous external inquiry into its constitution. Even in Dickens, whatever is wrong with them, most of the eccentrics have a right to their special languages, which baffle the stuffed shifts in authority. But the Verlocs are a powerfully disturbing family because, very simply, we can't place them: it isn't clear where they belong in the order of forced dialogue. Winnie's domestic "contract with existence" is itself forced, and she experiences it, wrongly, as free sympathy—forced dialogue disguised as sympathetic and free contractuality. Existence is for her a political family contract that breaks down when real political action comes in to expose it. When Stevie is killed, we hear: "She had her freedom. Her contract with existence, as represented by that man over there, was at an end."

Forced dialogue here subsumes all other relations. We seem to be shown first that the process of inquiry itself, by various forms of the state, is the sinister contaminant of the family; but then it seems equally true that the state has not exactly polluted them arbitrarily from the outside but instead only illuminates the forced structure they have made for themselves. They themselves have been a forced dialogue: their bathetic private language weakly mimics the state's sympathetic-coercive political order. Any tragic "dialectical" tension between state and family threatens to collapse if both state and family have analogous forced dialogical orders. But does this family deserve or invite annihilation for that? The novel's refusal to decide this question makes the book what it is. Certainly the Verlocs are not fully "innocent," any more than the investigation of them is: Verloc's political work is stupid and cowardly; Winnie's manipulation of life is bad family politics. They are an unhappy, funny, and ugly family to start with. The disorder in their time relations implies incestuous distortion, with no clear generations but a kind of age blur from the mother to Verloc to Winnie to Stevie. But for all this, nothing would have happened without Vladimir's primary imposition, the embassy inquiry into Verloc's home and "fat-pig" activities; and each time another inquiry is conducted, or someone in authority enters the Verloc home to objectify the mood of inert domestic forced dialogue, the annihiliation of the family comes closer. We might say that the plot of the book is this: tragic inquiry causes the death of a low comic family. They have nothing to offer against—nothing with which to fend off—the state's inquiry except weaker forced dialogues which they misconstrue as "sympathy." The world is a totality of pseudosympathetic forced dialogues, domestic and political. The dialectic here drowns in forced dialogic; inside the family, and outside from the state, this dialogic shapes all relations. It subsumes what is experienced as domestic sympathy. The family has no comic, lively, or sentimental language of its own—like the domestic, sympathetic languages in *Bleak House* which oppose Chancery inquisition—to set against state-forced dialogue. The domestic dialogue order is only a weak imitation of the "familiar" investigatory scene. The novel is an "investigation of investigation": investigation itself, the necessary forced order, seems finally to have caused the tragedy it exposes. Fiction, as an "art" or craft or method, does not stand outside this Oedipal (in Sophocles' sense) order. "Man may smile and smile, but he is not an investigating animal. He loves the obvious. He shrinks from explanations. But I will go on with mine."

One last thing needs to be said about Conrad's stake in the tragicomedy of Stevie's death, the "absurd explosion" which earlier in this chapter was identified as a mixed allusion to Euripides and Dickens.

There is one major comic element in Stevie's death—the means of his identification afterward—not found in either forebear. Winnie has sewn an address label into his coat so that if he gets lost someone will direct him home—a ridiculously ingenious clue. Inspector Heat finds the scrap among the fragments. This leads—if we can treat *The Secret Agent* itself as a story needing some absurdly oblique detection of our own to find Conrad's autobiographical stake—to a last famous scene, in which a young man torn apart is identified by a coat. It's obvious: in Genesis, Joseph's brothers sell him into exile and bring their father the envied coat dipped in goat's blood, and Jacob laments that his son Joseph has been "rent in pieces." This last ancestor of the story of Stevie's disintegration has no meaning to the novel as a novel: but it is important if we want to understand the element of autobiography, and the wild laughter in the tragedy. Jacob's lament is pitiful, but there is the secret romance irony that Joseph has in fact not been torn in pieces but is instead in exile, where he'll prosper and become the provider. If names are for Conrad carefully considered, perhaps his ordinary first name, Józef, had more importance for him than the more obviously allegorical name Konrad. The Joseph pattern in Genesis, not the epic story of Konrad, seems in fact closer to his life: though torn in pieces psychically, he managed to survive and then achieve mastery in exile. When he first chose his pen name, it perhaps meant for him that he would be the Konrad, or Polish hero, who was a Joseph, or successful exile.

Stevie, then, as an autobiographical deflection, is tragic but funny. His death *mis*represents the comic fact that the young Józef Korzeniowski himself didn't die but survived the political destruction of his immediate family. Stevie's idiocy and the confusion of his age represent Conrad's actual childhood and lack of political understanding when his parents died. Within the novel's plot, the "mystery of identity," the corpus delicti problem, is solved by the coat, which tells who was killed; but the mystery of the novel's functional identity in relation to its author—who was clearly having a good time writing it—is also solved by this "coat." It is the one detail in the whole book that reminds us of a young "Joseph" who was not killed, and therefore of the author, who otherwise seems to be absent from the book, an omniscient, "scornful and pitying" narrator. There are many novels in which an author invents a destroyed youthful self-image who fails or suicides just where he or she managed to survive. This one marks out, with the actual reverse of detachment, and with a kind of despondent triumph, the line of difference between Conrad and the destroyed idiot Stevie (compare Saint Stephen as young martyr), a line which must have continued to seem to him very hard to draw. Read as a deft composite allusion to Euripides' Pentheus and Dickens' Krook, the explosion gives a glimpse of Conrad's recombinatory power, as it insists on the force of low tragedy and the bathos of political reality. But read with the Joseph story also in mind, it becomes something else in addition. The pitying and laughing author has a secret stake in the work. He wrote the book as a Joseph, or exiled survivor of a family destroyed from within and without by politics. In the book itself, the family has no such survivor.

V

The Anti-Conversational Novel:
Under Western Eyes

AMONG CONRAD'S WORKS *Under Western Eyes* is the most consistent presentation of the logic of forced dialogue. The action draws attention steadily away from rhetorical persuasion toward an alternate set of "political language arts": making people talk; overhearing, involuntarily and as a spy; calculated silences; interpreting silences; renaming oneself; and causing deafness by "detonating" the eardrums. Listed, this sounds a lot like the old dialogue repertoire of spy melodramas and realpolitik intrigues, and in some sense it is, deliberately; but the novel has in fact been arranged to contemplate this order of melodramatic scenes with an unexpectedly abstract power. The idea of dialogue that emerges is nonconversational, that much is obvious; nonrhetorical, if we define rhetoric as requiring some initially voluntary association and identification between speaker and listener; and finally even nondramatic, as a meditation on the political order of coercion to speak. The novel undermines conventional dialogue categories to make them all appear as the sublimated expressions of coercive dialogic, which itself becomes the final aesthetic object. In Razumov's life the conversational, the rhetorical, and the dramatic appear as illusory expressive surfaces of a constant reality of forced participation. The dialogue plot is that he is forced to talk with everyone he meets but is simultaneously prevented from conversing or arguing freely with anyone. He is repeatedly unable to escape the bare reality of imperative participation in dialogues that have no real final category except their own forcedness. He is Conrad's purest image of the forced speaker and listener. Conrad's most difficult objective is to make this seem more sadly ordinary than thrillingly coercive, so that Razumov becomes not only a great figure in the line of ordinary heroes but an unusual critique of the "thrilling" aura of coercive drama.

To begin simply and rehearse the novel's action by focusing on the "gridlock" of forced dialogue scenes in his life: he is the unacknowledged bastard son of a Russian prince who never sees him but gives him support enough for marginal survival. "Razumov" (like Dostoevsky's "Razumihin") connotes Reason, and as the novel opens, he is a solitary, profoundly lonely university student, looking forward to examinations and to writing a scholastic essay for a silver prize medal. As someone vaguely outcast who wants to rise by writing in academic forms, he obliquely resembles Rousseau, who wrote his first prize essay relatively late, and perhaps, more obliquely, the younger Dostoevsky and Conrad himself. At the start, then, Razumov welcomes the ordinary forms of forced discourse that make up "education." He sees them as his planned route out of poverty, and we get the sense that this attitude signifies his normality, and that he has every reason to be hopeful about making an academic name. This is one of the novel's apparently mild but in fact stark ironies: though scholastic examination is the ostentatiously "rational" form of forced dialogue, it is sadly unreasonable, childishly fantastic, to rely on it, or place one's expectations there, if the world in fact takes shape as a far more political and total forced dialogue into which one is thrown. In fact, the two forms Razumov encounters at the start—school examination and political inquisition—are incommensurate, disproportional: school examination doesn't begin to anticipate the force of political anacrisis. In the next scene, when Haldin comes to his room after the assassination and naively forces Razumov to talk, making him a post facto accomplice, he propels Razumov from forced dialogue as innocent scholastic examination into the unlimited "experience" of political forced dialogue.

Each makes ideological statements during their talk, but Razumov is right when he later defensively corrects Mikulin: "He talked and I listened. That is not a conversation" (92). Razumov, feeling himself linked by this nonconversation to the assassination, at first decides to help Haldin escape. He goes out to find the peasant driver Ziemianitch for the scheduled getaway, and we have a scene of purely physical forced dialogue. Ziemianitch is in a drunken coma—an extreme and tragicomic arrest, meant to be allegorical of the Russian peasant's historical stasis—and Razumov in despair beats him furiously, but can't wake him up to speak or drive. After this failure with the symbolically immobile peasant, Razumov converts, during a strained, rationalized inner dialogue, to the principle of czarist autocracy, and decides it is supremely right to betray Haldin. To do this, however, he has to violate the central taboo of his life by going to his father to force an interview. First horrified at his bastard son's arrival, the father, having heard him through, agrees that he did right, and they go together to report. Haldin is arrested, interrogated, and executed.

Razumov's academic plans are wrecked in spite of his safe negotiation of this crisis. Fellow students believe he was Haldin's coconspirator, and they force him into degrading pseudorevolutionary dialogues about his heroic role; at the same time, the state police, having smelled a potential lifelong Judas in him, want him for the intelligence. Mikulin, obviously under orders from General T——, calls him in for an interview. This interview, which is the finale of part 1, is probably the most allusively complete scene of coercion to speak in Conrad, containing the feelings at once of genteel Socratic dialogue, paternalistic sympathy, inquisitorial torture, and job interview. It is a masterpiece of dialogical construction in which many different kinds of coercion to speak—rational-philosophical, theocratic-totalitarian, and mundane-practical—are fused matter-of-factly for a sense that we are overhearing the world's central dialogue form, which for all its inquisitorial mystique is primarily a mode of hiring.

This is Part First. It might be called an exercise in "inquisitorial chamber music." It is clearly both a causal sequence of forced dialogues—the forced dialogue with Haldin leads to the other forced scenes, with Ziemanitch, the Prince, Kostia, and Mikulin—and a juxtaposition of the varieties of forced dialogue. Conrad described it as the inspired section. The rest of the novel develops the same theme. Parts Second and Third—a series of "many conversations" (237) which seems oddly vised between the more violent parts 1 and 4—set Razumov in Geneva, ostensibly a place of free political expression, where he engages in slow, sometimes funny, sometimes almost unreadable, always inescapable political "conversations" with various real and bogus revolutionaries around the Menippically named Boulevard des Philosophes. These sections revise what Turgenev called "smoke"—frustrated exiles' talk. While alluding to Turgenev's lyricism, they subvert his tone by an imposition of the crude framing fact that Razumov, having accepted Mikulin's offer to become "intelligence," is now a forced spy among his interlocutors. The power of the "many conversations" in Parts Second and Third comes less from their specific ideological content than from the various ways in which Razumov is forced to hear it all out and to let others speak while remaining as silent as possible. The revolutionaries misread his silences. "Conversations" is an ironic designation for these masquerades, in which the involuntary spy pretends to be a mysteriously silent revolutionary leader.

As the tempo slows painfully in these parts, Conrad also introduces the portrait of the revolutionary amanuensis Tekla, and through her the image of forced writing. Tekla, modeled partly on Sonia in *Crime and Punishment,* is the novel's insulted and injured, but her brand of prostitution is to take dictation daylong in a statuary, frozen posture from Peter Ivanovitch, a radical feminist author, who insists that she stay motionless while he composes. She is not as disillusioned, however, by this abuse, or coerced arrest, as by her discovery that his writing, which sounds like free inspiration, is forced, strained, rewritten. Beyond the interest of this in the line of images of abject scriveners, Tekla is in the novel for the same reason that Mrs. Neale is in *The Secret Agent:* her writing slavery resembles Razumov's forced spy writing, much as Mrs. Neale's servility is a metaphor for Winnie's, or the sterile beasts of burden in *Nostromo* resemble Emilia Gould.

The main action closes with Razumov's attempt to break out of this forced language totality by a confession. The afternoon before the confession, writing a spy report under a statue of Rousseau, he clearly resembles Tekla, forced to write under Peter. During this meditation, shaped as a forced dialogue with the self, he is implicitly weighing, among other things, whether to coax Natalie Haldin to meet and talk with Peter. Razumov has the spy's obligation and the lover's power to effect this: to force her into an implicitly obscene dialogue (though all this, like the pattern of forced dialogue, is never overstated). This is the major, rarely noticed "forced dialogical" crux of the resolution: Natalies has in fact gone once reluctantly to visit the revolutionary grotesques, has instead talked with Tekla, seen her mistreatment, felt revulsion, and left. So far she is innocent—that is, she has not been forced to speak with Peter. The whole is presented, in a sexual way not unlike that of Dickens in *Little Dorrit,* as a matter of subtle pimping. She is rescued not from rape but from debasing coercion to speak when Razumov protects her from this lowest forced dialogue by his confession to her. But he is still undecided whether to confess when he goes to the little island to write reports under the statue of "the author of the *Social Contract*" (291). The statue itself, a persecutory muse, is Conrad's harshest image of the world order as arrested freedom, and of his own condition as a forced writer.[1] Under this statue Razumov argues with himself: as in Decoud's suicide, even a talk with oneself is in reality shaped by outside forces.[2] The course and terms of his decision are not shown clearly, but later that evening he confesses twice. "Nikita nicknamed Necator," after punching out and "detonating" both his eardrums, boasts that Razumov will never talk or listen again. In contradiction to this boast, the last news of Razumov puts him in

Russia, talking with the more lowly and implicitly more authentic revolutionaries, who now see him as a martyr for having confessed voluntarily to them as well as to Natalie. We hear that these last talks occur, but get no details.

In its framing, the novel starts with two bomb "detonations" in the snow and ends with two "detonations" of Razumov's ears.[3] Double detonation, like two raps of a drum, makes for a percussive, ironically "musical" opening and closure. Another symmetry, less obvious but more profound, is that Parts First and Fourth are full of coercive dialogic—inquisitorially violent—while Parts Second and Third, between them, are made up of philosophical and ideological talk that is less obviously forced.This framing of political philosophy (Parts Second and Third) within coercive dialogue drama (First and Fourth), as if the Boulevard des Philosophes (political discussion) were only a scene imbedded in the more forceful patterns of terror, inquisition, and confession, is one of the most important structural gestures of the novel.

This summary of the action highlights forced dialogical turning points; but I think that these are, more than in any other of Conrad's works, the plot itself, and that they should indicate that Conrad here has finally found the pure story of forced dialogue for which he had been looking. The story *is* the tale of how one forced dialogue leads to another until a final deafening "detonation" that makes clear the meaning of the word *detonation* itself. As a dialogue novel, *Under Western Eyes* resembles some brilliant minor works by other writers also more famous for other things—Goethe's *Elective Affinities*, Turgenev's *Smoke*, James's *Awkward Age*—works in which power struggles infiltrate apparently gentle conversations. But *Under Western Eyes* differs from that conventional irony by its much more absolute forced negativity of dialogue form. Conrad amplifies James's "question of our speech" into a steady political negation of the ideal of conversation. There is the assassination, and Razumov falls in love with Natalie; but nothing else, by the ordinary standards of adventure and romance, happens. The entire book can only be called a set of anti-conversations—scenes of apparent talk which come about asymmetrically and by force—and in which it is made persistently clear that though there is no conversation, any one anti-conversation will lead to and resemble others it produces.

Some major issues regarding this novel about which critics have long been quarreling can be redefined through this perspective. The deliberate resemblance of *Under Western Eyes* to *Crime and Punishment* has to be grasped as part of a "forced dialogue" with Dostoevsky, intentionally presented as such, as I shall show. And the word-weary narrator, the tired old language teacher, whose purpose has often been debated, also illuminates the order of forced dialogue. First of all he flattens the prose style into a documentary tone without much dialect or other dialogue fun so that instead the *forms* of dialogue can be seen bare. Though he tells us that he is both a polyglot and a naif, the surface of his prose is neither; he writes a careful standard English that allows for the abstraction of drama. In a deeper and more personal way, however, he himself mediates between the "English" idea of humane conversation and the "Russian" reality of coercive dialogic. As the story progresses, "England" and "Russia," the imaginary places of conversation and of forced dialogue, are gradually brought together in his own conflicted person. Though he protests that he finds violent Russian speech manners alien and incomprehensible, the protest seems at least a little forced or dishonest as it turns out—though not until page 187—that this "Englishman" spent his childhood in St. Petersburg. Like his inventor, he remains elusive about his own nationality while being convinced that nationality is the determining factor in others. This duplicity enables him to personify what is in Conrad and in us a split response to and feeling about forced dialogue. In the world he reluctantly describes, scenes of conversing as spying, making the other talk, interpreting silences, acquiring documents, and so on far outnumber scenes of conversation or persuasion. The "English" part of him repeatedly insists that this world is insane and incomprehensible, and the "Russian" part of him seems to feel that it is so familiar as to be boring. The narrator allows Conrad to assume—half praising, half blaming—that the particular English audience reading in 1912 or 1913 somehow knows little or nothing about, or repressively forgets, the repertoire of forced speech; believes that dialogue is essentially conversation; has, like the narrator, drolly timid ideas of what it means to *force* the other to talk;[4] and must be carefully guided through such an anti-conversational world of force and silence. At the same time, through him Conrad suggests that under masks of quiet astonishment everyone knows this scene too well. The narrator duplicates the lifelong mixed politeness which Conrad personally assumed, forcibly political, and approximately insulting. He is close to Conrad's own mask, a stiffly conversational tone alluding ironically to its own origins in forced dialogue. Through him the novel finds an extraordinary tonal triumph, making coercion to speak at once "thrilling" and "boring." As someone who hides, and hides from, the fact that he grew up in Russia (put abstractly, that his polite conversational manners have their origins in forced dialogue), he reflects the desire to make and sustain a distinction between humane conversation and inquisition. But his own comical consciousness, divided between an assumed conversational gentility and a real personal knowledge of inquisitorial force which he tries to forget—a struggle which has tired him out into a "documentary," matter-of-fact, informational voice, a voice that goes flat and resigned whenever it faces its own origins—is split in two. He expresses both naive surprise at force in discourse and final boredom with it; amazement and weariness; irreconcilable notions—that the inquisitorial is inaccessibly strange and that it is overfamiliar. The narrator, by this conflict, allows Conrad to posit, but then cancel, the alleged gap between Eastern and Western speech worlds.

In political melodramas—perhaps also in Foucault's writing[5]—the scene of coercion to speak or write is usually supposed to thrill the audience, and it does so, as we shall see in Chapter VI, partly by exploiting preconscious awareness of the scene of coercion to speak as Oedipal. Conrad's genius here discloses the Oedipal pattern of self-destructive inquiry beneath ordinary conversation, but at the same time refuses to exploit that insight for politically sensationalistic thrills. But this description makes the achievement seem a little more coldly controlled, perfect, and ahistorical than it is. Throughout the novel Conrad himself, still at work on this dialogical theme, has a contradictory intention: somewhat as in *Nostromo*, he can't decide whether to write a historical novel (as he ambiguously asserts in the Author's Note[6]) about a unique local nightmare, his idea of Russia as "the horror," or to picture a more abstract, intuitive, universal fact of dialogue itself, which is only made clearest for him within "Russian" relations, and which itself "returns upon" the Western scene of speech. Though it would be easy to fall into a long disquisition on whether forced dialogue is logocentric—that is, whether Conrad makes coercive force in dialogue the pessimistic proof of speech as presence—that would be the wrong question to ask. Our first question, like his, has to be historical and dialogical, not deconstructive or philosophical. Does the novel here primarily display a Russian anomaly, as he probably first intended, or did he once again, with dangerous self-critical honesty,[7] write himself into a corner, describing "all dialogue" as somehow essentially coercive, and therefore his own condition as a contractually "Western" author also? Or does he leave the novel open, so that both interpretations, as Russian history and as dialogical universal, work disconcertingly together?

This problem of forced dialogue as either a universal logic or a local reality has to take precedence over a reading of the book as another satire on political rhetoric. On the novel's first page, the idea that political language is "all" only endless rhetoric is presented as a commonplace, a sort of weary banality, by the tired language-teacher narrator. "Words, as is well known, are the great foes of reality." This proposition is not the novel's moral served up at the start. Like the narrator, we begin with a knowledge of the rhetorical indifference of words, but we still go on receiving and compiling the documents, and taking a forced part in various language scenes. "Responsibility" is consciousness of this "forced dialogue," and not of rhetorical illusions alone. The classical opposition between words and realities becomes, it is hinted, a half-truth if the forced speech scene is ignored. It is "well known," perhaps in the Shakespearean sense that certain half-true, tired commonplaces are well known: "All this the world knows well" (Sonnet 129). As in *Hamlet*, dismissal of words is itself a melancholy assertion in context, a pathos, a forced speech act, dramatized as taking place within a violent political dialogic, which itself includes a lot of spying, interrogating, and overhearing. This dismissal of words can become a denial of the context of force—a retreat into sighing. Conrad's narrator, when he complains of the inconsequence and irreality of "words" himself makes that somewhat banal complaint inside a political force field, within a relay of texts, documents, and reports. The differences among the scenes in which people happen to be forced to produce (empty) spoken or written language remain, and they retain dramatic interest in spite of grayness and flatness. Knowledge that ideological language can be dissolved into "empty chimes" is expressed in this book as powerfully as in any of Conrad's works, by yet another series of disturbing chimes—Razumov, Russia, Rousseau, reason, and *roseau*. But the novel's dialogues imply that such a knowledge of the unreality of ideological terms does not derealize the forced dialogical relations in which they are produced.

The novel concludes, struggling, that it *may* make a real, concretely historical, limited difference to Razumov (or anyone) in which scene he is forced to speak and write, which social "bargain" he makes. That is, there are limited local differences on the general horizon of forced human relation. These differences cannot be proven or absolutized. They are not Dostoevskian, Russian, Rousseauist, and they yield no complete freedom. Razumov has only a limited forced option, and even when he confesses unexpectedly, under no obvious coercion to do so, he still seems much more limited and constrained than Raskolnikov, of whom he is a revision. His situation is closer to a classical tragic "dilemma," in which both choices are intolerable, than to Raskolnikov's liberation through confession (or to Waverley's dialectical wavering between two somewhat appealing alternatives, romantic rebellion and legal order). That is, Razumov takes no absolute liberty. We are not meant to read his confession in particular or confession in general as achieved community.[8] His confession is not so much an act of pure freedom as one reasonable and admirable, but forced, closure of his own scene of coercion to speak. Implicitly, his original Raskolnikov, of whom Razumov is a trope of coercion, moves through an inwardly and outwardly forced process of confession toward authentic freedom. But Razumov can only choose where to "end" his involuntary "contract"— continuing to be a spy is one choice, a confession interposing himself in the totality of forced dialogue to rescue Natalie from one of its worst aspects is another—and though there remains a sense of moral difference among these choices, it is not as simple, or pleasing, or exciting as a question of achieved spiritual freedom. That this is one main point of the novel in its attempt to revoke Dostoevsky was noted, in somewhat different terms, long ago by Jocelyn Baines.[9] Dostoevskian, "Russian" freedom is refuted. But likewise, the self-congratulatory reading, which would see the novel as a reminder to Western free beings, a warning to us who are so free that we forget the reality of unfreedom, is partial and finally false; the novel is not, in its deepest structure, a reminder that we are forgetfully free in our transcendence, but a reminder that the West's supposed discursive freedom (freedom of speech) is illusory, and has the same final "human" ground of coercion to speak as the dialogue scene in more obviously coercive societies. Though Conrad may have set out at first to paint Russia as radically different from the West, his honest art by the end made Western conversation and Russian inquisition appear—partly through the agency of the narrator, and partly through other devices to be explored—similar. The action argues that one may and should make choices—for "the constitutional bargain" over the autocratic state—but should not deceive oneself about the coercive ground of all relation. And it would be bizarre if Conrad, after writing the books examined in the earlier chapters, were really trying here to present Russia as the unique scene of coerced language.

The intellectual purpose of the novel is therefore to set up a grammar of political language on the ground of coercion to speak, write, and listen, but in a style that criticizes the "grand inquisitorial" tone and the "thrilling" power of this vision as it is usually expressed. The more one knows Conrad's work, the more *Under Western Eyes* becomes a remarkably subtle culmination. But it has obvious flaws in pacing and suspense. If not exactly his best novel, it is probably his clearest and strongest dialogical composition. In what follows I want to look at four specifically dialogical questions: (1) the meaning of the deafening of Razumov; (2) the allusions in the interview with Mikulin and in the dialogues that lead up to it; (3) Conrad's relation to Dostoevsky's dialogues; and (4) the meanings of the scene in which Razumov writes spy reports while sitting under the statue of Rousseau.

The entire action of *Under Western Eyes* moves with a relentlessness unusual even for Conrad toward Razumov's deafening. When Nikita, showing off a hit man's gimmick, punches out Razumov's eardrums, it may look only like Conrad's gimmick also. The action can now close with an allusive poetic dumb show, Razumov wandering Geneva in a "detonated" storm, lightning without thunder. This silenced *Sturm und Drang* is perhaps the clearest expression of middle Conrad's own forcefully muted romanticism. Historically, also, the scene alludes cleverly both backward to the Elizabethan dumb show and forward to the silent film, fusing the past and present of dramatic technique together into a single "detonated" drama: "Silent men, moving unheard, lifted him up, laid him on the sidewalk, gesticulating and grimacing around him their alarm, horror, and compassion. A red face with moustaches stooped close over him, lips moving, eyes rolling. Razumov tried hard to understand the reason of this dumb show" (370). At its most allusive, this mime perhaps prophesies the coming of poetic "imagism" as an ideogrammatic blitz of the reader having a concealed political philosophy of visual force even more violent than that underlying "impressionism."

But the deafening has a much more specific set of meanings as a tragic mutilation within the novel's action. While transferring Oedipus' mutilation from sight to hearing, it makes suddenly clear how, as the novel unfolds, Razumov has a growing figurative or symbolic wish to be deaf—figurative, not physical. Throughout the novel he has been the overhearer, forced to talk with Haldin, Mikulin, and the revolutionaries. During this negative progress he has wanted absolute silence, at least in human relations, to rescue him. Writing his spy reports, he has thought that only "natural" sounds, like wind and water, are tolerable, while "all the other sounds of this earth" bring "contamination to the solitude of a soul" (291). The fantasy of silence is not exclusive to him; it determines the political metaphors of the other characters also. Natalie says, in an unconsciously totalitarian metaphor, "I must own to you that I shall never give up looking forward to the day when all discord shall be silenced" (376). Natalie's mother withdraws into a kind of psychotic silence. The narrator, who calls himself, inaccurately, "a mute witness of things Russian" (381), verbosely attacks words at the start of the novel in a way that is not identical to authorial intention, but instead introduces the theme of hatred for noise and speech as the symptom of a forced dialogical world. The characters have this hatred in reaction: hermeticism, mutism, purism, and so on are not in fact pure but are reactive functions of forced dialogue. They offer total silence as a mystification within the world as forced dialogue. Nikita, the hit man, in an ironic closure, is the one to enact this purist and absolutist ideal.

"(For silences have their character)," we are told during the Mikulin interview (86). Parenthesis is used sparingly in this novel, and this remark has roughly the same place in *Under Western Eyes* as the apparently throwaway remark that "the force of sympathy . . . is a form of fear" in *The Secret Agent.* Far from asserting that Silence is a transcendent good, the whole dramatic texture of *Under Western Eyes* implies that a plurality of silences exists, each with its own character, and that the fantasy of a perfect, indeterminate Silence, the modern fantasy of "perfect detonation," is only a fantasy within the scene of forced dialogue. Conrad wants the reader to attend, as an exercise in poetic and social imagination, to a plurality of dialogized rather than transcendental, mystical, or ineffable silences. The deafening scene is great, for example, not only because of its kinetic conviction and physical precision as a frightening punishment (a kind of grotesque wit), but also because of the fine balance it achieves between the abstract desire for silence as freedom, and the plain reality, even the "pop" brutality, when deafness is physically effected. Silence loses its transcendental aura when physically realized in simple torture. The result is not the ineffable, or the free, but only one more political silence among many, the specific, limited silence when someone's ears are punched out.

The deafening of Razumov, then, is a tragic closure the point of which is that no silence transcends the forced dialogue of which it is a part. This is also why the novel ends with the ostensibly "weak" scene in which we hear that Razumov now chats with the revolutionaries. Nikita's claim to have silenced Razumov totally is his own variant of the illusion of Silence. The picture of Razumov speaking again, though feebly, is meant to detonate the completeness and finality of Nikita's "detonation" (379). The talk continues. Often Conrad's supposedly weak endings are thoughtful triumphs over banal high closure, and here the decrescendo in the last scene, itself delivered to us as supposedly trivial hearsay, is necessary as a criticism of final solutions.

This does not mean, however, that Conrad draws a "sociolinguistics" of plural silences. K. H. Basso writes in that mode: "Although the form of silences is always the same, the function of a specific act of silence— that is, its interpretation by and effect on other people—will vary according to the social context in which it occurs. For example, if I choose to keep silent in the chambers of a Justice of the Supreme Court my action is likely to be interpreted as a sign of politeness or respect. On the other hand, if I refrain from speaking to an established friend or colleague I am apt to be accused of rudeness or harboring a grudge." [10] This is common sense, but not Conrad's theme. His theme is that while characters (and probably Conrad himself as an individual) do attach transcendental, ineffable, and mystical values and expectations to silences, and while these tropes are inordinately powerful, pathetic, and understandable, their ultimate causes are themselves secular. Gould, Nostromo, Winnie, Heyst, and others try to make silence into redemptive strength. Razumov is the starkest of the set, because he is throughout the most fully conscious of the limitation and the forcedness of his own silences, even while he has little recourse but to practice them and to want more from them. To work only as a sociolinguist of silences in dialogue would be paradoxically unrealistic: people do in reality attach transcendental signification to their silences, continually. The contrast between this imaginative signification and the real "contractuality" of each silence is one of Conrad's most uncompromising themes.

If the deafening of Razumov dramatically criticizes the mystical-political desires for Silence throughout the novel, the interview between Mikulin and Razumov absorbs and criticizes all the forced dialogues that precede it in Part First, and becomes Conrad's single most complete scene of forced dialogue. But in order to understand the scene, we should first look at some of the previous dialogues, each of which leads up to and contributes something to the meeting.

Preceding the interview, Kostia, a rich student (Razumov thinks Kostia only wants revolt added to his other thrills, but he may seem more likable and pathetic to most of us), begs "to be of some use" to Razumov, whom he sees as a great revolutionary. He offers to take his father's money to get Razumov safe passage out of Russia. Razumov refuses (later he will accept the offer under government orders to appear revolutionary). The scene is a neat, cold, deliberate travesty of the *Crito*. Razumov is forced to play Socrates, refusing safety, while Kostia insists on seeing him as "a man of ideas—and a man of action too" (81). The more he tries to escape the Socratic role, the more he seems to play it. His refusal of the money only feeds Kostia's idea of his austere courage. As a result of this degraded, coldly Lucianic dialogue (a travesty of the Socratic sublime), in which Razumov cannot converse, argue, or prevent Kostia from misreading him, he concludes that he is now likely to come in for similar "revolutionary" encounters endlessly.

The scene ends with one of the most important sentences in the novel: "He lost all hope of saving his future, which depended on the

free use of his intelligence" (83). Razumov's practical notion of "freedom" is stated here explicitly. The best life, he feels, would be "the free
use of intelligence" that has become for him politically impossible. The
meeting with Kostia shows that Razumov, now conscious of having lost
this possibility, will go to see Mikulin half prepared to sell or reuse his
"intelligence"—that is, to work for the foreign "intelligence." This does
not mean, however, that we are to regard the phrase "free use of intelligence" with easy irony as simple utopian or innocent nonsense, which
Razumov now abandons, or to assume that the word *intelligence* must always be cynically politicized into its lowest meaning as spying. On the
contrary, the phrase captures Razumov's realistic, even morally intelligent, ideal, analogous to the concept of "practical forms of political liberty" (104), which the narrator later brings up against "Nathalie" 's[11]
strong charge that the English parliamentary constitution is only a satanic "bargain." Here the slight contrast or semantic oscillation between Razumov's idea of "free use" and the narrator's idea of "practical
liberty" is worth considering. The narrator's substantive word, or noun,
is *liberty*, with *practical* the modifier. That is, perhaps in the line of J. S.
Mill, he argues that the basis of Western social constitutions is or
should be "liberty"; "practical" only modifies, is open to interpretation,
and can refer either to insidious limitations (resigned demonic bargains, according to Natalie) or, if one likes the phrase, to communal
judgment and common sense about violence toward others. So the
narrator takes a "classical liberal" position. When Razumov, however,
resigns his ideal of himself, he thinks in the even simpler words—
ostensibly similar but in fact reversed—*free use*. The main word or noun
is *use; free* only modifies.

When the narrator describes the social constitution as a whole, the
governing concept is liberty; when the concrete individual thinks of
himself, the governing concept is use. From this we can glean Conrad's
own wavering political notion, to the degree that it is articulated, in its
slight but crucial difference from a libertarian individualism like Mill's,
and its uneasy (for him) proximity to Rousseau. Mill of course celebrates individual variety and the unpredictable rewards of legally allowed difference and idiosyncrasy. Apparently useless freedoms will
turn out, as in a romance, to be of social use, in the final account; if not,
they are still desirable. For Conrad, whatever his sometime desires to
affirm this kind of feeling, as in his attack on the Censor,[12] the intelligent individual, like Razumov, starts instead from the awareness that
the main fact of social life is being used or employed, not freedom of
expression. Whatever he says, in various letters, about his own liberal
sensibility, Conrad in fact lacks any full pleasure in personal idiosyn-

crasy, variety, and freedom for their own sake. By comparison, Dickens loves eccentric variety, and expresses something very like Mill's liberty as multiplicity of character, even though there is also a more tragic undertone of involuntary mechanical diversity. But Conrad is unable to think about liberty at all playfully. He tries, but is temperamentally closer to Rousseau's idea (which he despises) of obligatory freedom, or, less threateningly, to Wordsworth's "stern, independent liberty." [13] So, if we put the two oscillating statements together—"practical liberty" and "free use"—we see that in Conrad's thought "liberty" is the state's negative obligation not to interfere; but usedness is in fact the first term of thoughtful personal existence, not because it ought to be that way but because it is. His aesthetic reflects this: art is not "pure play" but, in a slightly unfamiliar variant of the Kantian aesthetic, "work itself"— work made clear in the abstract as forceful, productive action. Art is almost the abstraction of all other jobs, the communion of all "work." It enacts the pleasure of a pure work with sensory materials for the whole working order of society. This sense of the social contraction in aesthetic activity can be vital, but it is never exactly "playful," and unfortunately (as Conrad knew) never completely joyous or ecstatic.

Having been forced to participate in a debased *Crito* with Kostia, Razumov goes to the interview with Mikulin newly conscious of his unfreedom and half prepared to have his intelligence put to political use. The most important point for us to grasp, however, is that the man he encounters, Mikulin, is himself forced to participate in the dialogue, though we are given only a subtle indication of this, and that as a result Mikulin is himself a mirror image of the forced reuse of intelligence which will be Razumov's fate. In this sense, the two of them stand toward each other in a kind of symmetrical, rather than conscious or sentimental, sympathy. Sympathy itself is redefined, throughout this scene, as common immersion together in forced dialogue, rather than as a psychic capacity, or a detached feeling of understanding for the other. The strongest, most strikingly ironic phrase in the whole portrait of Mikulin is "something resembling sympathy": "In his passionless persistence there was something resembling sympathy" (86). This startling proposition, quietly overwhelming in a novel of harshly repressed ironies, withholds any clear indication whether Mikulin inwardly feels sympathy or not, and thereby puts the reader into an interpretive quandary allied to Razumov's terror of him as an inquisitor. The question of *our* sympathy for Mikulin—our ability to get a hold of his "inner state"—is here raised and left unanswered. He has been constructed to make us as interpretively discomforted as Razumov. The reader trying to operate by the cognitive terms of ordinary dialogical "sympathy" will be defeated. One sympathetic reading will make Mikulin a pensive, compassionate liberal, caught in an autocratic role: his job nullifies the real sympathy he feels. The contrary reading will make him an enlightened despot wearing a calculatedly passive and tragically despondent sympathetic face in order to "snare" Razumov, as Morton Zabel puts it.[14] In that reading, to be anachronistic, he's a sort of Szaszesque shrink. The construction of the scene, however, while it intentionally makes these opposed readings available, bypasses them. The point seems to be a redefinition of "sympathy" itself. Sympathy is not, as in Dickens, a cognitive force futilely opposed to power but a relation that power uses and that power even creates. Nor is aesthetic or psychological sympathy, as is implicit in several things said by both Zabel and Fleishman, a positive mental function, in the service of real "community" or "participation."[15] The strangest irony, and the most difficult to articulate, is that Mikulin's "something resembling [traditional] sympathy" for Razumov *is* "sympathy," restructured. Calculated, genuine, or merely the structural sympathy that stems from their symmetry as forced participants in an anti-conversation—it does not matter. What resembles sympathy here, and what *is* sympathy, what has displaced older sympathy as the energy of meeting, is the pathos of symmetrical forcedness in all human relations, and the power to fix all human relations.

Mikulin's involuntary sympathetic tyranny, and its disorienting effect on the reader's own desire to understand sympathetically, is foreshadowed in the very opening scene by the curious actions of Minister de P—— of the "Repressive Commission" during his assassination. Zabel and Karl note that the scene resembles the murder of Plehve; but the poetic double "detonation" seems to have been taken also from the assassination of the "kindest" and most "liberal" czar, Alexander II, which likewise involved two bombs within minutes, the first unsuccessful, drawing the czar out of his carriage to look after wounded servants, the second successful.[16] After the first "detonation muffled in the multitude of snowflakes" fails to wound him, the man we have been told is a fanatic autocrat, P——, leaves his cab, and, while seeming to appear "there" before us for the first time, says to the crowd surrounding his dying servant, "For the love of God, I beg of you good people to keep off." Then, while he stoops (though he doesn't kneel) over his dying servant, he is killed by the second bomb thrown by Haldin (7–10).

These unexpected sympathetic details can serve as opening dramatic hints about the novel's entire attitude toward the disjunction between sympathetic and political representation. Almost certainly, Conrad wants the reader to despise P—— as an exemplary absolutist despot, perhaps of the kind who tormented Conrad's parents. His moral monstrosity as recorded by the narrator is to be believed. Yet Haldin kills P—— just after he has mentioned the "love of God" and "begged" the crowd (which we would expect him to hate), calling them "good people." The speaking mass murderer in his last moments seems also to have "something resembling sympathy." These gestures, disturbingly—or is it ludicrously?—almost add up to a conventional moment of grace. Haldin, then, is no Hamlet: he kills his Claudius however he finds him. And we could be satisfied with this as a moral ambiguity and elusive mystery, adding to a general sense of "Russian tragedy." But as with Claudius, there is no real hint here that P—— is really a "good soul," or that the reports about him were wrong. A contrary, sharper reading suggests that Conrad is jeering at Tolstoyan, Dostoevskian, "Russian" pseudo-complexity about moral monsters and their final moments of repentant grace. This sort of thing, for Conrad, is a little belated. It is cant. He includes the Christian gestures of P—— in the midst of crisis not so much to make P—— pious as to remind us that P—— and Haldin are symmetrical, both theocratic madmen. In the two of them, he finds a Russian symmetry of absolutist imagination, whose gestures of sympathy are themselves grotesque. Haldin's bomb kills a comrade whose sheepskin coat can signify either his Christianity or his naivety and *bêtise*. The final reason for all this ambiguous imagery is not to set the reader into a vaguely "complex" moral, religious, political quandary but to introduce, at the start of the novel, a representational dilemma: that the modes of political representation available—melodramatic dialogue and documentary reporting—are grossly inadequate, even when they are combined or carefully syncopated, and that traditional "sympathy" between the characters or on the reader's part is not adequate to the political question. It would be false, sentimental, to assume that P——'s "last spoken words" somehow count more than his acts. But they suggest that he—like Mikulin—is a figure not knowable by sympathetic representation because he is immersed in some power field that makes "sympathy" itself over into something else.

Though the necessary spotlight on Razumov's dread of him makes Mikulin's own forced condition hard to see, and gives him an aura of omnipotence, the prior action in fact specifically tells us that Mikulin acts not on his own but under orders from General T——. He is melancholy, heavy, and unclear, partly because he is himself forced into the dialogue. In an earlier scene, when Razumov, blinded by fear, believed that he was primarily a suspect, he failed to see that in fact General T—— was sizing up his malleability, not his guilt. "Mr. Razumov is quite safe with me. I am interested in him. He has, it seems, the great and useful quality of inspiring confidence" (49). The heavy irony on the word *interest* is T——'s, not Conrad's. Whether General T—— suspects Razumov or not is of no consequence; he sees that he might get Razumov to reenact the present scene of betrayal perpetually. The reuse of Razumov is determined at this moment of T——'s "interest"; it is clear that T—— instructs Mikulin to interview him, and almost as clear that Mikulin somehow does not want to.

If, no matter how terrific he seems to Razumov, Mikulin himself is only involuntarily engaged in a forced dialogue ordered by General T——, and is forced to force Razumov to talk, then the main irony about Mikulin is that his aura of absolute fatal power derives from his own powerless fatalism. This fatalism is expressed by his broken syntax, aposiopeses, aborted clichés, such as, "Religious belief, of course, is a great—" (90). His final verdict of infinite incompletion, "Where to?" articulates not only a main truth of the novel but also his own resignation and entrapment.[17] The whole scene, then, is somewhat less Kafkaesque or uncanny, and more concerned to outline a clear dialogical symmetry of forcedness, than comparison to other nightmares in modern inquisitorial fiction might lead us to think. Mikulin is immersed symmetrically in the same forced dialogue with his interviewee. As Razumov could not explain himself to Kostia, Mikulin cannot explain himself to Razumov. The whole scene, with remarkable compositional restraint, balances Razumov's apprehension of Mikulin as absolute power against Mikulin's reality as an interviewer quietly and resignedly forced to force his subject to speak.

Dostoevsky describing Porfiry Petrovich pictures a shrewd comedian, a Menippean Socrates in "a dressing-gown" and "trodden-down slippers," "stout even to corpulence," with "a large round head, particularly prominent at the back. His soft, round, rather snubnosed face was of a sickly yellowish color, but had a vigorous and rather ironical expression." He has a piercing expression "strangely out of keeping with his somewhat womanish figure," and so on.[18] When Conrad describes Mikulin, who is a revision of Porfiry, he gives his figure a more burdened quality, making him a heavily, rather than playfully, Menippean Socrates.

There was nothing formidable about the man bearing that name. His mild, expectant glance was turned on the door already when Razumov entered. At once, with the penholder he was holding in his hand, he pointed to a deep sofa between two windows. He followed Razumov with his eyes while the last crossed the room and sat down. The mild gaze rested on him, not curious, not inquisitive—certainly not suspicious—almost without expression. In its passionless persistence there was something resembling sympathy. (86)

The penholder signifies the forced writing that pervades the whole novel (later Razumov will be writing forced spy reports to Mikulin). Razumov, the future forced writer, here becomes, grammatically, "the last," the most abject, crossing the room. As the scene continues, there is an open allusion to Mikulin as a Socrates, so that both Mikulin and Razumov—symmetrical if we recall Kostia's *Crito*—are now involuntary travesties of Socrates, meeting. The two, similarly burdened, are forced together into an autocratic interview: "Razumov noticed a thick forefinger clasped by a massive gold band set with a blood-red stone— a signet ring that, looking as it would weigh half a pound, was an appropriate ornament for that ponderous man with the accurate middle-parting of glossy hair above a rugged Socratic forehead" (90).

Conrad's version is not an entertainment. Dostoevsky's Porfiry, a master of anacrisis, entertains and flatters Raskolnikov to extort his ideas about crime. Porfiry is brilliant, awful, shallow, funny—Dostoevsky's image of "Western" reason as a process. Though he obviously enjoys anatomizing Porfiry's strategies, Dostoevsky finally makes him the rational externalization of a "deeper" process, that of conscience, just as Western reason is to him a clownish travesty of the soul's growth. Porfiry, of course—or at least this is Dostoevsky's plan—has no real place in the final register of guilt: he lacks the evidence to convict Raskolnikov.[19] The punishment relies not on his rational method but, in the end, entirely on Raskolnikov's conscience, whose correlative is Sonia. This was the purpose: if rational state inquiry and spiritual conscience meet in a contest, the inquiry, with all its antics, may appear to be stronger, more dramatic, and more enthralling, but the resolution will show the final motive superiority of internal conscience over the grotesque, comical, external tactics of anacrisis in the production of the confession. Police interrogation in Dostoevsky loses to a spiritual compulsion that is finally freeing.

Conrad rejects this dialectic, which makes political coercion to speak a subplot, a secondary and almost merry comedy inside the true confessional process. In detail after detail, Mikulin is an atonal version of his original: nowhere as pleasing or funny, nowhere as playfully thrilling, not as personally free, but in fact the bearer of a much more determining power. The blood-red stone reifies the name Porfiry; what was playfully "purple" and intoxicating in Dostoevskian naming becomes a material symbol of binding contractual relation: a heavy ring. To Conrad, *Crime and Punishment,* as a view of "liberating" forced dialogic, makes the narrative argument that great spiritual freedom and wild energies can emerge from the milieu of "enlightened despotism." The comedy of Porfiry is therefore crudely ideological—part of a defense of police autocracy as the harmless spawning ground of spiritual freedom. If this were so, then Conrad would have been wrong to leave Poland. And part of the pain in the novel comes from his fear that Dostoevsky might be right. But in answering, the novel insists that the choice is not one of spiritual liberation through immersion in force on the one hand, or a great Western liberating constitution on the other, but a choice between somewhat different bad "contracts," immersions in force, neither fully liberating. There is no Socratic or Christian or confessional dialectic; there is only forced dialogic. This dialogic replaces the more familiar organizing principles of human relation, "sympathy" and "dialectic."

In *The Prelude* Wordsworth describes the "social principle of life, / Coercing all things into sympathy." [20] A similar uneasiness that "sympathy" and "coercion" may somehow collapse into a single principle, "the social," runs through the Mikulin interview. Razumov, seeing Mikulin, seems to enter the inner sanctum of social power, about to find the "key" to the forced dialogue pattern, which in this novel replaces "sympathy" as the secret reality of dialogue itself. For better or worse, everything will come clear here. All forced dialogue as it has been progressing through Part First will make itself explicit. This ominous totalizing mood is the carefully engineered result of the progress of forced dialogues that precedes. Recall again the causal sequence of dialogues: Haldin forces an interview with Razumov, which leads to Razumov's failure to force Ziemianitch to awaken, which leads Razumov to force himself on his father; this brings about the interview with General T——, which leads to Haldin's arrest, silence under interrogation, and execution; after this there are rumors of Razumov's collaboration with Haldin, and the forced interview with Kostia. This momentum of *sequentially* causal forced dialogues generates the Mikulin-Razumov meeting, which is the most frankly coerced interview, so that we might expect from it at least a clarification of the process itself. And in this scene, a kind of musical summation, there is an effort to convince the reader, by allusion and structure, that all dialogue process, from Socrates' rational pedagogy to the Inquisition, is somehow the same and *simultaneously* gathered "at once" in the autocratic interview: that everything from rational inquiry to Inquisition is in fact meeting here in one total format.

Ironically enough, we do make a kind of discovery of what all this forced dialogue "is" here; but the answer is skeptical and labor contractual. Within the scene itself there is a surprising review of forced dialogues both in Razumov's consciousness and in the reader's: Razumov hallucinates the Inquisition momentarily; his own talk with Haldin is discussed and defined as not conversation; the classical art of making people talk is mentioned by Razumov himself; there are allusive echoes of Mephistopheles, Faust, and the temptation of Christ; the reference to Mikulin's Socratic forehead reminds us of the most rational, classical, civilized art of making others talk; and we learn from Mikulin that Haldin under interrogation remained absolutely silent though tortured—a complex silence in regard to Razumov's conscience and his fears. These many forced dialogues—ostensibly differentiated as theocratic, political, philosophical—are juxtaposed diachronically and synchronically, in order to make them seem like one total scene, whether marked by dialectic, theology, poetic drama, or political anacrisis. But while this collapse of dialogues into one fearful world scene is effected by allusion and analogy, the mastery of the scene lies in the instrumental frame: for all the terror—encapsulated in Razumov's hysterical-historical hallucination of the Inquisition—the real scene here is only what we might call a "job interview." The difference from the Inquisition at Goa in Marryat's romance, or even from the inquisitorial tortures in *Nostromo*, lies in this new, skeptical, labor-contractual frame. The aim here is to hire, not to convert, teach, or torture. A brief encyclopedia of strong Western dialogic from Socrates to Torquemada is summoned only to enlist Razumov in the state intelligence. Conrad quietly condenses these highlights of dialogical history in order to "contract" them, and remake them into a modern scene of contractual forced employment, impression, "mild" slave labor. Thus we really have entered an inner sanctum of the dialogic, the *summa* of the whole dialogical plot of Part First; but we discover that the entire grand inquisitorial and Oedipal machinery of coercion to speak, as it works on the conscious and the unconscious, is in fact not a mystery but a contract, and that all this scary historical hoopla has been neatly designed to make the young person work.[21]

To the sense of personal exploitation and reuse pervading *Under Western Eyes* can be added Conrad's harsh reuses of the plot of *Crime and Punishment* and of Dostoevsky's themes and biography to write the novel itself. His main motive for this reuse was to enter a forced dialogue with Dostoevsky, and insist that Dostoevsky was wrong about dialogical order. Preliminary to a discussion of their comparative ideas of dialogue, it would be helpful to rehearse quickly some of the narrative parallels. Major characters are stolen and changed. Raskolnikov commits the murder, and next day visits his good friend Razumihin; Haldin commits the assassination, and immediately visits Razumov. Raskolnikov's mother and sister arrive in St. Petersburg shortly after the murder, and Razumihin falls in love with the sister; Razumov, after in fact betraying Haldin, who is thought to have been his close comrade, goes to Geneva, meets Haldin's mother and sister, and falls in love with the sister. The mothers of Raskolnikov and of Haldin gradually go mad. Raskolnikov, under interrogation by Porfiry, and having taken up with the prostituted, pious Sonia, moves toward confession; Razumov, interrogated by Mikulin, only becomes more implicated in a life of constant betrayal of the revolutionaries, in which he seems to be about to become a perpetual forced spy and forced correspondent. Raskolnikov is accompanied throughout by his companion the prostituted Sonia, whom he loves, and who emerges from the typical Dostoevskian family of Marmeladovs; Razumov at the end does not have Natalie, whom he loves, but only the pathetic, familyless, unappealing Tekla, who leaves her job as a forced secretary just as he leaves his job as a forced spy, and follows and tends him in his last days—which are not, for him at least, romantic.

Conrad's reuse of Dostoevsky here, beginning with his decision to focus on the struggles of the Razumihin (reasonable) figure rather than on the passions of the transcendental murderer, has raised many questions—for instance about Conrad's knowledge of Russian, a language he denied knowing just as the narrator denies being able to comprehend Russia.[22] But the reuse also raises a simpler but more dialogical issue: how obvious did Conrad think the parallel was? Was it obvious to him? Is this a petty theft, to give Conrad, exhausted producer of many commercially unsuccessful novels, some working pattern against which to play his creative hostility? Is it "influence," in Harold Bloom's sense, a "strong" work repressing a debt to Dostoevsky? Or is it open and conscious travesty, with "the reader" (whoever that is) meant also to see the obvious contrast? The questions themselves sound vaguely mismatched, and a little trivializing, in regard both to the argument between the books and to the complex reality in which each was written. To answer them one must resist either/or stances, and try to imagine Conrad's situation of writing for an English audience.

Bloom's theory of influence probably does not apply here. Looking for ancestors of that sort for *Under Western Eyes*, we might go first to Scott's *Waverley*, or possibly to *The Ambassadors*, to discuss the ways in which an onlooker caught between dialectical alternatives is forced to change. With *Crime and Punishment*, however, parallels in the plot and also in the naming are too explicit for Bloom's notion of largely unconscious "influence," *agon*, and sublimely repressive troping. We need something more like *Widerruf*—the term used about those poems Paul Celan wrote by making alterations in the poems of his contemporaries, so that he provoked the charge of plagiarism.[23] In English the word might be *revocation* or *repudiation*—the explicit reform of someone else's text to criticize it and make it radically different for a programmatic purpose.

To revoke someone else's writing is obviously an aggressive dialogical act. The writer sets out to reshape the other's work, and to make the audience see the process. Can we say that this is happening in *Under Western Eyes*? The answer is not easy to give, because in Conrad's historical context, the politics of openly reusing Dostoevsky's text to write his own novel were themselves complicated. When confronted with the parallel to Dostoevsky, or with the charge of being Slavonic in temperament,[24] he of course became heated in denial, for many reasons. But in what available terms could he have defended the method of the novel if it was in fact a conscious reconstruction or revocation? If he had pointed to Shakespeare, who also "stole" or reused contemporary plots to "raise" their dialogical and dramatic intricacy, he would have been making things worse by comparing himself to the Bard, and by noting that the Bard also was a thief. While poets may have always known what Eliot, and in a different way, Bloom, later argue, that great poets steal rather than borrow, and while one could point to many examples of allusive novelistic revision before Joyce, like Hardy's *Mayor of Casterbridge* as a revision of David and Saul,[25] to rewrite a near contemporary's plot is not the same as recasting the Bible or the Odyssey. Conrad's contract was in any case not a poet's, but to write novels for the public, not to effect political revocations or conduct a secret anti-Dostoevskian polemic. He would have been open to the charge of running out of material. Further, he had no abstract theory on which to base his method of reconstruction, which, as scholars like Norman Sherry have shown, became increasingly important throughout his middle period.[26] There is, then, a complex political scene behind his dialogical (though Conrad fortunately had no such term) reuse of Dostoevsky, which makes this use neither simply open nor simply buried. That is, he did, partly, want some readers, a "friend here and there," to see the parallelism, but he had to muffle the parallelism also. Challenged, his only recourse was simply to deny that he had been influenced by Dostoevsky, which sounds like a lie, and to insist that he found Dostoevsky unacceptable, which comes close to the truth. With a little attention, we can see that he is asking the audience to reconstruct with him Dostoevsky's vision of events and dialogue. A pragmatic reuse of Dostoevsky is however a coherent, not simply a repressive act, and it makes sense precisely because in this novel Conrad argues that the world is itself dialogically a place of pragmatic contracts and forced reuses rather than of transcendent freedoms. The writer and reader themselves are not obliged to transcend, only to reuse, rethink, reapply.

In a formal dialogue criticism we want to find recurrent patterns in dialogue form and then show their connection to the writer's deepest assumptions. To compare Conrad and Dostoevsky in this way, we have to take risks, paying less attention to the interesting plot contrasts than to the sense of dialogue form in the two novels. Many of Dostoevsky's critics have emphasized his dialogue, though in different ways. To take only two examples, Merezhkovsky called Dostoevsky a tragedian who happened to employ the form of the novel, and said that the real action begins when the talk begins; and Bakhtin's first major work argued that Dostoevsky had been the one modern writer to "dialogize" fully, to evoke equally convincing and irreconcilable forms of language, social existence, and consciousness.[27] Bakhtin's word *dialogic* describes an intricate field of relations in which words are polysemous, voices comprise and are subverted by other voices (no speaker has one voice but instead has put together many voices, some of which are those of his enemies), and consciousnesses are irreconcilably plural. All this, and also the implicit and by now traditional opposition of dialogic to dialectic, dialectic being construed as the philosopher's way of appropriating drama and making it monologue, has much to say concerning Conrad's sense of language as well.[28] But in comparing Dostoevsky to Conrad, I want to focus on something more modest than Bakhtin's dialogic, and consider only Dostoevsky's patent formal devices for making dialogue exciting.

If Conrad's dialogical bias or signature is the scene in which one person tries to force another to speak, and finally provokes a "detonation," Dostoevsky's is the scene in which someone unwanted or unexpected shows up at a gathering, and in which, also, people say things which (they say) they did not plan to say. The mood of Dostoevskian dialogue is surplus—surplus of presences and surplus of statement. For example, Luzhin in *Crime and Punishment*, after a violent quarrel with Raskolnikov, calls a "conference" with Raskolnikov's mother and his sister, Dounia, at this point Luzhin's fiancée, but tries to forbid Raskolnikov's presence. Dounia insists on that presence and, compounding the affront to Luzhin, also invites his poor friend Razumihin, who is in love with her. This surfeit of people of course becomes the issue of the meeting itself, and the encounter breaks apart when Luzhin, a malicious figure delineated largely by his addiction to slander, learns that Raskolnikov recently had his sister and mother sit down and converse with Sonia—an earlier "ensemble," as Mochulsky calls Dostoevskian gatherings. The two scenes are mutually constitutive: notions of who may speak with whom, who may sit down with whom, define Luzhin's consciousness. The fact of the first meeting's having taken place at all breaks up the later meeting, or serves as the excuse. To this constitutive quarreling in *Crime and Punishment* may be added many others of even greater comic and prophetic energy: the underground man's decision to invite himself to the party of his ex-colleagues, where he remains a surplus presence throughout, and cannot help saying outrageous things; the several gatherings in *The Possessed* where everyone plus one seems to show up, as when, for example, Lebyadkin and his sister appear in Varvara Petrovna's drawing room, make havoc, and turn out to be members of the family; Prince Myshkin's presence as a mysterious addition to the human scene itself, altering everything and nothing; the wild meeting of the Karamazov clan at Father Zossima's; and most curiously, the seemingly whimsical decision made by the Savior himself, in Ivan's prose poem, to "gate crash" the Inquisition, not for a Second Coming but only for a surprise visit, as an added unwanted presence whose silence is the transcendental addition that disrupts the typical secular human scene of coercive interrogation.

Dostoevskian dialogue achieves an extraordinary feeling of willful participatory addition. To call this "confessional" is to single out only one action. It does not matter how many readers have thought Dostoevsky confessional; he was in fact an additive dialogist. Dostoevsky's interest in the comedy of speech surplus that surprises the speaker himself, or seems to, and also in what we call colloquially "gate crashing" made into a grand comic gesture, is much more than the morbid, guilty intentionality implied by "confession." On the contrary, Dostoevsky's surplus of presence and speech is ingeniously funny.

The common ground between Dostoevsky's dialogic and Conrad's should be apparent. Each tends to ignore "conversation"—warm meetings of approximate equals who can share thoughts and metaphors—in favor of confrontations which keep returning to the preconditions of their own occurrence, so that the very meeting of the characters is felt to be unlikely, and thematic. That is, they are both writers who dramatize the structures of participation and take their energy from the awkwardnesses of inclusion; and the characters display their consciousness of the problem. This might seem to say little more than that both are dramatic. Yet there are dramatic conflicts in which questions of the right or desire to participate in the conflict at all, to take part in the dialogue, are not at stake. While Conrad and Dostoevsky share a formal emphasis on problems of social inclusion, and while each has come up with what must be called his own formulaic idea of the process of inclusion, their formulas run contrary. Dostoevskian form presumes that everyone desires to break in. It is emancipatively expansionist. The spiritual world's abject serfs are always breaking into its drawing rooms. Conradian form presumes that everyone is already in—there is only the world, in spite of illusions that some are more "worldly" or secular than others. Dostoevskian form assumes that there is a profound dialectic between the worldly and the unworldly, the secular and the transcendent. Conradian form indicates that, on the contrary, since everything is flatly secular, the ritual of forced participation in the "world" may continue, but has no ontological basis; it is in fact only a sort of contract. People imagine the difference between worldliness and unworldliness, between being outside and inside; imagine ritually that they are forcing others into the world, or being forced in; that they are bringing "out" someone withdrawn; but in fact this process is an illusion. The forced dialogue in Conrad is therefore a ritual of inclusion which continues to be conducted as a contract long after its substantial reality has vanished.

Dostoevsky's format of inclusion, grounded in desire rather than coercion, has so much more immediate appeal than Conrad's, and his additive method has so much more apparent energy than the contractual pathos of the forced dialogue, that it seems as if we ought to give up right here, accept the comparison as an embarrassment, and make no attempt to defend Conrad's implicit critique of Dostoevsky's dialogic. But sides should not be taken too quickly. We should instead consider the two feelings for dialogue, one positively inclusive, the other ironically and negatively inclusive (in Dostoevsky people break in, in Conrad people are forced in even though they are already in), as themselves in dialogue with each other, and with respect for the power of each. The case for Dostoevsky, I think, makes itself, or at the very least has been made undeniably by Bakhtin; it is one expression of that "surfeit" which is perhaps the genius of the novel. To state the anti-Dostoevskian, critical, and skeptical case as it is implied in *Under Western Eyes* is much more difficult. Conrad's implicit charge is that Dostoevsky assigns his characters their vital outspokenness without acknowledging his own role in this—how and why he himself "makes them" speak out—and without fully acknowledging what systematically compels his own productive authorial impulse—what *makes him make them* speak. To Conrad, what makes him make them speak out—"fierce mouthings"[29] was Conrad's strong, stupid, dismissive phrase for Dostoevsky, but it lets us hear that he objected to Dostoevsky primarily as a kind of regressive speech—is the denial of the autocratic scene in which he is immersed. The phrase "fierce mouthings," though itself a little insane, implies that Conrad saw the dramatic energy in Dostoevsky, the outpourings of speech, as an overcompensation against the political actuality of his own being compelled to speak; a pretense that what is being written under a complex of compulsions is "free." By contrast to Dostoevsky, Conrad in his own careful speech work seeks to inscribe into the text the process whereby the characters force each other to speak and write, and also, in a variety of metaphors and analogies, to point back to the conditions of this own forced production of writing, his own "social contract" as an author.

An anecdote from David Magarshack's *Dostoevsky*, describing a forced confrontation between Dostoevsky and Turgenev, might be useful here in regard to Conrad's claim that he was not simply biased about Russia or Dostoevsky when writing *Under Western Eyes*. At a dinner in honor of Turgenev, Magarshack tells us, after Turgenev made a speech hinting at a constitutional monarchy by using the phrase "to crown the edifice," Dostoevsky jumped madly to his feet, demanding that Turgenev repeat those words. Turgenev, the taller man, reared up and replied that he would not submit to an *"interrogation"* (Magarshack's italics, suggesting an extreme emphasis in Turgenev's voice). This emphatic word implied that Dostoevsky might turn police informer. Dostoevsky rushed, injured and defeated, from the room. Magarshack then notes that this accusation must have been especially "galling" to Dostoevsky the ultrareactionary because he himself was the incessant object of police surveillance, against which he repeatedly protested by citing his writings, till near the end of his life. " 'On hundreds of pages,' he wrote to the state protesting this surveillance, 'I have been and still am expressing my political and religious views, which, I hope, are such as to give no cause to suspect my political propriety.' His request was ignored by the ministry and the police stopped opening his correspondence only a few months before his death."[30]

This miserable scene may not be an accurate report. But if it is, it may show only that Dostoevsky remained so terrified, after his youthful near execution, of being in any way linked to anticzarist activity that he always overplayed his czarism in liberal company. Magarshak implies that the galling surveillance is pathetically ironic: it is ironic that Dostoevsky should have defended a regime persecuting him. But perhaps there is less irony than bare coercion here. Our sense of irony, Conrad's work shows, is often a defense against recognizing simple coercions in the production of "civilized" discourse. In this light, the surveillance is the strong, simple *cause* of Dostoevsky's outburst. Still being watched, he makes sure to shout out his czarist devotion. There may be informers present. And someone, after all, has in fact reported this scene to us; the gathering was not totally private.

This is not to say that Dostoevsky's czarism was only a conscious protective mask. A comparison of Dostoevsky and Conrad as they understand dialogue might lead to the psychoanalytic thesis that Dostoevsky, in the melodramas of his father's murder and his later, last-minute reprieve by the czar, experienced a world which overplayed for him, externally, grossly, the Oedipal scene (see Chapter VI), while Conrad's parents disappeared before he could begin to work out his relation to them in real terms. The result is that Dostoevsky represents and lives out an overdone dialogue of interrogation, a histrionic, melodramatic, surplus world in which madly forced speech shouts itself into freedom, while Conrad has to go out into the world to find any terms of inclusion at all, which terms he can see only as a "contract," never entirely satisfying or original, yet always all that there is. But however we read the difference between Conrad's contractual forced inclusions and Dostoevsky's ecstatic additions, the main thing is that the scene above, as is, could not appear either in Dostoevsky's work or in Turgenev's, while something like it shows up all the time in Conrad. Dostoevsky and Turgenev, pressed into dismal mutual baiting and *interrogation,* confront each other on a horizon of forced relation which neither, in his own novels, represents tonally. The scene is too harsh and drab for Turgenev, too shabby for Dostoevsky.

Certainly Ivan's "Grand Inquisitor" implies, as does Foucault later, that the "human" scene without God is in essence inquisition, not conversation; but even there confessional speech keeps its potential as freedom, and the world has a transcendental, silent horizon in the savior who arrives to add everything and nothing. He says nothing, but just by being present he breaks open the inquisition, and also makes it in our sense "Oedipal," since in his presence, the Grand Inquisitor *himself* feels forced to speak, obliged to decribe and to condemn himself; that is, he becomes the subject of the inquiry he has heretofore conducted: the inquisitor exposed, Oedipus. "The Grand Inquisitor," though there is no time for a close reading here, in its tripartite structure of speeches and silences also makes for a remarkable contrast to the typical Conradian scene.[31] But the main difference is that Dostoevsky there affirms the existence of both a confessional sublime and a transcendent silence. Forced confession, taken to the fullest spiritual limit, becomes something else: freedom, as also, curiously enough, for Rousseau. Yet the figure of Dostoevsky in Magarshak's sordid scene is neither confessionally free nor simply silent, but only a man under life-long secular surveillance, who feels immersed in a drab, permanent, secular inquisition which he must hysterically defy. In this ugly, and what Conrad would call "stupid" context, Dostoevsky produced two sets of texts—his great novels on the one hand and his reactionary journalism (probably the referent of the "hundreds of pages" above), over-proving his loyalty, on the other. As a producer of two kinds of writing, this biographical Dostoevsky resembles the fictive Razumov, who also writes two parallel texts—his private, personal journals, which are the documentary source of the novel, and his "forced" spy reports. Conrad may have seen this pathos of "doubleness" in Dostoevsky's biography—the "doubleness" which is not a mystifying hallucination but a self forced politically to write two texts—and intended Razumov as a compassionate analogue of Dostoevsky's own history: arrest for being implicated in radical politics; rescue by the state (the czar's reprieve, Mikulin's recruitment); self-deceptive conversion under stress to a reactionary politics; and a final life of forced double writing.

It would, probably, be fair to say that Conrad has no stylistic gift comparable to Turgenev's pure prose lyricism or Dostoevsky's un-equaled momentum. He lacks the clear tonal definition each of them gets from an imagined release from forced dialogue. Turgenev achieves release into lyrical conversation, Dostoevsky release into surplus as freedom. Conrad instead corrosively analyzes that desire for release itself. That his approach is stylistically biased in its own formal obsessions is obvious: to negate free conversation as thoroughly as *Under Western Eyes* does is one-sided. At the same time, the strength of *Under Western Eyes* lies in the uncompromising organization of this unpleasant insight into a nearly systematic deidealization of dialogue.

Part Third closes with a prose poem about forced writing:

He went back to a garden seat, dropped into it. This was the place for making a beginning of that writing which had to be done. The materials he had on him. "I shall always come here," he said to himself, and afterwards sat for quite a long time motionless, without thought and sight and hearing, almost without life. He sat long enough for the declining sun to dip behind the roofs of the town at his back, and throw the shadow of the houses on the lake front over the islet, before he pulled out of his pocket a fountain pen, opened a small notebook on his knee, and began to write quickly, raising his eyes now and then at the connecting arm of the bridge. These glances were needless; the people crossing over in the distance seemed unwilling even to look at the islet where the exiled effigy of the author of the *Social Contract* sat enthroned above the bowed head of Razumov in the sombre immobility of bronze. After finishing his scribbling, Razumov, with a sort of feverish haste, put away the pen, then rammed the notebook into his pocket, first tearing out the written pages with an almost convulsive brusqueness. But the folding of the flimsy batch on his knee was executed with thoughtful nicety. That done, he leaned back in his seat and remained motionless holding the papers in his left hand. The twilight had deepened. He got up and began to pace to and fro under the trees.

"There can be no doubt that now I am safe," he thought. His fine ear could detect the faintly accentuated murmurs of the current breaking against the point of the island, and he forgot himself in listening to them with interest. But even to his acute sense of hearing the sound was too elusive.

"Extraordinary occupation I am giving myself up to," he murmured. And it occurred to him that this was about the only sound he could listen to innocently, and for his own pleasure, as it were. Yes, the sound of water, the voice of the wind—completely foreign to human passions. All the other sounds of this earth brought contamination to the solitude of a soul.

This was Mr. Razumov's feeling, the soul, of course, being his own, and the word being used not in the theological sense, but standing, as far as I can understand it, for that part of Mr. Razumov which was not his body, and more especially in danger from the fires of this earth. And it must be admitted that in Mr. Razumov's case the bitterness of solitude from which he suffered was not an altogether morbid phenomenon. (290–292)

While writing his spy letter, Razumov has a conversation with himself which in its riddled tripartite rhythm resembles all the other major scenes of forced dialogue we have considered. In this formal coda to Part Third, he speaks three times—trying to make himself accept his work as a spy—and in effect denies himself three times. In three progressively more conscious statements, he tries to legitimize the "extraordinary" compact of a police informer. The first statement—"I shall always come here"—is simply false comfort: Razumov will not come back to this place of contemplative "arrest" but will confess the same evening. The tone is mock sacred, as if Razumov were a wanderer finding a holy site and promising himself to return. The second statement, presented as inner speech—" 'There can be no doubt that now I am safe,' he thought"—refers obliquely to Ziemianitch, the news of whose suicide has been interpreted by the revolutionaries as proof that *he* had been Haldin's Judas. This is a fiction, yet it is not unlike the confession which Razumov is in fact himself about to make. Razumov's "there can be no doubt," is, of course, unconvincing in a novel that is a construction of doubts, and from a character who likes to quote Pascal. Put differently, his "fine ear," mentioned in this same paragraph, which can detect "faintly accentuated murmurs of the current," resembles the reader's solicited attention to the faintly accentuated current of propositions running through Razumov's almost inaudible—and strangely reported—dialogue with himself. His verdict—"Extraordinary occupation I am giving myself up to"—is by far the most important. The phrasal verb *giving up to*, like the scene itself, has three parts, increasingly abject. He begins with the false notion that he is "giving" himself this job, making a willed covenant (I shall come here). Then it becomes clear that all this is only "giving up"—surrender and resignation (I am safe). But last, this is not even a simple resignation, or a private despair, but one which is made over "to" the state—a deliberate echo by Conrad of Mikulin's question "Where to?" which closed Part First. Razumov is a study in writing, dialogue, and even speech with the self as *given up to:* forced and contractual. Conrad in this period is not a poet of "the horror," or of simple despair and "giving up," but of the condition of being "given up to."

The scene ends with a quiet, scarcely audible forced confession, made not by Razumov himself but by the nearly omniscient narrator, who has been recounting the scene from Razumov's journal. At the end it is the narrator, standing for the audience, who "must admit" something while contemplating this arrested meditation of Razumov's—that is, who is forced to a logical conclusion. We are forced to admit that this scene of coerced inner monologue is not exceptional, not hyperbolic literature, theologically splendid, politically dramatic, or poetically extreme—not a "morbid phenomenon"—but instead a secular and ordinary political scene. In the typical temptation battle of the Western tradition—the temptation of Jesus, Goethe's *Faust*, the trial of Joan of Arc, Flaubert's *Tentation de Saint Antoine*, Dostoevsky's "Grand Inquisitor," and in more sardonic and cagey examples like "Bartleby the Scrivener" or Peretz's "Bontsche Shweig"—a saintly, ascetic, scholarly, or minimal figure, who in some way refuses to participate in the world, is forcibly offered the world. Such temptation crises, between the "world" and the unworldly saint, or between "everything" and the little man, often have a "morbid," phantasmal, hilarious, and/or hallucinatory aura. The worldly and the unworldly, as two radically opposed categories, are kept in grand dialectical tension. Conrad's method here radically secularizes and mutes the entire scene of temptation and statuary persecution into a social and political contract, lacking dialectical grandeur and deliberately lacking intense tonality. The scene is not "daimonic"; it is a formula, ironically, a *social contract*. This reduces the glamour of temptation itself, the grand struggle between spirit and world, heaven and earth, or even state and subject. If there is only, behind the temptation scene, the pattern of forced dialogue, which is not spiritual but social, then there is no literary grandeur. Razumov, the narrator sees, is in danger "from the fires of *this earth*" (my italics); his temptation is not Mephistophelian. What we must admit, then, along with the narrator, is that this scene of forced writing is purely secular, fairly common, and not even infernal—despite the underlying joke that Russia is hell on earth. The narrator, however, is in fact admitting that Russia is not as exceptional or mysterious as he has been insisting. For the reader, it amounts to a renunciation of melodramatic and spiritual thrills from the forced production of language. *Under Western Eyes*, then, denies that there is any grand dialectic between the worldly and the unworldly, and insists that there is only the world, as a plural forced dialogic, which includes everyone. No one is more "in the world" than anyone else; the melodramatic thrill in the representation of forced dialogue is itself *our* temptation as writers and readers.

But the above scene, for all its purposes within the action, is also clearly a self-portrait as forced writing—a picture of writing as a forced action accompanied by forced "inner" speech, the two of them not identical but polyphonically related. Edward Said wrote that the reader of Conrad is often "almost forced" to consider autobiographical elements in the work.[32] Conrad himself might have written the words *almost forced* so that the *almost* would be left to the reader's irony to slash. This is one of the set of Conrad's formally organized scenes about coercion to produce language, probably the last major scene, placed like many of the others at the end of a narrative movement, and in a very clear prose frame. It reconsiders writing in exile itself in the worst light, as a forced and servile spying. The bronze statue, perhaps like Pushkin's Bronze Horseman, contributes the symbolic backdrop of an immobile nightmare-muse. In this scene of arrest, by contrast to the pious aesthetics in the *"Narcissus"* preface, arrest is fully political as well as psychological. Razumov is indeed immobilized, "under arrest"—aesthetically, as in sculpture—but also literally and socially. While it would be wrong to make a simple equation between the condition of Conrad the writer in England and the pictured condition of Razumov the writer in Geneva, it would be equally wrong to deny any possible symmetry between them as writers who "must" write. This must be the crux of permanent disagreements about the novel. Is it a critique of Russia, or does it, again, turn back critically on the author himself, as a self-portrait, in precisely the way that Marlow is criticized as an imperial speaker? Is there a suggestion that the unseen, shabby little island is, indirectly, England? The whole scene is informed by Conrad's most involuntarily negative feelings (though of course he had others) about writing as an oblique form of slavery, so that, once again, we are as far as possible from Nietzsche and later notions of writing as freedom and play.

But one obvious crux of the passage is the extremely ironic appearance of the phrase *Social Contract,* italicized amid all the coercive machinery and imagery. At the very least, it becomes obvious that the "contract" here, as elsewhere in Conrad, is seen as coercion rather than as free choice. Razumov's own social contract is his forced writing. The strongest jolt, however, in this forced dialogue poem—though it is by no means central to the public fable, and as an "overheard" echo isn't necessary to our sense of the passage as a bitter and deflected self-portrait—is Conrad's obliteratingly ironic act of "signing" the novel here, in a corner, by noticing, I think for the first time while he wrote the passage, the assonance between his pen name and the phrase *social contract.* Note how the article *the* is absent from the italicized words. He detonates and rehears his sonorous, romantic pen name, "Joseph Conrad," in alignment with the order of ideological cant and "Social Contracts." That is, he signs himself, as in a corner, *Social Contract.* If he originally wanted his pen name to mean that he would be the Konrad, or Polish hero, who was a dreaming but somehow practical man successful in exile, he now dismisses that hopeful and perhaps naive self-image to tell us that the author writing this novel is himself only a "social contract," a reused man, in the forced sense. He may not be identical to Razumov as a forced writer, but he lives in the same world with him. All this is a historically grounded "detonation" of his pen name, not a simply textual and playful "deconstruction" of it.

The chime is overdetermined: a pen name is a kind of contract with the audience, and the name Joseph Conrad "contracts" or shortens his given name. He once described his pen name as a "neutral pseudonym" designed to disguise his national origins from the English audience.[33] As a name, that is, it was always the reverse of an "intonation," or national, ethnic inflection; it was always a contraction and detonation of Józef Teodor Konrad Nałęcz Korzeniowski. In various parts of this book, I have already shown how names throughout Conrad's work point semantically and formally to their own condition as "namedness," social contracts, identities given by relation rather than from within: Almayer, Heyst, Nostromo, Mrs. Neale, and so on. In Catholic ritual, of course, the giving of the Christian name occurs at baptism, a dramatic rite corresponding to Stein's recommendation for destructive immersion. As late as *The Rover,* Peyrol receives his name in a baptism which is a forced dialogue: the nameless orphan stows away, is discovered aboard, and is violently interrogated. Babbling in terror, he mentions the name of the farmer at whose house he worked, Peyrol; so he is baptized, at sea, in a scene of violent interrogation, and becomes Peyrol.[34] There is no point in rehearsing here all the ways in which these and other names indicate themselves as the outcome of coercive social relations rather than as freely expressive identities. What should be emphasized is that Conrad has his own very powerfully conceived onomastics here, which is a little too easily confused with the uncanny or "alienation." Frederick Karl, though writing eloquently and compendiously on naming in Conrad's work, wrongly concludes that Conrad's onomastics mainly prefigures the "anonymity" and "nobody-ness" found in later modernism.[35] Conrad in naming was not a weak forebear of Kafka. For him, names are predicated on concrete human relations, and are not comical signifiers of alienation. Even the names Prince K—— and General T——, in this novel, and Tekla's discourse on the fear of being named, designate specific reasons for anonymity in a world of force. By this signature in italics, in the phrase "the exiled effigy of the author of the *Social Contract,*" Conrad completes the take-over of the novel's action by forced dialogical processes. The order of forced dialogue has already subsumed the narrative order; now it also subsumes the order of personal naming, including the author's name.

We can find a famous name in Conrad's earlier work which formally resembles a secret joke on the contractuality of his pen name. Kurtz was a contraction of Korzeniowski, as many people have noticed; but it also means "brief," so that it makes a semantic joke about its own abbreviation. Frederick Crews, during a one-sided but important Freudian critique of "Heart of Darkness," long ago saw Kurtz as Conrad's "patronymic," referring to the father, Apollo; Marlow's journey upriver to find Kurtz performing obscene rites in the darkness is not good political writing but a neurotic replay of the primal scene.[36] This is a strong criticism, but not complete. First, it seems very unlikely that the name Kurtz, in regard to Korzeniowski (Ford also notes that the first syllable was pronounced *Kurz*), was unconscious. From our angle, the naming seems much more consciously witty than Crews allows, since it means "curt" and was created by "abbreviation." Something like Kurtz, used as a joke, might even have been Conrad's nickname as a schoolboy in Cracow (we call him short for short) because for speakers of Germanic languages his name was too long to pronounce easily—as he tells us was true for at least one of his examiners, baffled by the name, in *A Personal Record*. Thus the name Kurtz semantically and comically refers to the process of its own contractual production. Recall also that Kurtz, throughout "Heart of Darkness," is himself an elaborate picture of bizarre extremes of alternate wordiness and brevity. He always says and writes either too much or too little. But if all this is so, then the name Kurtz, as a conscious if dark autobiographical joke, does not refer mainly to the father, Apollo Korzeniowski, and does not exactly equal Józef Korzeniowski either, the author's given name, but most resembles, in the way it was produced, the shortened pen name "Joseph Conrad." Kurtz, in the conscious part of the allegory, is not simply Conrad's father, the Polish poet, but the contractual "author" in exile whose works we read, and who is, like the rest of us, caught up in moral and political dilemmas of disproportion in communication. The forced contractual resolution of "Heart of Darkness," further, is arrived at by a forced dialogue with personified Intention: the nonnaming phrase "your name." "Your name" is *not* the Intended's name, but a general namedness tactfully or grotesquely substituted for her personal one. Why the substitution? And why the feeling that this polite, contractual, forced substitution is both a fraud and the essence of civilization? The force of circumstances renames, and gives a new "name of name" ("Nom de nom, quelle bête de vie!"), which means everyone, and has the status of a universal "forced contract."

To the "familiar reader," the overheard chime says that the whole scene of spy writing above is an oblique picture of Jospeh Conrad as forced to write, and a picture of what a novel, as a "social contract," really is, and is like in its production: it is a forced writing embodying and reenacting the historical forcedness of other relations. This grotesque and cryptic but deliberate pun turns our attention violently away from the many perspectivist, rationalizing questions about the "narrator's" role in this novel, back to the questions concerning the relation of the person now renamed Joseph Conrad to these political and social materials.

This account of an echo between the pen name and the cant phrase is not meant to be a provocative misreading, a bad joke, a parody of modern overreading, play, or an unconscious event—although Conrad's sardonic signature of the scene of forced writing here perhaps anticipates and includes reactions like these. The echo is instead part of the poetics of overhearing which has to be, to most of us, the most alien part of Conrad's forced dialogism. That "Joseph Conrad" and "Social Contract" sound alike is a matter of subjective judgment, perhaps, or at the extreme border of overhearing—but in fact is there any common English phrase that sounds so much like the writer's name? "White

Elephant"? They are, in fact, easily off rhymes; if the phrase were emphasized (as here italicized) in the dream of a psychoanalytic patient named Joseph Conrad, the patient would not be making wild associations to connect it to his name. The main reason, in fact, for our not wanting to hear the proximity of the *sounds* is the distance between the two lexical orders—personal naming and political ideology, or more abstractly, name and number—to which they belong. We want to resist the forced assonance between the two phrases because we want to keep personal names and ideological cant separate. By middle-class convention, to name a child for a food or a place, say, is only comical, but it is offensive to name a child ideologically. Yet Razumov, and in fact also Józef Teodor Konrad Korzeniowski *and* the renamed author Joseph Conrad were all from the start names chosen ideologically. The separation is illusory. Conrad's bitterly depersonalizing fusion of himself and Razumov to the order of "forced social contracts" in the scene of spy writing is precisely his political point. The author is the historical product of nearly annihilating political circumstances, and the survivor-exile is now, authorially, only a social contract, not the free, exotic author his English audience takes him to be.

"Poetry," Robert Champigny writes, "does not name things; it things names." [37] That may not be the last word on poetry and names, but it is a useful dogma. Deliberate reification of names has a major role in the novel's critique of an oversimplified idea of individualism. Conrad's gesture is not unique, by any means, but only somewhat more complex than others, harder to hear, and more outrageous. "Mark Twain," for example, may mean not so much sounding for depths on the steamboat as, more simply and sardonically, "Name Two." And there is an analogous, desperately comic, if not quite so bitter authorial signature near the end of *The Mayor of Casterbridge*, when Henchard's spontaneous lie to keep his stepdaughter is referred to as "this hardy invention of a moment." [38] Trying to repress the conscious, intentional, personal character of the onomastic detonation, one could cite Freud's comments on names as important to the unconscious and to dream work,[39] or Foucault's assertion that "classical" discourse typically progresses to an act of naming as closure (discussed by D. A. Miller in relation to renaming and wedding as the goal of Austen's *Emma*).[40] But neither approach is exactly right. Conrad knew what he was doing. This action should be compared instead to self-critical play with their own names by writers as different as Twain, Shakespeare, Donne, Blake, Stevens, Burke. Many great middle-class authors have variously needed to debunk their own names, or at least subjugate them with detached irony to the general diction, in order to escape a certain kind of foolish namedness.

In Blake's terms, the job is not to see into but to see through one's own name and the ways one has cathected it. When Conrad rids himself here of the romantic connotations of "Joseph Conrad" to bitterly subsume his name to the general will and the "Social Contract," he gives a devastating *account* of himself, violating rules of detachment, insisting that he is another forced exiled participant in the novel's Russian scene. Prose with unexpected, indecorous, "tolling," or shocking rhymes is particularly suited to an art concerned with the disproportions between history and the individual subject. The disproportion between "Joseph Conrad" and "Social Contract" (person and order) is the intended theme of the chime and of the scene itself—the disproportion between intended theme of the chime and of the scene itself—the disproportion between Razumov and the forced writing he has to do. John Ashbery in a recent poem, "Punishing the Myth," describes the "snow having second thoughts," an image of prose turning into poetry[41]: the discourse seems to be prose, but then resettles. Conrad at the close of Part Third, with a more caustic intention, shifts all the abstract, perspectival questions to the more radically historical question of the immersed author himself, by rhyming in an ugly and *bête* way on his own romantically sonorous pen name. It is a historical reminder that the author was another forced subject.

This whole scene, then, works as one of his most unusual and disturbing prose poems about the forced production of language on all levels. (1) The idea of the "social contract" is here revised into a present bondage of writing itself. The implication is that "social contracts" are real enough, but not in the past; their reality is that whoever writes involuntarily writes one. (2) In a kind of anticarnival, Rousseau in bronze is enthroned not as freedom but as a perpetual effigy of the confusion between compulsion and freedom. (3) Razumov's inner speech is not a free or mad or morbid talk he has with himself (contrast Raskolnikov's monologues) but is permeated with the demands of others; this forced inner dialogue is in turn *accurately misrepresented* by the forcedness of the writing he produces. (4) The author renamed Joseph Conrad insists in italics that his own renaming in English was at least in part a forced social contract rather than a simple triumph of individual choice. The power of the form I have called forced dialogue reaches a kind of final verdict here, with the novelist able to "sign" the novel ironically, indicating himself as one of its forced contractual subjects. The author's—not the narrator's—own forced history is inscribed in the scene.

Usually the recurrent Conrad plot is thought to be a betrayal followed by some sort of expiation or self-punishment. This obviously can apply to *Under Western Eyes*. But there is an equally important and near-universal Conrad plot, more abstract, but perhaps deeper, which has to do with contracts, and which has two parts that are, as seamlessly as possible, fused. In the first part, often a comic or ironic study, the central character finds work under contractual conditions which limit, humiliate, or compromise him or her. It is a grim comedy of "the mere force of circumstances" (vii). This initial forced contractuality applies, in diverse ways, to Whalley (the long study of the origins of his contract with Massy), Verloc (his contract with the embassy versus his other, conflicting contracts with the police and the anarchists), Winnie (her marriage to Verloc as her pathetic contract), Marlow (his grotesque hiring), James Wait (his contract aboard the ship, and his anticontract with the crew to histrionically violate that contract, entertaining, annoying, and enthralling them), Jim (his contract as Tuan in Patusan), Nostromo (his contract as Capataz and his later compact with himself over the stolen silver), Amy Foster (her marriage to Yanko), the almost nameless young hero of "The Shadow-Line" (his new contract as captain), and Razumov (his contract to be a spy). In most of these cases, the contract is not presented as given; we follow at length how slowly and particularly it comes into existence, and how much compromise, forced relation, self-limitation, and loss of illusion go into its creation. This part of the story might be called a contractually realistic "beginning."

The second half of the story is much harder to execute, and is more often deprecated by Conrad's critics, but is equally necessary. In contradiction to all the prior comical groundwork which seemed to show how the contract involved some pragmatic compromise and self-limitation, the contract itself turns on the person to demand "everything," or in some other way becomes catastrophically again a "forced dialogue." Against the contract, which was a sublimation and limitation of the forced dialogue, a new forced dialogue appears which breaks it open. There is considerable variety in this pattern, but in most cases— Lord Jim, Whalley, Nostromo, Razumov, Verloc, Winnie, James Wait—the contract, which has been forcibly accepted with a sense that it will bring some practical autonomy, turns out to demand more than was originally expected. New forced dialogues intervene to redisclose the forced dialogical character of the contract and of human relation itself. The object of Conrad's art now is to make the shift from the first part—the limiting, ironic contract—which exposes the forced circumstances of employment, to the second part—the retotalization of the contract—as seamless as possible. Marlow makes a freebooting contract to travel the Congo and then finds himself in a totalizing scene, bound to his image of Kurtz. Jimmy pretends contractually to be dying, and then, seamlessly, is dying. Verloc makes a contract to be an agent provocateur who does little, and is then forced to deliver terrorism. Winnie chooses a contractual, businesslike marriage with Verloc, which turns out to be the contract of annihilation. Nostromo's contractual heroism as Capataz de Cargadores forces him into the life-threatening mission; and his second identity appears as a contract with silence and silver that also turns annihilative. Razumov contracts with Mikulin to be safe, but the contract turns out to demand his entire existence. Thus contracts, themselves attempts to stabilize forced dialogue, become total and are then disrupted by even more intense forced dialogue. The irony of contracts is that they are not freely realized agreements but forced dialogues which attempt to deny their own ontological ground as coerced relation; pretending to be expressions of choice and freedom, they are burst open again by reappearances of the forced dialogue. One enters them to escape forced dialogue or control it, and one fails, because the essence of contractuality is that it is not voluntary agreement but forced mutuality. This relation always reappears.

The difficulty in realizing this double ambition, the movement from ironic contractual naturalism to tragic contractual retotalization, is that Conrad must each time find a way to realize the second movement convincingly, and with as little absolutist afflatus as possible. The first half of the action—for example in Part First of *Under Western Eyes*, where we see the elaborate chain of events by which Razumov comes to be hired—is often more obviously successful. Conrad is a master ironist of contractual realism, showing how strange new contracts emerge and assume a false appearance of having been chosen, an air of "forced freedom." But he is less simply successful at the retotalization. By conventional criteria of "prose fiction" as "showing not telling," his most uncertain moments are those in which he assigns the character the task of insisting on the new totalization. Thus he has trouble getting across Marlow's idea that Kurtz is all-important, Nostromo's sense of the total danger of his mission, the young captain's concern for his crew in "The Shadow-Line," Razumov's sense of immersion in Geneva. In each case the reader is likely to feel that something is happening by assigned fiat rather than by realized representation. Nevertheless, this leap from the first part to the second is not only absolutely necessary to Conrad's art as a whole, which is, if it can be defined at all, "tragic contractuality," but is powerful even in its fall back onto poetic fiat, assigned to the hero as itself the voice of such tragedy. The point may be stated as an argument about identity: the contractual self is as total as any other. Chosen contracts are not in essence different from tragic forced dialogues. The two halves are adjunct and mutually necessary.

The strange jobs of Conrad's heroes might be criticized as the vehicles of this idea of process. Most people, it might be said, aren't hired heroes: don't become foremen in charge of a whole working class, lords of foreign peoples, double agents, sea captains. Work like this is unusual in its contractual totality. The hero's loss of freedom is double: first he willingly accepts the loss of freedom by becoming a hired "master," but then the job demands more than was expected, exploding the self which was altruistically renounced. A somewhat easy and cynical order of metaphor would see this as a self-pitying representation of the writer: one contracts oneself to write, and then ends up having "to give too much of oneself." But the conclusion that everything refers to its own textuality and that the other jobs are simply metaphors for the demands of novelistic writing is too easy here. On the contrary: in Conrad's work, writing is represented as being only one sort of skilled labor or mastery, contractually total, but not mystifyingly more so than many other kinds of labor. Authority itself is understood as the ability to bear the conscious recognition of forced relation. All authority seems to be a practical acceptance of, and self-abnegation toward, the totalizing forced dialogue of community. Such master workers, by definition, are those asked to give all of a self which, because it has become mature by contracting into mastery (as opposed, say, to expanding into pure genius), is no longer exactly there to be given. The story becomes that of a figure who has accepted this authority within forced relation, but whose acceptance does not protect him from a reappearance of that forced relation in a more intense form that will annihilate him. The real order, in fact, behind this pattern of the reemergence of forced dialogue in a contractually masterful life is not an idea of writing but Sophoclean tragedy. The rupture of the contract by a forced dialogue, the sense that, despite appearances, contractual power grows out of forced relation and is destroyed again by forced inquiry, can be found expressed first, most clearly, and most abstractly in the drama of *Oedipus.* Oedipus is the contractual king who has acquired kingship and the judicial power to conduct the investigatory "forced language scene" by his rational triumph over the Sphinx's irrational forced questioning. When the play opens, he is playing out, contractually, the role of judicial investigator, the "new Sphinx," the speech-forcer, trying to discover the criminal agent, repeating the scene of violent inquiry; and in the action, he loses a contractual self he never really had to the process that always was.

VI
Oedipus: The Punishment
of the Speech-Forcer

THE PRECEDING CHAPTERS have described Conrad as a novelist who pays steady formal attention to scenes of coercion to speak and write, and who explores the historical recurrence, the institutional variety, and the psychology of such scenes. The readings have moved toward the conclusion that, in spite of his reputation for writing about solitaries, he is in fact preoccupied with a type of relation that takes place not so much inside the consciousness of relatively isolated persons as between them: forced contractuality. This idea of forced relation becomes most clear in scenes where persons are forced to produce some speech or written language. His sense of this forcing is, further, more direct and radical than the "pressures," for example, in Henry James' dialogues, and more fully and abstractly conceived than Scott's in *The Heart of Mid-Lothian*. Although this formal fascination with coercion to speak might seem to lead to a bare determinism in dialogue, Conrad emphasizes not the successful catechism but the unexpected, mutedly violent, almost toneless answer that briefly shocks the speech-forcer, redefines the relation, and passes a "sentence" upon the scene preceding. We are looking not at a mechanical determinism or pessimism in dialogue but at something else, more difficult to label.

This flexible format of coercions to speak has already led to a redefinition of a large set of relations, and in starting to consider what this idea of dialogue finally represents, it might be useful first to think of it as a dramatic and critical version of "intention." "Intention" here is the necessary directive force between persons that nevertheless leads to unpredictable results; it becomes most fully clear when it fails to produce exactly what the forcer has demanded. A forcing intention makes dialogue strong, holding interlocutors together; but at the same time it makes for the possibility of an unpredictable response, unlike what either side planned, and not "free" for either of them. The dramatization of intention, as opposed to the dramatization of determinism, depends on a partial and mutual failure of realization. In what was probably the first scene of the whole set of Conrad's forced dialogues, the figures whom Marlow politely calls "the Intended" rids him of his ideal image of discourse and dialogue by making him lie; in addition, he substitutes for her personal name the general and contractual phrase "your name." He refuses to name her personally and instead names her generally. He arrives at the civilized "name of name." A newly displaced, contractual, forced mutual identity is realized in the strained dialogue between them; and this bizarre "civilized" contract itself resembles the pervasive forced contractuality throughout his novels, the general mood of "forced political intention" between persons as they act on each other to produce responses. The loss of a comforting, free, or personal "tone" in this process "detonates" the ideal of free intentional contractuality, and is in several ways more despondent than Freud's idea of necessary self-repression; but the scene at the same time refuses to condemn—it has no single verifiable tone, not even the mock tragic—this process it displays as necessary.

The last step (implicit in some of the above readings) is to show that the pattern of surprised coercion to speak is neither peculiar or idiosyncratic, nor simply part of a conventional "dialectic" in which forced contracts repeatedly emerge and dissolve in response to the "force of circumstances." It has something more crucial to say to our ideas of dialogue than to our ideas of dialectic. It has its origins in tragic drama; and Conrad's anomalous power as a writer of novelistic dialogue comes from a quiet, formal return (within his relatively "minor" and "detached" representations) to consciousness of Oedipus as the "first" surprised inquisitor, the most circularly punished speech-forcer in the dramatic tradition. The result is that Conrad's work hints that there is an Oedipal dialogue format (understood at first, as by Conrad himself, more in relation to the plan of Sophocles' drama than to Freud's Oedipus, though we will come back to Freud) at the core of dialogue. This format, for all its power in Sophocles, might appear also in small and ordinary moments. For language as "truth" to be produced, persons have to make each other speak, but those who force speech most actively are also most vulnerable to shock and punishment by the language that then appears. This possible closure, both as the immense Sophoclean format of the punished examiner and as a smaller daily possibility, is one of the ultimate formats of "humanist" and "democratic" dialogue process, and a format we have lost sight of because we are preoccupied with more idealized notions of dialogue.

The premise that our preconceptions about what dialogue "is" are among the main topics of the novel as a genre will probably seem reasonable; but the specific attention to coercion to speak here will probably seem more stubborn, excessively narrow, or cynical. But this narrow focus is necessary, as in Conrad's writing itself, because forced dialogue eludes the two most familiar contemporary classes of ideas of dialogue. The first could be called dialogical idealism, as in Buber and his ancestors and in many contemporaries such as Habermas, Rorty, and Ong. This is a great tradition beyond and in spite of some easy dismissals of it. For these writers, of course, "dialogue," or some variant like "conversation" or "the ideal speech situation," is a central term, even a principle metaphor. The second, conceived as the critical opposition or analysis of such relational idealism, sometimes regards dialogical idealism as a kind of rhetoric or even a cant. The critique takes many forms, the most well known of which *seems* to be Derrida's concept of "logocentricity." Yet Derrida, Foucault in his discussions of "excitations to discourse" and "infinite examination," and Lacan in his breaks with the conventions of therapeutic dialogue in fact have some marked affinities to dialogical idealism. Conrad's idea of dialogue as necessary coercion to speak with unstable results looks as if it has something in common with both the idealisms and the critiques, but is finally unassimilable to either. Because it intuits that there is an Oedipal format of dialogue, a ritual dramatic inheritance, it may be the basis not so much for criticism of the other two (dialogue idealism and skepticism about dialogue) as for a third way of thinking about dialogue form, which allows us to ask why we project ideas about dialogue, idealized and negative, in the ways we do.

It might be useful, before going on to the question of Conrad's "classical" idea of dialogue and its somewhat unusual place in modern writing, to sketch, very briefly, these two stances of dialogical idealism and skepticism about dialogic in contemporary writing. The dialogical idealisms—sometimes nearly "utopias"—try abstractly to describe, posit, project what dialogue is or ought to be. They are among the most typical and representative works of the twentieth century. A small but various sample has already been cited: Buber's *I and Thou;* Habermas' image of the "ideal speech situation"; Paolo Freire's *Pedagogy of the Oppressed;* Gadamer's readings of Plato; Laura (Riding) Jackson's prose work *The Telling;* Paul Goodman's belief in the scene of the speech as the antidote to the scientization of relations; and Mikhail Bakhtin's superb work on dialogic and the novel.[1] Since these belong to different genres (philosophy, political theory, the prose poem, literary criticism, pedagogical theory), and since the writers are diverse and would reject the grouping, the list must seem incongruous. In fact, however, they make for a modern genre (often explicitly antidialectical, or seeking to correct something "missing" in dialectics) of critical prose that seeks to describe, and often also to enact by a meeting with the audience, a regenerate idea of "dialogue" as the model of human order, restoring life or coherence or legitimacy to fallen human and political relations. The modern essays on dialogue are, in one sense, new abstractions or distillations of a conversational idealism that has a long history in literature and philosophy since the Renaissance. In English literature the dialogical conviction of the lyrics of Shakespeare, Donne, and Herbert was novelistically elaborated in what Leavis calls "the great tradition." American literary dialogism—to Whitman and beyond—often reflects the egalitarian religious meeting forms and liturgies of radical Protestantism.

By contrast, corrosive doubts concerning the ideological uses of dialogue run through the work of all the major figures vaguely identified as post-structuralist; but they are at the same time difficult to locate in relation to dialogue as a utopian idea, in Mannheim's sense of the two terms *ideology* and *utopia*. Though specialists remind us that they are not at all alike, let's assume momentarily that Lacan, Derrida, and Foucault have something in common, as they seem to from the outside, and that in part it is a rigorous, even positivistic detachment from ideological concepts of dialogue as the term is ordinarily used, and yet a slightly stronger incline toward utopian dialogic. Jacques Lacan, for example, popularly known partly for discarding some formal conventions of the analytic dialogue, supposedly once told students considering a dialogue with the government in 1968, "There is no such thing as dialogue, it is a swindle." [2] A strong enough statement, its spirit is not brand new, and not exactly outside the range of earlier "humanist" insight: it could be a header for Melville's *Confidence-Man*, for example. Bitter doubt about the invitation to dialogue as ideological swindling runs from Thucydides' Melian Dialogue to "The Walrus and the Carpenter." Classical irony, after all, often traces the most extreme and the most minor mutual opacities in dialogue. There is an English tradition of skepticism about dialogue that runs from Swift's *Polite Conversation* through Austen and Lewis Carroll; and there is a long French tradition of scrutinizing dialogue to see the "contract," rather than the soul, beneath it. The very writing out of dialogue in the novel implies a plain skeptical scrutiny of it. James, overstating the contrast in the preface to *The Awkward Age*, protested that Anglo-Saxon audiences want heaps of dialogue in dramas but refuse to look at dialogue as form, the idea of which fills them with "horror," while Parisians want the texts of plays that get popular or "loom large." In the history of French political theory, the strongest linguistic model of social order has been, of course, not "dialogue" but "contract"—that is, it has for a long time been, before Derrida, a metaphor derived from writing, rather than speech, and the metaphor of the social contract was perhaps always tinged with irony about the more Hebraic and dialogically responsive notion of society as "covenant." My only point is that the contemporary division between idealized and critical attitudes toward dialogue ideas is not new and not easy to define historically: *both* positions have been anticipated by various kinds of "humanism."

Further, dialogical idealism has a way of returning in action after being dismissed in critique, and neither Derrida nor Foucault exactly dismisses, or evades, dialogue idealism. On the contary, one seemingly unusual way to describe their styles—forget their propositions for a moment—is that they are not at all indifferent to, but are in melancholy reaction against, dialogical utopias, which are the only projects they would accept, if they could accept any. While each implicitly and explicitly criticizes some versions of dialogical idealism,[3] at the same time they remain closer to it, and more indebted to it, by a kind of nostalgic enmity, than to any other metaphysic. This is one reason why the work of Bakhtin, for example, has often been confused with deconstruction, though his dialogic is in fact incompatible with deconstruction. Derrida cannot accept such idealism for the same reasons he cannot accept any metaphysic of presence, but at the same time his work is closer to that of Emmanuel Levinas, for example, who might be called an absolute dialogist, than to that of many other thinkers; his writings, that is, read otherwise from what we are told they assert when redacted into theses. To overstate only a little, they read in part like elegies for dialogical idealism. Foucault, likewise, obviously rejected dialogical idealism because it so flagrantly denies the reality of produced "discourse," and instead sought to describe the modern world as "infinite examination," a model which is (and this should make us suspicious) virtually the contrary of the ideal, an Oedipal totality with no resolution; but he admired Bakhtin, in practice interviewed easily, and seemed to want public exchanges of ideas in a way not entirely different in spirit from Habermas' "ideal." Foucault, from this angle, took a complex stance about dialogue as utopia versus dialogue as ideology. Lacan's angry moment, "There is no such thing as dialogue, it is a swindle," stands for their common position athwart rather than simply without dialogical idealism. Perhaps the unconscious in Lacan's advice to the young can be translated, "Be afraid of dialogue: Oedipus loses everything." Yet Lacan's advice is certainly not cheap cynicism, but only part of the on-going rift about "dialogue" as a term that is itself often cynically ex-ploited.

It seems naive, and even forbidden, to talk about Buber and Derrida as similar. But one simple way would be to compare, for example, Der-rida's use of the word *écriture* to Buber's use of the word *dialogue*. Each takes a word that ordinarily signifies one part of all language produc-tion and makes it, with a certain amount of deliberate difficulty, the metaphor or image of an antithetical "social contract." That is, Derrida perhaps places *écriture* where Buber and his romantic ancestors placed dialogue: it is the part of language production to be privileged as "free-ing" in its powers. Derrida's *écriture*, like Buber's dialogue, is the ideally antiauthoritarian social contract beyond the given constitution. Derrida would almost certainly reject this picture of his writing as a transcen-dentalism of writing as freedom, but it is possible that where Buber makes an image of "dialogue" as the indeterminate "covenant," Der-rida makes an image of open and infinitely various *écriture* as potentially emblematic of freedom or at least its hint. He is another poet of the so-cial contract, whose social contract is "writing" itself, which cancels ex-clusionary and inclusionary orders. You analyze local constitutions down to their contradictions and also imagine an ultimate constitution of infinite tolerance and undecidability. The motives are as clear as they are logical, humorous, sane, compassionate. No one is a more compas-sionate reader of others than Derrida in his deconstructions. Structur-alism, especially in Lévi-Strauss, had hinted, perhaps even demonically proven, that structure works by exclusion, elimination of someone, the creation of gaps in series.[4] In his remotely bitter way, Lévi-Strauss was suggesting the origins of genocide. Derrida's deconstruction is a re-statement of the battle against exclusionary order, a moral project which has to be conducted in an absolutely antiabsolutist language. It is nihilistic only in the mask it wears for conservatives.

There is another, less easy way to compare Buber and Derrida. This would be from the "Oedipal"—that is, forced dialogical—perspective that Conrad's writing gives. From this standpoint, both Buber and Der-rida repress or sublimate the scene of the punishment of the speech-forcer, the Oedipal scene to which Conrad was productively resigned. Buber transcends it to turn it into a perfectly dual, covenantal "I and Thou" alterity beyond any forced closure; Derrida, though in fact equally Judaic in his final sublimity, works more from "inside" the classical tradition, and comically makes the dramatic punishment or undoing of the speech-forcer something that "language," by a kind of sleight of hand, does to itself. That is, Derrida's hero, "writing," does to itself playfully what Oedipus does to himself tragically in the drama: analyzes and interrogates to the point of self-dissolution. The dramatic disintegration of the central figure—the "Oedipus dialogue"—is sublimated as the deconstruction of the text by itself. In Foucault, Oedipus (the principle of self-annihilating inquiry) is distributed everywhere and nowhere, a depersonalized "infinite examination" whom we cannot locate; in Derrida, Oedipus is troped into the playfulness of linguistic deconstruction. Each can be seen as the dramatic Oedipus dialogue monologized, or at least redistributed along a lyrical axis.

Conrad as presented throughout this study occupies a fairly singular place in this field of twentieth-century dialogics. Conrad is not assimilable to conversational idealism, to a tradition of novels of intimacy and personal realization, to deconstruction, or to a vision of all dialogue as inquisition. It is hard for us to place the meaning of his bizarre dialogue formalism, of his continual and obsessive return to the scene of dialogue as coercion to speak. He has neither an ideal picture of dialogue as sympathy, "betweenness," or "encounter," in Buber's or George Eliot's sense; nor exactly a skeptical picture, as in Lacan and Melville, in which there is no discoverable dialogue except an illusion of it and a swindle; nor, though he may seem closest to this at first, a Foucauldian or pre-Kafkaesque picture of the world as a vast system of impersonal pressures to produce "discourse." Instead, he revives and rearticulates, in a strangely musical and formal mode, what I will try to show is the classical, dramatic, and Oedipal picture of the "most human" dialogue as it "must" be. This idea of dialogue has, among other things, some refreshing elements of vulgarity and obviousness. To put it a little comically, it answers the abstract question What is the origin of speech? ironically and dramatically: people forcing other people to talk. This is a meaningless, even stupid answer, by the criteria of metaphysics, of linguistics, even lyric poetry. But it is a powerful answer in the context of the novel, which for Conrad describes contractual "illusions," among them ideas about free conversation.

Insofar as his writing argues the existence of acting "persons," agents, and forces, it will seem a humanist illusion to some. Conrad's art presents persons having effects on each other as agents. There is not good ground for suggesting that he believes that discourse produces us, rather than vice versa. But insofar as he also denies that "true" speech is what is produced freely, or from within, or in deep, intimate conversation, he seems "antihumanist." Speech instead is "force"—what he calls the perceived "force of words"—and "truth" is what is produced not when we speak freely but when we are circumstantially forced to speak. Truth is to be seen most strongly in the contours of a forced, lying response. The response provoked is not, as in a totalitarian (or successful) catechism, identical to the response sought. Conrad also pictures neither an "ideal speech situation" like that found variously in Buber and Habermas, nor a negative world of "excitations to discourse" like Foucault's. "Dialogue" does exist, and is not a metaphysical term, but it is neither a scene of freedom and equality nor one of simply perfect and fatal domination, of making the other say exactly what you want, nor even one of fruitful pedagogical disproportion, as in Plato and Valéry. It is a scene of coercive disproportions, in which question and answer are asymmetrical to each other, and the outcome is partly unpredictable in spite of being "caused" by forceful mutuality. Dialogue is, in essence, not meeting, not philosophy, not conversation, not dialectic, but only persons making persons speak in a continuous, unresolved, and finally unresolvable field of force.

Why is this formal, rudimentary realization of this idea of dialogue and drama as a sort of broken forced catechism—as persons making other persons speak but without being able to determine the words spoken—important? Why isn't it just crude? We might want to say, polemically, that it is important because it allows us to take a position that is neither unconvincingly sentimental, humanist, and unforced (something we sentimentally call Dialogue is open and free and a good in itself) nor depersonalized and systemic (the idea of conversational dialogue masks a world inquisition, a discursive system of forces). But Conrad's formal idea of dialogue does not really forbid or refute these other positions. It is important only because it opens to us the possibility that our ostensibly political ideas of dialogue can also be psychoanalyzed, and specifically, that there is an Oedipal dialogue—the punishment of the speech-forcer—which we have overlooked in these other theories; for instance, which Habermas overlooks when he projects an ideal speech situation for new, legitimate democracy. This radical position would suggest that all idealizations of dialogue, but *also* all thrillingly negative theories that present a world of inquisition and antidialogue, are repressions of the Oedipal insight—that dialogue is caused by forcing, in which the one who forces is potentially redefined or destroyed by the outcome.

There is and should be a plurality of ideas of dialogue; no one form of dialogue is the "essence" of all dialogue, and there can always be new kinds. But I want to use the notion of an "essential" dialogue here pragmatically, as a model, in order to emphasize that coercion to speak has a place in the classical vision of dialogue which we have tended to forget, and to suggest that it is an object of unconscious repression by philosophies, conversational idealisms, deconstructions, and theologies. This idea of dialogue is found fully acknowledged only by certain dramatic imaginations. I do not mean to propose that the dramatic idea of coercion to speak is finally the essence of all dialogue, the ground; but in this essay I want, for dramatic purposes, and to clarify Conrad's powers as a novelist, to write "as if"—to use a verbal mood ironically—it "might" be. It is this feeling of a possibility—that coercion to speak might be the repressed essence of all dialogue, and that dialogue becomes most "human" not when we let each other talk but when we make each other talk—that I take to be the major critical meaning of Conrad's work in relation to the poetics of dialogue.

What did the Athenians see when they watched the *Oedipus Tyrannus?* Most of the great answers, including Freud's, emphasize a dialectic of knowing and ignorance and its attendant metaphors; Girard and others emphasize ritual scapegoating as encapsulations of general violence. I don't mean to replace or argue with any traditional or psychoanalytic readings but to turn our attention elsewhere, toward the tragedy as dialogue form, and to notice that the audience was also being shown a model of public dialogue as forceful inquisition. The play, from this perspective, was also about the judicial institution whereby certain persons are empowered, or seize the power, to force others to speak. The specialized (not intended as total) answer here to the question is: they saw the judicial power of coercion to speak, embodied in the person of Oedipus, brilliantly and startlingly prove its neutrality and legitimacy by exposing and destroying the person of Oedipus. That is, they saw an ingenious justification of that power to force witness which is perhaps, from the common viewer's standpoint, one of the aspects of the legal process which is most disturbing or anxiety producing. We generally hate or fear being made to speak ourselves and are thrilled and disturbed to watch forced witness in its many forms. In Sophocles' play the force is so objective that it incriminates the person who bears it. The figure of Oedipus at key points in the drama—when he provokes the prophet Teiresias, and when he forces the shepherd to reveal what he knows just before the full recognition—exercises this power heroically, personally, and uninhibitedly, with what can fairly be called great dramatic force.

Oedipus, then, is a secular logos: not the Logos as the great transcendental concept, not the sublime core of dialectic, but the logos as a legal institutional power to make the other talk and bear witness to the community. The logos defined this way is legitimate coercion to speak. To illustrate from contemporary experience, bearers of such a logos include teachers in the classroom, interviewers and journalists when they approach people with questions, judges, talk-show hosts, and so on. I use the lower-case term *logos* and these examples here not to debunk this secular power, or to make fun of the higher idea of Logos, but because some term is needed for our ideas about what makes social language happen, or what lies "behind" it, and this is the conventional one; and because in Conrad's novel the logos—that is, the origin of speech and its substance—is not transcendent but secular and coercive. In addition, this sense of logos as a secular force is not entirely unusual in standard studies of the idea.[5]

Oedipus is the *tyrannos*, and he is, partly because of his history with the Sphinx, the contractual possessor of this specific institutional power to "riddle," to make others bear witness, a ritual power which he has perhaps inherited from the Sphinx he destroyed, and now bears (to the Athenian audience) in a more rational, less "matriarchal" or "primitive" form. The play, as a dialogue action, and as a defense of inquiry, works to prove that this power to make the other speak—about which the audience is torn—is finally legitimate and rational, for all its power to fascinate and horrify. That the power to make others speak is a usually ignored major theme of the play is reinforced by the uncanny parallelism between Oedipus and the Sphinx in their life histories. She was the speech-forcer finally punished by the answer she provoked, in the legendary past, and now, during the course of the "rational" play, he undergoes a parallel process. When Oedipus answered her correctly, of course, he said, "Man"; that is, he overthrew the archaic power of the Sphinx by rationality, by the answer of "humanization," and perhaps to the audience by a ritual defeat of the matriarchal past and the old gods. But the power which she had to force speech did not disappear, any more than the terror the Furies bring simply disappears when they become Eumenides. He became himself the rational, humanized substitution for her more primitive, chthonic, maternal power to force speech. Oedipus, then, did not simply rid Thebes of the Sphinx but instead came to bear a new, supposedly more humanized form of this mystery. His replacement of her allows us, at the very least, to imagine what Aeschylus might have done in his lost version: Oedipus' rational but still forced inquiry replaces the Sphinx's riddling force much as the Eumenides grew out of the Furies. As *The Eumenides* studies the retention of fear in the *polis*, *Oedipus* treats of and justifies another fear-ridden feature of the laws: the power to force witness, the "primary" power to make the other speak. Oedipus is the Sphinx turned into the practical logos of coercion to speak in the *polis*; he is the democratic neutrality of violent inquiry as justice; and he suffers the same (roughly) democratic fate of being destroyed by the answers he forces. The drama assigns Oedipus as inquirer the worst crimes, and then proves to the audience that this new logos is neutral, absolute, fair.

When Teiresias answers Oedipus' taunt, "Who has taught you truth?" by saying in effect, "You, for you have made me speak against my will," this retort is put in his mouth precisely because the play argues that the process of forced inquiry has final authority over the language of prophecy. The power to make the other speak must be put, as a logos, into the hands of human officers, not divine prophets. Where *The Eumenides* ends with the goddess Athene conducting a transparent inquiry—the scene of the trial as a glass bubble of clear witness and plain language after all the dark language preceding—inquiry in *Oedipus* is more politically humanized. No Athene makes witness transparent; Oedipus himself as a human agent has to force transparency out of those who are highly reluctant for his sake. The process must be conducted by human force, not by a god; but this immediately puts the issue of human force in dialogue at the center. How can it be as neutral and objective as Athene's? (The setting in Thebes, not Athens, is secondary here: it allows the playwright to make the *tyrannos* more sensationally and primitively coercive.) The most brilliant, even mathematical, way to justify the exercise of judicial force is to construct a perfect dialogue recoil, in which the process condemns the forcer himself. The people are being taught that coercion to speak, which is the constant vestige of violence in the court, is just. Of course all this is also presented not as shallow rationality but as deeper, pious rationality which knows its own history: in some sense, the rational inquiry has the same form as the old rite of killing the Sphinx. Rational process recognizes its irrational origins, which only proves how rational it is. With another kind of piety also, Oedipus in the play undergoes a *nostos*, or homecoming, purely by dialogue. By standing in the same place, he comes home, through the process of forceful questioning alone. He has appeared to be the contractual king; forced dialogue shows him to be the blood king of Thebes at the same moment that it dethrones him.

This reading should not conflict with the Freudian reading of the drama but should only add the disturbing (and ultimately Conradian) suggestion that what Freud calls the "Oedipus complex" is enacted in the public sphere in rituals of coercion to speak. A culturally important proposition can be derived from this, as from Conrad's work: coercion to speak is the public form of an aspect of the Oedipus complex which is to be found in Sophocles more clearly than in Freud. For example, one would have to read the transcript of the McCarthy hearings or the television show *60 Minutes*, as well as literary performances like the opening to *King Lear*, Kafka's *Trial*, Dostoevsky's "Grand Inquisitor," or Edmund Gosse's *Father and Son*, not as "symptoms" of the Oedipus complex in Freud's sense but as the complex itself in a dramatic sense—the set-up, always a highly emotional ritual, in which there is a speech-forcer who is then actually or in fantasy destroyed. That is, the "Oedipus dialogue complex" is the process of coercion to speak in which the secret aim of the dialogue action is to somehow punish the inquisitor.

But instead of broaching a discussion of this pattern in politics and social ritual, here we should look only at the pattern of the punished speech-forcer in literature, a literary history which Conrad grasped and reinterpreted within the boundaries of the novel. Let us say, more abstractly, that in regard to dialogue, Sophocles' play realized a formidably unrepeatable dialogue pattern for later writers, an "Oedipal dialogic," a perfect closure in which the inquisitor is violently revealed and punished by the process he institutes. No one later can duplicate this. This is a dialogue that can be described and pictured, here as a circle. There are other stark dialogue patterns of equal power that come to mind: for instance, the Hebraic pattern of the Book of Job, not exactly "dialogue" in the Greek sense, but the collective mutual amplification of a set of questions, until God speaks, not answering but only further amplifying Job's questions, to make him "apprehend." Job "makes" God speak, yet the answer does not punish Job but rewards him as speech-forcer. This is not Hellenic debate. Another strong, highly picturable and paradoxical dialogue format is that of mutual conversion, or "chiastic persuasion," in which by the end two originally opposed speakers have exchanged places, so that they still don't agree. A Protestant and a Catholic debate and convert each other, as Kierkegaard jokes; Hardy uses this form powerfully in *Jude*.[6] These are illustrations of other strong primary dialogue "types," whose form can be "pictured," if one wants to use that term. The punishment of the speech-forcer—the type here heuristically assigned the status of classical and Oedipal—is one among many formal options. But it begins to seem, in Conrad's work, the picture of dialogue itself rather than only one reusable form among others. This may be an irrational intuition, but it is one which Conrad's work in the middle period explores.

Having set up this hypothesis about Oedipal dialogue form, and having implied that Conrad's own work leads us back to this scene but gives it a strange new light as a "contract," I want to consider some other scenes of coercion to speak in classical literature: (1) Clytaemnestra's unsuccessful attempt to make Cassandra speak in the *Agamemnon*; (2) the Dialogue at Melos in Thucydides; (3) the vexed question whether Socrates is mainly maieutic, a midwife of other people's thoughts, or eristic, someone forcing the opponent out of positions while ironically disavowing his own combativeness. These three scenes are interesting in themselves; but they also pertain to things said here earlier about the meanings of forced dialogue in Conrad's novels.

Cassandra takes center stage in two scenes of very disproportionate length. In the first, brief and prologuelike, Clytaemnestra orders her into the house, and the Chorus urges her to obey, but she remains silently unmoved. In the second scene, of course, she speaks her gradually less obscure prophetic lament. The first scene, though only a kind of prologue or frame, has signal importance, because it shows Cassandra's unique response to being forced to speak by a political, secular figure. Though the device of "speech after long silence" (keeping a character mystically mute on stage for a long time so that the words finally spoken will seem profound) is one that Aristophanes makes Euripides ridicule in *The Frogs* as Aeschylus' typical "gimmick" for generating pseudoprofundity in the absence of real dramatic art,[7] that shrewd dismissal does not make sense here. By not answering, Cassandra provokes Clytaemnestra into two face-saving rationalizations: that Cassandra must be ignorant of Greek (which is nonsense), or that Cassandra is mad. For the first time, that is, she fumbles and lies *to herself*, or at least makes weak excuses in the face of the only figure in the drama who, despite her enslavement, manages to resist her direction. Clytaemnestra has just succeeded, of course, in making Agamemnon obey her by entering the house on the purple carpet, symbolically reenacting his murder of Iphigeneia, and in many other respects she directs the play's language and silences. But Cassandra's success in oppositional silence establishes her prophetic stand against political direction. Aeschylus' use of the forced dialogue here, then, is precise, and in keeping with the dominant classical meaning of the scene as "humanization"—that is, forced participation in society. When Aeschylus wants to make Cassandra's speech seem inspired, or to set her speech, for all its suffering humanity, apart as obscure prophetic truth, he first shows that unlike everyone else's, and in spite of her abject condition, her speech is not governed by the *polis* and cannot be generated by the ruling tyrant. Cassandra's silence, of course, also contains all her ordinary "human" despair, and is not "free" in the ordinary sense. But her speech functions on its own. By contrast, nothing could indicate the more secular horizon of Sophocles better than the fact that the tyrant Oedipus does successfully make Teiresias speak, and that Sophocles has Teiresias ironically and angrily affirm this coercion as his education.

Cassandra repudiates the coercive logos as a colonized subject. Insofar as she manages to fend off forced dialogue, she stands outside the human political order, and is the prophetess. When she does speak, she reworks the dialectic of dark and clear speech, which in the rest of the *Agamemnon* appears as political deception and calculation, into her own religious-poetic mode of dark clarity. She may seem to us very "human," in a sentimental-transcendental sense, a Joan of Arc, but the play itself divides her starkly into two parts, each of which is classically *in*human: slave and prophetess. The play underscores the tragic symmetry of her prophetic transcendence of the human government of speech to her simultaneous position "below" the human order as a slave. She is at both extremes at once. Her speech transcends human coercion (though not Apollo's coercion), while in every other way she is powerless and degraded. To be inside the human order is to be forced by other human beings to speak. One might think of Simone Weil on force in the Iliad.[8] But the strongest comparison available is to Thucydides, who does close studies of degraded speech forms during imperial wars. Conrad assimilates into his novels, as no other novelist had, and explores with some modern distance, the Greek theme, which runs from Homer through the tragedies to Thucydides, that to be "human" is not to be free in dialogue, as in Renaissance and modern "humanism," but to be immersed either in a *polis* or in an imperial tangle of polities, and therefore to be caught in multiple forms of dialogue as coercion.

There is no more famous or bitter instance of this intuition than Thucydides' Dialogue at Melos. According to Rudolf Hirzel, this scene startled ancient as well as modern commentators by its sudden textual shift into dramatic form.[9] (The analogy for us would probably be the night scenes in *Moby-Dick* and *Ulysses*, in which prose suddenly becomes theatrical script, in part because voices prevail at night.) Hobbes, by contrast to Hirzel's emphasis on the drama of the scene, believed that it had been overinterpreted, and was not much more than the picture of a tough negotiation,[10] in which the Athenians, who present blatant arguments for force as the law of history, are themselves forced into a brutal policy destined to do them harm. Extermination, Hobbes implies, is never good realpolitik. But where Hobbes pays attention solely to political arguments, we should look, more like Hirzel, at the dialogical setting, but unlike him, not idealize it as "dialogue."

The Athenians approach Melos, a Spartan ally, with more than enough power to destroy it, and ask to argue their case for immediate Melian surrender before the Melian populace. The leadership refuses. Prevented from appealing directly to popular fears of extermination, the Athenians suggest a format for negotiation with the leadership:

"Suppose that you, too, should refrain from dealing with every point in detail in a set speech, and should instead interrupt us whenever we say something controversial and deal with that before going on to the next point?"[11] The Melians accept this open format half-heartedly, objecting that while "in a calm atmosphere" the form would be reasonable, it is "scarcely consistent" with "the certainty of your making war on us" (401). During the debate, the Athenians argue for the law of force in history, dismissing, accurately, the hope that Sparta will come to Melos' aid, as well as moral notions of the injustice of imperialism. They claim that they themselves are, in fact, because of "a necessary law of nature" (404), forced to force Melos to submit, themselves the slaves of a law of force in history. After the debate, the Melians again refuse to surrender, and in the war that follows they are in fact exterminated.

The scene could be used as a primary tool in any critical study of dialogue, to teach wariness about universalizing the term *dialogue* in the easy way which treats it as a simple good. The formal irony is at least double. First of all, Thucydides makes it implicit that the Athenian proposal for open eristic discussion smacks of Athens itself, not of a universal logos. Whatever his cultural limits, he does of course know that there are different ways of organizing political speech. Among the best-known parts of the history are the entertaining descriptions of the Athenian taste for talk or disputation, the Athenian *Redelust*, as opposed to proverbial Spartan silence. Much of the first level of irony here comes from the sense that the Athenians offer Melos not an objective, rational form of disputation but instead a dialogical export, a home-grown talk game, mutual interrogation and interruption rather than oratory, which in fact is an Athenian cultural sport. From this angle—which reminds us again not to use *dialogue* as a universal term covering all possible scenes of talk together, but as culturally specific—the Melians are quite right to say that nothing could be more off base than to suggest a fair, equal "dialogue" when an unequal war is about to occur. But this, of course, is only half the irony. Fully registering that the Athenians propose some sort of eristic format redolent of the verbal contests back home, Thucydides at the same time structures the scene so that we feel that dialogue does indeed objectify; only what it objectifies is inequality, not equality. Dialogue is not in essence egalitarian: who could have thought so? The form of dialogue is objectifying because it too is disproportional, like history. Its use is not liberating but representational. Dialogue *is* forced dialogue, *is* the Dialogue at Melos—it *is* the forcing of political "reason" on the other. The word *dialogue*, which has been the object of so much excessive pacifist optimism, like the word *communication,* is one that in political reality tends to be used and imposed by imperial powers, or people in the position to impose "dialogue" and "communication" on those who do not want it. Thucydides' scene dramatizes what, since the quattrocento, we have more or less repressed in defining *dialogue.* We are back again at a starker form of Valéry's principle described by Lazaridès: "La communication ne s'établit, en effet, que si l'inégalité est supposée." [12]

A grim ethnography showing "dialogue" as an Athenian custom and export, created by an aggressive, competitive society, and not as a simple universal form, the Melian Dialogue has permanent power. A final reading of the scene is impossible, but we should note that some critics have thought it the centerpiece of the whole history, or the turning point at which Athens begins her final fall. Some think the scene shows the first major descent of Athens into the late, degraded phase of cynical rationalization of imperialism. But by our first formulation, that of the Oedipal dialogue, note that these readings support the idea that there is some strange connection in Athenian representation between being the speech-forcer and being the final victim.

In any event, these patterns take us to the clearest, most "vulgar," most important, and most Menippean issue of all, and the one which Conrad himself raises in *Under Western Eyes:* the place of Socrates—that is, of philosophy—in coercion to speak. While the relation between Socratic method and combative eristic is a vast question, and many writers have taken many sides, it is arguable that the Socratic "irony" relies at least in part on the consciously sly disavowal of his own force and combativeness. This goes against some major modern strains in readings of Socrates—against Nietzsche's image of Socrates as resentment, and equally against those humanist admirers who see a kind of saint, employing a purely maieutic and liberating technique to allow the intellectual rebirth of the other. [13] Gilbert Ryle, extremely subtle on this issue of Socrates as bully-inquisitor or as gentle midwife, brilliantly manages to emphasize Socrates' social immersion in an eristic world, and at the same time to deny what he sees as our common and mistaken image of Socrates as a kind of coercive inquisitor himself. Ryle insists that no one talked with Socrates unwillingly, and that Socrates could not in fact have "made" anyone talk with him. [14] But Ryle's feeling that this image of Socrates the forcer needs correction implies that he considers it a common one. Most teachers will recognize that students—and in this they resemble Conrad—often react to Socrates with simple resistant dislike, not because like Nietzsche they think him deviously humble but because he seems to them to force conclusions out of the other. From this split response it is certainly possible to consider Socrates a figure consciously shot through with the dilemma of speech-forcing. Richard Robinson says of the early Socrates that his "denial that he is conducting an elenchus is insincere, and constitutes what is known as the Socratic slyness or irony." [15] That is, Robinson implies that Socrates knows the coerciveness of the format within which he works, and that his irony is often a complex, humorous attempt to moderate this necessary force, a desire to confess and transcend this condition together, and find the dialectic beyond the eristic.

So there are at least grounds for questioning the idea that Socrates as represented by Plato knows nothing of coercion in dialogue. He is not naive about the dangers involved either. Those dangers are political, but also, in the complicated sense traced here, traditionally Oedipal in Athenian culture: the speech-forcer may be destroyed in an Oedipal ritual. The Socratic irony, a broad humor really, is based on acknowledgment of this complex of coercive speech as the trap which even the philosopher can't finally escape. By his account in the *Apology*, Socrates was brought to trial not for corrupting youth but for examining famous people, making them speak in front of others and embarrassing them. That is, by this sublimely ironic, purportedly autobiographical account, Socrates' life obeyed, though at a slant, the Oedipal pattern in its closure, the punishment of speech-forcer. Perhaps we misread him, misdefining him as gentler and more resentful than he is in fact presented to be, because we need for various reasons to forget his conscious working relation to the Oedipal scene, the disproportion and force in dialogue which he is quite ready to activate, the social and sometimes petty reality beneath the greater Logos. Modern readings of Socrates which deny him this active consciousness are pretty but false. The ironic tone of Socrates, on the contrary, is grounded in laughter about his own immersion in eristic, which he thereby "shares" with the other, and tries, not entirely successfully, to get past. He knows that he is caught in coercion to speak. And he knows about what is called here the "Oedipus dialogue," not in Freud's way but as the inevitable scene of coercion to speak as the logos, and the subsequent punishment for speech agency. From a psychoanalytic standpoint, however, Socrates' mysterious sublimity as inquirer perhaps lies in his ability to repeat Oedipus as dialogue *form*, without having actually committed the primary crimes of which Freud makes so much. Socrates is, psychoanalytically, an "innocent" Oedipus. The primary crimes are repressed out of consciousness by "philosophy," but the Oedipal pattern of self-knowledge as a high, dangerous process is retained for an even more sublime thrill. It is in Socrates that the Oedipus dialogue sheds its specific Freudian insight (incest and parricide) and becomes an abstracted forced dialogue, or "dialectic."

These selections have deliberately emphasized this one scene in order to show that classically the concept of "dialogue" is more violent and coercive than it has come to be in most modern usage. Since the Renaissance, for many reasons, *dialogue* has become a term for the absence of force. But contemporary use of *dialogue* to mean only positive, tolerant freedom comes, after all, from later philosophy, or from radical Protestant liturgies, or from the conversational novel, not from drama or poetry. These ideal notions of dialogue are conditioned by humanism and enlightenment. They are not native to the dramatic or poetic traditions, or even to Plato. Gilbert Ryle writes, in *Plato's Progress*, that after Plato philosophical dialogues "smell proleptically of the reader's lamp" (23–24), as opposed to Plato's, which retain the sense of combative circumstance. There are many possible historical reasons for the pacification of *dialogue* as a term, until it now means something akin to equality, nonviolence, and tolerance. In the present context, some of the best dialogics—Buber's, Freire's, Habermas'—certainly recognize force, but in a place secondary to conversational otherness and egalitarianism. While these projects, insofar as they are explicitly philosophical and projective, are important, criticism of them should not be "deconstruction," but the reminder of the dramatic insight into the coercive, Oedipal format of dialogue as the shadow, the repressed reality, of such high, optimistic definitions of dialogue itself.

In modern dialogics, it is not uncommon to find a kind of blurry sense of coercion to speak which preserves traces of the drama but still represses the classical intuition. Here, for example, is Gadamer describing the process in Plato's dialogues by which Socrates reveals not a general truth but a personal truth for his interlocutor:

> The thesis that only the person addressed really understands, it seems to me, hardly needs justification for students of Plato. After all, who else but Plato said that Socrates, whatever he might begin to discuss, ultimately demands an answer from the individual whom on any occasion he has right in front of him, and that he forces the latter to account for what he is saying? The methodological primacy which the literary form of the dialogue has for an interpretation of Plato's philosophy derives from the same principle. In these dialogues, we ourselves are the ones . . . who find ourselves addressed and who are called upon to account for what we are saying.[16]

In this we can hear how a vocabulary of force may be used just far enough to excite a sense of personal drama, but not so far as to revive the starker insight into dialogue as coercion and appropriation found in at least some major Greek literature. To repress the dramatic is to repress Oedipus as coercion to speak. But a further irony is that if philosophy, rather than dramatic and poetic literature, has ignored forced dialogue as process (even for those who, like Gadamer, want to deemphasize dialectic and empower dialogue), then when philosophy is supposedly "unmasked" as a coercive discourse, the unmasking itself can magnify coercion to speak into the totality of the world if we continue to forget Oedipal dialogue. Foucault's writings, for example, also repress the Oedipal scene; why don't we notice how the epistemological breaks, the gaze, the examination rehearse Sophoclean plot and imagery? Why the insistence that nothing like the modern answer "Man" could have been given until the eighteenth century, the great break, somehow "later" than we all thought, after which everything became a diffuse inquisitorial scene? Isn't this the myth of Oedipus, a little reorganized and discursively abstracted? In Foucault, Oedipus is distributed everywhere and nowhere as an impersonal universal examination scene without a clear answer. Of course this does not prove Foucault wrong; on the contrary, modern institutions may in fact depersonalize and diffuse the Oedipal drama in examinatory and inquisitive scenes. But it is possible to accept some of Foucault's models, and even to admire his critical analysis of the ideological "myth" of repression, while still wondering if his writing does not repress and amplify the Oedipal dialogue scene, to evoke a dishonest ominousness by hiding the *Oedipus Tyrannus* in a monologue about the whole world order. Abstract dialogics, positive or critical, may derive "mysterious" sublime "force" from the scene of the punishment of the speech-forcer, variously reworked, redistributed, sublimated. Freud's own therapeutic dialogue does not make explicit when to "force" or lead the patient to insight and when not to; Freud may not have fully psychoanalyzed his own dialogical methods. A formalism like Conrad's, though it must defend itself from the scene by "contracting" it, nevertheless faces the scene consciously and usefully.

The punishment of the speech-forcer also appears in several strong moments in English literature which Conrad is likely to have known. For the purpose of imaginative comparison—not to do a systematic survey of such scenes in English or to suggest direct influence—let us look at some scenes from Shakespeare, Wordsworth, and Marryat. *King Lear* and *The Winter's Tale* both begin with punishment of the speech-forcer. Lear presses his daughters to declare love and meets resistance from Cordelia; Leontes orders Hermione to talk their guest Polixenes into staying longer, and then goes mad with jealousy about the two of them, whom he perceives whispering together: "Is whispering nothing?" (1.2.330) Each scene has been criticized and admired, and is arguably either "naive" in a bad sense, or directly in touch with some primary dialogue idea that makes questions of motive and psychology relatively trivial. From the present standpoint, if Sophocles constructed a "perfect circle," in which the drama traces the punishment of the speech-forcer, Shakespeare alters this scene in two ways. First, he "contracts" it, so that it is only the beginning of a larger exploration of a king's humanization; second, as a Renaissance artist, he breaks open the Oedipal circle *partly*, by exploring the meanings of a man forcing a woman to speak, an issue which had already arisen with unparalleled force in the trial of Joan of Arc. Specifically, by making the scene of coercion to speak a struggle between the sexes, he tries to show that what we have called the Oedipal process, the classical scene of coercion to speak and punishment, is the dramatic as *only* the dramatic—only part of a larger natural order which transcends drama itself.

When Lear tests his daughters and Cordelia resists, we have the beginning of humanizing drama as the rupture of catechism. The father forces the children to speak, but instead of being catechized, one daughter says something unexpected. Cordelia's "Nothing" is, however, significantly not a pure silence but a spoken word. That is, she does not remain simply silent, as Cassandra does under pressure from Clytaemnestra, but in fact names something which she calls "Nothing." In Shakespeare's English, "nothing" is always potentially more substantive and less abstract than in our use. In Hamlet's juvenile teasing of Ophelia, "nothing" is mildly obscene, the "nothing" in Ophelia's lap, a substantive "nothing." Lear, equally childish, tries to conduct a ritual of inheritance with three daughters in place of one son. Forced to speak in this bizarre deflection, Cordelia answers, "Nothing," and is a little less prudish than many modern readers think. She insists on naming her sexuality as it appears to him, and as he misconstrues it. That is, in regard to the love which he asks for from his daughters, she can only offer his mistake about his daughters' sexuality as "nothing." This is a complex sexual answer, not just a metaphysical one, and is less prudish than we sometimes think when we criticize Cordelia's reserve. If Sophocles' Oedipus, even at Colonus, seems primarily to be discovering only his own identity, Lear discovers the world outside catechism by being made to confront first the "nothing"—the sexuality, but not available to him—of his one true daughter; and then, through this refusal of the feminine to submit to forced dialogue, he can begin to discover what Shakespeare calls Nature. Shakespeare reworks the restricted Oedipal process of forced dialogue within male social order to try to "include"—but fail to include—women and Nature in its contract. This frees the drama from the closed circle of Greek recognition, and opens the possibility of a larger natural order, another recognition. For Shakespeare, the word *nothing* remains dramatically and dialogically personal, arising between father and daughter as the result of a forced dialogue; it then leads the way not to the transcendent but to Nature. Shakespeare's Renaissance idea makes the essential classical dialogue, the forced dialogue, a failed attempt to appropriate women, which failure is hopeful. It promises that one might leave the restricted dialogical circle of a purely Oedipal drama.

The opening movement of *The Winter's Tale*, in many ways the late companion play to *Lear*, also takes up the question of forcing a woman to speak. In the first brief scene of the play, the polite talk of courtiers introduces the discrete language styles of Sicilia and Bohemia: Leontes' court is plain spoken, those attached to Polixenes are florid. The two courtiers forecast the opposed styles of their kings: Leontes, leonine, is blunt, curt, imperative to a fault; Polixenes is so polite, prolix, and florid that he seems too exquisite in his oratory. Like Homer's overpossessive hosts, Leontes wants Polixenes to prolong his royal visit, and makes his demand gruffly and stubbornly, while Polixenes' refusals are perhaps equally insulting in their ornateness. At this rhetorical impasse Leontes turns rudely to Hermione, demanding that she use her own inviting skills: "Tongue-tied our Queen? Speak you" (1.2.36). She obeys and flatters Polixenes into compliance. Leontes then unintentionally insults her in his thanks: she never spoke more to the purpose, he tells her. At this, she coaxes him to admit that at least once she spoke well before, when she agreed to marry him. This seems, however, to open an old wound, that she made him wait three months for the answer. His character is outlined as the vulnerable need for immediate answers from others in forced dialogue.

Leontes of course suddenly goes mad just after this in a great scene about the spontaneous, "uncaused" onset of madness. The scene is strong partly because it presents an insanity unexpected and inexplicable at first glance. But while Leontes' madness arises out of "nothing" (like Lear he raves about "nothing"), we are also meant to feel some subtle and irrational causes. The subtlest is that Leontes is the speech-forcer upon whom the scene he directs recoils. As in *Lear*, the speech-forcer, whose prototype is Oedipus, has to be punished virtually "by" the language extorted—in this case Hermione's courteous talk with his friend—and "humanized" into nature by suffering. The dialogue pattern is the cause. A sophisticated reading of this pattern might see a struggle between author and character, in which the tyrant dramatically assigned to make others speak—to seize direction from the start—must exist in order to drive the drama, but also must be checked or destroyed by the author for his usurpation of word-creating or authorial power. But Shakespeare's art, without any naivety, transcends this battle with his own characters to study a deeper qualm about dramatic authority itself. He seems, instead, to want to resolve this authority to make others speak (in one form the authority of the playwright) back into what he designates Nature. Dramatic authority by itself, without Nature, is only Oedipal forced dialogue, which includes the playwright's specific craft, and is by itself the contract of insanity, if there is nothing beyond it. Throughout the play, "silence" becomes the emblem of femininity, healing, organized innocence, nature. While time passes over a long, feminine silence, apparently passive, in fact that silence effects, through Paulina, Perdita, and Hermione, a restoration, though one in which the dead son, Mamillius, remains unresurrected. Most critics have seen Perdita's speech about "Great Creating Nature" as one of the central statements of the play, and there, when Shakespeare tries not to abdicate his authority but to resee it as part of Nature, he seems to be seeking absolution from the claustral, Oedipal drama (the dramatist's crime, making others speak, makes him what Othello pathetically calls "the cause," a power to project that becomes jealousy and paranoia) into a natural order more whole than dramatic power. This power is at the same time not repressed but understood as the contract of the tragic, the narrowly dramatic. Making the other speak is itself the Sphinx (the closed circle, the power to riddle) that must be dissolved— the tyrannical, the classical, the dramatic, the logos as social inquisition—and the way to do this is not to deny it but to show it as a contract, set small in a larger frame.

This is one way in which Wordsworth has more in common with Shakespeare than with Milton.[17] In Wordsworth, reticence about making the other speak combines strangely with a recognition that talk with strangers, and pilgrim dialogue in general, must be initiated, out of nothing, crudely and directly. At the same time he seems to feel that the young speaker, who inquires directly, needs to be forgiven for his assault; and apostrophe in Wordsworth is often more hidden and retarded than in any other major English poet. Wordsworth also of course rejects what to him seem mechanical rhetorical devices that force the audience to feel, and pictures an audience that is trying to force him to force it to feel; his technique repeatedly frustrates that demand by the withholding of conventional narrative catharsis. In keeping with this, it seems that to his temperament institutional pedagogy is a scandal because it is a forced dialogue; questioning is often badgering; precocity may be the most dangerous forced poison; universities are places of forced activity and feeling—and that all this is Rousseauist.

But unlike Rousseau, Wordsworth in fact has a dramatic sense which contradicts this moralism, an ability to face and accept coercion to speak as part of existence. His best scenes of encounter attempt not to avoid but to recognize and then outsmart the forcedness of learning itself. The chillingly entitled "Anecdote for Fathers" (*Lyrical Ballads*) is the most explicitly and complicatedly Oedipal of his early poems according to this definition. The speaker is a father who has moved from "Kilve by the green sea" to "Liswyn farm," and implicitly feels melancholy about the move, and about time itself. Out walking with his son, unable to own these feelings, he turns the melancholy into an arm-twisting interrogation of his young son, asking him where *he* would rather be. I will quote the second half of the poem.

> Birds warbled round me—and each trace
> Of inward sadness had its charm;
> Kilve, thought I, was a favoured place,
> And so is Liswyn farm.
>
> My boy beside me tripped, so slim
> And graceful in his rustic dress!
> And, as he talked, I questioned him,
> In very idleness.
>
> "Now tell me, had you rather be,"
> I said, and took him by the arm,
> "On Kilve's smooth shore, by the green sea,
> Or here at Liswyn farm?"
>
> In careless mood he looked at me,
> While still I held him by the arm,
> And said, "At Kilve, I'd rather be
> Than here at Liswyn farm."
>
> "Now, little Edward, say why so:
> My little Edward, tell me why."—
> "I cannot tell, I do not know."—
> "Why this is strange," said I;
>
> "For here are woods, hills smooth and warm:
> There surely must some reason be
> Why you would change sweet Liswyn farm
> For Kilve by the green sea."

At this my boy hung down his head,
He blushed with shame, nor made reply;
And three times to the child, I said,
"Why, Edward, tell me why?"

His head he raised—there was in sight,
It caught his eye, he saw it plain—
Upon the house-top, glittering bright,
A broad and gilded vane.

Then did the boy his tongue unlock,
And eased his mind with this reply:
"At Kilve there was no weather-cock;
And that's the reason why."

O dearest, dearest boy! my heart
For better lore would seldom yearn,
Could I but teach the hundredth part
Of what from thee I learn.[18]

The clear lesson of the poem is stated in the Latin epigraph, which translates, "Restrain that force of yours, for I shall lie if you press me." Do not make children explain their moods, and also, do not press children to invent or label moods in the first place. The child's first answer—that he prefers Kilve—seems a "lie" tailored to his father's hint ("On Kilve's smooth shore, by the green sea, / Or here at Liswyn farm?" is not a neutral parallelism). The triple riddling—"And three times to the child I said"—and the double arm twisting emphasize the formulaic and ritual elements of this coercive scene. The father may be slightly satanic in his "very idleness," even though rest is often a good state for Wordsworth. The absurd, childish reason given—the weather-cock—is a touch of dry folk laughter. In all this we seem to have a Rousseauist poem against enforced precocity, learned dejection, bad teaching. But obviously, while pressing home the image of this unconscious projection with great power, Wordsworth also seems much more dramatically conscious than Rousseau in *Émile* that the scene may be inevitable and necessary. The world is with us, late *and* soon: enforcement of *soonness*—precocity, the imitation of parental moods, the too fast or too early—on the child may be as universal as the self-pitying lateness felt by the father. Time as soonness and forced precocity, in addition to Harold Bloom's "lateness," may be the theme of romantic poetry (consider Keats's Odes); and in Conrad's apprehensive time structures what is forced is the future. Here in Wordsworth the child, contrary to the epigraph, does not simply lie, and the father professedly learns from the confrontation.

The childish surprise answer, "weather-cock," could be thought of in a plainly sexual or crudely "Freudian" way, the cruder the better. Is it random, or just plain apposite in the dialogue—the punishment of the speech-forcer—which is here being reduced to an Oedipal *anecdote?* Annoying or funny the choice may be, but it has to be considered: either it's nothing, a random choice, or unexpectedly appropriate in its randomness. For the apparent Rousseauist moral, of course, the weathercock is "nothing," a random choice made by a desperate child forced to find a precocious reason for a feeling he does not even have. The obvious absurdity of the explanation teaches the father that he has been forcefully projecting melancholy onto his child. The boy chooses it as the first thing he happens to see that seems likely to get him off the grill. This seems like the correct reading. A second subtler reading might see the weathercock, which indicates the direction of the wind (motions of the spirit, as in the Gospel of John, or of feeling, as elsewhere in Wordsworth), as being the emblem of the father's desire to have directional "evidence" of the free, careless shiftings of the child's soul. A third reading might try to reduce the poem to unconscious symbolism: the five-year-old son and the father (or father figure, for Wordsworth was in fact talking to a friend's son during the scene which led to the poem) have now fallen into the Oedipal relation; but Wordsworth doesn't know that. The boy says "weather-cock," and the father, identical to Wordsworth himself, who is reporting an actual dialogue, not wanting to face the depth of the son's awareness, goes instead into slightly artificial and strained ecstasies ("dearest, dearest") about the child's power to teach, while actually evading the point of what has just been taught.

But a fourth reading, combining all these, would give more credit to Wordsworth's consciousness. He is reducing the whole strict format of the *Oedipus Tyrannus*—the punishment of the father as speech-forcer—and startlingly, comically, wisely scaling it down into an anecdotal folk ballad. Here the weathercock that becomes the turning point between them signals the inevitably directive and forced dialogue between father and son. When the son answers he means, "At Kilve there was no such coercive, directive dialogue." The weathercock becomes the sly, folk-tragic emblem of the father-son dialogue when it shifts—as it must—to coercion. The shock lies in the power of the scene to contractually reduce: in Wordsworth's "English" power, inherited from Shakespeare, to see the Oedipal reversal as a limited struggle within a greater "natural" environment. The poem scales the ordinary agony down into an anecdote, and the speaker, not Wordsworth himself, ends shrieking, almost as if afraid, like a questioner in Blake told what he does not want to hear. Thus by this account Wordsworth "knew" much of what Freud says (it is folk wisdom) about sons and fathers and symbols, but used it here with dialogical rather than mechanically symbolic emphasis. And the true Freudian reading also is the dialogical one, not the crudely symbolic one, as Freud himself decribed the symbols as occurring in a dialogue. Note the simple structural parallel between the scene from Lear and the anecdotal poem: whenever the father forces the child to speak, the child answers with a displaced figure for the genitals, which horrifies the father, not the child. As Shakespeare's Cordelia was forced to shock her father by answering, sexually, "Nothing," this son is forced to startle his father by answering "weathercock," which also seems to be, but is not, "nothing." There is a comical physical health in this English reduction of classical process.

Shakespeare and Wordsworth were able to look directly at the punishment of the speech-forcer. Each sees it, though in different ways, as an Oedipal contract, beyond which lies a natural order larger than this one formal struggle. The idea reemerges vividly in Scott's *Heart of Mid-Lothian.* In the last section (curiously enough the section Scott was forced to write), Jeanie's wild-child nephew assaults his mother and then kills his father; Jeanie when freeing him tries to force him to speak, to civilize him, but fails, and instead he sets fire to everything. The plot of the novel is first the successful sublimation of tragic forced dialogue by one sister, one "plain-spoken" feminine principle, Jeanie, and then its failure, and the return to Oedipal crimes, in her romantic sister Effie (Euphemia)'s family. These English versions seem conscious of a (nonpsychoanalytic) connection between forced dialogue and Oedipus. Arguably, however, Freud himself did not fully psychoanalyze this dialogue or his own dialogue practice. His hints about therapeutic method sometimes imply absolute neutrality—no forcing of the patient in any direction—and at other times recognize the inevitability of some forcing. From the present standpoint, if the Oedipus dialogue is the punishment of the speech-forcer, then an analyst who never "forces" the patient somewhat would be one afraid of being Oedipus—of being the punished speech-forcer. His neutrality would mask his own lack of resolution. By this account, psychoanalysis never fully analyzed its own dialogue form; and so one of the lingering problems in all analytic therapies is the question of the degree of "interference." Dramatic awareness like Shakespeare's, Wordsworth's, Scott's, or Conrad's is much more ready to face this issue. This kind of dramatic intelligence can face the Oedipus complex—the universality of forcing in human relations and of danger to the forcer—without at the same time falling into a pessimistic projection of this fact into the vision of a universe of mechanical and fatal force. It can face the thought that dialogue is forced and dangerous without being overwhelmed into mechanical fatalism.

So there is a certain dramatic perspective which reminds us of unfreedom in dialogue as a potentially good thing. For a daring, completely unembarrassed answer to anxiety about forced dialogue, we can look not at a slice of life but at a slice of Captain Marryat, who wrote extremely readable and lively adventures. Ford claimed that Marryat was the real, unknown key influence on Conrad. That's nonsense, but his ideas of dialogue are worth exploring. In *The Little Savage*, one of Marryat's two last unfinished books, Frank Henniker is stranded from infancy on an island with Edward Jackson, who, we later learn, driven by desire for the mother, killed both parents after the shipwreck. At the start of the book we know little of this. The two are "Boy" and "Master." They survive together on this *Crusoe*-like island, but Jackson, bullying and almost entirely mute, tells the boy nothing. When the boy is about seven, however, lightning blinds Jackson during a great storm, and the first major turn comes: " 'No,' replied I, 'do you come here. You have been master, and I have been boy, long enough. Now I am master and you are boy, and you shall find it so.' " Though at first Frank weighs killing Jackson, he soon realizes that he can now force information: "for now he shall answer all my questions, tell me all he knows, or he shall starve . . . He shall now do what I have ever tried to make him do, and he has ever refused." [19] Learning begins. Jackson tells the little savage about language, about England, and about the past. Lying at first about his relation to Henniker's parents, he finally, just before dying, tells the truth about this also. After his death, Frank is alone for a while missing his "father"; and then, through a complicated piracy plot not worth detailing, a missionary's wife is left alone with him on the island, to *sivilize* him where Jackson had only informed him. She explains Christian ethics and English patriotism, and tells the story of her husband's martyrdom by savages he tried to convert.

This tale is a blustering conservative protest against the picture of education as bullying. Marryat's little savage bullies his reluctant blind master into giving him an education. The child himself forces the pedagogical dialogue, which would not exist without his energetic initiation. Learning, he almost comes to love his "father's murderer," and gets from him the rudiments of social history; then the missionary's wife appears, to give him more subtle, ethical, boring instruction. Marryat's genius in effecting such a reversal of the romantic protest against pedagogical coercion should not be scanted. Though elsewhere, as already mentioned, Marryat gives a vividly angry description of the Inquisition—which the anti-inquisitorial, romantic Stevenson loved—here he makes coercion to speak not in essence an authoritarian distortion of natural order but a positive scene initiated by the wild child. The story roughly says that, left untaught in the wild, children would—force their elders to teach them. What is "human" would take form as coercion to speak, initiated by the younger generation, if the elder generation were unnaturally uninstructing. Marryat's scene has a kind of simple, if fantastic, health. The closest thing to this in Conrad is the scene of homage to his master's examinations in *A Personal Record*.[20] In Marryat, of course, all this takes place within a naive justification of imperialism, and Marryat could be said here to take all the anxieties about forced dialogue and simply ignore them, turning all the generational conflict into free will and gratification. His defense of Frank's demand to be taught runs dead parallel to his notion that natives need to be converted. But they are not in fact the same: Frank's early education makes good reading, his later conversion is unreadable. As for Conrad, the sense that "forced dialogue" may be a positive energy is linked to a knowledge of physical action and pleasure in physical work. Forced dialogue here is simply a form of natural energy, as Marryat himself had no trouble writing to meet public demands.

This set of examples above is meant to show the persistence of another, dramatic "humanism," not conversational, for which force in dialogue must be recognized as part of what is most human. Conrad himself belongs in this critical dramatic tradition, and he finally, if very qualifiedly, defends a kind of "humanism" which does not have the illusion that it can deny or eliminate its own coerciveness. The broad use of the term *humanism* here to mean any view that puts agency, and self-consciousness about that agency, at the center of things, so that coercive dialogue can surprisingly be regarded as "humanist" (or at least "humanizing"), will legitimately raise scholarly—and moral—objections that cite the history of the term, and its specific Renaissance meaning in association with freedom and against coercion. But there are several reasons not to confine the term to that historical definition. One is that the term is already politicized and broadened by common use well past its Renaissance meaning. Contemporaries in the United States who attack "secular humanism," for example, are not condemning Pico della Mirandola, but a range of beliefs which includes deterministic ideas far removed from the narrower definition of "humanism" as a philosophy of the free potential of human beings. But even more, it may be that Renaissance humanism, in regard to dialogue, was itself repressing or forgetting some important elements of classical "humanism." The examples above should at least open the question of whether the "other" dramatic humanism from Sophocles onward has not always known itself as problematically involving the process of coercion to speak as a core ritual of "humanization." As a result, a fair portrait of this broader, self-critical humanism would see persistent tensions in it between efforts to limit coercion by "contract" and critical visions which argue that the contracts all fail, and that secular dialogue is an inquisitorial nightmare of "discourses."

Conrad, of course, refused to define his own art clearly as humanist, impressionist, romantic, realist, or classical. But he did not so much reject them all as include them all, pragmatically. The artist, he implies in the Preface to *The Nigger of the "Narcissus,"* makes use of whatever methods seem right during the work of composition. Even "art for art's sake" is ony a practical stance that can be of use in allowing him to work. He was a "dialogist" who saw them all as ways, useful at times, of meeting the forced condition, and at other times not so much dangerous as pathetic denials of that condition.

Evidence that he knew "classical" literature in our sense, and that he had a practical familiarity with, for example, Sophocles, Aeschylus, Thucydides, and Plato, can be found in many allusions in the fiction and the letters. In a late letter about H. L. Mencken, Conrad in violent language tried to answer Mencken's characterization of him—meant to be praise—as a Slav. Torn about this, since Mencken was his laudatory herald in America, Conrad lamented that such "a really ruthless mind, pitiless to all shams and formulas," should lapse to "parrot" the notion of his Slavism. In rapid sentences full of strong phrasal verbs ("snatches him away," "harping on," "ramming into," and so on) he insisted angrily that Polishness and his intellectual origins were ultimately liberal and Western European. Then he added, "While I was a boy in a great public school we were steeped in classicism to the lips, and, though our historical studies were naturally tinted with Germanism[,] I know that all we boys, the six hundred of us, resisted that influence with all our might, while accepting the results of German research and thoroughness." [21] This sentence tells of his education as a process of influence, resistance, and final approximate acceptance of a classical education. His classical education, whatever it was, was also a variant of forced dialogue. The German scholars forced classicism on the boys (who sound, oddly, almost like the "we" in the *Narcissus* forecastle), and they resisted but accepted.

The metaphor "steeped in classicism to the lips" recalls forced dialogue as well as Stein's famous advice to immerse in the destructive element. To be steeped in a certain tradition "to the lips" means, possibly, to be made to speak by it, or to have one's language influenced by it forcibly. *Steeped in . . . to:* obviously this English idiom translates the Latinate word *immersion.* This phrasal verb accompanies other similar verbs of physical force in regard to both Mencken and Conrad. It is a violent letter against verbal violence. To refute Mencken's charge that Conrad is a Slav, Conrad accords him similar barbaric praise, suggesting that Mencken's writing resembles "the crackle of blue sparks like those one sees in a dynamo house among revolving masses of metal that give you a sense of enormous hidden power." To answer Mencken's charge of primitive dark force, he tells us, in one of his key metaphors, that of incomplete immersion, that his own quasibaptism, insofar as it took place in education, was in something he calls "classicism," and that it was to the lips. He does not say that a whaleboat was his Harvard and Yale, or that he had no real education except life. He was schooled and did receive something he calls a classical education; and of course it took form as a variant of the scene of coercion to speak.

The same letter uses a related but weaker metaphor of partial immersion to refer to "romanticism." "I am a child, not of a savage but of a chivalrous tradition, and if my mind took a tinge from anything it was from French romanticism perhaps." This is a double reticence: "to take a tinge . . . perhaps" does not have the same force as "to be steeped in to the lips." One could argue that, if we take Conrad at his word, his tinge or coloration was romantic, but his force or immersion was "classical." But the reference to "classicism" in the letter is of course vague. From the context it could be argued that by "classicism" he means the classics of the French and English novel, which shows how little of a classical education, how much of a popular, romantic education he in fact had, since he regarded Balzac, Hugo, et al. as "the classics." But this quibble goes too far. Conrad almost certainly meant by "classicism" Greek and Latin literature, and while he may not have known them in any scholarly way, it seems unlikely that his German education at Cracow, his father's early influence, and his later reading excluded Sophocles, Plato, Aeschylus, or Thucydides.

Steeped or tinged, immersed or drowned—metaphors of forced participation: clearly it is easiest to think of Conrad as a late romantic, steeped in classicism like most other romantics, but full of contradictory romantic drives and classical forms. The labels, however, do not matter so much as that Conrad's language, even in its metaphors, is preoccupied with forced speech. As we have seen, his sentences are filled with gestures such as "I confess" and "I submit." Traditional myths are also restated in these terms. The for him related myths of baptism and Narcissus' drowning, for example, take on the quality of forced dialogues, between self and community, and between the self and its ideal image. Baptism brings the individual forcibly into the community and names him (as with the early forced naming of Peyrol when he takes to sea as a boy). The drowning of Narcissus describes an individual who tries to force a merger between himself and his ideal image of himself and is destroyed. These are two stories of identity as a forceful process. In the first, the individual submits to a communal immersion; in the second, the individual seeks an ideal identity and fails. Lord Jim's story, for example, might be read as the impossible juncture of the myth of baptism and the myth of narcissistic drowning; it tells us that the baptism of a Narcissus is his death. To put it more conventionally, it tells us that primary narcissism (in Conrad a strikingly emphasized feature in most central characters) must, but cannot, engage the world. When it tries it "drowns." We have a kind of detached and narcissistic temperament which knows that the world is real (Jim, Nostromo, Winnie, Razumov, Heyst), and seeks honorably to act on that premise, but lacks some final capacity for realism. To be immersed is to be destroyed: Narcissus immersed dies. This is one reason why, in dealing metaphorically with his own forced education in "classicism," Conrad insists that he himself was "steeped" only "to the lips." That is, it was still possible for him to breathe. To protect oneself, one transforms the "sea" into a "mirror" and stops there: immersion becomes representation. No one tradition or place has been fully allowed to immerse or suffocate him.

This detached perspective on forced participation gives Conrad his special tone regarding the Oedipal drama of forced dialogue. His novels treat the scene repeatedly, and make it extremely important, but with a sort of contractual distance. He recognizes the scene as the Oedipus dialogue, and writes it out repeatedly, but makes it seems as much a common contract as a high drama. The form of the novel, which can represent "dramatic dialogue" as a visible "form" or "contract" on the page, is particularly amenable to this. Conrad's work seems to assimilate the suggestions about forced dialogue that I have been tracing throughout this chapter in works by Sophocles, Thucydides, Shakespeare, and Wordsworth, but to view them through a fisheye. The final effect of adding scene on scene of various quiet rather than grand inquisitorial forced dialogues, in history, and in various social institutions, and in his picture of his own circumstantially determined writing, is to remind us that there is a practical dramatic logos—the power to make the other speak—and that it is minor, local, and contractual, as well as "terrific." Instead of overwhelming the reader with immense scenes like the Melian Dialogue or the opening to *Lear*, he distributes the form of a more petty inquisitorial pressure throughout many different institutions; coercion to speak and the punishment of the speech forcer take place in many smaller crises. The Oedipal dialogue is "contracted" in modern democracy and dispersed into many little scenes. Speech-forcing, everywhere in the contracts and institutions of modern life, includes the irony of authorship as a kind of forced telling.

Conrad, as a result, for all his apparent solemnity, has in fact a strange, unique prankster's sense of humor about the logos, because he sees it not as a profundity, or an enormous metaphysical illusion, but as a strangely persistent contract in which human relations small and grand are caught up. To summarize three main points about what I call here, a little ironically, the Conradian logos: (1) defined dramatically, it is not mainly the authority or presence of the speaker's own personal voice as intention or action, but it does in fact exist as the unstable social power to make the *other* speak, a power that appears in many forms, from subtle authority to explicit violence. To have the strength to see this logos is to reach the "heart" of civilization and to touch on the problem of "humanism as force." (2) The logos becomes most "democratic" not in egalitarian scenes but in the scene of the punishment of the speech-forcer. This dramatic democratic closure is the "Oedipal" and most classical dialogic. (3) Conrad's work in the middle period repeatedly displays this circular pattern on an oddly reduced, skeptical, even degraded scale, as the contract of "being human." If the scene appears in many institutions, and seems to be something like a universal or a constant, it is also a "contract" or contraction, a little petty, and seems as a result both total and local.

To illustrate specifically, let me close this study by discussing a very local, minor, droll story of Conrad's, his only "ghost story." Though usually disparaged, "The Black Mate" is one of the shrewdest examples of a small "popular" tale about coerced speech in Conrad. The story has been noticed by Conrad scholars not for this theme but usually because Conrad and his wife, Jessie, disagreed about its date of composition. He insisted that it was his first story, written in the 1880s and then revised in 1908; she insisted that it was entirely new in 1908 when she gave him the idea for it. This reported dispute between the couple lends a kind of special interest to the story for Conradians and a chance for some prying into his unreadable marriage. In the anecdote he appears to be—contrary to his stated hatred for lies—a fibber, sticking in a childish way to a whimsical assertion that it was his first story. Some critics, however, do lean toward Conrad's claim; others accept Jessie's version.[22] As a result it becomes a "mystery" of dating.

Putting aside the question of dating (which is by itself somewhere between boring and funny), the story, even without close reading, proves to be full of devices, forms, and ideas, though of course very sketchily realized, that lie at the heart of his methods of composition. These include the forced dialogue, here reapplied casually but in fact brilliantly to the raising of ghosts and the dialogue of séance (raising ghosts is obviously a forced dialogue with the other world, and therefore, from Conrad's skeptical standpoint, with nothing); getting a job as contractual degradation and compromise; contrasts between black and white, here organized temporally as a joke about "aging overnight," or having one's hair turn white overnight; and the central Conradian idea of a man who has two ages. As a result, while it is a light exercise, not well executed either, the conception of the story is very fine and witty and has something important but lighthearted to tell us about his main themes.

The tale also is fun, the way a piece for "Maga"—Conrad's name for the magazines—should be. The main action (leaving out the narrator as the device by which the reader is kept in the dark about the hair dye) goes as follows: the hero, Bunter, an older seaman, once a captain himself, is now down on his luck. To be hired as mate, he has dyed his white hair black, because the captain, Johns, is notoriously prejudiced against the old, and will hire no one over forty. (Bunter's name may suggest the German *bunte*, "variegate," or "many colored.") Johns has one other obsession: he believes passionately in ghosts. The two obsessions are assigned to Johns, the "little man" of the story, by fiat, and since both are there to make for the gimmicky outcome, they seem to be one of its weakest points at first. Yet the belief in ghosts and the neurotic avoidance of workers over forty add up, of course, to a terror of death not unlike that on the *Narcissus*. During the voyage, Johns keeps trying to force Bunter into conversation and an admission that ghosts exist. Ghosts have, he says, been photographed. Exasperated during one of these (implicitly recurrent) forced dialogues, the silent Bunter finally answers him with a threat. Johns has accused him of being capable of denying "the possession of an immortal soul to your own father." Bunter erupts and says, "You don't know what a man like me is capable of" (103). This threat only increases Johns's conviction that Bunter, impressive because of his stark black hair, his white skin, and his heroic stature, is a demon.

During this scene the real Bunter, not a demon, is in fact a worried man. In a storm, the bottles of the hair dye which makes him seem younger (autobiographically analogous to Conrad's author's ink) have broken; he dreads being exposed and becoming a cosmetic laughing-stock when his hair turns white. Shortly afterward, however, when he suffers a serious fall owing to negligence aboard ship, he has time to think while laid up. He concocts for Captain Johns the claim that he fell because he saw a ghost, and he tells Johns, as the weeks go by, that his hair is now turning white from the intensity of the momentary fear. His hair is the proof—implicitly, even more black and white than a photo-graph, or than print—that ghosts exist. He maintains his tone of con-tempt toward Johns, however. It was a powerful ghost, he says (though he refuses to describe it), who could make a man like him afraid, as opposed to the "tea party" sort of ghost that would visit a Johns. In all this, the man moved to dye his hair to get a job, then forced to make up a ghost to keep it and avoid disgrace, is justified by the narrator and by Conrad. He had to dye his hair and to make up a mystifying tale to support his wife. There is no trace of condemnation—as there is with Whalley for his forced dishonesty. Bunter is, in fact, "in the force of his age" (87), a capable seaman come aboard relatively late in life (as Conrad began to write also late in life), and only Johns's idiocy drives him to fabricate the nonsense for survival. Bunter, like Conrad a mid-dle-aged sailor turned author, first refabricated himself, dyeing his hair, or making himself a bit of black on white which is half true, and which contains two ages in one time; and then fabricated a tale tailored to the weakness of a specific audience, audience weakness being always one thing—denial of death.

Despite the usual evaluation, this seems to me to be one of Conrad's key minor pieces. But whatever the evaluation, there is at least one odd fact that has not, so far as I can find, been noticed. That is the symmetry between the scholarly problem of dating we now have and the temporal comedy of the story itself. While Bunter, the hero, lies about his age, Conrad, the author, according to our information, may be lying about the age of the story. That is, his story about the story resembles the story. Or to put it a little more subtly, where the Black Mate as a man has a composite age, each age in its own way true, so Conrad's story, because of his claim that it was his first, also now has for us two unrec-onciled ages, and we can't be entirely sure—unless the piece turns up some day in print—whether some version was first printed in the 1880s, or if it came directly and entirely from the period of forced dialogue that began about 1898. This immediately makes Conrad's "lie" more interesting, more droll, potentially a question of tone as much as schol-arly dating. Though we might come up with all sorts of deep motives for the lie, *if* it was a lie—such as that Conrad feared seeming to make fun of the "Master" Henry James (Captain Johns?) by writing such a crude antighost story which dismisses the origins of ghost stories themselves as fabrications for fools afraid of death; or that Conrad was psychotically unable to distinguish between himself and his heroes— nevertheless the most entertaining explanation is that Conrad's "lie" it- self was a kind of impulsive prank or game, a response to a literary "in- terviewer," with its own kind of truth about the nature of stories and their dates, and the nature of the "author" in a Conrad story. Conrad's "lie" tells us the truth that the "story of the story" (the story of its con- tradictory production) will sometimes resemble "the story" itself in in- teresting fiction. The story (like "The Black Mate") may be a complex metaphor for the way it was itself forcibly and circumstantially pro- duced. Conrad made a story for "Maga" about Bunter producing a story for Johns. Fiction like this also has several ages, not one, and has no simple "date." It is produced, under constraint, like answers to liter- ary inquirers, by writers who have to produce it, and who in part ex- ploit and represent their own youth by "dyeing" their age.

There is a strong temptation to take one side or the other, and seriously answer the problem of the date, to display one's knowledge of Conradiana. We could find remote data to support the idea that the story is early—for instance that the name Johns can be found also in Sienkiewicz's famous Polish patriotic chestnut "Latarnik" ("The Light- house-Keeper," 1882), a story Conrad may have been more likely to imitate in the 1880s than in 1908.[23] For this study, there is the even stronger temptation to argue at solemn length that the shrewdly dis- missive use of the forced dialogue as centerpiece of the tale (Johns *does* conduct a séance, with Bunter, and does force a ghost to appear) shows that the story must have been substantially rewritten, or fully con- ceived, well after 1900, since it was only in this period that Conrad began to write formal forced dialogues. If it was an old story, this argu- ment runs, Conrad revived it only because he saw his chance to include the séance among the astonishing variety of modern scenes he delin- eated as forced dialogues. But beyond this question of dating there is the simple and most important fact that the story is a portrait of the storyteller as circumstantially coerced to make up a story he despises. The storyteller may be as much a hired man as a master. "The Black Mate" details circumstances that would force a highly capable but so- cially compromised man to produce a ghost story for personal survival. What, that is, would lead someone who hates mystification to con- sciously mystify other people? There are circumstances that put an au- thor under contract to assume the role of power, or mystery, to take the role of the father, to "impress" mysteriously, displaying ghosts for his "children," or intellectual inferiors, who demand that he mystify them. These ghosts themselves are a displacement, both of their fear of death and of their fear of the father himself. The teller compromises his own realistic powers, putting them in suspension, inventing something which he and ultimately they also know to be unreal, because the audience forces him to. The author puts the ghosts there because under "contract" with his audience about his own powers; the ghost is his own power as a realist in suspension. Where Ibsen or James focuses on the repressed eros and the lack of full dialogue in the *characters* that lead to the production of "ghosts," Conrad makes the ghost a function of the coercive contract between author and audience. The audience wants the dream, not the reminder of the contract, and is not ready to accept the fact that all writing is a contract. And so the author is, paradoxically, forced to appear unforced, spontaneous, mysterious, magisterial, poetic, and has to do this to make a living. The "ghost" is finally the denial of the reality of forced dialogue. It is not, as in James, interesting because psychic. It is interesting because it is social contractual, a nexus where anxieties about domination can be repressed.

The "lie" about the date of composition, then, implies not that Conrad was deluded, or lived in a dream world, failing to distinguish between himself and his character, but primarily that he saw fiction as a literary form full of metaphors for the author's own productive servitude. This kind of fiction (as opposed to the simplest tales) has a metaphoric fidelity to the author's own servitude. People within the tales work as forced servants much as the writer himself does. The novelist creates narrators or voices not primarily (as in the Flaubertian and Jamesian theories, to which Conrad was only technically loyal) in order to gain objectivity, comprehensiveness, and final detachment, but more for the reverse reason: narrators figure as representations of the circumstances that generate his own compromised writing. Narrators are the figures of authorial servitude more than of authorial distance or control. When Conrad writes a "cheap" ghost story for the magazines, it is a story about a worker's forced production of a "cheap" fib. He later commits the prank of leaving us uncertain about the age of the story, as we are uncertain about the age of the hero, because he is also talking about fiction as production which makes the author have two ages, or combine his youth with the present. Fiction itself is not a free act but a complex of forced dialogues that registers itself as such a complex: the author "must" produce for his public on terms they make for him in great part, and must exploit his own past life.

"The Black Mate" makes a lighthearted, buoyant sketch of the forced creation of a ghost story for a solemnly superstitious audience. The story is crudely antitranscendental and reductive, and this is one reason why no contemporary school of criticism would like it as much as it deserves, or see its refreshing place in Conrad's work as a quick, dismissive, scornful application of the process of forced dialogue to the occult. The plot is what Todorov in an essay on James calls a "determinist" dismissal of ghosts.[24] Whether early or late, the story troubled Conrad because it showed his hand so clearly, and could be seen as an insult to James. The occult is only the nauseous and the stupid here, the socially coerced. There is nothing psychological or unconscious or playful about it. The storyteller appears as a canny working man who panders to his audience's taste for the uncanny in order to survive. And he is *not* (as with James's Selah Tarrant or Dickens' Chadband) a charlatan. He is morally justified in making up black and white, occult nonsense for the other's consumption. Authors have no exaggerated responsibility to tell the truth, because they are also only workers. They cannot create the listener.

There is, then, a plainer truth hinted at in Conrad's wavering insistence that "The Black Mate" was his "first" story, or by extension his initial idea. Whether or not it was in fact his first story, the insistence is a metaphor about the theme of his fiction. The story is about someone circumstantially forced to make up a false and mystifying story for someone stupid and in a position of power. At its most extreme, such a forced writer is the paid political hack helping to justify state crimes. How to come to terms with this element of degradation in all writing, even the supposedly most pure, is one of the obsessive themes of early modernism. Denouncing literature in the furious "Fourth Prose XII" (1929–30), Osip Mandelstam describes "writerdom" as "a race with a revolting smell to its hide and the very filthiest means of preparing its food . . . yet anywhere and everywhere it is close to the authorities . . . For, anywhere and everywhere, literature carries out one assignment: it helps superiors keep their soldiers in line, and it helps judges to dispose arbitrarily of the condemned."[25] But this attack on "literature" as evil collaboration with the state opposed to true "poetry" becomes meaningful, and Dantean, only when we hear that Mandelstam dialogically denounces hack writing in the lowest style of hack writing itself, that of the racist pamphlet. In calmer times, Mandelstam wrote the dialogically idealizing essay "About an Interlocutor" (1913), in which he argued that "there is no lyric without dialogue" (62–63), and claimed that symbolist poetry had "completely neglected the, as it were, contractual relationship, the mutuality that accompanies an act of speech. (I speak, and that means that I am listened to, and not for nothing, not out of kindness, but because there is an obligation)" (58). Each of these comments on the obligatory production of language—one scabrous, one idealized—is tonally conditioned by the historical period in which Mandelstam wrote it. There is no way to choose one over the other.

There can be, though perhaps only in less extreme historical periods, less extreme modulations between the two images—of poetry on the one hand and literature on the other. Somewhere in a poem by Ashbery a cranky older voice says to someone younger that it's allowable to write poetry, but please, no literature. This is an innocent American spoof of Mandelstam's type of passion; the older voice attitudinizes the "poetic life." But the distinction between lively personalist poetry and all the rest of the stuff written under resigned constraint is at the same time a dogma which, I think, Ashbery partly believes, for good reasons. His work doesn't simply make this distinction, but it finally enacts it dialogically, like all great poetry. Obviously he often recombines clichés into an insidious sublimity. Less obviously—though we talk about speakers we are unused to talking about the implicit dialogical background in any lyric—the half-hidden scene of Ashbery's poems is sometimes the forgiving answer to some typical bad, silly, forced conversational question or writing assignment ("What did you do for summer vacation?"). Ashbery's poetic action is to accept, parry, and reprieve the "worst assignments," understood, however, in a more innocent American sense and not in Mandelstam's desperate political sense.

The tone of Conrad's detonations, his modulation of forced and unforced writing, falls somewhere between the two of them, probably because his historical situation does. The sure difference between poetry and forced hack literature—the sense that we know for certain the real poem from something too forced and too "literary"—is often collapsed with defiant historical clarity in his work. His writing often deliberately challenges or aggravates any possible complacency about this ideal and apolitical difference. Partly through its own expressive constraint, Conrad's work tries to demonstrate and enact the ways in which all writing and dialogue must be forced. This forcedness itself becomes the secret theme; like Baker's "ough," inspiration as a kind of forced working effort rather than as free breathing, Conrad emphasizes the awkward work in language. If we accept a perfect distinction between poetry and literature, then Conrad in his prose works is often too forced, overwrought, too much of a high hack who indulged in seeming mysterious or hazy or sententious or deconstructed by turns to flatter our various ideas of the profound. A more accurate reading acknowledges that he is mocking these profundities and often teasing the demand for poetic mystification. If we reject any easy self-congratulatory distinction between poetry and literature, it becomes possible to say

that in his carefully extended forced scenes he finds the clearest expression of an original and unmatched contractual energy. The image
of forced dialogue can itself be read either as a complex historical commentary on coercions to speak or as a cheap fictive device; and both
readings are necessary. When he takes us back to this "familiar"
demon of his, his anti-conversational, obsessive idea about what all dialogue "is," he rebelliously cancels the ideal and necessary distinction
between pure poetry and forced literature. The truth of his writing is, in
part, this bizarre courage of visible forcedness. The forced magazine
tale "The Black Mate" should be kept in mind when reading the major
pieces, because, as Conrad tells us himself, it was his "first" fable.

Notes

I. Ideas of Dialogue and Conrad's Forced Dialogue

1. See Joseph Conrad, *Notes on Life and Letters,* "Some Reflections on the Loss of the *Titanic,* 1912," pp. 213–228, and "Certain Aspects of the Admirable Inquiry into the Loss of the Titanic, 1912," pp. 229–248. This and all subsequent citations of Conrad refer to the Canterbury Edition of the *Complete Works* (Garden City, N.Y.: Doubleday, Page and Company, 1924).

2. Ibid., p. 240.

3. Ibid., p. 215.

4. Ibid., p. 234.

5. For "ingenuities" see *Jude the Obscure,* pt. 1, chaps. 2, 5, and 6.

6. In "Flanagan and His Short Filibustering Adventure," a piece that may have had some influence on Conrad for various reasons including its theme of Cuban gunrunning, the engineer says the "old biscuit-box will never see port again" (*The Portable Stephen Crane,* ed. Joseph Katz, New York: Vintage, 1969, p. 356). Crane's usual pet word for dialogue was *pow-wow.* It shows up in the fiction and in a letter to Conrad about their first long meeting (see R. W. Stallman, *Stephen Crane,* New York: G. Braziller, 1968, illus. 18). Though a primitivist mannerism, "pow-wow" avoids the gentility of "conversation" and the abstraction of "dialogue" to describe talk as common force and noise. Conrad writing back to Crane does him a typical little gesture of homage by calling their recent meeting "our powwow" (Jocelyn Baines, *Joseph Conrad: A Critical Biography,* New York: McGraw-Hill, 1960, p. 204).

7. Many discussions of the Menippean, including those by Northrop Frye and Mikhail Bakhtin, emphasize parody of philosophy, the skeptical perspective of the dialogue of the dead, and Lucian's laughter. I will use the term here primarily to refer to formally comic or antiphilosophical dialogue in the novel.

8. *Typhoon,* p. 5.

9. "Certain Aspects of the Admirable Inquiry," p. 239.

10. Norman Page, in *Speech in the English Novel* (London: Longman, 1973),

contrasts "dialects" to "idiolects," or individual speech habits. Discussing Hemingway, Page calls the forms of cross-examination and catechism "the simplest . . . available to the writer of dialogue." Here, catechism will be taken not to be "simple" in this pejorative sense but imaginatively primary, with its varieties, including punishment of the catechizer, of extreme importance for drama and for surprise.

11. There have been no major studies of Conrad's dialogues because, by handbook notions of natural, spontaneous conversation, he does not write much good dialogue. The following articles are valuable: Owen Knowles, " 'To make you hear . . .': Some Aspects of Conrad's Dialogue," *Polish Review*, 20, nos. 2–3 (1975), 164–180, in which Knowles emphasizes, in a fairly traditional way, that Conradian dialogue is a scene of mutual misunderstanding; Eugene Hollahan, "Beguiled into Action: Silence and Sound in *Victory*," *Texas Studies in Literature and Language*, 16 (1974), 349–362; John Hagan, Jr., "The Design of Conrad's *The Secret Agent*," *ELH*, 22 (1955), 148–164. This last excellent piece gives a good account of formal dialogue recurrence and its importance to the reader in this one novel. Ian Watt, in *Conrad in the Nineteenth Century* (Berkeley: University of California Press, 1979), p. 128, writes, "He was particularly weak in dialogue," but this refers only to "The Return," an unsuccessful story, and probably not to Conrad's dialogue in general.

12. No full bibliography of modern dialogue idealism is possible here. See, for a few major and ideologically diverse examples: Mikhail Bakhtin, *Problems in Dostoevski's Poetics*, trans. R. W. Rotsel (n.p. [Ann Arbor]: Ardis, 1973); Jürgen Habermas, *Communication and the Evolution of Society* (Boston: Beacon Press, 1979), for an attempt to apply speech-act theory to a new picture of the "ideal speech situation" for legitimate public discourse; Walter Ong, *Ramus: Method and the Decay of Dialogue* (Cambridge, Mass.: Harvard University Press, 1958), for a study of Renaissance pedagogy that sees a decline of dialogue in Protestantism; Paolo Freire, *The Pedagogy of the Oppressed* (New York: Herder and Herder, 1970), for an attempt to supplement Marxist dialectic with a practical humanist dialogic; Martin Buber, *I and Thou* (New York: Scribners, 1970); Hans-Georg Gadamer, *Dialogue and Dialectic* (New Haven: Yale University Press, 1980), and *Truth and Method* (New York: Crossroad, 1982); Paul Goodman, *Speaking and Language* (New York: Random House, 1971), for shrewd criticisms of what he sees as fallacious denials in modern linguistic science and modern philosophy of the actual scenes of speech; and Laura (Riding) Jackson, *The Telling* (New York: Harper and Row, 1972), for a peculiarly American prose poem trying to enact a new "telling." For more skeptical discussions, see Jan Mukařovský, *The Word and Verbal Art* (New Haven: Yale University Press, 1977), chap. 3, on Gabriel Tarde's thesis that "conversation" is not a universal but a historical development of the Renaissance (92), and Paul de Man, "Dialogue and Dialogism," *Poetics Today*, 4, no. 1 (1983), 99–107, a concise and witty critique of contemporary "dialogic" as a cover term for almost everyone's thought, except his own strong rhetorical criticism.

13. Ford Madox Ford, *Joseph Conrad* (London: Duckworth, 1924), p. 185; citations in the text are to this edition. Their collaborative novel, *The Inheritors*,

begins with a dialogue scene with this comment interpolated: "In conversations of any length one of the parties assumes the superiority" (3).

14. *Leopardi: Poems and Prose,* ed. Angel Flores (Bloomington: Indiana University Press, 1966), p. 244.

15. See Habermas, *Communication,* esp. chap. 1, "What Is Universal Pragmatics?" for an overview of theories of legitimate dialogue.

16. Robert Louis Stevenson, *Virginibus Puerisque and Other Papers* (New York: Scribners, 1918), p. 347.

17. Important comments on the chaos of dialogue can be found in the Preface to *The Awkward Age.* In the lecture "The Question of Our Speech" (Boston: Houghton Mifflin, 1905), James describes common speech as a near chaos—but James's own sentences reflect on, rather than reject, that chaos. L. C. Knights, in *Explorations 3* (Pittsburgh: University of Pittsburgh Press, 1976), pp. 24–37, argues that the main theme in James's work is "domination," and that the theme is embodied in speech and dialogue *forms* (his italics). He does not go on to say what the forms are. The domination, "pressure and coercion," in Knights's version of James's dialogue, however, have to do with themes and issues the characters discuss, not with speaking itself. The plain dramatic coercion to speak found in Scott and Conrad is unusual in James, whose scenes are generally "conversations," and whose characters, with few exceptions, want talk. Domination is apparent between them, not in primary struggle about the production of speech itself, although *The Bostonians* (see n. 22 below) may be a partial exception.

18. Richard Gunter, in *Sentence in Dialog* (Columbia, S.C.: Hornbeam Press, 1974), pp. 81–98, discusses the possibility that connections between sentences of dialogue indicate ideas of order.

19. Hagan, "The Design of *The Secret Agent,*" p. 149.

20. For an anthology of articles, including some on ritual dialogue forms, see Richard Bauman and Joel Sherzer, eds., *Explorations in the Ethnography of Speaking* (Cambridge: Cambridge University Press, 1974); see esp. articles 3, 5, 7, 11, and 15.

21. Bakhtin emphasizes clearly the difference between dialogue form and his concept of "dialogic," as when he writes, in *The Dialogic Imagination* (Austin: University of Texas Press, 1981), p. 279, that the "internal dialogism of the word . . . does not assume any external compositional forms of dialogue." See also Mark Lambert, *Dickens and the Suspended Quotation* (New Haven: Yale University Press, 1981), and Stanley Rosen, *Plato's Symposium* (New Haven: Yale University Press, 1974).

22. *The Confidence-Man* tries to define the typical American *dialogue* scene—not exactly the same thing as the typical rhetorical scene Sacvan Bercovitch has described as jeremiad (or intense moral criticism covertly reinforcing the idea of the chosen people). The study of American dialogue and its literary representation would have to consider events such as religious meetings and talk shows. James's portrait of the precocious, ecstatic public speeches of Verena Tarrant in *The Bostonians,* and of her ambiguous forced rescue from their "phoniness" via dialogues with Basil Ransom, is one example.

23. "Certain Aspects of the Admirable Inquiry," p. 234.

24. Gerard Jean-Aubry, *Joseph Conrad: Life and Letters*, 2 vols. (Garden City, N.Y.: Doubleday, 1927), I, 258.

25. See Alexandre Lazaridès, *Valéry: Pour une poétique du dialogue* (Montreal: University of Montreal Press, 1978), pp. 9–53. "La communication ne s'établit ... que si l' 'inégalité est supposée' " (12).

26. Richard Ohmann, "Reflections on Class and Language," *The Radical Teacher*, no. 20 (n.d.), 19–22. Ohmann refers to and criticizes the work of Basil Bernstein (also criticized by Goodman) and Claus Mueller on disproportion in dialogue between classes.

27. Gilbert Ryle, *Plato's Progress* (Cambridge: Cambridge University Press, 1966). See especially chap. 4, "Dialectic," and chap. 6, "The Disappearance of the Eristic Dialogue," for discussions of Plato's dialogues as immersed in a social context of "force." Ryle's hypothesis is that Plato at first practiced, and later sublimated, the "force" of eristic dialogue, in which speakers try to drive each other into elenchus, or self-contradiction. The state, he says, itself at some point forcibly stopped the real practice, and the censorship was fruitful: "What forced Plato to find out the secret of solitary debating was the suppressing of his practice of conducting eristic Moots ... He became a philosopher because he could no longer participate in questioner-answerer Moots, or any longer be their dramatic chronicler. No longer had the Other Voice to be the voice of another person" (208–209). That is, philosophy is sublimated forced dialogue. Ryle uses the term *force* often to describe Athenian dialogue scenes, and less quietistically than, for example, J. L. Austin, writing of "illocutionary force"; but of course he makes no cultural connection to Oedipus as the dramatic inquisitor and speech-forcer.

28. *An Outcast of the Islands*, pp. 95–96.

29. See, for example, the Last Supper in Hölderlin's "Patmos." *Friedrich Hölderlin: Poems and Fragments*, trans. Michael Hamburger (London: Routledge and Kegan Paul, 1966). Jesus' speech there is a continuous goodness that generates future speech as plenitude: "Vieles wäre zu sagen davon" (466), the poem says of Jesus' talk and death, "Much could be said of [from] it" (477). Hölderlin's own continuous syntax in this poem is itself meant to be regenerated, a continuation of Jesus' speech as the inexhaustible source of further speech in time.

30. See *The Red Badge of Courage*, chap. 3, for a brief example of speeches clustered together.

31. Bakhtin, *Problems of Dostoevski's Poetics*, p. 91: "Syncrisis was understood as the juxtaposition of various points of view ... Anacrisis consisted of the means of eliciting and provoking the words of one's interlocutor, forcing him to express his opinion, and express it fully. Socrates was a great master of the anacrisis; he was able to force people to *speak*, i.e., to put into words their hazy, but stubborn, pre-formed opinions, elucidating them by means of the word (and not by means of the plot situation as in the 'Menippean satire')." Bakhtin's emphasis on verbal, physically nonviolent coercion in his definition of *anacrisis* is not shared by the dictionaries. See, for example, *Webster's Third:* "an

investigation of truth in a civil law case in which the interrogation and inquiry are often accompanied by torture." In New Testament Greek dictionaries the word seems to imply *preliminary* examination—what leads up to (*ana*) the crisis of the trial itself. Bakhtin's sublimation here of the term *anacrisis* into Socratic nonviolence is curious, since he is otherwise not usually finicky about physical life, the body, or violence. In this context the possible psychoanalytic explanation is that he is repressing, in a different way from Ryle, the connection between coercion to speak and the figure of Oedipus. Oedipus, unlike Socrates, gets others to speak by *both* verbal provocation and the threat of physical violence. In this light, Socrates' rich humor stems from his mock denial that he forces the other to speak: he does it all gently and slyly. From one perspective at least, both Oedipus and Socrates cause their own downfalls by following through—by continuing to press the inquiry and to make others speak—even after it becomes clearly dangerous to do so. Ryle argues that Plato himself was punished for conducting eristic debates—for being a speech-forcer—and that this aspect of Socrates' self-portrait in the *Apology* really belongs to Plato; but of course Ryle sees no connection to Oedipus here. The punishment of the speech-forcer is not for Bakhtin or Ryle a specific pattern: but the punished speech-forcer may indeed be a classical figure, first Oedipal and then Socratic, whom Conrad imports into the novel.

32. See Frederick Marryat, *The Phantom Ship*, in *The Works of Captain Marryat*, vol. 14 (New York: Peter Fenelon Collier, n.d.), chap. 36, and the opening chapters of *The Little Savage*, in *The Works of Captain Marryat*, vol. 17, whose scenes of coercion to speak are discussed in Chap. VI.

33. See, for example, Mickey Spillane's anticommunist novel *One Lonely Night* (New York: Signet, 1951). The paperback cover shows a naked woman hanging by her wrists. Forced questioning is of course frequent in detective novels but is also often the motif on the cover.

34. See the French translation of Bakhtin's study already cited in English: *Problèmes de la poétique de Dostoevski*, trans. Guy Verret (Lausanne: Éditions de l'Age d'Homme, 1970), p. 133. The phrase *rire resorbé* is clearer than its English equivalents, "reabsorbed laughter" or "muffled laughter"; it means that serious works steal or absorb comic ingredients while suppressing the laughter.

35. "The police, in the course of a persistent inquiry, could find not a single document compromising him, nor did they wrest any useful information from him." Eloise Knapp Hay, *The Political Novels of Joseph Conrad* (Chicago: University of Chicago Press, 1963), p. 41.

36. Borys Conrad, *My Father: Joseph Conrad* (New York: Coward-McCann, 1970), pp. 11–12, describes silence as the first rule in the family. Ford (*Joseph Conrad*, p. 21) describes how Conrad listened to him read their collaborative work aloud: "For the first chapter or two ... he was silent. Then he became—silent. For he seemed to have about him a capacity for as it were degrees of intensity of his silence." But the contrary image of him as a good storyteller and talker can be found with equal frequency.

37. Frederick Karl, *A Reader's Guide to Joseph Conrad* (New York: Farrar, Straus, and Giroux, 1969), p. 155, quotes an early comparison of Conrad's plu-

ral silences to those in Maeterlinck. R. L. Megroz, *Joseph Conrad's Mind and Method* (New York: Russell and Russell, 1964; first published London: Faber and Faber, 1931), which has important comments by Conrad on language, quotes George Gissing's response: "How, in Satan's name, do you make their souls speak through their silence? Nay, it is as though the very soul of the world spoke for them—as in that voice of the sea, which makes all the world 'like a tolling bell' . . . This is your glorious power, to show man's kindred with the forces of earth . . . Only a poet can do the like" (94). Gissing's corny rhetoric seems in its way more accurate than criticism which has been made cautious by deconstructive conscience.

38. The inquisitorial meaning of *familiar* appears italicized in Marryat's *The Phantom Ship*, p. 413: "There is also a public accuser, a procureur of the Inquisition, and lawyers, who are permitted to plead the case of the prisoners, but whose chief business and interest is to obtain their secrets or betray them. What are termed *Familiars* of the Inquisition are, in fact, nothing but this description of people; but this disgraceful office is taken upon themselves by the highest nobility, who think it an honor." The scene of "familiar" coercion to speak remains an obsession as late as *Chance*, where Marlow—who, after all, might be considered Conrad's figure of confession itself—bursts out into an uncharacteristically violent diatribe against confession: "Never confess! Never, never!" (212)

39. See, for example, the examinations of Madge Wildfire and Effie Deans in chaps. 16 and 17 of *The Heart of Mid-Lothian*.

40. George Gissing, *New Grub Street*, chap. 9.

II. Dialogue and Labor

1. A. J. Ayer, *Hume* (New York: Hill and Wang, 1980), p. 26.

2. Not one but three apparently unrelated minor characters in *Sylvia's Lovers* are named Donkin: a tailor who describes a recent anti–press-gang riot to Sylvia's father (chap. 5); the captain of Kinraid's merchant ship, mentioned only once (chap. 18); and a lawyer who will prosecute Sylvia's father for his own rowdy insurrection against impressment (chap. 25). It is not clear why Gaskell repeats the name, whether out of sloppiness, or as a comic observation about kinship in provincial life and the scarcity of names, or because it seems to her a spicy lower-class variant of Duncan, or as a kind of quiet joke: there are Donkins—ordinary working people mysteriously related—everywhere. Conrad's interest in this strong novel would have been prompted by the historical period (the Napoleonic Wars), and by the clear treatment of the domestic lives of seamen. If Conrad's low name Donkin comes from Gaskell, however, it is probably because she is a nineteenth-century novelist often associated with the sympathetic treatment of strikes and riots and resistance to work in general; he would have lifted the name partly to allude to her sympathies. Gaskell herself seems to make a thematic connection between masculine "impressment" and feminine "impressionability," writing of Sylvia's "impressible na-

ture." Both the lower-class seaman and the lower-class woman are easily "impressed," politically and psychologically. Note the skeptical relation this has to romantic "imagination" as the privilege of a freer class of people.

3. Baines, *A Critical Biography*, p. 205, concedes the possibility of Crane's influence, but dismisses it as unimportant.

4. John Berryman, *Stephen Crane* (New York: William Sloane Associates, 1951), pp. 200–201. While Berryman asserts Crane's influence, he also quotes Crane's retort to Harold Frederic, who had jeered at Conrad: "You and I and Kipling couldn't have written *The Nigger!*" (205)

5. *Almayer's Folly* on the first page announces Conrad's lifelong device of splitting phrasal verbs to create a sense of continuity within sentences: *"Leaning with both hands on the balustrade of the verandah, he went on looking fixedly at the great river that flowed—indifferent and hurried—before his eyes"* (my italics). While this splitting is obviously readily available in English, Conrad exploits it continually. "Flowed . . . before," for example, is not strictly a phrasal verb, but the verbs preceding in the sentence make it seem so. Conrad uses this particular device more consistently than either Dickens or James.

6. See Robert Caserio, *Plot, Story, and the Novel* (Princeton, N.J.: Princeton University Press, 1979), pp. 81–132, for a discussion of varieties of rescue in the English novel.

7. V. S. Pritchett, *The Tale Bearers* (New York: Random House, 1980), p. 52.

8. Jean-Aubry, *Life and Letters*, I, 208.

9. Ibid., p. 222.

10. *Letters of Joseph Conrad to Marguerite Poradowska*, ed. John A. Gee and Paul J. Sturm (New Haven: Yale University Press, 1940), p. 48.

11. See Carlyle's "Occasional Discourse on the Nigger Question" (1849), in *English and Other Critical Essays* (London: Dent, 1967), pp. 303–333, for comparison with the subdued racism in Conrad's portrait. Carlyle writes: "No Black man who will not work according to what ability the gods have given him for working, has the smallest right to eat pumpkin . . . however plentiful . . . but has an indisputable . . . *right* to be compelled, by the real proprietors . . . to do competent work for his living" (309). Whatever resemblance there is between Carlyle's work ethic and Conrad's is never simple. Ford, though he may be wrong, notes (*Joseph Conrad*, p. 89) that Conrad disliked Carlyle. Jimmy "Wait," as in cockney pronunciation, seems to function more as an image of the "white's" projected laziness than as a direct image of black labor itself. But, as with Hirsch, the critical displacement of the racism is incomplete.

12. *A Personal Record*, p. xxii.

13. Watt, *Conrad in the Nineteenth Century*, p. 77.

14. See John Dozier Gordan, *Joseph Conrad* (Cambridge, Mass.: Harvard University Press, 1940), pp. 96–173, for a discussion of Conrad's sentences.

15. Conrad went through various stages of emphasis: the word *see* was first followed by an exclamation point, then italicized *and* followed by an exclamation point, and finally italicized without an exclamation point.

16. Tzvetan Todorov, "Connaissance de la parole," *Word: Journal of the Linguistic Circle of New York*, 23, nos. 1, 2, and 3 (1967), 500–517.

17. *Oedipus the King*, trans. David Grene, in *Sophocles I* (Chicago: University of Chicago Press, 1941), l. 358. On this scene see also René Girard, *Violence and the Sacred* (Baltimore: Johns Hopkins University Press, 1972), pp. 70–72.

18. "Ough!"'s surrounded by dots very visibly dominate pp. 20–21; on p. 24 Jimmy coughs violently. In chap. 2, on p. 44, the "ough!"'s reemerge, and on the same page, in the next paragraph, Jimmy has a shattering fit of coughs. The juxtaposition is clear, then, by p. 44 at least, with one paragraph dominated by the "ough!" and the next by the cough. This is one of many transitions by the "force" of a sound, rather than by conventional logic or action, in Conrad's style—what he elsewhere calls an "accord." (The scenes of the "coffin" and of the "coffee" may be musically related to the ough-cough theme; the difference between "crew" and "crowd" is pivotal.) A useful essay could be written on the imagery of forceful breath and forceful wind in the story, on the sense of "practical inspiration," via the sails, Jimmy's lungs, dropped *h*'s, snores, whistles, whispers, violent and calm winds, and even a small but powerfully expressive detail like Singleton's progress from the initially aspirated word *hold!* to the word *old*. This notion of "forced inspiration" locates Conrad both within and against the Romantic idea of breathing as freedom and energy.

19. *The Prelude* (1805), bk. 11, ll. 138–184.

20. Megroz, *Joseph Conrad's Mind and Method*, p. 33.

21. See Uriel Weinreich, *Languages in Contact* (The Hague: Mouton, 1966).

22. For some particular scenes of overhearing see *The Secret Agent*, chaps. 3, 9, 11; *Lord Jim*, chap. 6; *The End of the Tether*, esp. chap. 7; *Almayer's Folly*, chaps. 1 and 4; *The Nigger of the "Narcissus,"* chap. 2; "The Shadow-Line," pt. 5; *Victory*, pt. 2, chap. 1.

23. Mikhail Bakhtin, *Rabelais and His World* (Cambridge, Mass.: M.I.T. Press, 1968), p. 106.

24. *Notes on Life and Letters*, p. 14.

25. Jean-Aubry, *Life and Letters*, I, 268.

26. Ibid., pp. 257–258.

27. Ibid., p. 89.

28. Baines, *A Critical Biography*, p. 278; Zdzisław Najder, *Congo Diary* (New York: Doubleday, 1978), p. 155.

29. Karl, *A Reader's Guide to Joseph Conrad*, p. 144k.

30. Baines, *A Critical Biography*, p. 279.

31. See the letter to David Meldrum, in Lawrence Graver, *Conrad's Short Fiction* (Berkeley: University of California Press, 1969), p. 116.

32. See David Thorburn, *Conrad's Romanticism* (New Haven: Yale University Press, 1974) pp. 106–108, for a discussion of Conrad's taciturns as romantic heroes. Thorburn's reading has specific value to his argument, but the later works, which he does not discuss, elaborate very differently on silences.

33. Graver, *Conrad's Short Fiction*, p. 116.

34. See *Hard Times*, pt. 2, chap. 2, for Harthouse's "honesty in dishonesty" as the typical modern vice. Hardy uses the same phrase in chap. 19 of *The Mayor of Casterbridge*, where it refers specifically to Susan Henchard's silence about her daughter's birth, but more broadly to many major actions in the novel.

35. Though the term *unrest* is easy to find in labor histories like G. D. H. Cole's, the *OED* is largely and curiously silent on its connotations. It is safe to say, however, that Conrad, from the evidence in the story itself, heard this word in the way we do.

36. Jean-Paul Sartre, *L'Idiot de la famille* (Paris: Editions Gallimard, 1971), pp. 612–648; *The Family Idiot*, trans. Carol Cosman (Chicago: University of Chicago Press, 1981), pp. 592–627.

37. *Letters to Poradowska*, p. 39.

38. Jean-Aubry, *Life and Letters*, I, 285.

39. Ibid., pp. 251–252.

40. Ibid., p. 266.

41. Ibid., p. 230.

42. This bad praise he calls a "kick from a donkey." Ibid., II, 70–71.

43. Baines, *A Critical Biography*, p. 205, quotes a contemporary review that saw in Crane and Conrad "the same jerky and spasmodic" prose rhythm.

44. *Letters to Poradowska*, pp. 48–49.

45. *A Personal Record*, p. 15.

46. See the French version of the letter, until 1983 only at the Beinecke Library, Yale University, New Haven, in *The Collected Letters of Joseph Conrad*, ed. Frederick Karl (Cambridge: Cambridge University Press, 1983), I, 118–119.

47. Watt, *Conrad in the Nineteenth Century*, pp. 112–115.

48. See Leo Bersani, *A Future For Astyanax* (Boston: Little, Brown, 1976).

III. Silver and Silence

1. F. R. Leavis, *The Great Tradition* (New York: New York University Press, 1964), p. 200.

2. Avrom Fleishman, *Conrad's Politics* (Baltimore: Johns Hopkins University Press, 1967), pp. 3–5.

3. Jean-Jacques Rousseau, *Oeuvres complètes* (Paris: Editions Gallimard, 1964), III, 959: "Commencez par resserrer vos limites, si vous voulez reformer votre gouvernement," and so on. Rousseau recommends the contraction of Poland—smaller boundaries—as one step toward a secure republic. This to some degree resembles Decoud's plan for secession and contraction. Rousseau also discusses the need for rules to reduce harangues and *flagorneries* in the Diet.

4. Edward Said, *Beginnings* (New York: Basic Books, 1975), p. 110.

5. Fernand Braudel, *The Mediterranean* (New York: Harper and Row, 1972), p. 196.

6. Graver, *Conrad's Short Fiction*. See especially the Preface, quoting Ford on Conrad's "long-short" stories.

7. R. B. Cunninghame Graham, *Mogreb-el-Acksa* (London: Heinemann, 1898). The book is full of asides and anecdotes on names, language, and word change.

8. Ernest Bufkin, "Conrad, Opera, and Nostromo," *Nineteenth Century Fiction*, 30 (1975), 206–214.

9. Conrad, writing to George Keating (Jean-Aubry, *Life and Letters*, II, 288–290), discusses his education; see also Chap. VI here.

10. Graham, *Mogreb-el-Acksa,* pp. 52–53. Immediately after a passage giving Conrad's work high praise, Graham calls himself someone with a filibustering reputation. Conrad may have scoured Graham's prose for diction; Graham, for example, uses the word *villegiatura* ironically for his imprisonment in Morocco; the word shows up a decade later in *The Secret Agent* in regard to Stevie's stay with Michaelis in the country.

11. *Webster's Third International Dictionary,* p. 849.

12. See Albert Guerard, *Conrad the Novelist* (Cambridge, Mass.: Harvard University Press, 1958), p. 194, for concise comments on Decoud's attitudes toward parliamentary hubbub.

13. R. C. K. Ensor, *England, 1870–1914* (Oxford: Oxford University Press: 1936), pp. 55–56.

14. Angus Fletcher, *Allegory* (Ithaca, N.Y.: Cornell University Press, 1970), p. 305, discusses Northrop Frye's contention that resistance to allegorical readings shows a dislike for being "compelled" toward one meaning. Conrad in one letter attacks allegory in a way that implies, ambiguously, that he himself is mortally immersed in it, and sick of it, just as Dickens attacks old allegory but practices a new kind of urban allegory of contagions in *Bleak House.*

15. See Jean-Aubry, *Life and Letters,* II, 30–31, and 129 for examples of this ongoing lament about the mass production of words. "I must try to get up some strength . . . I must write some 20,000 words." During the composition of *Nostromo* Conrad wrote to Galsworthy about magazine pieces, "I've discovered that I can dictate that sort of bosh at the rate of 3,000 words in four hours . . . So in the day *Nostromo,* and from 11 to 1 A.M., dictation." These are only two examples of a common self-accounting in the letters.

16. In the very last sentence of p. 2, Nostromo swims ashore without his boat: "He saw it vanish, as if jerked under, and then struck out for the shore" (304). The phrasal verb *jerked under* here marks Nostromo's entry into the silences from which his own naive continuity and force has so far exempted him. The verb *jerk* has been used to mean the lash of a whip in punishment; a tic or slight bodily convulsion; a lack of fluidity in prose rhythm; and, most interestingly, a moment of harsh satire; see *OED,* s.v. "jerk."

17. A flier advertising Jean-Aubry's *Life and Letters* includes a series of paragraphs like this: "You have read Conrad's stories—he has made you live them. You know Ricardo, fierce, half-crazed fighter,—Almayer, the treacherous,—Lingard, rough, South Seas trader,—Heyst, the idealist,—passionate, inscrutable Nostromo,—Kurtz, the killer, whose heart was darkness,—and Conrad's women!—Dona Rita, the bewitching plotter,—the brave little outcast, Lena,—the subtle Mrs. Gould,—Aissa, the seductive Malay princess, for whom a white man sold his soul!"

18. In addition to *Dostoevski's Poetics,* see *The Bakhtin Newsletter* (Department of French Studies, Queen's University, Kingston, Ontario), no. 1 (1983), for a descriptive bibliography of articles and books on Bakhtin. I do not mean to suggest that this criticism of Bakhtin is simply "correct"—only to state it plainly to suggest the different spirit in which Conrad as a Pole regards the polyphony of some novels. Interestingly, Paul de Man, in "Dialogue and Dialogism" (see Chap. I, n. 12), insisted on finding a note of inescapable

"imperialism" in the mutual interferences of Bakhtin's dialogic. For a structural and linguistic study of second-language speakers see Weinreich, *Languages In Contact*.

19. Charles Rossman, "A Note on Puns and the Spanish in *Nostromo*," *Modern British Literature*, 1, no. 1 (1976), 88–90, sees Gould and silver as simple mutual reinforcements.

20. Adam Mickiewicz, *Pan Tadeusz*, trans. G. R. Noyes (London: J. M. Dent and Sons, 1917), pp. 31, 338 n.

21. Adam Mickiewicz, *Poems*, ed. G. R. Noyes (New York: Polish Institute of Arts and Sciences, 1944). See *Forefathers' Eve*, pt. 3, pp. 247–368. On p. 259, the hero, Tomasz, describes the "inquest" as the worst of the Russian persecutions. The story of Cichowski, who learns silence in prison, "his sole defense," but then never speaks after his release, is in Part III, sc. 7, ll. 75–189.

22. Thorburn, *Conrad's Romanticism*, pp. 106–118. The notion, however, that "silence" simply corresponds to virtue, either in Conrad, or in nineteenth-century "romances" in general, seems a vast oversimplification. Silent figures in Stevenson, to take only one example, are often evil.

23. Heinrich von Kleist, *Sämtliche Werke und Briefe* (Munich: Carl Hanser, 1961), II, 338–345.

24. Jean-Aubry, *Life and Letters*, I, 213.

25. Ibid., p. 218.

26. Ibid., p. 247.

27. Ibid., p. 251.

28. Ibid., II, 117.

29. Claire Rosenfield, *Paradise of Snakes* (Chicago: University of Chicago Press, 1967), p. 51.

30. For further discussion of critical picturing of one's own most common speech act or voice (in Blake, lamentation) see my article "Pictures of Speech: On Blake's Poetic," *Studies in Romanticism*, 21, no. 2 (1982), 217–242.

31. Wayne Booth, *The Rhetoric of Fiction* (Chicago: University of Chicago Press, 1961), p. 18 n.

32. For the word *sub-ironic* see Conrad, "The Planter of Malata," in *Within The Tides*, p. 29.

33. "A Familiar Preface," p. xx.

34. Hay, *The Political Novels of Joseph Conrad*, p. 161.

35. *Notes on Life and Letters*, p. 17.

36. Karl Kroeber, *Styles in Fictional Structure* (Princeton, N.J.: Princeton University Press, 1971), chap. 11.

37. Ibid., p. 169.

38. Mark Lambert, *Dickens and the Suspended Quotation* (New Haven: Yale University Press, 1981). For moments in which assonances within the "tags" seem to link the narrator, by a kind of singing or burden, to the singing quality of the speaker, see pp. 28–29, and p. 36. When Pip, for example, says of his sister's "forced" and blackmailing hysteria ("O! O!"), "Each of these exclamations was a shriek," the high *e*'s in his comments echo her repeated "O!"s of lamentation. While he criticizes her, he also joins in, or as Conrad would have it, "chimes" in with her. And Dickens not only interrupts others, he often in-

terrupts himself also. These participatory chimes and structures are among the poetic effects which set off Dickens'—and Conrad's—prose from more plainly prosaic novels of social criticism like those of Gissing or Gaskell, for example. Though it is true that Dickens, mimicking Carlyle, attacked Parliament repeatedly, Dickens' remained a parliamentary, or choral, imagination.

39. See Ronald E. Martin, *American Literature and the Universe of Force* (Durham, N.C.: Duke University Press, 1981), for a discussion of Herbert Spencer's influence on American writers like Dreiser, London, and Henry Adams. Conrad periodically lapses into a nineteenth-century rhetoric of force, but often does so ironically, applying it to language events and the ironic "force of words." Conrad's forced dialogues, as already indicated, are not simply determinist, or part of a mechanical picture; scenes in which persons "force" other persons to speak focus not on mechanistic forces but on mutual agency, persons as both caused and causers, in a way that is finally dramatic and Oedipal rather than mechanical. To apply a diverse imagery of "force" to dialogue is itself ironic, altering our idea of force as much as our idea of dialogue. The Marxist position on this, which Martin does not mention, is given clearly in Engels' critique of Dühring's prefascist picture of history as force. Conrad's relational forcings have little in common with Dühring or even Spencer, except the mood of the epoch in which all of them wrote. In spite of the obvious problems in such force philosophies, however, Martin seems too convinced that the image of force is simply naive, an example of cheap popular metaphysics and sloppy thinking. What makes the term ludicrous and dangerous to a logician like Peirce or a thinker like William James—that "force" can refer to apparently different events and is not one scene—is what might make it a useful "complex word" for a dramatic writer like Conrad.

40. Irving Howe, *Politics and the Novel* (New York: Horizon Press, 1957), p. 113.

IV. The Fragmentation of Sympathy in *The Secret Agent*

1. Megroz, *Joseph Conrad's Mind and Method*, p. 25.

2. See the account of parental anxiety by Jessie Conrad, *Joseph Conrad And His Circle* (London: Jarrolds, 1935), pp. 197–198; and Conrad himself in Jean-Aubry, *Life and Letters*, II, 217.

3. Stevie is fourteen when he sets off the staircase explosion at the close of chap. 1. Verloc appears in their lives *after* this; and later we learn that the Verlocs have been married for seven years. Conrad does not exactly hide Stevie's real age, but he plays with it. Student responses indicate to me that a fair number take Stevie for about sixteen—that is, as underage. Seven is important among the many numbers in the book: the Verloc marriage seems to be related to the "seven years hard" labor of imprisonment in Heat's thinking (chap. 5); allusively, seven is the typical duration of servitude or work in the biblical tradition in Genesis (this has some relevance to the "young Joseph" motif I mention at the end of this chapter).

4. Hitchcock's *Sabotage* translates Stevie from a retarded twenty-one-year-

old into an ordinary if dreamy boy. "I made a serious mistake in having the little boy carry the bomb . . . the public was resentful" (Hitchcock in an interview in François Truffaut, *Hitchcock*, New York: Simon and Schuster, 1967, p. 76).

5. Jean-Aubry, *Life and Letters*, I, 213.

6. Ford Madox Ford, *Portraits From Life* (Chicago: Gateway, 1937), p. 89.

7. "The Life Beyond, 1910," *Notes on Life and Letters*, p. 70.

8. See particularly Hagan, "The Design of *The Secret Agent*" (see Chap. I, n. 11). R. W. Stallman, in "Time and *The Secret Agent*," *Texas Studies in Literature and Language*, 1, no. 1 (1959), 101–122, gives the now standard discussion of time in the novel, which has generated others. He is wrong, I think, to conclude that Time is *"the* Secret Agent," a reification which draws attention away from the time consciousness and political responsibility of the characters in dialogue to a structural "ingenuity." Caserio, *Plot, Story, and the Novel*, pp. 264–274, gives a succinct discussion of the "home" question, and sees "domestic" order as the key theme of the novel.

9. Hagan, "The Design of *The Secret Agent.*" Hagan's word *interviews*, for all its ironic detachment, seems to me to lead to an excessive neutrality in his account of the novel's dialogue "design." The marriage dialogues are not interviews but forced dialogues: this marriage is politicized. "Interview" does not adequately label what happens in the Verloc bedroom, and is too forceless a term for what happens when Vladimir summons Verloc, or the assistant commissioner grills Heat.

10. Stallman, "Time and *The Secret Agent*," p. 102.

11. See Pietro Pucci, *The Violence of Pity in Euripides' Medea* (Ithaca, N.Y.: Cornell University Press, 1980), pp. 169–174, for a discussion of the thesis that Aristotle himself meant to suggest that pity is a kind of terror. It is unlikely that Conrad would have had this unusual sense of Aristotle's theory, however; he probably thought he was reducing the theory sardonically.

12. *A Personal Record*, pp. 124ff. When Megroz asked for Conrad's favorite authors, Conrad hedged, then named Dickens first; he also named Dr. Johnson, and, when coaxed, the sermons of Jeremy Taylor. Conrad's aim in the "interview" with Megroz was clearly to emphasize his own Englishness, or literary patriotism. Throughout this interview one can also hear him playing skillfully against the gentle forcing. He professes delight that Megroz has mentioned Taylor. In regard to the *Bacchae*, Conrad may have been influenced by Shaw's *Major Barbara* (1905), with its study of the Bacchic in modern politics. For "Spontaneous Combustion," see *Bleak House*, chap. 32, and Dickens' mockdocumentary Preface.

13. See, for example, Adam Gillon, *Joseph Conrad* (New York: Twayne, 1982), and Norman Sherry's *Conrad's Eastern World* and *Conrad's Western World* (Cambridge: Cambridge University Press, 1966, 1971), for extensive work on allusions and on sources.

14. See Bruce Johnson, *Conrad's Models of Mind* (Minneapolis: University of Minnesota Press, 1971), chaps. 2–3, for an extended discussion; and for a brief comment, David Daiches, *A Critical History of English Literature* (New York: Ronald Press, 1970), II, 1156.

15. See Max Scheler, *The Nature of Sympathy*, trans. Peter Heath (New Haven: Yale University Press, 1954). Scheler tries to make a phenomenological yet hierarchical classification of various kinds of sympathy; though often unconvincing or biased, his thinking about sympathy is invaluable.

16. See Mickiewicz's *Forefathers' Eve*, pt. 3, and Juljusz Słowacki's *Anhelli*, trans. D. P. Radin (London: Allen and Unwin, 1930). There is no space even to suggest the relevance of these writers to Conrad here in relation to themes of silence, suffering, coercion to speak, and arrest. Czesław Miłosz, in *The History of Polish Literature* (London: Macmillan, 1969), gives concise discussions. Not *all* pathetic or martyred sympathy in Conrad is a parody of Dostoevsky. On the contrary, there is a Polish tradition which deals with rescuing pity from an angle that might seem to resemble Dostoevsky's, but which to Conrad may have seemed radically different, if only because it was Polish.

17. Albert Guerard, *Conrad The Novelist* (Cambridge, Mass.: Harvard University Press, 1958), p. 226.

18. Patricia Spence, "Sympathy and Propriety in Adam Smith's Rhetoric," *The Quarterly Journal of Speech*, 60, no. 1 (1974), 92–99.

19. *Paradise Lost*, bk. 10, ll. 539–540.

20. In *The Idiot*, chap. 2, Myshkin imagines the guillotine: "When you lay your head down under the knife and hear the knife slide over your head, that quarter of a second is the most terrible of all. You know that this is not only my fancy, many people think the same" (trans. Constance Garnett, New York: Modern Library, 1935, p. 20).

21. Conrad may have had in mind the strangely comical indecision and fragmentation of the Chorus in the *Agamemnon* overhearing the murder inside the house. Some critics have read Winnie's murder of Verloc as full of allusions to the *Agamemnon*; the second chapter portraying the anarchists talking to themselves alludes to this choral anarchy.

22. *The Bostonians*, chap. 4.

23. *Bleak House*, chap. 4.

24. See Gadamer, *Truth and Method*, pp. 17–19, for a discussion of tact and *Bildung*.

V. The Anti-Conversational Novel

1. See Roman Jakobson, *Puškin and His Sculptural Myth* (The Hague: Mouton, 1975), for an account of the image of the persecutory, nightmarish statue in Russian tradition.

2. See Erving Goffman, *Forms of Talk* (Philadelphia: University of Pennsylvania Press, 1981), chap. 2, for an interactionist, pragmatic, witty study of the ways in which speaking aloud to oneself, for instance after stumbling, is actually addressed to a social other. My analysis of this scene, later in this chapter, is closer to Bakhtin's "dialogical" premise that all speech, even monologue, is addressed to, and amalgamates, the voices of others. Conrad might be said to differ from Bakhtin in that his art replicates this "dialogism" without celebrating it.

Notes to Pages 184–188

3. Jacques Berthoud, *Joseph Conrad* (Cambridge: Cambridge University Press, 1978), p. 183, briefly mentions this symmetry, but omits the word *detonation*, which Conrad has added to the historical accounts.

4. In one forced scene between the narrator and Razumov (186), Razumov asks, "What is the meaning of all this?" and the narrator replies, "The object, you mean, of this conversation, which I admit I have forced upon you in a measure?" Razumov answers, "Forced! Object!" His exclamation means in part that after his earlier encounters it is astonishing to have someone as polite as the narrator describe himself as forcing conversation. Razumov's exclamation is in the same tone as Conrad's "If one must . . . !" to Ford's English pressure.

5. See, for example, Michel Foucault, *Discipline and Punish* (New York: Vintage, 1979), p. 189.

6. The first sentence of the Author's Note to *Under Western Eyes* reads: "It must be admitted that by the mere force of circumstances 'Under Western Eyes' has become already a sort of historical novel dealing with the past." Throughout the Note there is a tension concerning the status of the novel as a historical portrait of Russia or a more universal study of political psychology.

7. Conrad's nervous collapse during the last stages of composing *Under Western Eyes* has been discussed at length. See, for example, Baines, *A Critical Biography*, pp. 372–373, and Frederick Karl, *Joseph Conrad: The Three Lives* (New York: Farrar, Straus and Giroux, 1979) pp. 680–686, for an account of various theses, not quite accepted by Karl, which cite the breakdown as the start of Conrad's alleged decline. We can reject the idea of a simple decline while at the same time noting that in *Under Western Eyes* Conrad confronted his own "forced contractuality" more severely than in any other work and then put a stop to the self-criticism.

8. Marlow's attack on "confession" in *Chance* (212) argues that all confession is "untimely" because it arouses feelings of superiority in the hearer, and because the "sympathetic" are so rare as to be practically nonexistent: one in ten thousand. Dostoevsky in chaps. 12–14 of *The Idiot* parodies Rousseau's story about the maid he accused of a theft he had committed. Dostoevsky is not accurately described as confessional; but he shares with Rousseau, and with Conrad, the sense that among speech acts, confession most blatantly contains the orthodox dilemmas of necessity and freedom. He also shares (as Conrad does not) Rousseau's sense that by taking compulsive confession to its limit, one can paradoxically free oneself and others. This is why the two are, for Conrad, roughly the same as forced speakers, confusing their forcedness with their freedom. Even if audible to him, Dostoevsky's laughter and Rousseau's irony were not the issue for Conrad.

9. Baines, *A Critical Biography*, pp. 369–370: "Their confessions emphasize above all the difference between the two authors. Raskolnikov's confession is the beginning of a process which leads to full repentance and to regeneration, whereas Razumov's confession is a culmination and is conclusive; Raskolnikov finds his god, but fot Razumov, as for Conrad, there is no god . . . *Under Western Eyes* is an indictment; its mood is fatalistic . . . *Crime and Punishment* is an assertion of ultimate human goodness."

10. See K. H. Basso, " 'To Give up on Words': Silence in Western Apache Culture," in *Language and Social Context*, ed. Pier Paolo Giglioli (Middlesex, England: Penguin Books, 1972), p. 69.

11. Slight duplicities in the novel include oscillations in the spelling of Natalia, in Mikulin's protean job titles, and in the narrator's nationality. To these can be added the fact that while Razumov is first described as having an Oblomovesque, vague face—"as if a face modelled vigorously in wax . . . had been held close to a fire till all sharpness of line had been lost" (5), this waxiness aligning him to Waverley and other heroes of extreme impressionability, and to the ironic idea of impermanent sculpture—later we are told that "his features were more decided than in the generality of Russian faces; he had a line of the jaw, a clean-shaven, sallow cheek; his nose was a ridge, and not a mere protuberance" (179). Certainly this contradiction is not sloppiness but a joke: Razumov's face is vague and indefinite, but much clearer than that of most Russians. Conrad himself is duplicitous here: either he satirizes Russians as a race of vague potato people, featureless, depersonalized, among whom the waxen Razumov seems unusually delineated; or he charges that Western eyes see Russian faces only as a blur.

12. See Fleishman, *Conrad's Politics*, pp. 37–40, for an excellent discussion of the essay "The Censor of Plays" (*Notes on Life and Letters*, pp. 76–80). Fleishman notes that the intense denunciation of censorship in Conrad's submitted draft of this essay was itself, ironically enough, censored—or softened—by the liberal Garnett, who had invited him to write it. Conrad's opposition to the censor was absolute—he wanted to eliminate the office—and Fleishman reasonably uses this as one indication that Conrad's politics were by no means simply conservative. But the question is complex. This essay gives one of his few images of the censor, who does not appear in the fiction. The censor is the enemy in the liberal imagination, as the speech forcer is a typical figure in the tragic scene. Further, even in this liberal essay, for all its emphasis on expressive freedom, Conrad cannot refrain from modulating to the idea that art is servitude, not free expression. The public will "judge . . . the work of its free, independent, and conscientious servant—the artist," he writes first; but then, omitting the freedom, begins the next paragraph, "Only thus can the dignity of artistic servitude be preserved" (77).

13. *The Prelude* (1805), bk. 1, l. 219.

14. See Morton Dauwen Zabel, "Introduction," in *Under Western Eyes* (Garden City, N.Y.: Anchor Books, 1963), p. lvii.

15. Ibid., p. xlvi; and Fleishman, *Conrad's Politics*, pp. 217–242. Fleishman's "Speech and Writing in *Under Western Eyes*," in Norman Sherry, *Joseph Conrad: A Commemoration* (New York: Harper and Row, 1977), pp. 119–128, takes up some themes discussed here, such as silence, but does not deal with coercion to write and speak as a major theme.

16. For a recent account of the assassination which strikingly resembles Conrad's scene, see Robert K. Massie's popular history *Nicholas and Alexandra* (New York: Dell, 1967), pp. 15–16. Other histories confirm the resemblance. The closeness to the historical accounts adds weight to the idea that the choice

of specific words like *detonation* is important: Conrad is rehearsing the famous event in his special terms. See Karl, *Joseph Conrad*, p. 69n.; Zabel, "Introduction," p. xxvi. The letter *P——* in the oppressive minister's name is *not* Kafkaesque (grotesquely empty and depersonalized) so much as dialogically full, and a historical joke: there were several repressive Russian ministers in the last part of the nineteenth century whose names began with *P*; Conrad seems to have been joking about this fact. As Andrzej Busza, in Sherry, *Conrad: A Commemoration*, notes, Pobodonotsev is as important as Plehve among the "documentary" sources of this character.

17. See Howe, *Politics and the Novel*, pp. 86–93. Howe insists it is "to Razumov's credit" that when he betrays Haldin he does not claim to have been "forced to walk over his chest" by the State and the revolution. That is, he defines Razumov as having a conscience beyond his own determinacy. This seems only half true, given Razumov's reference to himself as the victim of "unthinking forces." Howe then goes on to affirm Mikulin's "Where to?" as Conrad's indication that "in the modern world politics is total" (p. 89). Two of Howe's terms throughout his discussion—*dialectic* and *sympathy*—are precisely the concepts of the inherited historical novel which the book succeeds in expelling, if regretfully, from its main action. Howe criticizes the novel for failing to show a real dialectic of opinion about revolution. But Conrad was working out a more unusual and rebellious political "dialogic," which is, as much as possible, not dialectical. It is marked not by a progress of ideas but by the sense that everyone is forced into an ideological nondebate, mutually immersed. If *Nostromo* can be taken as Conrad's reuse of Thucydides, and *The Secret Agent* an ironic adaptation of Euripides, this work is something like a critique of *The Republic*, showing that consideration of politics in dialogue cannot overcome forcedness, in the subject under discussion and in its own format. It is more important to see how the sides are immersed in destructive dialogue than to work out a complex understanding of the ways in which they predicate the future together. Howe is right, then, to emphasize that the book "fails" as dialectic, but is wrong to see this as a sign of a lack of dialogical power.

18. *Crime and Punishment*, pt. 3, chap. 5, trans. Constance Garnett (New York: Airmont, 1967), pp. 210–211.

19. Konstantin Mochulsky, *Dostoevsky* (Princeton, N.J.: Princeton University Press, 1967), p. 273.

20. *The Prelude* (1805), bk. 2, l. 409.

21. This forced dialogue includes a detonative renaming: Razumov protests, a little sophomorically quoting Pascal, that he is only a "thinking reed," caught among "unthinking forces" about to annihilate him. This reed is ironically and pastorally English but is also a reminder, by the reader's overhearing, of the original French *roseau pensant*. When he calls himself a reed-*roseau* under the interrogatory stress of the meeting, there are many meanings, but one strong irony is that Razumov, who spent so much time being educated, can't help taking the opportunity now to quote his authors—that is, to treat the political scene as if it were the academic exam he has anticipated. Also, however, the self-renaming generates a "hollow" set of echoing /r-s/ names—Razumov

(Reason), Russia, Rousseau—detonating these categories of identity in the novel. The *roseau* is a "hollow" instrument; tones are made by the force of air traveling through it and the graded, forced stops. Razumov, Reason, Russia, Rousseau become secondary to *roseau*. An /r-s/ group, an "onomastic duo," can be found in *Crime and Punishment* itself: Raskolnikov and Razumihin as sons of Russia. Balzac's Rastignac may be *their* ancestor. More curiously, Rousseau's essay *Considérations sur le gouvernement de Pologne*, which applies the ideas of *Du contrat social* to an outlandish sketch for a new Polish constitution, deploys a sharp /r-s/ pun about Russia in one of the first passages. Speaking to the Poles, he writes: "Vous aimez la liberté, vous en êtes dignes; vous l'avez défendue contre un agresseur puissant et rusé qui feignant de vous présenter les liens de l'amitié vous chargeoit des fers de la servitude" (*Oeuvres complètes*, p. 954). "Russia" has not yet appeared in the essay. Conrad, who almost certainly read this far into *Considérations*, would have noticed and no doubt enjoyed Rousseau's strong implication that Russia is in regard to Poland too despicable to name, and is only *rusé*, "wily," a distorted Reason. He would also have thought, however, that the same pun refers us to the author's name, Rousseau, collapsing them all into the same irrationality. If modern readers of Rousseau, aware like Dr. Johnson of Rousseau's sometimes global irony, might read this powerful rhetorical *rusé* as potentially conscious (Rousseau warning his readers that some of the constitution to follow is also Rousseau-*rusé*, a modest proposal by an outsider), Conrad could not have heard this irony as being at all within the range of Rousseau's polemical intention.

Onomastic plotting is not hermetic, is probably not unconscious in the manner of Freud's chains of associated words in the *Traumdeutung*, and is quite common to many novels taken to be "realistic." Novelists obviously can invent names to fit characters; there are also ways in which the names in some novels fit, or are coordinated to, each other—dialogized to each other. Consider the homes of Dorothea's two suitors at the start of *Middlemarch*—the impotent old scholar from Lowick and the raw young fool from Freshitt. *Under Western Eyes* is of course accessible even if the reader does not "overhear" the term *reed* back into the French *roseau* and then see how it "hollows out" some other key names. I relegate this to a note because at least some readers have no doubt had enough of this point about Conrad's thinking in chimes. But the real question is why we have been trained culturally to deny and dislike patterns of names, to think them heavy-handed. It is partly because they reveal a certain unfreedom in composition. The fact is, however, that these chimes are in Conrad anything but hermetic. They echo the language of history. Newspapers like the *Daily News* or the *New York Post*, for example, embody an old tradition of popular journalism—nicknames, puns, catchy language, scabrous word play; and the punless texture of the *Times* may in fact belie or even repress the contagious language of history, politics, and social change found in the "cheaper" papers. "Nikita nicknamed Necator," a catch phrase Conrad obviously relished, figures as a part of this onomastic contagion, in which every name becomes *rénommé* by entering new dialogues of force. The only difference from popular journalism is that Conrad organizes these name sets with a kind of conscious hollowness, which is not a melodramatic "despair" about history. Articles by

Joseph Dobrinsky in *Cahiers Victoriens et Edouardiens*, no. 11 (April 1980), and no. 16 (Oct. 1982), which I had not seen during most of this book's composition, reflect a similar sense of Conrad's interest in names and echoes.

22. See *Conradiana*, 12, no. 1 (1980), for a set of articles on Conrad's knowledge of Russia and Russian.

23. For a brief English account of *Widerruf*, see Jerry Glenn, *Paul Celan* (New York: Twayne, 1973), p. 25: "The technique consists of an allusion—often extended over several lines or even through an entire poem—to a religious or literary work or works, for the purpose of denying or poetically 'refuting' the work in question . . . The literary work generally expresses some form of optimism and affirmation, which is contradicted in Celan's poem." Glenn includes references to important articles on *Widerruf*. Though Conrad did not distrust English in the way Celan distrusted German, his "overhearing" is somewhat similar, and as a Pole he was writing in a genre—that of the political-historical novel—whose dialectic he needed to "refute." Andrzej Busza, in Sherry, *Conrad: A Commemoration*, discusses the parallels between Conrad and Dostoevsky as "sufficiently numerous and obvious to suggest that Conrad meant the reader to make the connection" (111). This is accurate and essentially correct, but the term *the reader* seems too singular. Conrad like most novelists imagined and simultaneously addressed different classes of readers and a plurality of readers in time also. Thus it is not an evasion to say that he meant the parallels to be both obvious and hidden. Busza cites an excellent essay, Ralph E. Matlaw, "Dostoevskij and Conrad's Political Novels," in *American Contributions to the Fifth International Congress of Slavists* (The Hague: Mouton, 1963), II, 213–231, which insists that this kind of aggressive relation between "two great novels" is "unique in literature" (218). But as Busza says, that is an exaggeration: as a revocation, *Under Western Eyes* also seems typical of all writing.

24. See Jean-Aubry, *Life and Letters*, II, 288–290, for a violent late letter protesting Mencken's characterization of him as "Slavonic." The explosion shows that Conrad to the end of his life was still volatile on this issue.

25. Julian Moynahan, "*The Mayor of Casterbridge* and the Old Testament's First Book of Samuel," *PMLA*, 71 (1956), 118–130, reprinted in the Norton Critical Edition, ed. James K. Robinson (New York, 1977).

26. Norman Sherry, *Conrad's Western World* (Cambridge: Cambridge University Press, 1971), studies various textual sources of, for example, *Nostromo*.

27. D. S. Merezhkovsky, "Dostoevsky and Tolstoy," in *Russian Literature and Modern English Fiction*, ed. Donald Davie (Chicago: University of Chicago Press, 1965), pp. 75–98.

28. Whether *dialogic* parodies and carnivalizes *dialectic* was the first question raised after Donald Fanger's 1983 lecture on Bakhtin at Boston University. It seems clear that at the very least Bakhtin's work is open to a reading as dialogical subversion of dialectic, just as he pictures one of the primary origins of the novel as Menippean satire of philosophical dialogue.

29. Jean-Aubry, *Life and Letters*, II, 140.

30. David Magarshack, *Dostoevsky* (London: Secker and Warburg, 1962), pp. 475–476.

31. Very briefly: the Grand Inquisitor speaks, the Savior remains silent. There is a rhythm of three temptations like that in the Gospels. These three temptations met by three silences come to an end when Jesus, instead of speaking, kisses the Inquisitor and goes away. Dostoevsky makes the parallel between the story and the scene of its telling explicit when Alyosha, who has remained largely silent during Ivan's poem, interrupting only occasionally, kisses Ivan and leaves. Ivan's poem exists not only by itself but "as between" the two brothers. *The Brothers Karamazov*, bk. 5, chap. 5.

32. Edward Said, *Joseph Conrad and the Fiction of Autobiography* (Cambridge, Mass.: Harvard University Press, 1966), p. 5.

33. Jean-Aubry, *Life and Letters*, II, 336–337, quoted by Jeffrey Berman, "Introduction to Conrad and the Russians," *Conradiana*, 12, no. 1 (1980), 3.

34. *The Rover* (1923), pp. 7–8.

35. Karl, *Joseph Conrad*, p. 28.

36. See Frederick Crews, *Partisan Review*, 34, no. 4 (1967), 522 ("Kurtz amounts to a vindictive reconstruction of Conrad's father"), and Watt, *Conrad*, p. 238, for a skeptical view of psychoanalytic readings. But psychoanalysis does not have to debunk Conrad; he can be read as a strong self-analyst who objectified his own feelings about the political scenes of coercion to speak and write, and made a contribution to the psychoanalysis of ideas of dialogue.

37. Quoted by Walter A. Strauss, "Rilke and Ponge," in *Rilke: The Alchemy of Alienation*, ed. Frank Baron et al. (Lawrence: The Regents Press of Kansas, 1980), p. 85.

38. Hardy, *The Mayor of Casterbridge*, p. 225.

39. Sigmund Freud, *Totem and Taboo*, trans. James Strachey (New York: Norton, 1950), p. 56: "The taboo upon names will seem less puzzling if we bear in mind the fact that savages regard a name as an essential part of a man's personality . . . : they treat words in every sense as things . . . They are never ready to accept a similarity between two words as having no meaning . . . Even a civilized adult may be able to infer from certain peculiarities in his own behavior that he is not so far removed as he may have thought from attributing importance to proper names, and that his own name has become to a very remarkable extent bound up with his personality . . . psycho-analytic practice comes upon frequent confirmation of this."

40. D. A. Miller, *Narrative and Its Discontents* (Princeton, N.J.: Princeton University Press, 1981), pp. 44–45.

41. John Ashbery, *Shadow Train* (New York: Viking, 1981), p. 2.

VI. Oedipus

1. See Chap. I, n. 12. Tolstoy's *What is Art?*, a black mass against high art, is one of the earliest major tracts of modern dialogical idealism. Though there are of course many older Renaissance and Romantic works affirming dialogue and colloquium as activities, genres, or cultural ideals, none have the highly self-conscious theoretical and abstract character, privileging dialogue as the ground of existence, that becomes explicit in modern writing.

2. Sherry Turkle, *Psychoanalytic Politics* (New York: Basic Books, 1978), p. 86.

3. See especially Derrida's essay on Emmanuel Levinas, "Violence et métaphysique," in *L'écriture et la différence* (Paris: Editions du Seuil, 1967), pp. 117–228; and Michel Foucault's work on "examination" in *The Birth of the Clinic* (New York: Vintage, 1975), and *Discipline and Punish*, previously cited. It remains a question whether Freud in his therapeutic dialogic, his theory of resistance, and his statements about forcing and not forcing the patient—so that we are left with the sense that finding the moment to "force" insight is an art—had himself seen or resolved the relation between the figure of Oedipus and the act of making the other speak. This leads to large questions, beyond the scope of this discussion, about the Freudian dialogue. The collection of interviews with Foucault in *Power/Knowledge: Selected Interviews and Other Writings*, ed. Colin Gordon (New York: Pantheon Books, 1980), record Foucault in conversation. In the second interview, Foucault and his interviewer agree at the start that no "history of the practice of examining" (37) has ever been written. That is, I think, they collaborate eloquently in forgetting the Sophoclean *Oedipus* and the many pictures of the history of examination to be found in the novel, the drama, and in sociology like Max Weber's; and they are partly right.

4. See *The Raw and the Cooked*, trans. John and Doreen Weightman (New York: Harper and Row, 1970), pp. 52–53, where Lévi-Strauss interprets a Bororo myth of punitive depopulation not unlike the biblical flood as meaning that "a discrete system is produced by the destruction of certain elements or their removal from the original whole." See also *Race and History* (Paris: UNESCO, 1958).

5. See Anathon Aall, *Geschichte der Logosidee* (Leipzig: O. R. Reisland, 1896–1899), on Logos as immanence versus Logos as force. Jehuda Halevi's Logos in *Kuzari* was translated—inadequately according to the editor, Isaak Heinemann—as "force" (see *Three Jewish Philosophers*, New York: Atheneum, 1973, p. 54). See also H. A. Wolfson's *Philo*. I use the term because it seems the best for Conrad's sense of what, practically, *makes* a dialogue happen.

6. Søren Kierkegaard, *The Concept of Irony*, trans. Lee M. Capel (Bloomington: Indiana University Press, 1971), p. 93. In *Jude the Obscure* the lovers Jude and Sue exchange positions on religion in the course of their lifelong quarrel.

7. Aristophanes, *The Frogs*, ll. 907–908. Franz Rosenzweig in *The Star of Redemption* typically interprets Aeschylean silences as sublime and as transcending the dramatic.

8. Simone Weil, *The Iliad, or the Poem of Force*, trans. Mary McCarthy (Wallingford, Pa.: Pendle Hill, pamphlet 91, 1976).

9. Rudolf Hirzel, *Der Dialog* (Hildesheim: Georg Olms, 1963, reprint), I, 43–48.

10. *The English Works of Thomas Hobbes*, ed. Sir William Molesworth (London: John Bohn, 1843), IX, 110.

11. See Thucydides, *History of the Peloponnesian War*, trans. Rex Warner (London: Penguin, 1954), pp. 400–408.

12. Lazaridès, *Valéry*, p. 12.

13. Robert E. Cushman, *Therapeia* (Chapel Hill: University of North Carolina Press, 1958), pp. 230–232.

14. See *Plato's Progress*, pp. 176–179, for Ryle's insistence that the "eristic duel" is "a voluntary undertaking," that Socrates was not an inquisitor, that his answerers were "eager" to participate. This, Ryle says, contradicts "our habitual picture" of Socrates as forcing people to talk with him. I mean to argue that Conrad, rightly or wrongly, had precisely this "habitual" picture of Socrates as a speech-forcer, and that, culturally and psychologically, he was right to exploit this image of Socrates, whether it is intellectually accurate or not.

15. Richard Robinson, *Plato's Earlier Dialectic* (Oxford: Oxford University Press, 1953), p. 8.

16. Gadamer, *Dialogue and Dialectic*, p. 128.

17. This is not the place for a dissertation on Milton and speech-forcing. Briefly, Milton in *Areopagitica* conceives of tyranny as censoring, not forcing language.

18. See *The Poetical Works of William Wordsworth*, ed. Ernest de Selincourt (Oxford: Oxford University Press, 1940), pp. 241–243, for the text here. This is the later version. The first version (1798) is a little less coercive.

19. *The Works of Captain Marryat*, XVII, 21.

20. *A Personal Record*, pt. 6, pp. 106–126. This section moves from a discussion of critics as public examiners needed by any writer and at least not silent or indifferent; to a discussion of Conrad's examination for master in the merchant marine; to a final scene about Madame Delestang, who subtly examined him in his youth and warned him that he might spoil his life. This great chapter of parallel examinatory scenes receding progressively into the past accepts and even celebrates examination, though often in a mock-solemn tone. The theme of the chapter might be called the mystery of necessary examination. Thorburn, *Conrad's Romanticism*, p. 65, has a good discussion of the section.

21. Jean-Aubry, *Life and Letters*, II, 288–289. In Jean-Aubry there is a period, not a comma, after "Germanism." If this was Conrad's own punctuation, it might show resistance to writing a long, "Germanic," "dialectical" sentence, even while he was remembering and recording this dialectical scene.

22. See Najder, ed., *Congo Diary*, p. 156; Said accepts the idea that the story was almost certainly composed early, and so does Karl.

23. See *Tales from Henryk Sienkiewicz*, trans. Monica M. Gardner (London: Dent, 1931), pp. 194–208. Johns appears at the end of the story to fire the lighthouse keeper for negligence; engrossed in a copy of Mickiewicz's poems, the old man had forgotten to light the tower, causing a shipwreck.

24. See Tzvetan Todorov, *The Poetics of Prose* (Ithaca, N.Y.: Cornell University Press, 1977), pp. 179–189.

25. *Osip Mandelstam: Selected Essays*, trans. Sidney Monas (Austin: University of Texas Press, 1977), p. 166.

Index